ROUTLEDGE LIBRARY EDITIONS:
EDUCATION MANAGEMENT

Volume 10

THE MANAGEMENT OF EDUCATIONAL INSTITUTIONS

THE MANAGEMENT OF EDUCATIONAL INSTITUTIONS
Theory Research and Consultancy

Edited by
H. L. GRAY

LONDON AND NEW YORK

First published in 1982 by Falmer

This edition first published in 2018
by Routledge
2 Park Square, Milton Park, Abingdon, Oxon OX14 4RN

and by Routledge
711 Third Avenue, New York, NY 10017

Routledge is an imprint of the Taylor & Francis Group, an informa business

© 1982 H.L. Gray, selection and editorial matter

All rights reserved. No part of this book may be reprinted or reproduced or utilised in any form or by any electronic, mechanical, or other means, now known or hereafter invented, including photocopying and recording, or in any information storage or retrieval system, without permission in writing from the publishers.

Trademark notice: Product or corporate names may be trademarks or registered trademarks, and are used only for identification and explanation without intent to infringe.

British Library Cataloguing in Publication Data
A catalogue record for this book is available from the British Library

ISBN: 978-1-138-48720-8 (Set)
ISBN: 978-1-351-04158-4 (Set) (ebk)
ISBN: 978-1-138-48788-8 (Volume 10) (hbk)
ISBN: 978-1-351-04114-0 (Volume 10) (ebk)

Publisher's Note
The publisher has gone to great lengths to ensure the quality of this reprint but points out that some imperfections in the original copies may be apparent.

Disclaimer
The publisher has made every effort to trace copyright holders and would welcome correspondence from those they have been unable to trace.

THE MANAGEMENT OF EDUCATIONAL INSTITUTIONS

Theory Research and Consultancy

Edited by HL Gray

 The Falmer Press

A member of the Taylor & Francis Group

© 1982 This selection and editorial matter copyright H.L. Gray.
All rights reserved. No part of this publication may be reproduced,
stored in a retrieval system, or transmitted, in any form or by any means,
electronic, mechanical, photocopying, recording or otherwise, without the prior
permission in writing from the Publisher.

First published 1982

ISBN limp 0 905273 24 9
       cased 0 905273 25 7

Jacket design by Leonard Williams

Printed and bound by Taylor and Francis (Printers) Ltd
Basingstoke
for
The Falmer Press
(*A member of the Taylor & Francis Group*)
Falmer House
Barcombe, Lewes
Sussex BN8 5DL
England

Contents

Foreword	iii
Introduction	1
The Management of Education in its Social Setting L.E. *Watson*	15
A Perspective on Organization Theory H.L. *Gray*	29
The Performers: Higher Education as Theatre I.L. *Mangham*	45
Mysticism, Management and Marx R.I. *Simon*	63
The Nature of Managerial Activities in Education P.C. *Webb, and* G. *Lyons*	85
The Emergence of the Politics of Education as a Field of Study D.H. *Layton*	109
What Business Management can Teach Schools C. *Brooklyn Derr and* T.J. *DeLong*	127
Organization Development for the 1980s R.A. *Schmuck*	139
Training Internal Change Agents for Schools M.M. *Milstein*	163
Consulting with Education Systems is about the Facilitation of Coordinated Effort W. *Mulford*	179

Management Development for Headteachers 219
H. Heller

Research into Educational Innovation 245
M. Fullan

Problems of Institutional Management in a Period of Contraction 263
Tom Bone

Contributors 285

Index 287

Foreword

This book is a collection of specially commissioned papers by writers who are closely involved in education management as practitioners, researchers and trainers. The purpose of the book is not to offer a blue print for educational administration but to provide readers with an insight to some of the major theoretical considerations in managing educational institutions.

Education management is barely recognized as an area of study in its own right, and indeed there are many reasons for not wishing it to become a separate activity, certainly not a distinct 'discipline'. What the education manager aims to do is to understand the kind of organization for which he is responsible and to use the best practice in his administrative behaviour. It is important, therefore, for him to have a good understanding of theoretical concepts – organization and management theories – upon which to base the decisions he has to make.

There are good grounds for believing that education until quite recently has not been managed so much as roughly guided. During the period of expansion up to the end of the 1970s, managers needed to do little more than add on new activities, resources and people with little regard for the disciplines of organizational management. We are now, in the 1980s, suffering the consequences of largely untutored enthusiasm as managers are required to deal with different issues such as falling rolls and the attendant early retirements and redundancies among quite young staff, teachers as well as administrators. It is hoped that this book will provide some guidelines for a rethinking about the nature of education management and the development of an appropriate rationale and philosophy.

The selection of authors naturally reflects the editor's own concerns and interests but it is hoped that a reasonably coherent perspective emerges from the book. None of the writers is concerned with mechanistic approaches to management but on the contrary much concerned to describe management practice as having as a basic responsibility for the needs and demands of people. The chapters on OD (Organization Development) illustrate this even if the definitions of OD differ somewhat.

Readers will hopefully obtain a flavour of humanistic approaches to education management and gain an understanding of how the complex organizations called schools and colleges etc. can be sensitively managed not just by the appointed managers but by using the considerable resources of consultants, many of whom have wide experience not only of education but of industry as well. Additionally, it will be seen that industrial perspectives are more sensitive to the needs of education than is often thought – frequently more insightful and concerned than those of theorists who have only educational experience.

All the contributors have published widely elsewhere and readers interested in individual approaches might well care to follow up what is written here by seeking out other writings. It may also be worth commenting that writers usually welcome contact with their readers (only too often they remain totally anonymous) and would welcome correspondence on their topics. Thinking about education management is in a very lively phase of development and dialogue; discussion and the sharing of views and experiences is an essential part in this development.

H.L. Gray
Netherthong, March 1981

Introduction
H.L. Gray
Huddersfield Polytechnic

There seem to be two large classes of people interested in education management, the theorists and the practitioners, and they do not often come together. Of course, there are those who straddle the division, generally practitioners reaching out to theorists. In higher education the managers may be more serious about theory than those in primary and secondary schools, but by and large the theorists and the practitioners live in quite separate educational worlds.

There are understandable reasons for this. Educational institutions are complex organizations in which a large amount of managerial preoccupation is with the present and immediate. Schools and Colleges are not organizations where strategic planning is perceived as enormously important. Nothing very much happens if targets are not met – there is no product to sell in a fickle market, no violent fluctuations in demand, no competitors to keep a sharp eye on. Heads and Principals are involved in a much more personal organization than those of almost every other institution. Schools have no *essential* technology which has to be maintained, developed and supplanted. By and large industrial and commercial models of organization and management are not applicable to education. So heads are right to be sceptical about much management theory, especially when it has its origins in industrial techniques rather than general theory.

The theorists, on the other hand, have tried to make sense of educational organization and this can only be done in the first instance by over-simplifying the situation. In North America there developed an urgent concern to discover a respectable theoretical base for administration in education and for a very long time there appeared to be a firm orthodox line that a certain kind of sociological theory was the only acceptable basis (Greenfield, 1979). The theory building side of the divide has been dominated by North American scholars, both Canadian and American, abetted by a number of Australian writers. American literature dominates the field in unabated profusion and the British literature which has taken a slightly different turn, hardly shows up against it. (See Baron, 1979).

One of the problems of dealing with the literature and the theory is that it originates from a number of different standpoints each of which has a different,

The Management of Educational Institutions: Theory, Research and Consultancy

and not necessarily compatible, concern from the other. First of all there is the administrative concern. In the United States the school system is decentralized into School Boards, separately elected, and the primary management concern is with the administration of the local system as a whole. Superintendents are the key figures and they occupy a career profession distinct from other governmental professions. Training has always been an important element in the Superintendent's career and the American educational career structure is quite distinctive from, say, the UK structure. In the UK, schools' systems are a part of the local government system and the education department is a unit of local government. Schools in the UK tend to be more independent of politics and the heads have been, until the current economic recession, almost autonomous in the management of their institutions.

In other parts of the world, educational systems tend to follow a pattern copied from one of the European systems, even where there was no colonialism, simply because nineteenth and twentieth century history was dominated by the European powers. At any rate, African and Asian systems tend to be centrally administered, highly structured, authoritarian and paternal and greatly vulnerable to economic and political change and influence. As a consequence, many African and Asian educators are looking for a theory of universal application to administration rather than, like the English, a theory which helps the head to run a school, or a principal to run his college.

Most of the American theory of educational administration has been concerned with schools because it is the school situation which has dominated the picture; thinking and writing about schools and thinking and writing about colleges and universities have been kept apart and in the North American context bridging this gap has been very difficult. In the UK on the other hand, and in the European countries in general, there has been much less of a preoccupation with schools alone. But even in the writing there is a language, or terminology, problem. For example, although Americans use the word 'school' to mean 'university' in the phrase 'going to school' there is no collective word in English to describe schools, colleges, polytechnics, universities, etc. except the rather clumsy and pedantic sounding 'educational institution' so writers tend to use the word they find easiest to deal with and in line with their experience – school or college. In the context of UK education it is very difficult to write about schools, colleges, polytechnics and universities, etc. at the same time.

Where training programmes in educational administration or education management are offered they tend to divide even more into the sectors of primary, secondary, further education and higher education. This is as true of short courses as higher degrees. Courses for primary heads are of quite a different order from those for Further Education College Principals. (e.g. FE Staff College courses, Coombe Lodge, Bristol). The more basic the school in the system, the more trivial the content, though the complexity of content offered for some university managers goes far beyond anything most of them can comprehend. It should be noted, too, that in the UK context the word

Introduction

'head' is used for the head of primary and secondary schools while the word 'principal' is usually confined to heads of institutions where students are over the age of 16. There are no 'principals' of English primary schools only 'heads'.

Furthermore, writers and practitioners are themselves located in some part of their national educational system and are naturally preoccupied with one part rather than the whole system. In the UK there does appear to be an attempt to keep all the sectors together and a good deal of credit must go to the British Educational Administration Society for attracting into membership quite a wide representation. (See *Educational Administration*, Vol. 1, No. 1, 1973 onwards). International bodies, on the other hand, tend to keep the sectors, especially elementary and higher education, apart and the emphasis seems to be more largely on Higher Education, a term subsuming Further Education (sometimes under the ambiguous term Tertiary Education). With the terminology for describing the systems so unclear, it is hardly surprising that the development of theory and the description of practice is so difficult.

Another important distinction – or, more properly, confusion – is over the concepts of management and administration. These terms are often used interchangeably though they do represent different ways of looking at the problems of education. (See Hodgkinson, 1978). Added to this is the growing interest in policy making and governance which form yet another perspective. For when one is talking or writing about education it is always from a particular viewpoint. Education management is rather like a prism in which the rays diverge rather than converge. The four major viewpoints appear to be political and economic; administrative and sociological; institutional and organizational; curriculum and content.

The word administration is the most confusing. Its general meaning refers to the way in which a system or institution is run in accordance with agreed procedures. Superintendents, chief education officers, etc. are administrators in that they implement policy decisions made by their superiors. Keeping the system running is the task of administration. But some administrators make policy decisions and all administrators make autonomous decisions in the course of their administration. In national government, administrators may be the decision and policy makers though the term management, in English usage, generally refers to the process of making decisions and also deciding policy. Are heads of schools managers or administrators? Are principals of colleges and universities managers or administrators? Why do we use the term 'education management' in the UK where the Americans use the term 'educational administration' though in neither country is the term exclusive or consistent. In France the terminology is different yet again with different usage implying different perspectives.

It seems as if we are a long way from a unified view of theory and practice and so long as there can be an open, continuous and intelligent debate, it hardly matters. But there is a tension between, on the one hand, those who engage in a political, economic and social debate and those who take an essentially humanistic stance. The sociologists take a more serious look at Marxist philosophy than the organization theorists and it can be argued that much of the current literature in 'Educational Administration' that is school based ignores almost entirely a political perspective. For example, there is not much of a Marxist awareness in literature on school administration and there is only just surfacing an awareness of phenomenological and existential perspectives on the organization of the school, though we shall see a considerable increase in this aspect of debate in the next decade.

It seems, too, that there has been little concern in educational administration about reform of the system, a grappling with fundamental ideological issues, in spite of the currency of ideas from Illich, Rheimer, Holt, Postman and Weingartner and others. Educational Administration has been concerned largely with maintaining the system not changing it in spite of the spate of writings about educational innovation. It has often been overlooked that innovation and reform are by no means the same. Much educational innovation has left the system and the institution essentially unaltered in that the social and economic power structure has been unchanged. Reforms in the Swedish, Norwegian and Danish systems have been a consequence of political ideology and consistent with the dominant political theory of the countries. In America the origin of reform has been the same but the more conservative nature of American society has determined the extent to which reform has been possible. In the UK the amount of educational reform has been much less than anyone supposed when secondary comprehensivization was introduced for it is significant that UK educational 'reform' left the social class structure almost untouched.

These last paragraphs have contained gross generalizations and the sentiments are highly contentious but the purpose is to emphasize the complexity and uncertainty of the context in which we talk about education. Not only are the terms in use varied in their meaning and connotation, but the intellectual frameworks in which they are used are of more significance than many writers about education management are able to take account. Is it possible to write about the theory and practice of institutional management without taking cognizance of the philosophical and political idealogy of the presenter? Are we right to look for a neutral theory or unbiased practice? The phenomenological standpoint would be that we should do, in so far as we can be aware of the subjective nature of objectivity. Our concern in seeking a generally valid theory is to deal with the subjective elements as openly as the objective elements – whatever they might be. To surface prejudices and biases and declare them so that assumptions are as clear as deductions is a necessary part of thinking about management and developing appropriate theory.

The two basic and polar grand perspectives in theory and practice of Educational Administration are open systems theory and phenomenology. These perspectives are expressed in ideological and idiosyncratic ways by each writer and overlaid with whatever other philosophical views he holds.

Introduction

One can be a Marxist or Christian open systems theorist, a humanist phenomenologist or a conservative phenomenologist. [It is perhaps not possible to be a Marxist phenomenologist though he has been called so by at least one writer.] By far and away the greatest coverage is open systems based and perhaps only a Hindu is capable of a phenomenological view of economics. Increasingly, writers add a phenomenological gloss to their open systems descriptions and few phenomenologists would go quite so far as to say that there is nothing other than pure existentialism. Stated briefly and crudely, open systems theory is concerned with the interrelation of parts and the assumption that what happens in one situation affects in some way what happens in related situations. Phenomenology is concerned with the personal and unique meaning that individuals give to situations and there is the assumption that what appears to be true for one individual may not be true for anyone else. Open systems theory is replete with charts, diagrams and statistics while phenomenology is concerned with personal and subjective interpretations and experiences of reality.

Historically, there is no way in which the significance of these two grand perspectives can be ignored because they affect the way in which all educational theory and practice is viewed and expressed. They have implications for every concept used in thinking about education, administration, schools, colleges, universities, society, the meaning and structure of life itself. We have entered a period of a new dialectic which exposes much theory and practice as being just too simplistic.

The phenomenologists may be tempted to opt out of the debate just because the controversy is not worth the hassle but that would be to lose the fight for truth. Many of the solutions proposed by humanistic psychologists are as questionable as those proposed by systems protagonists because they assume a universality which does not exist. Many of the problems of OD (Organization Development) occur because it is simply one value system being substituted for another and an examination shows that the solution is far too simple. For example, much early OD activity was concerned with seeking consensus on the assumption that general agreement could be usefully achieved among members of a group or team. Consensus seeking seems to imply that not only is agreement possible but desirable and is a way of avoiding conflict. But agreement may be neither possible nor desirable. Perhaps consensus arises from an idealogical view that people ought to agree. A phenomenological critique would be that individuals can never wholly agree and that to retain disagreement is more realistic than the pretence of accord. In American society 'consensus' occurs in a quite different way from 'consensus' in Nigerian society. It can be observed, for instance, that the acceptability of traditional American OD theory and practice in the UK is much less than some have supposed – Americans are much more inclined to seek expressed agreement while the English are more inclined to want to live with differences.

An open systems view of OD suggests a commonality of interest that a phenomenological view would not assume. Hence OD programmes organized by consultants using an open systems model would move to quite different conclusions from one organized by those who start from a phenomenological viewpoint.

Several references have been made to national cultural perspectives as if the UK, the US, Nigeria, etc. were each countries where everyone thought alike. While we perceive national differences and distinctive cultures overall, individuals within these cultures will perceive things differently. A Canadian and an Englishman may have more in common with one another than another compatriot. This is undoubtedly true in educational theory and practice. Both an Australian and an American may share the same open systems perspective while an Englishman and a Canadian hold the same phenomenological views. Nevertheless, the dilemma in looking at educational administration in an international context is that national characteristics, as embodied in an administrative system, have a tangibility which can only best be described in a largely universal national sense. It is clear, for example, that a description of the whole system of education in Malta can be best understood in terms of the politics of that country, for the behaviour of the individual Maltese derives from the cultural situation in Malta.

An example is the concept of leadership – a key concept in any theory of educational administration and management. The understanding of leadership is different in the USA, the UK and Nigeria. Americans are quite happy to talk about educational leadership and there have been programmes designed to develop various kinds of leadership. The term 'leadership programme' is quite acceptable in American society and in a slightly different sense in Canada. This is not the case in the UK where the term leadership raises apprehension and even amusement. The reason has to do with different concepts of democracy. The Americans see leadership as a characteristic of democracy while the British see it as a possible denial. The Americans may think of pioneers and developers of the great wide west but the English may think of Hitler and Mussolini and the denial of democratic rights. In Nigeria, leadership is seen in the context of a tribal and authoritarian social structure that is characteristic of Nigerian culture. To the Nigerian, there are few leaders and they are always bosses; the job of others is to follow and do what they are told.

Given these kinds of national and cultural differences, there are enormous problems with the terms and assumptions of theories of education management. How can we write about them in the context of one national culture and be understood in another? In one sense, the problem is greater with administrative theory and less with management theory. Administrative theory expresses very clearly the cultural premises on which it is based. For example, theories of staff development which include a description of the procedure throw an English view into stark contrast with the practices possible in Uganda, Nigeria or Malawi. A Ugandan just cannot contemplate doing things in the same way as an Englishman; his organizational context

Introduction

functions in a quite different way – it is much more authoritarian, much less sophisticated and the social objectives of the school are much more limited. Even after thirty years of Western aid to under-developed countries in Africa, where the European influence has been strong for centuries, foreign consultants and advisers still impose their philosophy on the indigenous peoples instead of entering a dialogue and exploration of perspectives.

Institutions exist within a wide socio-economic culture. This is never disputed in the literature although certain institutions may be seen as providing a counter-culture (for example, religious schools). And though this is well understood intellectually, it is not always remembered in the application of ideas to practice. We all tend to impose our values and way of doing things on others, especially when we move from one country to another. But we often, and perhaps more dangerously, fail to understand the ways in which our own institutions reflect social organization and expectations. In the early 1980s the economic recession in the UK throws into sharp relief the way in which schools are dependent on the current social and economic system even more than economic institutions. Schools have no way to go, it seems, but into retreat and into decline because they have never developed a value system which is in any way independent of the current general value system. Quite suddenly, schools are judged on simple economic criteria that put into question almost everything else they do. When faced with falling rolls, schools are able to contemplate a future little different from that of a large company faced with immediate cash flow problems and there are very few ideological resources to deal with a changed function and need. Not only are the institutions threatened as such, but there is no energy in the philosophy of education to cope with the exigencies of the time.

It is this world economic recession of the 1980s that will be the testing period for whatever theories of schools as organizations are current – whether it is open-systems based or phenomenological. On the face of it, open systems should have pat answers that can be quickly shown to work. One might extend the notional boundaries of the school and regroup the resources. But open systems theory has not led to a widespread view of education as a social process rather than an institutionalized activity. And the phenomenologists are still trying to persuade people that things are not what they seem – or rather that things are what they seem and not what you think they are.

This is where the distinction between administrative theory and management theory becomes important. If we become fixated on administrative considerations, then our preoccupation will be with how things are done and a standardization of procedures. If we concern ourselves with management theories then our concern will be to examine the decision-making process and the exercising of power and authority. The leading question for the practitioner is whether he sees himself as an administrator or executive, or a manager and policy maker. In periods of social and economic stability (if such can ever exist) perhaps administrative thinking is the more acceptable, but in periods of social and economic change, the dynamic stance of the management perspective would seem more realistic. However, by their very nature, expressed theories tend not to be dynamic, they represent little more than the worked out thinking of the theorist at the point when he sets his ideas down – and in academia that may mean several years prior to publication. If we teach managers management theory that others have developed we are behaving paradoxically. Management is not about the past but about the present (and a little bit about the future). If we are to train people to manage, we must train them not to learn and remember what others have thought but to think and decide for themselves. The training task is to bridge the gap between theory and practice by helping the learner manager to use the past (his own and others) only as a jumping off point for his own decision-making and not, as in most academic programmes in education, to see management theory as the sole basis for his actions. Unless our theoretical position in education management is pragmatic, it will be quite unable to deal with the situations managers actually have to cope with.

Management is an activity, a class of behaviour. Management theory is about how we might behave and its evaluation occurs in practical situations. Clearly the requirement for management theories to be workable and utilitarian is more pressing than with some other academic pursuits. One does not learn about management in order to store the ideas in the memory, nor is one interested in purely academic distinctions. Some academics believe that a true academic stance is not to take sides and as a consequence they become incapacitated when it comes to making management decisions or give managerial advice. The criteria for academic credibility are not quite the same as those for other academic disciplines – just as the criteria for each academic discipline differ, though academics sometimes fail to realize this. Management theory is good only in so far as it leads to good practice, to paraphrase Kurt Lewin's well-known sentiment. There is no luxury in management theory of simply indulging in the exchange of ideas for ideas' sake. The professor of education management who was delighted when he read a book purporting to prove that bureaucracy could be good had misunderstood the situation. The debate is not about whether bureaucracy is good or bad but about the usefulness or otherwise of the concepts and practice of bureaucratic systems. The management theorist cannot rest with his theories, he must try them out. The saddest feature of many departments where 'Ed. Admin' is taught is that 'Ed. Admin' is never practised – just as Faculties of Education often have the worst educational practice.

It may well be that the academic value system in management is significantly different from that in other faculties of universities. It is quite reasonable for this to be so and it is no accident that business schools are organizationally different from other university departments. In the UK the Business Schools (the alternative term is 'management' schools) are often partly separated institutions like the London and Manchester Business Schools and the quite large number of private Management Colleges. In the UK, USA, Canada and Australia, education administration is securely situated in the universities

Introduction

and polytechnics (the distinction between polytechnics and universities in the international context is perhaps not significant at this point). In some instances, separate centres or units have been set up to give freedom for experiment but the longer tradition in 'Ed. Admin' has been to go for academic respectability – which it can never have in traditional terms as the sociologists and psychologists have painfully learned.

But the dilemma goes further than this even. Schools, colleges, etc. are perceived as part of the academic tradition themselves, a tradition that is essentially conservative. The central core of educational institutions extends from kindergarten to graduate school and the thread is that of academic excellence. Here is the essential paradox of education. Though most people will spend their lives in industry and commerce, the major influence on organizations supposedly preparing people for the realities of life is one of rarified academic distinction. The situation is at its worst in the UK and France, less pernicious in other European countries but not much different in Canada, Australia and the USA. We organize educational institutions on a highly competitive basis with only one ultimate yardstick of success – the first class honours degree preferably obtained at a prestigious university. That is why the English are so derisive about the American University – because a student can obtain a degree in a non-traditional, non-cerebral subject like football. The origins of this view lie in the social system that still coheres around the British university and the English class system.

This is not intended as a digression nor as a petulant sideswipe. Unless we can critically examine the educational system to which we belong we shall never move towards a theory of educational organization. In different situations in different countries, there are remarkable parallels. For instance, in India it is said no one fails a degree, certainly not a first degree (in Italy anyone can gain one simply by persistence). The reason is that it is embedded in the Indian way of life that people do not fail – not just for personal reasons but for family reasons. The honour of the family is at stake and the marriage possibilities for an individual depend on his honourable achievement. An Indian parent of a child at a school in England wishes his daughter to be in the top class because she is *his* daughter, her success is *his* success and the honour of *his* family is at risk. He is not interested at all in academic achievement as such, only that his daughter work hard, be obedient and receive the appropriate rewards.

Before the English deride this as a caricature they should examine the Oxbridge system where entry is still a matter of privilege and family connection (often via the public school) and where the class of degree matters very little so long as a student has been to the 'right' college, met the 'right' people and made the 'right' connections. Schools, colleges and universities have one primary social role and that is to preserve society as it is, to maintain privilege and distinction and to ensure that the political system is strengthened and perpetuated. Once we understand this as axiomatic we may consider what a theory of school management would be and how it relates to a theory of educational reform. Should we believe differently, our theory of management will enshrine different values.

Much organization theory skirts round the problems of power and authority, although they are at the core of much of the practice of the British Tavistock Institute and the American National Training Laboratories. Authority is linked almost solely to issues about the management structure (the administrative structure) especially the role of the head. A great deal has been written about the nature of democracy and shared decision-making among the staff and there are hosts of programmes that purport to help managers to engage in power sharing. Much OD is concerned with a 'democratization' of the institution but issues of the authority of knowledge and the dictatorship of the institution are largely if not entirely overlooked in the literature.

The problem of authority within the institution takes us back to the place of the institution in society. In an earlier comment it was suggested that there was an authority inherent in the social system – the English class system, the Nigerian tribal system, the Indian caste system and the Jewish sense of nationhood and so on. Schools cannot function outside this authority structure and it is dangerously naïve to believe they can. The USA has a different form of social structure mythologized in the idea of the 'melting pot'; social divisions in the USA are different from those in Europe and the idea of social equality and acceptance is different. The idea of authority by right of birth or social standing is largely foreign to the Americans so that schools are democratic in quite a different way from the UK. The status of academic subjects in America reflects this differing starting point for authority and there is a much wider acceptance of achievement – in Europe worthwhile achievement is much more narrowly subscribed.

If there are these differences among the older English speaking countries and if they can be identified by English, Americans, Canadians, it is more than likely that there are differences of at least the same order in other countries of the world. Take for instance, the idea of guru in India. A guru is not a social authority, a master in social status, but someone from whom one's values and standards are taken. A guru is not at all the same as one's university professor or psychiatrist. The family patterns in other countries are quite different and socially significant from those in Europe (where the Italian family is differently organized from the Swedish family). How does one transpose these social values about authority in and out of the family into the school? In England the teacher is given parental rights (e.g. to administer corporal punishment) because of the tradition of the boarding public school. These rights are not given to the teacher in the French school and the position in Islam is different again.

In the English school system there is an identification of authority between the teacher and the subject; the authority of the subject is bestowed on the teacher. Essentially English teaching is authoritarian – pupils are told what is right, what needs to be learned. Perhaps all educational systems do this in some way but in some societies there is a yet higher authority in the church

Introduction

i.e. religion. To understand educational organizations properly, it is necessary to understand the significance of major philosophical concepts like authority, freedom, democracy and autonomy, otherwise we have no context in which to set the theory. The greatest and perpetual dilemma in education is on the question of authority and freedom. Not only is education culturally bound but it is required to fulfil the contradictory functions of preserving tradition and also changing society to take advantage of new knowledge. Teachers tend to be the more conservative members of society but also there are teachers who are among the more revolutionary in a political sense. But in the classroom, they are overridingly conservative and traditional in their methods. Some of the most politically revolutionary teachers are also the most authoritarian.

The major concern of most educational systems, most schools, is to transmit a conservative value system. Deviants do not last long as teachers for one reason or another and the most persuasive effect of the teacher is not the transmission of knowledge so much as the transmission of values. Could we make available more knowledge and remove as much as possible the values that go to its transmission, we should change the relationship between the student and the teacher. We should begin to transfer power from the teacher to the student. Now this is exactly what can occur with the development of the silicon chip and very inexpensive integrated circuitry in information storage and retrieval systems. If knowledge can be stored and made cheaply and readily available in a wide variety of forms, the cumulative effect is to decrease the values content. Furthermore, as students have increasingly free access to knowledge, the authority of the teacher as a purveyor of knowledge disappears and to remain in charge, he must change his style.

It is perhaps not expecting too much to foresee a change in teaching styles from didactic and authoritarian to facilitative and collaborative. In the new modes, the teacher will help the student to learn by learning how to learn. The teacher will act as personal counsellor and group facilitator rather than the sole source of knowledge. His concern will be to improve the affective self, help the student in his disposition towards learning and sort out emotional blockages and impediments. There will be a consequent change in the experience and concept of democracy in the classroom and institution because pupil-teacher relationships change radically (Gray, 1981).

Democracy in the Western World is a more complex concept than politicians generally give us to believe. In the UK, democracy appears to be simply majority will with considerable uncertainty as to what a majority is. In America, the position is similar but the underlying power structure is different – wealth rather than lineage. The two-party system obfuscates the issue of democracy which may be greater in one-party states so long as more interests are represented. But democratic government does not solve the problems of authority and representation and these are left even more unresolved in the power structure of the school. The earlier the stage of schooling, the greater the power of the teacher; the later the stage of schooling the greater the power of the administrative system. The further from the kindergarten, the more impersonal the power structure. Organization theory in education has not resolved issues about the location of power because one of the myths of education is that 'academic freedom' is paramount when it demonstrably is not so unless it conforms to the prevailing social value system. The only permitted freedom is the freedom to conform and agree.

Though the almost universal ideal of the well educated man is one who is autonomous (at least intellectually) we do all we can in the system to prevent this. That in itself is not bad. Freedom can only be obtained when it is hard won; there is no freedom as a gift. It is right that we should be made to fight for freedom though the resultant achievement should be welcomed not punished. Yet everything we do in education is to create dependency right up to the level of 'doctorates' which have to conform to 'standards' as much as any other work even though this educational conformity means it is almost impossible for really original work to surface. The issue is about who has control of learning.

The fear of freedom occurs in many other directions not least in the move for the increasing vocational relevance of education which means students will be able to learn only what social managers consider good for them. Control of qualifications is likely to develop frightening dimensions in the last decades of this century as the economic recession bites. How soon will we learn to see the student in a totally different relationship in the school from that which he has traditionally held? Can we really envisage education as being concerned with the dialogue of partners or must it always be the institutionalization of social control that the school embodies? The silicon chip may force some change in a new direction but it must be followed by a value shift on the part of teachers in general. A collaborative view of learning means a quite different model of organization for the school than those we have generally used in 'Educational Administration'.

The economic recession biting with unaccustomed sharpness in the UK of the early 1980s has coincided with, even if it has not been the cause of, a reappraisal of how schools etc. function as organizations. In a bleak process of experience and endurance the issues of responsibility and accountability have become unexpectedly clearer. The swingeing economic cuts suffered everywhere, and especially painfully in further and higher education, exposed very clearly where authority and power really lay in the English system; decisions that affected quite detailed and small matters of educational organization were clearly made by those who held the purse strings and the question of autonomy of institutions and collegiality of management have been raised. Such questions have always been raised in social and organization theory but the experience of non-collective decision-making is being experienced in a new way.

The polytechnics have shown the situation most starkly. There had been several straws in the wind, notably the consequences of stress on the heads of the institutions who were suffering a burden few of them were able to carry.

Introduction

The polytechnics were very large (by UK standards) institutions and were run authoritarianly on a simplistic administrative model. Quite suddenly, with the 1980 financial cuts, the question of shared responsibility was raised. Teaching staff at large were unaccustomedly expected to accept responsibility for implementing cuts when previously decision-making (often with considerable benevolent intent) had been largely reserved to the few (or even a single individual) at the top. But more than responsibility was at stake; there was also the question of accountability. Paternalism, patronage, benevolence and authoritarianism began to extort their price because there was a remarkable unwillingness of many teachers to accept responsibility when they felt they had never been properly considered as being responsible. Administrative structures began to fall apart as the effects of dependency came into play.

All forms of authoritarianism lead not just to depriving of freedom but lead to refusal to accept responsibility. It is not so much a question of shared decision-making by prolonging the process through debate and discussion in committees and working parties. Nor is it a question of consultation and participation. Rather the issue is how individuals can be helped to be fully responsible if they are never given the chance to learn that responsibility. In some institutions the whole chain of dependency has collapsed because no one was prepared to stand up against the decisions of his superiors when he believed them to be wrong. Hence, institutions suffered a classic dependency and the consequent inability of the membership at large to help the 'institution' back on the road to recovery.

No theory of organizations can avoid the moral implications of behaviour. Management by its very nature raises issues of values and the esteem in which members of organizations hold one another. Collegiality is not an indulgence but a necessity because it concerns all the members of the organization in the shared responsibility of seeing that the institution serves the needs of all the members. Perhaps these needs are incompatible but organizations are as much concerned with incompatibilities as congruence, agreement and uniformity. The reality of organizations is that they are composed of different people and no educational organization can reduce its members to a mean, or norm or single value system or set of behaviour patterns. Good management must perceive all situations as offering opportunities for growth and development and the last decades of the old century will be a period of testing whether educational institutions become agencies of opportunity and growth or of repression and retreat. These are the issues beside which all theories of education management must be assessed and evaluated. These are the issues to which it is hoped the papers in this book will go some way to helping us to find answers.

References

Baron, G. (1979) 'Research in educational administration in Britain', *Educational Administration*, 8(1) Autumn.

British Educational Administration Society (1973) *Educational Administration*, 1(1) and ff.

Further Education Staff College *Coombe Lodge Reports*, Blagdon, Nr. Bristol, Coombe Lodge.

Gray, H.L. (1981) 'Teacher education in the 1980s and '90s', *Experiential Learning in Teacher Education*, London, North East London Polytechnic.

Greenfield, T.B. (1979) 'Research in educational administration in the United States and Canada', in Hughes, M.G., *Research in educational Administration*, Bristol, BEAS/Coombe Lodge.

Hodgkinson, C. (1978) *Towards a Philosophy of Administration*, Oxford, Basil Blackwell.

Holt, J. (1969) *How Children Fail*, Harmondsworth, Penguin.

Illich, I.D. (1971) *Deschooling Society*, New York, Harper and Row.

Lewin, K. (1951) *Field Theory in Social Science*, New York, Harper and Row.

Postman, N. and Weingartner, C. (1971) *Teaching as a Subversive Activity*, Harmondsworth, Penguin.

Reimer, E. (1971) *School is Dead*, Harmondsworth, Penguin.

The Management of Education in its Social Setting

Leonard E. Watson
Sheffield City Polytechnic

It is a truism that education (and therefore the management of educational institutions) exists and operates within a social setting: even though it is often less than clear in writings on education management what precisely is meant by the term *social setting*. What is clear, however, is that in any place and at any time, those who have responsibility for management in institutions (in varying degrees, according to their level of responsibility, and the nature of the educational system within which they work) have to discharge their duties in the light, not only of their own preferences and the situations they find within their organizations, but with reference to the context of their institutions. Put into the terms of systems theory, they are concerned with *boundary transactions*.

This is not simply because schools and colleges are historically, geographically and administratively placed 'within' society, however true this may be: for in an important sense they are creatures of that society, established for ends which, even if still current and relevant (and they may well not be), are unlikely to be either clear or generally agreed. The meaning of the institution for significant elements of its society, and the expectations which are held for it, are critically important to the senior management of institutions. Especially is this so when schools and colleges are having increasingly to compete for resources (both economic and political) with other social agencies.

The literature of attempts to provide policy-makers and management personnel with an understanding of the context and setting of educational

---

Editor's note: Len Watson is a trainer and consultant with very considerable experience of educational administration in many parts of the world. His standpoint is practical and pragmatic, trying to deal with educational problems as his clients perceive them and trying to deal with them in terms they can handle from within their own experience. He is less concerned with academic theory than practicality. But he raises the kinds of questions that may be correctly defined and appropriately answered.

Watson's chapter is strictly a theoretical one in that he does not write from an ideological standpoint as many other contributors do. In a way his chapter provides a bench mark to measure theory development against because theories should increasingly provide relevant answers in the areas where Watson raises questions.

institutions have broadly gone in one of two directions. On the one hand, there have been theorists who have attempted to provide grand overviews, theoretical perspectives and models, with a view to encompassing conceptually all of the material covered in this paper, only in much fuller explanatory detail. Such an emphasis is upon a comprehensive understanding of social, economic and other processes, and their accompanying structures. The second approach, typically found in the literatures of industrial management, public and educational administration, has been more prescriptive. While attempting understanding, it has tended to assume that there are 'right' and 'wrong' (or at least 'better' and 'worse') ways of going about management, and that the relationship between theory and practice, therefore, essentially comprises theory producing 'principles' for managers to apply. The assumption here is that specific guidance can be provided to practising managers in advance of the specification of any particular situation.

The social scientist, looking at the situation within which the manager works, takes a number of parallel situations and abstracts from these certain characteristics or elements, and analyzes them along certain dimensions, with the intention of being able to make valid generalizations about classes or categories of situations. In order to do so, he pays attention, of necessity, only to a limited number of situational characteristics – he concentrates mainly upon that which situations have in common, rather than on what makes them unique. By contrast, the practising manager is concerned with the complexity and uniqueness of a particular situation within which he carries responsibility, and is only indirectly concerned with other similar situations. What is particularly important to him is not only the presence or absence of particular features (this also would interest the social scientist), but the particular way in which these elements are combined together to make up a complex, unique whole. For the manager has to manage within this situation, and to take into account all of those elements which he considers relevant, however complex these may be – and certainly, in any significant situation, they will be much more complex than current social science can accommodate within its thinking.

For these reasons the analyses and prescriptions of social scientists are frequently less than adequate: while the exhortations of practising managers for each other ('This is the way I do it – go and do thou likewise') also carry little conviction ('That may work in your situation, but my situation is different, if for no other reason that I am different from you').

If then the 'answers' to management situations have to be found through an understanding of the complexities and uniqueness of the actual situation, then what can be done to assist managers to gain from the experience of others, or from 'theory'? A list of specific prescriptions can have only limited validity – there are likely to be many situations in which these prescriptions may be most inappropriate. The practical problem (both for the practitioner, and for those concerned with the professional development of senior staff in educational institutions) centres here upon the issue of how one can assist those with

The Management of Education in its Social Setting

management responsibilities to develop criteria and skills in knowing when, or when not, to follow the traditional 'rules'. If the problem is to act *appropriately*, then how does one go about determining what is appropriate within a specific situation? General statements provided for guidance are likely to be so general as to be of little use as guides to action in particular situations. This is particularly the case with respect to the manager's relationships with the organization's social environment.

How then can the volume and complexity of the organization's environment be reduced in order to be manageable? Certainly it is not of use to restrict, in advance of the specification of the situation, the range of variables which shall be examined, because in any particular situation a datum which is not normally important may take on critical significance. Rather than *a priori* reduction of the data in advance, what is needed is some way of assisting the practitioner to conduct his own sifting and sorting when faced with the particular problem or issue in the field. This requires the development of a 'map' or other way of organizing complex data without arbitrarily reducing its richness too soon. The purpose is that the practitioner be in a position to explore the 'geography' of a situation in advance of any knowledge of what is most important within that situation, and in such a way, and using such concepts, as will illuminate his understanding of what he may actually *do about* the situation. For any analytical framework, to be useful, must be couched in terms which can be used in the development of strategies for action.

It follows that the academic has to provide the practitioner neither with overall theoretical models (descriptive or explanatory); nor 'tips for managers' (however useful these may be in particular circumstances). Rather, he should assist the practitioner in developing:

> diagnostic skills in identifying the most significant elements within the situation which confronts him;
>
> an understanding of a range of possible strategies;
>
> an ability to match strategies to the salient elements of a situation so that 'closest match' choices can be made;
>
> the skills of operational planning and implementation (including monitoring and control).

This chapter is concerned only with the first of these, with the problem which the practitioner has in identifying the most significant elements within the situation before him.

It follows from what has been written above that there is at the present state of our understanding, little possibility of any model being developed which will, like a complex algorithm, state both the critical elements within a situation, and the weighting to be given to these elements; all within a model which will, when worked through according to a standard set of procedures, provide the 'answer', the specification of the 'correct' decision. Such clearly is at present not possible. An alternative is to restrict such a model to a small number of variables which experience has suggested will often be most significant. A major difficulty here is that in many cases it is the particular mix of variables, rather than the variables themselves, which is critical for determining what constitutes appropriate action.

This chapter, therefore, attempts a much more modest task. Rather than providing 'pre-packaged' procedures and answers, all that is attempted here is to provide a framework for the practitioner himself to identify what seem, in his judgement, and with his inside knowledge of the situation, the most important variables and the relationship between them. Clearly this involves the exercise of considerable judgement; but a real difficulty at the moment for many experienced practitioners attempting to improve their ability to diagnose situations, especially those outside of the immediate organization for which they are responsible, is the lack of a reasonably understandable framework. This chapter is a first attempt along a particular road in that direction. It brings together concepts derived from many different disciplines, and attempts to put them together in a way which will allow the matching of 'strategies'. Space only allows an outline of the framework.

It should be noted that although some use is made of the terminology of systems theory, the approach described is not dependent upon the assumptions underlying the work of many systems theorists. Specifically, there is no suggestion in this framework that social systems are teleologically oriented, or that their goals are 'givens'. The approach is specifically developed below with respect to the management of the educational institution within its social setting.

The Framework in Outline

It is assumed that the setting of educational situations can be thought of as comprizing seven systems, each overlapping. These do not form discrete categories, but relate to each other in complex ways. The 'systems' are:

1. The spatial or geographic system
2. The task system
3. The social system
4. The cultural system
5. The governance system
6. The economic system
7. The political system

Each of these is approached via certain key concepts: and leads to the generation of questions which relate specifically to that system, and which alert the manager to managerial aspects of the environment of the organization. Each system may then be related to others, generating more complex questions

The Management of Education in its Social Setting

of interrelationships, and sensitizing the questioner to more subtle aspects of the system at which he is looking. These may be summarized and briefly illustrated as follows:

1. The Spatial System

This refers to the geographic or spatial distribution of the institution in relation to its environment, and includes therefore its physical characteristics. Key concepts include:

* spatial distribution (the extent to which, and ways in which, buildings and other artifacts are distributed in space);
* built form (things (e.g. buildings, roads) built by man).

Key questions which relate to this system are, for example:

> Where is the organization in relation to its physical environment, with respect for example to transportation and other means of communication?
> What buildings and other 'built forms' comprise the physical setting of the institution? How appropriate are they, and how adequate?

2. The Task System

The arrangement of tasks which the organization attempts to achieve, and the ways in which it is organized to do so. The key concepts include:

* task;
* technology (the ways in which resources are organized for the achievement of tasks);
* division of labour (the ways in which tasks and roles are allocated among organizational members, or members of the environment, in relation to task and technology).

Key questions may include:

> What are the tasks towards which the organization is oriented? How far are these in conflict? In what ways are they related to the environment?
> In what ways are roles allocated? To whom? By what processes? With what results?
> What are the organization's characteristic technologies? How do they relate to tasks, and to the division of labour?

3. The Social System

The pattern of interaction among persons in the organization and in its environment, and the ways in which these are structured in social groupings.

The Management of Educational Institutions: Theory, Research and Consultancy

Key concepts include:

* social interaction (the extent to which, and the ways in which, people interact together);
* social structure (the structures or groupings of people which arise out of these interactions);
* roles.

Use of these concepts may lead to the asking of such questions as:

What are the key groupings in the setting and in the organization as they relate to the setting, from the point of view of the presenting issue?

What is the origin of these groupings? On what patterning of interactions are they based?

What is the significant patterning of social interaction within the groupings?

4. *The Cultural System*

Drawing especially upon the insights of anthropology, this refers to the patterning of norms and expectations within the environment, the 'culture' of the organization and of organizations in its environment, including the symbols and the meanings attached to them. Key concepts include:

* expectations (what individuals expect of those occuping roles, or of groupings including organizations);
* prescriptions (what individuals believe *ought to happen* (as compared with what they expect to happen) with respect to roles or institutions);
* norms;
* values;
* symbols.

Key questions may include, for example:

What are the norms, expectations and prescriptions of various groupings as these relate to the situation being examined?
What is the symbolic significance of relevant objects, and to whom?
What meanings are attached, and by whom, to objects or structures?
What functions are served by these symbols?
What values are inherent in the normative system and sub-systems as these develop in various sub-groupings, with respect to the situation under examination?

5. *The Governance System*

This comprises the legal and administrative framework within which the

The Management of Education in its Social Setting

educational organization exists, both with respect to the content of law (whether legislative or administrative), to forms and traditions of administrative behaviour, and to the structures and processes whereby education is governed. Most of these matters have their origins within the environment of the school or other educational institution, and serve in important ways to link the school to its context. Key concepts include:

* law (formally enacted prescriptions);
* legal/administrative framework (of procedures, organizational structures, personnel, etc., concerned with the formulation and implementation of law and regulations);
* governance (the processes and structures whereby policy of relevance to the educational organization (which may lie well outside of the normal educational circles) is formulated and determined).

Key questions which arise may include:

What is the law and the legal position with respect to the issue in hand?
What is the governance process and structures which relate to it?
To what extent do the legal and administrative arrangements act as a constraint upon what is possible in the situation?

6. *The Economic System*

This refers to the processes and structures whereby economic resources are acquired, distributed and allocated. These resources mainly come from the environment of educational organizations, and therefore serve particularly to link the school or college to its context. Key concepts may include:

* resource (things which can be used to supply wants). While the most obvious economic resource is money, and the financing of education is of central importance, the meaning of 'resource' goes considerably further to include other material resources (e.g. buildings and staff) and such intangible resources as information, reputation and time.
* cost. An important cluster of concepts in the economics of organizations relates to costing. Terms such as Unit Cost, Marginal Cost and Opportunity Cost have precise (but not always fully agreed) meanings in the economics of decision-making and of management, and represent important concepts which must be taken into account in looking at situations in which the organization relates to its context.

When applied to the context of educational organizations, key questions may include:

> What are the most important resources with respect to the situation being considered?
> From whence do they come in the environment? By what process are they allocated? Is the method of their acquisition significant for the issue in hand?
> What are the likely economic costs and benefits of alternative courses of action which might be taken in the situation?
> How are resources defined in the situation? Are there some resources which are not identified as such, and therefore neglected?
> How does the economic system operate with respect to the organization?

7. The Political System

This refers to the processes and structures through which power is mobilized in order to influence the operation of the organization in relation to its environment (and *vice versa*) and the ways in which these processes and structures are legitimized. Key concepts may include:

* power (the ability or potential for mobilising resources to desired ends);
* influence (the successful mobilization of power);
* legitimation (the process whereby a structure or action comes to be considered as legitimate);
* authority (the legitimate exercise of power, or the recognition of its legitimacy).

Key questions with respect to the institution in its social setting may include:

> What is the basis of power being exercised in the situation under consideration? Upon what political resources is it based?
> What are the patterns of influence in the environment, and how do they impinge upon the organization? To what ends are this influence directed?
> How are decisions in the community and organization legitimized? To what extent is authority operating in the situation?
> What is the basis of the authority as recognized by various political groupings? How far is this significant in determining influence patterns?

The Next Stage: The Framework Developed

Thus far the analysis has been decidedly uni-dimensional, taking each of the identified 'systems' and looking at it essentially on its own. In practice, in looking at a 'real' situation, the next stage is to relate each set of concepts

The Management of Education in its Social Setting

and questions to each other, with a view to developing insights into what may be particularly significant in the organization's setting as it relates to the managerial issue of the moment. Examples of how this generates questions are suggested below.

The Political System in Relation to Other Systems

When considered in relation to other systems, the Political System suggests, for example, the following questions which could be considered in relation to a particular situation faced by the 'manager' in education:

> What is the basis of legitimacy of the educational organization, and its relationship to the value-system in the wider community? What is the legal basis of the organization's authority? To what extent, and in what ways, does the administrative and legal framework delimit or circumscribe the possible action a manager may take in the particular situation? This may involve legal constraints quite outside of the normal educational sphere – as in the United Kingdom at present, the constraints set on building programmes or the utilization of buildings by the Health and Safety at Work Act; or on the employment of staff by the Employment Protection Act. If the management need to get a decision or a change of policy from the wider community, what are the procedures for doing so? And what are the organizational structures which will have to be worked through in order that such policy changes may be introduced and legitimized?

> What is the relationship between the allocation of power and the allocation of economic resources? Who gets what and how? Specifically, with respect to the particular situation, what are the mechanisms which relate power and influence on the one hand, to the acquisition and allocation of financial, staffing and other resources on the other?

> While the political system is concerned with the 'how' of power and authority, it is the cultural system within which is specified the values which underlie these, the direction which such influence shall follow, and the ends to which it should be used. The relationship therefore between the political and cultural systems is critically important. How far then is the political system embedded in the cultural system, and how congruent with it – or are they, in the particular situation potentially in conflict? Are the people who hold expectations congruent with those of the management also those who have the most influence? Or is power in the hands of those whose purposes are most antithetical to those of the manager?

> What is the relationship between the social structure and political structure in the educational institution's environment? Is power concentrated in certain hands, in a systematic way? Who are the

'influentials' in the community and in its various groups, as these relate to the issue being considered? What is the form of interaction within and between these groups, and how does this relate to their influence?

In what ways do power, influence and authority relate to the spatial system? It can be important when involved in such areas as communication; where there is a considerable literature on the relationship between geography and innovation, and the relationship of built form to social interaction and social structure. Is the placing of units (e.g. in a split-site school) significant with respect to the situation?

The Economic System in Relation to Other Systems

The Economic System is not the only one concerned with resources and their management; most of the other systems are concerned with some aspect of resources. When related to other questions, the following are suggested, each to be considered in relation to the specific situation under consideration:

What is the relationship between the economic and governance systems? What are the formal laws and regulations governing the ways in which resources are acquired and allocated? What are the formal structures through which these legal controls are developed and executed? What are the policies relevant to the economics of resources, and how are these formulated and determined?

As in the case of the political system, there is an important relationship between the economic system and the cultural system, and for similar reasons. What are the norms governing economic activity, including the ways in which activities are costed and their benefits identified? Are there norms which set limits to the ways in which resources may be used?

The relationship between the economic and social system can be explored by such questions as: Which groups are the 'haves' and which the 'have-nots' in financial or other resource terms? What is the significance of this, if any, for their commitment to alternative values? Are the costs of alternative courses of action similar for different social groupings? How do these relate to ways in which the social context of the organization relates to the organization?

With respect to the geographic system, are there certain geographic areas particularly significant economically? Do distances create costs? What is the relationship between the organization's buildings and other material resources, and economic factors to do with costs of production, and so on?

In what ways do the political and economic systems relate to the task

The Management of Education in its Social Setting

system? What resources are needed for alternative methods of achieving tasks? In what ways do these relate to value systems, and to the norms governing the task system?

The Governance System and its Relation to Other Systems

The ways in which educational and education-related policies are formulated and determined, and the legal and administrative frameworks within which the educational institutions operate, are both significant for their functioning, and are frequently significant factors in the analysis of a management situation. This significance can be explored through the use of such questions as:

> What are the relationships between the cultural system and the governance system as these relate to a particular management decision? What is the normative position of the various sub-systems of the governance system itself, and their significance for relation in practice to this system – for in practice the governance system is made up of sub-systems associated with various governance organs. When it comes to operating with those outside the organization in order to influence what happens, it is important to understand the significance and meaning of what is seen: the meanings for those within a system (such as a legal system) are not necessarily the same as those attributed to them by outsiders.

> What are the ways in which the legal and administrative system limits the normative system, and serves to re-define meanings? What limits do they set to what is realistically possible in the situation?

> It is likely that the legal and governance systems are related to the spatial system through the ways in which local government, or the development of some district organization, operates. Legal and governance systems are usually based upon some type of geographic boundary distribution, and this may be highly important for certain purposes. For example, jurisdictions may not cross district lines in certain cases. Thus it is important in the United Kingdom to understand the local by-laws operating with respect to particular situations; and it may be that the organization being managed covers in its activities more than one jurisdiction.

The Cultural System and Other Systems

The previous sections have already discussed the relationship between the cultural system and certain other systems; but certain further points can be made.

> What is the relationship between the cultural system and social structure in the particular situation? There is a very large literature

on this general question in both sociology and social anthropology. At present we are concerned only with identifying those elements which may directly relate to the matter in hand. In particular, attention might be paid to the following points:

(a) the cultural system may well be based upon sub-cultures identified with social groupings;
(b) these groupings may well have different power based upon different sets of values, and different political bases;
(c) the cultural system may well be itself stratified;
(d) the cultural system may be related to occupational groupings, as in the case of professionalism.

The cultural system is likely to be related to the geographic system through the mediation of the social structure and the way it is geographically differentiated. This may point up the significance, for example, of geographic isolation.

Conclusion

This paper has addressed itself to the question of the management of educational institutions within their social settings, by attempting to outline a conceptual framework which is designed to be open-ended, to be suggestive and not definitive, which is intended to apply to a wide range of situations, and which the experienced practitioner can himself use to identify the most important elements within his own particular situation, with respect to his own particular concerns, at a particular moment of time. It is an outline and initial attempt only, in need of much further development and testing.

It may be, however, that it may provide a way of linking the theoretical and conceptual interests of the academic to the decision-making and situation-diagnosis concerns of the practitioner, through a shared concept-based, situationally-relevant methodology. It is being used also, with some success, in the professional development of senior staff in educational institutions.

Further Reading

ACKOFF, R.E. (1966) 'Structural conflicts within organizations', in LAWRENCE J.R. (Ed.), *Operational Research and the Social Sciences*, Tavistock, pp. 427–438.

BENNETT, R. (1978) 'Orientation to work and organizational analysis', *Journal of Management Studies*, 15(2): 187–210.

BLAU, P.M. (1974) 'Parameters of social structure', *American Sociological Review*, 39(5): 615–635.

BLEGEN, H.M. (1968) 'The systems approach to the study of organizations', in AGERNSAP T. (Ed.), *Comtributions to the Theory of Organisation, II*, Copenhagen: Munksgaard, pp. 12–30.

DAHL, R.A. (1963) *Modern Political Analysis*, Prentice-Hall.
DAHL, R.A. (1957) 'The concept of power', *Behavioural Science*, 2: 201-215.
EASTON, D. (1965) *A Systems Analysis of Political Life*, Wiley.
FRANCES, C. and COLDREN, S.I. (Eds.) (1979) 'Assessing financial health', *New Directions for Higher Education*, No. 26.
GRAY, H.L. (1980) *Management in Education: Working Papers in the Social Psychology of Educational Institutions*, Nafferton Books.
HALL, A.D. and HAGEN, R.E. (1969) 'Definition of system', in LITTERER, J.A. (Ed.), *Organizations: Systems, Control and Adaptation*, Vol. II, 2nd ed., Wiley.
HARRISON, M., HOYLE, E., WHITE, J., WHITE, P., RUSSELL, T.J. and BONE, T.R. (1976) 'Barr Greenfield and organization theory: A symposium', *Educational Administration*, 5(1): 1-13.
HICKSON, D.J. and McCULLOUGH, A.E. (1974) *Power in Organisations*, Open University Press (Unit 3 of Course DT352, 'People and Organisations').
LANDIS, D., ANASTASIO, E.J. and SLIVAK, R.M. (1972) 'The educational system as a system', *International Journal of Production Research*, 10(4): 325-332.
LEAVITT, H.J. (1970) 'Applied organizational change in industry: Structural, technical and human approaches', reprinted in DALTON, G.W. (Eds.), *Organizational Change and Development*, Irwin-Dorsey, pp. 198-212.
LYNCH, B.P. (1974) 'An empirical assessment of Perrow's technology construct', *Administrative Science Quarterly*, 19(3): 338-356.
LYNTON, R.P. (1969) 'Linking an innovative subsystem into the system', *Administrative Science Quarterly*, 14(3): 398-416.
MACKENZIE, W.J.M. (1967) *Politics and Social Science*, Penguin.
MILSTEIN, M.M. and BELASCO, J.A. (Eds.) (1973) *Educational Administration and the Behavioural Sciences: a Systems Perspective*, Allyn and Bacon.
MOOS, R.H. (1976) 'The architectural environment: Physical space and building design', *The Human Context: Environmental Determinants of Behaviour*, Wiley.
PFEFFER, J. (1978) *Organizational Design*, AHM Publication Corp.
PUGH, D.S., HICKSON, D.J. and HININGS, C.R. (1968) 'Dimensions of organizational structure', *Administrative Science Quarterly*, 13(1): 65-105.
SALANCIK, G.R., PFEFFER, J. and KELLY, J.P. (1978) 'A contingency model of influence in organizational decision making', *Pacific Sociological Review*, 21(2): 239-256.
SARASON, S.B. (1971) *The Culture of the School and the Problem of Change*, Allyn and Bacon.
SCHMUCK, R.A. (1972) 'Organizational diagnosis', *Educational Administration Quarterly*, 9(1): 71-74.
SEILER, J.A. (1967) *Systems Analysis in Mrganizational Behaviour*, Irwin-Dorsey.
SIMKINS, T.J. (1981) *Economics and the Management of Resources in Education*, Sheffield City Polytechnic, Department of Education Management (Sheffield Papers in Education Management, No. 17).
STERN, G.G. (1970) *People in Context: Measuring Person-Environment Congruence in education and industry*, Wiley.
THOMPSON, J.D. (1967) 'Technology and structure' in his *Organizations in Action*, McGraw-Hill.
VICKERS, B.C. (1973) *Information Systems*, Butterworth.
WALBERG, H.J. (1979) *Educational Environments and Effects: Evaluation, Policy and Productivity*, McCutchan.

WHETTEN, D.A. (1978) 'Coping with incompatible expectations: An integrated view of role conflict', *Administrative Science Quarterly*, 23(2): 254–271.
WRONG, D.H. (1968) 'Some problems in defining social power', *American Journal of Sociology*, 73(6): 673–681.
YOUNG, O.R. (1968) *Systems of Political Science*, Prentice-Hall.

A Perspective on Organization Theory

H.L. Gray
Huddersfield Polytechnic

Every consultant and researcher has in his mind some kind of a model which influences the way he perceives the subjects of his investigation. For many people, the model is generalized, vague and below the level of logical consciousness but nevertheless it exists and provides a perspective on the world under examination (Berger and Luckman, 1967). In education management the models generally in use and at a recognizable level of consciousness tend to be sociological, economic and political in concept and systems models in structure and logic. Such models have the advantage of a broad tradition of expository writing and a high level of apparent tangibility – they have 'measurable' elements which makes them generally acceptable by scientific criteria. Administrators tend to like such models because they permit decisions to be made on the basis of quantifiable data though they tend to assume the values of non-quantifiable (qualitative) data.

In recent years there has been a reaction against the hard line approach in management and administration and an interest in the so-called qualitative aspects of organizations. Within the broad stream of psychology, an important body of scholars has espoused the 'humanistic' cause and developed a concern for personal values as against laboratory criteria. Among social scientists an interest in New Paradigms for Research (Reason, 1977) has an increasing

Editor's note: Many of the ideas in management applied to education are concerned with the tangible and measurable aspects of educational organization. There would appear to have been a great need for theorists to work on the basis of objective models and to develop theories of administration. Unfortunately, most organizational problems have to do with people and there are few technological problems in the organization of education because there is no basic technological process even though various technical systems like time tables and syllabuses have been invented.

In his chapter on a 'subjective theory' (some would call it a phenomenological theory) Gray tries to explore some of the practical implications of a perspective on organizations that sees them as essentially personally and individually constructed artefacts. The problem up to now with phenomenological theories is that they have inevitably fallen short in suggesting methods of application. In his twelve propositions, Gray tries to move some way to indicating how subjective theory can be applied in practice.

influence following on from interest in Action Research in its various forms (Clark, 1972). Action Research attempts to ensure the involvement of the client as an active participant in doing research.

Education management has tended towards a more conservative position as would be expected of a new field but after a long allegiance to a specific sociological school of thought (Greenfield, 1979) an interest in alternative methods of model building, researching and, as a consequence different models of consultancy, has grown and commands increasing support. The most significant event in the development of theory in the area of education management was Greenfield's paper at the International Intervisitation Programme (IIP) in Education Administration in the UK in 1974 (Greenfield, 1975). Controversy raged in the backwaters of education management theorists (hardly a mainstream group in the academic world) though comparatively little development occurred in spite of a general shift in opinion in support of Greenfield's basically phenomenological viewpoint (see *Educational Administration*, 1976 onwards). Largely ignored had been Dale's paper on Phenomenological Perspectives in the Sociology of the School published in 1973.

One reason for the apparent lack of activity in the new perspective was that in the European academic tradition, phenomenological approaches were comparatively well integrated into the general way of thinking. Europeans are perhaps more speculative and reflective than Americans who prefer action and visible evidence. Be this as it may, many writers in the UK at any rate have preferred to sit on the fence and have the best of both worlds – the phenomenological and the non-phenomenological – rather than help to develop a basically alternative approach to viewing organizations. One attempt was made by Gray (1980) in a paper entitled 'Organizations as Subjectivities' and it is broadly in line with this theory that the ideas in this chapter are developed.

A subjective theory of organizations provides a way of looking at organizations so that the uniqueness of individual perceptions is held in focus and becomes the major concern. Organizations exist effectively only in the experience of their members (i.e. those who experience them). A subjective theory is not very interested in whether organizations have objective existence or reality – they may or may not – the point is they can only be understood through the experiences individuals have of them. Because each of us is a different person (i.e. has a different self-concept, a different personality) each of us has a different experience of the same organization. Indeed it might be claimed that each member belongs to a different organization because experiences of 'the same' are different.

This is not to deny the physical existence of organizations since they clearly do exist otherwise no one could experience them. But the tangible and measurable is not the essential organization; there is always something else other than what is measured. For example a hospital building may be turned into a college. Physically the building is the same but its changed purposes lead one to think differently about it though the casual passer-by may still see it as a hospital. Even when we reduce an organization to people only (like a crowd in a football match) that which is observable from without (or above) is only a facet of organization since much of what is going on organizationally [the football match is the organization – organizational behaviour is everything related to the creating and experiencing of the football match so long as its occurrence can be attributed to the central activity of a football game] is invisible because it is in the minds of the members of the game and the spectators. Although everyone is at the same match, everyone experiences the events of the afternoon differently.

It is these individual responses that are of interest in subjective theory (Poole, 1975). Instead of examining organizations as aggregations, summations or majorities, the subjective theorist seeks to understand the meaning an organization has for each individual member. Of course there are enormous problems because organizational behaviour is by definition collective and so questions of agreement, consensus and control are problematical. One of the difficulties about Organization Development (OD) which as a technique for management appeals very much to individualists is that much of the emphasis appears to be on consensus and the avoidance of conflicting wishes in the greater interests of the organization or the collective good. But subjective theory does appear to provide a useful analysis of how individuals and collectivities or associations relate and no doubt OD and other management theories will respond.

If each individual has a different experience of a school, how can the school function when interests differ? There are two ways. One is for the organization to face up to the conflicts and resolve them in some way. Satisfactory resolution will lead to improved relationships; unsatisfactory resolution or avoidance will allow the conflicts to continue in some way. Of course, the organization does not do anything; the members do it, according to the way they have come to agree to work together. Usually this is in terms of the conventional positions that people hold such as manager, head, teacher, student, etc. These positions are expressed in terms of behaviour and a description of the behaviour is a role. Conventional and ritualized behaviours characterize role behaviour; that is, when there are common expectations about the appropriate behaviour for a position, that behaviour is ritualized as a 'role'. But all positions may be expressed in non-ritualized behaviour and in such a case an individual is often perceived as behaving inappropriately or denying his role (responsibilities). The rituals of organizations are explored in dramaturgical theories of organization (e.g. Mangham, 1978).

Another way of functioning is by doing everything to avoid conflict. In the normal way of things people manage to work together in an organization through a process of 'accommodation'. That is to say they reach agreement by default on all sorts of issues. In this way, two individuals of totally different personality with quite contradictory purposes may work together quite harmoniously because their differences just do not come into conflict; they can pursue their own lives as independently as passengers on a bus. The idea that individuals have to agree, have common purposes, objectives, values and so on is patently untrue although congruity in all these matters and others will lead to different and in some cases 'better' forms of association.

Relationships between individuals in an organization occur as psychological negotiations and contracts (Homans, 1961). In a perfect world these negotiations would be totally open but in practice they are generally constrained in some way. Nevertheless, all relationships are negotiated and the negotiations lead to some form of contract. Of course, these negotiations and contracts are unspoken, often subconsciously and for the most part unilaterally. Even mutual overt negotiations have a large element of unilateral reservation. When these psychological contracts are broken they are usually broken unilaterally and retrospectively. It is the unspoken nature of these negotiations that makes organizational life interesting because there is a constant element of surprise. Managers and administrators are disconcerted by these surprises because they upset their planning and control yet since they are one of the very essences of organizational behaviour a manager who is to be effective should be the kind of person to enjoy the unexpected rather than resent it.

If we pursue an interest in subjective theory, a fundamental concern is personality and how individuals develop a sense of themselves and give meaning to the world they live in (Hamachek, 1978). Personality theory is a confused area but organization theorists will tend to fall into two groups; those who believe personality is socially conditioned and those who believe personality is pre-existent but develops in terms of social opportunity. This is not the place to examine personality theory but on the whole, for a variety of reasons, organization theorists who are interested in subjective theory take a humanistic view of personality – humanistic or counselling psychology (e.g. Rogers, 1951). Much of their 'organization' theory is based upon their understanding of group behaviour, of group dynamics. My own position is akin to the latter. I see personality as a reflection of the self-concept; I believe the 'self' to be unique and pre-existent: I see organizations as opportunities for individuals to grow and develop through the process of self-discovery.

Formal organizations are simply one type of human organization but with all the characteristics of organization albeit formalized, ritualized and dramatized (Morris and Burgoyne, 1973). What happens in formal organizations happens essentially in informal organizations. Formal organizations are associations of individuals serving wider social purposes but at root having to deal with the requirements of individuals. Organizations are created by their members and do not have any inherent pre-existent form; they are not discovered, they are made and, being made by people, they are subject to people even when they are like Frankenstein's master and appear to be more powerful than their creators. They are always understood by their members differently, because they are experienced differently – a cause of perpetual exasperation to some managers.

Having very briefly outlined some of the more salient aspects of a subjective theory of organizations, I want now to deal with the implications for research and consultancy. If one views organizations from a phenomenological standpoint, there are certain quite clear imperatives for research and consultancy in which one will engage quite differently than if one has an alternative theoretical background. The presenting problems of organizations may appear the same but the explanations, solutions and approaches to solutions will be different. The researcher and consultant must approach his task with his theoretical perspective clearly in his mind or he will offer answers and explanations that are incompatible and inherently inconsistent.

I shall relate subjective theory to practice in terms of twelve propositions. Each of these represents an area of analysis and consideration and implies the terms in which an exploration will be expressed. Underlying them all is the idea that organizations exist for individuals only in terms of their experience and the understanding that comes from reflecting on that experience. Descriptions of organizational behaviour by an observer tell more about the observer than what he has observed. Interpretations and explanations are pictures created by the observer in terms that are consistent with his own intellectual framework. Objectivity is the understanding or meaning an experience has for another person in his terms not one's own interpretation of the same experience (Jehenson, 1973). What the subjective researcher and consultant is trying to do is to help his clients to understand their world better by exploring the terms in which they see it. The consultant is not explaining his own interpretation to them, though he may share his interpretations with his clients.

Such a client-centred approach has much in common with counselling and psychotherapy (Corsini, 1973). Indeed it may be called a counselling approach to consultancy (Gray, 1974) because the basic theory of the person is the same. The important element in the idea of counselling is that of listening to what the client has to say and the meaning he gives to the events and situations in which he is involved. In client-centred therapy the counsellor tries not to disturb the client's thoughts by substituting his own. That is what we need to try to do if we have a subjective theory of organizations because the solving of problems is dependent upon the correct insight into the self. Now for the propositions:

1. About Order and Disorder

'Order will always form and reform but in a different way'.

One of the deepest anxieties that people, especially managers, have about organizations is that somehow they will get out of control, that chaos will reign. Fear of losing control is pathological for some people but most managers justify strong controlling behaviour because they fear 'losing control'. Somehow 'being in complete control' is one of the expectations that managers have of themselves. The question is, what is the nature of order? In human terms there is no such thing as chaos. Chaos never reigns. Even when matters are 'beyond control' human behaviour is always purposeful. Those situations in which panic occurs are truly rare and quite special: they are not the general order of the day and, even when people panic, their behaviour becomes exceedingly purposeful.

All human behaviour is patterned in some way and responsive. When people gather together to do something they quickly organize themselves into some order. When the situation changes, they change their ordering. The problem with formal organizations is that they perpetuate a form of order suitable to a moment in time in their life and the need to perpetuate overrides other needs. There is no need to explain why this happens because it happens in many ways some of which are explained later but the authority and/or power given by a group or organization to its first leader is a matter for exploration because power tends towards consolidation and leaders tend to seek to retain power even at the expense of their followers. The question is not whether without leadership control there will be 'chaos' (because there will not; simply a more appropriate structure will emerge) but why the leader is perceived to have the power he is given. And why do leaders insist that power is not 'personal' but 'of the office' when all their behaviour is personal (because, of course, it cannot be anything else)?

2. About Structure

'Structure is a description of the behaviour of people'.

Many managers appear to be of the opinion that structure in organizations is pre-existent, that all organizations have a predetermined structure into which people must fit. This is not so. Structure is simply a description of what people do and how they relate; organization structure is a grossly simplified description of jobs and relationships. [Strictly speaking all 'organization charts' are little more than idealized representations.] A structure cannot be imposed on an organization, it can only derive from what people do. What people do is less determined by the nature of the job than the dispositions of the people doing it. Of course, some technical processes are highly determinative; there are a limited number of ways to stamp a die but most organizational tasks are complex and with increasing complexity there is a broadening of possible ways of doing things. No two people hold a pen in the same way or there would be no variation in handwriting.

To understand structure we need to explore not only what people are doing but what they believe they are doing and what kinds of explanations they give for their behaviour. It is not enough to observe people as if they were ants and to describe what the observer (believes he) sees – the problem with such writers as Desmond Morris who uses a biologist's perspective rather than a psychologist's (Morris, 1978). A headteacher will have an idea of what being a headteacher is and he will be attempting to reconcile that with the perceptions he has of himself. The conflict about position and self concept may not be observable from without yet in discussion the man may show himself to be in mental turmoil. The consequences of turmoil and uncertainty are certain forms of behaviour and a change in the individual's perceptions of role and self will lead to behavioural changes. To describe these changed behaviours is to describe the changed structures even though names of people and positions have not (apparently) changed.

3. About Objectives

'Organizations serve purposes, they do not have objectives'.

In subjective theory, because organizations have no corporeal existence apart from the experiences members have of them, there can be no 'objectives' for an organization only objectives for individual members. Furthermore, the nature of organizations as associations of people means that they are at best means to an end; that is they serve purposes. The purposes, however, are individual purposes – whatever members require the organization to do in order that something or other may be achieved.

But, more than this, individuals do not look to organizations to achieve simple and finite purposes. Human objectives are always negotiable. Whenever an individual fails in an objective, he substitutes an alternative – either an alternative solution, objective or retrospective expectation. People just do not reach a terminal point, point blank. So far as people are concerned, their contract with the organization is multiple, largely unexpressed, dependent on circumstances and on evaluation of experiences and outcomes and conditional upon the return being greater than the effort (a fair or generous reward; an unfair and punitive rebuff). To find out just what any individual wants (let alone wanted) of an organization is a difficult task because so many personal matters are involved but the answers have little or nothing to do with objective organizational goals or ascriptions.

4. About the Determinants of Behaviour

'The critical dimension in human organization is human behaviour not technology'.

On the face of it, this must appear fairly obvious but it is too often forgotten especially by managers. Time and again problems in organizations occur because managers require colleagues to respond to material and technical demands as if they were totally immovable. It needs to be remembered that human beings have an advantage over physical objects, they can always go round them. Material and technical blockages are, from the standpoint of subjective theory, no more, or less, than personal interpretations of the situation. In practice alternative strategies are always available, however disagreeable they may be at first sight. Since no situation remains static it is only a matter of time before attitudes and standpoints change.

In many cases, the constructing of technological structures has become a total impediment to perceiving the true nature of organizational relationships. Education is the classic case of non-relevant technology being imported into the system. For the essential process of teaching (more properly of education) no technology is necessary other than those present in the need-to-learn situation. Teaching/learning is a personal exchange with no essential materials other than those that are present on the occasion. (That is to say, you cannot learn to ride a bike unless you have one but you do not need a computer to learn arithmetical processes.) The false objectification of organizations will always be an intractable problem to consultants who look for 'real', 'tangible' and 'concrete' problems. But phenomenological approaches will deal with the fundamental blockages in the individual and then he will be able to proceed to deal with the objects that have meaning for him.

5. About Individual Interests

'Individuals always behave in terms of what they believe to be their best interests. Altruism is best understood in terms of self-interest'.

This is the concept of negotiation and contract described earlier. Would anyone claim that members of organizations do things in what they believe to be their worst interests? Clearly not. Since such behaviour would be pathological, it cannot be said never to occur but emotional sickness is a different problem. Just how people perceive their best interest is very complicated. Some people go around in a perpetual state of confrontation while others seem never to have a row with anyone. Observe the changeover from one trade union representative to another and the blockages of years can be cast away in seconds. Negotiating skills are not like steps in a dance or movements on the stage, though they often have those same surface characteristics, rather they derive from a disposition within the individual and the ways he conceives of himself.

One of the biggest lies in management is that a manager has only the interests of the organization or his colleagues at heart. Such statements are no more than attempted blackmail. The reality of self-interest is that it cannot be pursued without due consideration for self as well as others. Claiming altruistic interest is often no more than a consequence of identification of self and organization, a form of megalomania unfortunately not uncommon in organizations. True self-interest includes regard for others, generosity, care

A Perspective on Organization Theory

and affection but they arise out of a sense of contentment, with an acceptance of self. The consultant must explore the regard individuals have for themselves and how it conditions the regard for others. It cannot be done by observation, certainly not be aggregated data, but only by a mutual exploration of the meaning that collective activity has for the individual. Leaders are especially at risk because they may assume a responsibility for others that is only in the interests of the leader's self esteem not the good of his colleagues. Difficulties in counselling leaders often arise from their attempt to depersonalize and objectify their relation with the organization.

6. About Subjectivity and Objectivity

'Organizational experience is always subjective'.

By definition experience is subjective, though clearly the extent to which one is aware of others varies enormously. But being aware of others is not itself objective. This is not the place to argue the true nature of objectivity because the pragmatism of consultancy deals with a different relationship between the two concepts (objectivity and subjectivity). The individual's perceptions of organization are always richer in that they are subjective because reflection on one's own experience is possible but reflecting on another's is impossible. Of course, we all have views and opinions about others and we can make shrewd guesses about what they think and what they feel but we can never 'know' how they think and feel.

If the consultant is to help a manager, say the Principal of a college, to deal with a problem with staff colleagues, he can best do this by helping the Principal to understand why he sees a problem, how he constructs the problem, and interprets it, how it fills certain expectations about problems that he habitually employs, and how he perceives acceptable solutions. Obviously information about and from others in the problem situation can be obtained and discussed [many OD skills may be used such as feedback and paraphrasing: see chapter by Schmuck in this volume] but the essential task is to help the Principal to understand the way in which he perceives the situation because the problem is uniquely his; to anyone else it is uniquely different.

7. About Reality

'Organizations are personal constructs, artefacts or fantasies, existing only in the imagination of individuals'.

Obviously all organizations exist in themselves – though I am not very clear what that means – but each individual creates his own organization as an experience which consolidates in reflection. This proposition means that effectively two people working in the same school may well attend two irreconcilable institutions. I have used the term 'collective fantasy' (Gray, 1980) to describe this situation. One consequence is that the organization is capable of almost infinite development within the mind of an individual since we are all sharing a different reality in our membership. Our reality is our experience and no one's reality is greater than anyone else's.

For the consultant it means that he must help each individual client to explore what kind of an organization he has created. Many of the problems that managers have are a result of their expecting others to conform to their organizational expectations. They believe that the only permissible objectives and purposes are their own and that the validity of these expectations is directly related to position in the (fantasy) hierarchy of the organization. For some individuals a high level of fantasy is essential if the otherwise appalling reality is to be surmounted – that is, their belief that 'reality' is appalling. [This statement might be seen to imply that no level of fantasy would be 'reality'. In fact reality would be a state of maximum agreement between individual perceptions. There would always be other realities for other people. Reality is not an absolute state but a degree of congruity.]

8. About Organizational Change

'Organizational change occurs only as a consequence of changes in the individual self-concept. It is the individual's view of himself that changes, not the organization'.

Organizations do change in a lot of ways – they start up, close down, amalgamate, enter into new areas of activity. Conventional management theory is about such changes. But we need to know how and why change begins to occur. We explained earlier (proposition 4) that technical considerations are secondary variables. If a school building falls down, the 'school' may move into new accommodation. A company that starts off as a travel agents may finish up as an international bank. Such material changes still require explanation. From a phenomenological viewpoint the fabric and material is not the primary area of interest but rather the perceptions individuals have about the organization and their organizational perceptions are direct correlations of the self-image.

If we define the self concept (the self-image) as what an individual believes about himself, what he believes himself to be (the answer to the question, who am I?) then the organization to which he relates (i.e. which he experiences) will be experienced in terms of his self-concept because imaging self and others are part of the same world creation. Thinking about oneself and thinking about other than self are aspects of the same process. This is not to say the correlation between perceptions is direct and clear. An individual who likes himself may like or dislike other people according to other elements in his make up, the complexity of reasons for high self regard. High self regard may be selfish or unselfish in its effects and only deep analysis can uncover what is there.

The consultant and researcher concerned with organizational change can only deal with individuals anyway; there are no tangible organizations to deal with. Even when dealing with small groups, the *effective* changes occur in individuals never in the group. Group or collective dynamics are a different even if closely related dimension to individual behaviour and indeed there are many problems in working with groups when the individual emphasis is lost sight of.

By and large individual change occurs at what can conveniently be called the affective level of perception. That is to say cognition is a consequence of affective response. In group work it is customary to talk of 'feelings', 'gut reactions' and 'intuition' to refer to the psychological condition in which an individual says: 'Ah, now I see'. Invariably, this means he responds positively (i.e. by accepting) some feelings in his current experience and, as a consequence, sees himself differently with the further consequence that he sees the situation or organization differently. I have explained this process more fully in 'Training people to understand organizations: A clinical approach' (Gray, 1980).

9. About Organizational Functioning

'Organizations function as expressions of collective value systems and are inherently in a state of conflict'.

Much of this is inherent in what I have said already though the emphasis on values is expressed very adequately in a book by Christopher Hodgkinson (1978). On the face of it, however, it may appear to conflict with the idea of individual functioning. But each individual behaves on the basis of a personal value system, not expressed verbally but in behaviour – the underlying value system that relates to the self-concept. The strange position is that values are very often ignored as a major feature of organizational behaviour, as if values were trawled up after an expedition rather than being the very expression of relationships. In subjective theory the interest is in the variety and incongruence of individual value systems and the fantasies about organizational values. Organizational values, of course, just do not exist as an entity only the value systems of dominant individuals, a point which Hodgkinson makes very clearly.

The consultant and researcher will find considerable evidence of pervasive value systems in organizations but his first task will be to discover how they arise and which individual they reflect. The objective is not to seek common values but rather to discover what discordance there is. Value systems are highly personal and exceedingly complex and no two individuals share the

The Management of Educational Institutions: Theory, Research and Consultancy

same. Problems arise as individuals express personal values in behaviour with more than usual force or commitment. In organizations, as a general rule, accommodation takes place with regard to normal behaviour but, once behaviour changes, it changes the 'profile' of personal values, hence the need for renegotiation and new contracting. Inherent in this process is a realignment of values – changes in what is and is not acceptable. The ways in which individuals permit conflicts to be resolved depend on personal value systems – an aspect of organizational behaviour usually neglected because too personal and therefore too risky (Gray, 1975).

10. About Causation

'Activity is generated in terms of psychological exchanges between members'.

Changes within the individual's self-concept bring about a changed perspective on other people and a consequent change in the nature of psychological exchanges. The point here is just that the consultant needs to be clear about causation in organizations. It is not enough to say for example that changes in resources lead to changes in management practice. No doubt there are chains of causation that can be described in material or visible terms, but the nature of the energizing mechanisms must be uncovered. For example, the reason why a manager dismisses workers when he has a cash flow problem may be because he perceives the need to maintain the company in business as a preference to borrowing more money to tide him over a lean period. But why is he able to make such a choice? Had those to be dismissed been closely involved with him at a personal level the decision might have been different. But what makes it different? The phenomenologist tries to look for explanations in terms of the psychologically negotiated relationships and to uncover the nature of exchanges, rewards and punishments perhaps in the area of personal self-esteem.

In other words, a phenomenological stance to consultancy leads the consultant to work at as deep a psychological level as is possible and to understand organizational phenomena through some form of psychological analysis. In many cases, this leads him to embark on a psycho-therapeutic relationship with his client rather than a technological one, though technological knowledge may be used to facilitate the problem-solving processes.

11. About Authority and Leadership

'Organizations distribute roles and status without respect to individuals'.

There is an apparent paradox here but the idea is that activities such as leadership are 'functions of the organization' rather than the individual.

What happens in organizational terms is that situations require appropriate behaviours for their resolution and this can only be done by those best fitted to deal with them irrespective of their formal position or status in the organization. Does this mean that the organization does in fact function as a separate entity? Not so, because the very functioning is a consequence of the nature of personal relationships, themselves functions of individual behaviour determined by the self-concept. A group forms itself around an individual in affective terms but that does not mean that all initiatives and all authority are confined to that single individual. As relationships develop so everyone is brought into making important contributions and leadership is passed around and shared. One of the problems with charismatic leaders is that they do not allow the sharing to take place and so de-power their colleagues to the extent of incapacitation.

The consultant and researcher dealing with leadership and authority looks for the ways in which members of an organization regard each other and facilitates the sharing that goes on. He helps individuals both to accept and discard leadership behaviour according to the needs of the members of the organization.

12. About Management

'Managers can only react to events, they cannot anticipate them'.

Of course, much organizational activity is predictable in a broad sense but that is not the same as total prediction. But if an organization is running well, there is no need for any one individual to 'manage' others. Management is a form of control or (preferably) facilitation and support. Hence managerial behaviour (sc. leadership) is required only when problems arise – not only crises but the continual sequence of low level problems that are of the essence of relationships. Everyone in the organization is required to respond to problems as their skills and dispositions are appropriate. Individuals do not decide what others shall do, they can only work along with them in collective decision-making, a continuous collegiality. Sailing a boat may be a suitable analogy because sailing is a response to wind, tide and the characteristics of the boat, the captain having to be aware of what is at that moment going on, every bit as much as being aware of where he wants to go. And when conditions change, he changes his objectives, he does not abandon the boat and walk.

The consultant and researcher is concerned with discovering the prevailing condition of the organization, dealing with what is 'here and now' without being distracted by substitute and alternative desires that are an avoidance of present realities.

These, then, are twelve propositions about organizations that are important in a subjective theory of organizations. They are outlined only briefly and incompletely but provide useful questions to ask about organizations and the people who make them what they are. One idea, at least, has been left untouched; that is the idea of pathological behaviour, though the term has been mentioned. I would define pathological behaviour as self-induced behaviour which leads to the destruction of an individual or an organization. Some individuals and some organizations do seem to bring destruction on themselves and many more seem to want to. Pathological behaviour is not the same as bringing an organization to a useful end – it may often be the contrary, a stark refusal to terminate association. Much of the 'angst' of organization life is healthy and exciting and to resent and reject it is not nearly so helpful as dealing with it. In the end organizations only exist for their members and for their greater happiness. Presumably research and consultancy is about making people feel better – but that seems to be never mentioned in the literature, let alone the practice.

References

BERGER, P. and LUCKMAN, T. (1967) *The Social Construction of Reality*, Harmondsworth, Allen Lane.

CLARK, P.A. (1972) *Action Research*, London, Harper and Row.

CORSINI, R. (1973) *Current Psychotherapies*, Masca, Ill., F.E. Peacock Pubs. Inc.

DALE, ROGER (1973) 'Phenomenological perspectives in the sociology of the school', *Educational Review*, Vol. 25(3).

Educational Administration (1976, *et seq*) 'Symposium and follow up on Barr Greenfield and organization theory', 1(1) (*et seq*). Coombe Lodge, Bristol.

GRAY, H.L. (1974) 'Counselling and management', *Education and Development*, 15(1): 26–34.

GRAY, H.L. (1975) 'Exchange and conflict in the school', in HOUGHTON, V., McHUGH, R. and MORGAN, C. *Management in Education: the Management of Organizations and Individuals*, London, Ward Lock Educational/OU.

GRAY, H.L. (1980) *Management in Education*, Driffield, Nafferton Books.

GREENFIELD, T.B. (1975) 'Theory in the study of organizations and administrative structures: A new perspective', in HUGHES, M.G., *Administering Education: International Challenge*, London, Athlone Press.

GREENFIELD, T.B. (1979) 'Research in educational administration in the US and Canada: An overview and critique', Paper presented at BEAS Research Seminar.

HAMACHEK, D.E. (1978) *Encounters with the Self*, New York, Holt, Rinehart and Winston.

HODGKINSON, C. (1978) *Towards a Philosophy of Administration*, Oxford, Basil Blackwell.

HOMANS, G.C. (1961) *Social Behaviour*, London, Routledge and Kegan Paul.

HOUGHTON, V., McHUGH, R. and MORGAN, C. (1975) *Management in Education: the Management of Organizations and Individuals*, London, Ward Lock Educational/OU.

HUGHES, M.G. (Ed.) (1975) *Administering Education: International Challenge*, London, Athlone Press.

JEHENSEN, R. (1973) 'A phenomenological approach to the study of formal organization', in PSATHAS, G., *Phenomenological Sociology*, Chichester, John Wiley, Interscience.
MANGHAM, I.L. (1978) *Interactions and Interventions in Organizations*, Chichester, John Wiley.
MORRIS, D. (1978) *Manwatching*, St. Albans, Triad Panther.
MORRIS, J.F. and BURGOYNE J. (1973) *Developing Resourceful Managers*, London, Institute of Personnel Managment.
POOLE, R. (1975) 'From phenomenology to subjective method', *Universities Quarterly*, Autumn, pp. 412–440.
PSATHAS, G. (1973) *Phenomenological Sociology*, Chichester, John Wiley, Interscience.
REASON, P. (1977) 'Notes on holistic research processes and social system change', Centre for the Study of Organizational Change and Development, University of Bath.
ROGERS, C. (1951) *Client-Centred Therapy*, Boston, Houghton-Mifflin.

The Performers: Higher Education as Theatre[1]

Iain L. Mangham
Centre for the Study of Organizational Change and
Development, University of Bath

Somewhere beyond us, 'out there', is a reality which is invisible, incomprehensible and inaccessible to any of us other than through the efforts we ourselves make to render it less opaque. Reality is something each of us experiences, feels, and – in the final analysis – constructs; what we construct depends upon the metaphors we utilize to apprehend the world 'out there'. Our concepts structure what we perceive, how we act and how we relate to other people and there is considerable evidence that ordinary conceptual systems are metaphorical in nature.[2] Metaphor is much more than a literary device, an optional rhetorical flourish; much of what we call reality – our inner selves, our relations with others, our work and our social life – is not objectively given but defined by the metaphors we absorb from our culture. Some see the world in terms of systems, some in terms of machinery, others in terms of organisms; each of us has recourse to metaphor in defining reality. Without it, the spectacles through which we render our worlds less indistinct, we would see nothing; astigmatism is part of the human condition.

Some pairs of spectacles are, of course, judged better than others, though precisely why this should be the case is not always stated. Certain frames

---

Editor's note: For the most part, theories of organization and management have tended to be treated as more universally relevant than they warrant. The truth is that there are no adequate theories of organization, only ones which cast partial (but useful) illumination upon the ways people behave in organizations. The time is ripe for an exploration of many models rather than the seeking of a single complex answer. Mangham's chapter illustrates the importance and value of perspectives and simple models. If we really are to understand organizations, we must seek to understand how people give meaning to them and to appreciate the subjectivity of that experience. There is no objectivity in organizational experience.

Mangham's chapter is a reminder of how we should be looking at management theory and precept. If we wish to understand, then models for understanding should be within our comprehension otherwise they are no use to us. Read alongside the contribution by Webb and Lyons we can see just how personalistic and individualist managerial behaviour is. Hopefully, in reading these chapters we can obtain insights into our own selves and learn to use our own experience for verification of theories and the discovery of new and more relevant criteria of evaluation.

come into fashion and are regarded as the way of seeing until such time as someone declares them to be the cause of myopia and offers an alternative. Psathas[3] suggests that the utility of available frames may be judged along a couple of dimensions: first, do the consequences of seeing the world in a particular manner make sense to the ordinary social actors involved in the sphere towards which attention has been directed. 'If second order constructs were translated back into the first order constructs to which they refer, would the observer's report be recognized as a valid and faithful account of what the activity is really like?' In other words, can the natives recognize their world through your spectacles?[4]

A second and related test is whether or not other observers can find their way around the scene described (or the set of events) using the prescription of the original observer and that prescription alone, and whether or not the frame has the capacity to bring understanding to a range of events similar to the one directly addressed. Both criteria are essentially tests of plausibility which, ultimately, is the test to which all ideas in social science are subject, not excluding the ones to be presented in this chapter.

In brief, the argument presented here is that the metaphor which compares social life to drama serves to illuminate elements of behaviour in institutions of higher education that other metaphors cannot reach. I will begin with a brief history of the utilization of the metaphor in literature, social science and everyday life, continue with an outline of the major features of the metaphor as it is currently used and will conclude with an application of it as a way of seeing (and not seeing) behaviour in universities.

Literature and the Metaphor[5]

The idea that life is like the drama was promulgated almost as soon as drama itself appeared. In the Golden Age of the Greeks, many references to life as drama may be found – notably in Plato – and it seems reasonable to assert that wherever and whenever there has been a highly developed theatre, there has also been a recognition of the force of the metaphor. Burns notes that sixteenth century Spanish theatre stimulated the widespread use of the metaphor, so widespread that Cervantes has Sancho Panza remark of Don Quixote's use of the comparison: 'A fine comparison, although not so new that I haven't heard it on various occasions before – like the one of the game of chess'.

Not surprisingly, in England's great flowering of the theatre – the Elizabethan period – the use of the metaphor also burgeons. The works of Shakespeare are replete with drama/life allusions and the very construction of some of his plays (the idea of the play within the play) makes free with the notion. French dramatists utilized the notion, as in our time have German and Italian playwrights such as Brecht and Pirandello. Indeed, in the twentieth century the notion that 'All the world's a stage, and all the men and women merely players' has become a stale commonplace.

Sociology and the Metaphor

Part of this staleness may be attributed to the use the social scientists have made of the imagery of the theatre. Some of the core concepts of sociology, such as role theory, derive from the theatre and those writers in this discipline have not been slow to plunder drama for other concepts and for more general frameworks. In sociology the most comprehensive view of life as theatre is in the work of Erving Goffman, although his insights may be seen as the culmination of points made throughout the history of social science by writers such as Weber, Simmel, Cooley, Thomas and Mead[6].

Weber, while making no direct reference to life as drama, gave the impetus to the use of the metaphor by others by suggesting that action can only be understood by reference to the subjective experience of social actors as they seek to understand the behaviour of others by placing themselves in the others' position, a notion which was developed later in role theory. Simmel, who does make explicit reference to and comments upon actors and acting, noted that although people do perform certain roles there is always, waiting in the wings as it were, an actor behind the parts performed, a self beyond the social selves; again an insight that has been developed considerably by others. George Herbert Mead indirectly gave the metaphor more life when his ideas, later published in *Mind, Self and Society*, were given currency by his students and his colleagues, leading, eventually, to the development of a tradition of study which became known as 'symbolic interaction'[7]. There is considerable dispute as to whether Goffman actually belongs to any particular tradition, but there is little argument that his work is influenced by the figures mentioned above. His basic themes rely heavily upon the theatre and upon ideas culled from his predecessors, encompassing, as they do, concepts such as 'role', 'front-stage', 'backstage', 'role-distance', 'self as performer', 'management of identity', 'audience', 'stage fright' and the like.

Everyday Acting

The utilization of this particular metaphor throughout the centuries but in particular its popularization in the twentieth century by writers such as Goffman and others has had consequences for social actors in that, since the concept of life as theatre has entered everyday consciousness, to some social actors life may become theatre. It is arguable that for them, 'real' life is a theatrical production; everyday actions are construed in terms learned from the theatre and more particularly from the movies and the television.[8] Even the most cursory glances at popular magazines and journals will confirm that everyday conversation is spotted with references to 'acting out of character', 'performing', 'playing the villain', 'acting the fool' and so on. The fundamental features of this view of everyday acting appear to be fourfold: the first is that the social actors are conscious that they are 'on' –

they are playing parts; the second is that appearances matter – dress, posture, gesture and action may be manipulated so as to influence interaction; a third and related feature is that social actors not only perform, they also serve as a charitable audience for each other, as Goffman puts it, we are predisposed to cooperate to save each other's face (if you lay claim to a particular identity in an interaction – other things being equal – I am unlikely to challenge it and I rely upon you to be as charitable to me in my performances); the fourth feature is that the social actors in their interaction with others can and do become aware of themselves *as* acting out roles or parts – in such circumstances, they may signal their role distance and will be aware that they have levels of being other than the self being presented in that particular setting.

It is these elements of the dramaturgical perspective on everyday life, advanced by Goffman[9] and others, which give rise to much of the criticism of the perspective.[10] Fundamentally, the metaphor as currently utilized emphasizes *acting* natural to deceive both self and others and posits a limited, game-playing variety of human behaviour; if one reads closely enough, Goffman is telling actors how to become smashing successes *within* the given script, the structure of the bureaucracy. The perspective, as I have indicated, stresses presentation, packaging, manipulation and deceit, and, in this respect, does not accord with the perspective many social actors have on their own behaviour, whatever they may think about the behaviour of others.

This is not to say, however, that the utility of the theatrical metaphor is strictly limited: certainly not as limited as implied by the criticisms of Goffman's work. It is to state nothing more than the obvious; to date the metaphor has not been fully explored.[11] In what follows I wish to extend the metaphor by seeking to understand social life by reference to the theatrical concepts of possession and rehearsal, as well as to the more commonly accepted ideas of self-presentation and altercasting. I will begin with the latter, drawing heavily upon my own previous work and upon that of Goffman, Perinbanayagam, and McCall and Simmons.[12]

A Model and Some Consequences[13]

The first assumption of the model of behaviour that I am putting forward is that action can only occur and individual purposes can only be realized through the sharing of meaning about particular events, situations and relationships and such sharing is realized symbolically, rhetorically and dramatically. Theatre is at the heart of social life; interaction, and hence social structure, since the larger system is ultimately dependent upon the successful functioning of microscopic and episodic action systems, relies upon the acting ability of those party to it. People in each other's presence take steps to ensure that others, involved in the particular encounter or transaction, are made aware of their purposes and intentions as they want them to be 'taken account of'. In any given interaction social actors will take steps not only to present their own intentions and purpose, but also to determine the identity and purposes of the other social actors involved. Each social actor makes the other aware and, in turn, is made aware of the other's identity and purposes by the taking of necessary steps to publicize identities and intentions. Whatever the actor publicizes, either by dress, posture, gesture or speech, becomes the data that the other actors can 'take account of' and thereby can 'orient' their own behaviour accordingly.

> In other words the actor becomes aware of the other's subjective 'experiences' *only to the extent that these experiences are dramaturgically available*. Interaction proceeds as the basis of *whatever it is that one takes to be the other's* subjective experience ... [14]
>
> (italics in original)

The presentation of self is thus the key feature of all interaction. It discloses who we wish to be and how we wish to be treated; it also discloses who we wish others to be and how we wish to treat them. *Self-presentation*, that is, casts not only our own part in the situational script, it also casts others into parts. The roles made by participants in a particular situation are reciprocal – the role of interviewee played by an individual implies the role of interviewer, that of comedian, audience, and so on. The notion of presentation of self focuses upon the individual's effort to make a role and present an appearance of that role to others. *Altercasting* examines the other side of the coin, as it were, the effect that a self-presentation has upon the other party's ability to respond. Each self-presentation is in a sense an attempt to constrain the potential response; if I behave as a teacher, my presentation casts you in the role of pupil; if I present myself as helpless, I seek to impose on you the role of helper. Altercasting operates by seeking to place limits upon the capacity of others to play parts of their own choosing.[15]

Each actor acts on the basis of his particular definition; as he expresses what he takes to be the appropriate behaviour it becomes obvious whether or not his perspective is shared by others. In many cases the various definitions are compatible; people are familiar with the situational script, find few problems with the roles assigned to them and fit their lines and actions to those of others with little or no difficulty. Thus few problems arise where preliminary definitions and initial impressions are accurate predictions of the developing situation.

Occasionally definitions are incompatible and a process of improvization occurs, influenced by the physical setting, the props and purposes of others. The outcome is a compromise, an improvized reality which allows the interaction to proceed on at least a temporary basis. What usually transpires in problematic situations is that individuals are seldom allowed to perform exactly the role they would like nor do they comply exactly with the roles in which they are cast by others. Continuation of the interaction is dependent, therefore, on the ability of the participants to accommodate or at least to align themselves with some part of the projected and interpreted reality. What develops, in effect, is an agreement not to disagree; a working agreement that allows the participants to proceed, characterized not by consensus and clear agreement, but more by the absence of large scale disagreement. At the very centre of human behaviour, therefore, is definition and performance, compromise and improvization.[16]

All of this is, of course, a familiar perspective on social life as theatre and based upon the notion that acting in the theatre is characterized by self awareness, memory, a sense of direction and will. Social actors, on the other hand, do not always manifest such characteristics and, it may be argued, have much more a sense of being possessed by their roles than is implied by what has been presented so far in this chapter.[17] To themselves at least, they *are* teachers, not actors playing at, pretending to be or acting teachers. It seems to me that such views, although common, are an oversimplification both of what prevails in the theatre and in social life. Consciousness is not invariably or completely obliterated by possession nor, for that matter, are stage actors always totally in control of their performances. It is not uncommon to find them claiming that they have been taken over by the characters they are playing. Nor is it uncommon to find teachers consistently adopting specific strategies and techniques to sustain their performances as teachers. Actors strive to *become* their characters just as social actors strive to *become* the parts they are called upon to play; circumstances may call into doubt the spontaneity of any particular performance (more on this shortly), but for the most part social actors perform as if they had never played the parts before. Shaw's comment about professional actors may be as readily applied to social actors: '... even in the thousandth night, the actor can make the audience believe that he has never heard his cue before'. Social performance, like theatrical performance, may be informed by the entire spectrum of possible states of consciousness, from total unreflecting possession through to the cool, distanced manipulation of one's own performance and that of others.

The major concepts and assumptions of the perspective which I have put forward so far have stressed the creative participation of individuals in social and organizational process. I make no apology for this since I hold that the coordination of conduct in organizations or elsewhere depends, in the final analysis, upon how individuals present themselves and interpret the presentation of others. A significant part of the social order of any institution is based upon the definition of reality created and maintained by its members. The emphasis, however, does less than justice to the apparent patterned regularity of much social life; viewed from a distance the everyday conduct of members of any particular organization appears to be far from creative and individualistic. Like ants, people seem to be scurrying back and forth in an extremely routine and purposeful fashion, their behaviour so patterned and apparently culturally determined that notions of individuality and creativity may seem quite unnecessary. The daily round is not one of constant improvization, conscious interpretation and careful rehearsal, since much of what passes for everyday interaction has a taken-for-granted, well-rehearsed quality. Much of

The Performers: Higher Education as Theatre

what is deemed to constitute 'normal' interaction is non-problematic. Actors do not interact in a void and construct their social world *ab initio* on each and every occasion, but they approach interaction already influenced by past social experience and, to a marked extent, their choices (insofar as they are aware of them at all) are limited, if not determined, by the patterns of behaviour most frequently used by other social actors past and present, in what are taken to be similar circumstances. Such patterns of mutual accommodation arise as individuals seek to make the world more predictable by structuring their associations. For each person, an encounter with another constitutes an opportunity to reduce equivocality and to achieve some personal goal. Encounters, of course, also serve to maintain social order. When a relatively stable working agreement is arrived at, it may be in the interest of both parties to preserve it and in such cases we have the elements of what may be termed a joint act or a situational script.[18]

A great deal of behaviour is orderly and routine and has the character of being well rehearsed. Social actors know what is expected of them and perform, with minor variations, in line with the expectations. Our performance in management meetings, staff meetings, union branch meetings, parent/teacher associations and so on is adequate testimony that in many, many circumstances, we know how to conduct ourselves ritually and ceremonially. At the other end of the continuum are the circumstances in which expectations and parts to be played are much less clear and much more subject to improvization. The more novel or problematic the situation, the more consciously must those involved create and test out particular courses of action. The distinction between routine and the novel is, however, much less absolute than is implied above. In a number of routine circumstances, there is room for improvization and innovation and in the most novel of circumstances there is often an element of the stable and the predictable.

However, both the routine and standard responses to circumstances as well as the improvized ones depend upon the processes of interpretation. Just as the actor must arrive at a consistent interpretation of his part, which he does in association with his colleagues, essentially by a process of offering characterizations and adjusting those offered by his fellow players, so social actors, through the social process, improvize and sustain order.

> The meanings that underlie established and recurrent joint action are themselves subject to pressures as well as to reinforcements, to incipient dissatisfaction as well as to indifference; they may be challenged as well as affirmed ... allowed to slip along without concern as well as subjected to infusions of new vigour ... it is the social process in group life that creates and upholds the rules, not the rules that create and uphold group life.[19]

The last quotation contains the nub of the argument I am putting forward: *social process creates and upholds the rules, not the rules uphold the process.* Clearly this is an overstatement, since the relationship must be interactive; process influences rules and rules process. The emphasis, however, is chosen to highlight the fundamental and occasionally overlooked importance of process. Put another way, organization may be seen as a process – a continuous exchange of definitions and affirmation or otherwise of working agreements – and not simply as a structure of rules, regulations and procedure within which all is order. All shared understandings lack permanence and must be continually reaffirmed or renegotiated; rules, procedures, order and structure are not automatic occurrences (however taken for granted they may appear) but rather must be worked at and sustained by the repeated acts of participants. The working scripts which characterize organizational life arise from and are dependent upon the processes of interpretation and self-presentation, altercasting and improvization.

Performance and Rehearsal

It is clear that the framework outlined above differs from role theory in that it stresses interpretation and improvization far more than does the work of Parsons, Merton, Gross, or, for that matter, Biddle.[20] It differs from the work of Goffman in that I have indicated that much of social life *and* of theatrical performance may be characterized as informed by variable amounts of consciousness or self awareness. Social actors may be possessed by their roles, may experience their performances as spontaneous, in the same way that actors do. For role theorists, role performance consists in meeting the expectations of members of one's role set with the intention of attaining positive sanctions or, at the very least, avoiding negative ones. Such a mechanistic conformity to a role script may indeed be observed in the classic theatre where action and character are prescribed and inviolable. In Japanese Noh theatre, for example, the actor is limited to the precise gestures and inflections which have been handed down for centuries – no deviation is permitted, expected or attempted. My argument has been, and is, that while scripts may exist for a number of relationships within an organization, for a great many circumstances no detailed script exists and therefore the individuals concerned must improvize a performance within relatively broad limits. At the point where this occurs, the behaviour of the social actors concerned may be said to have the character of a theatrical rehearsal. As professional actors build towards a performance, they take advantage of the fact that their fellow actors are, in effect, the first audience of the work being created. An actor playing Hamlet, for example, may play the scene through once, seeking to project in his performance the impact of what he takes to be the essence of what should be expressed. The actress playing Gertrude (or whoever) will be able to perceive what the actor playing Hamlet has in mind and either agree with it or not. In turn, through her improvized performance, she can offer an interpretation. In the course of the rehearsal, each actor, perceiving the work of their colleagues, comes to understand and is expected to accommodate or influence, the developing conception of the scene as a whole. Of course, there is much more to rehearsal than this, but access to the theatrical metaphor even at this simple and, perhaps, simplistic level allows us to consider social life as having the character of performance – a finished product played through with an air of spontaneity and naturalness – or as having the character of rehearsal wherein the social actors struggle to define and pin down the nature of the most appropriate performance. For the role theorist, social and organizational life tends towards the ritual or classic drama, whereas in the perspective adopted above, I have tended to emphasize the improvized, the extemporaneous aspect of rehearsal.[21]

Both are, of course, exaggerations and, indeed, one begets the other; that which begins as improvization in rehearsal may persist in classic form. It may be more useful to conceive of performances within organizations and across organizations as varying along a continuum with classic, ritual drama at one end and improvized theatre at the other. Clearly a great deal of activity within universities may be fairly characterized as ritual or classic drama. The formal conferment of degrees, for example, has all the hallmarks of a rite of passage and is scripted and acted out accordingly; distinguished scholars dressed in splendid and outmoded gowns adorned with anachronistic headgear and preceded by functionaries bearing seals of office, royal charters, maces and the like parade solemnly through a hushed and expectant audience. Although many present may be aware that they are 'on', taking part in an elaborate performance, many others may be possessed by their roles and few depart from the sacred script. The purpose of the drama is transcendental since all involved recognize that they are foregathered to give substance to the notion of graduation; whatever the differences of principle, of emphasis and objectives manifest elsewhere, here the idea of a collectivity united in scholarship is celebrated.

Classic performance is, of course, clear in other settings within the university but is not necessarily marked by such obvious attention to costume and conduct. Writers of fiction such as Kingsley Amis, C.P. Snow, David Lodge and Malcolm Bradbury have given us some very fine examples; Roger Holmes provides an example from the perspective of a social psychologist in his paper 'The university seminar and the primal horde'.[22] Writing about the formal university seminar (where there is a chairman and sometimes a vote of thanks), he uses Freud's notion of the primal horde to illuminate some aspects of the behaviour that may be observed in such settings. For present purposes, I have taken the liberty of recasting his analysis in more theatrical terms. He notes that 'most of the speaker's – and the follower's – behaviour has been so encroached upon by ritual' that it cannot be analyzed usefully in any other terms. He notes that in rituals, the leader is surrounded by a quasi-magical aura and yet is 'simultaneously wholly emasculated in that their behaviour is rendered totally predictable'.

The seminar leader, argues Holmes, is often required to read his paper and acknowledge his sources, thus becoming – to all intents and purposes – a performer and, literally, a follower of a script. Seminars have little of the quality of improvization mentioned earlier but rather are marked by a ceremonial order, a format within which the principal actor is constrained to perform. He must read his paper, quote his sources, acknowledge that he is aware of the great honours heaped upon him by being asked to speak to such an audience and simultaneously declare that he is unworthy of them; there are so many in the room so much more fit than he to hold forth on this particular topic and he must appear to mean it.

The members of the audience also know their parts and faithfully carry them out. Such parts are marked by an ambivalence which may be part of all ritual; the members of the audience, Holmes argues, cannot tolerate the thought that the speaker has been called upon to talk on a subject upon which they, as members of the audience, are supposedly expert: someone else pontificating may serve to underline their own inferiority. They may thus be predisposed to derision and conduct themselves accordingly. On the other hand, the speaker may actually have something to contribute so derision must not be pressed too far, must not become contempt. However, taking the speaker seriously may lead to attack and derision from fellow members of the audience ('How could you still believe in that sort of outdated nonsense ...'). So a part in the audience has to be approached with some care; one must carefully signal attendance but not conviction and must give the impression that although open to persuasion one is not so naïve as to believe in everything that is being presented by the speaker. On the one hand, one must take care not to draw upon oneself the magical retaliation of the speaker and on the other, one must not risk derision from one's fellows. Both of which constitute good reasons for not sitting in front.

> How much better to join the Doubting Thomases, who – once they have turned up – take up their defensive/aggressive positions along the back, round the sides, and, best of all, near an exit. From there, of course, they can pour scorn upon the speaker and the gullible alike, and, by the barbed tones of their ostensibly polite questions reveal their superiority to those to whom alas! they cannot remain indifferent.

All such questions and answers are, of course, directed with elaborate ritual through the Chair and herein lies the clue to much of the ceremonial order of the University.

Classic theatre uses a special language – preferably archaic but certainly formal and heightened; it is also concerned with authority and formality. In the university, many circumstances are informed by carefully scripted references to authority and by a heightened sense of formality. The Vice Chancellor in the Senior Common Room may be Tom, Dick or Mary but in the Senate Chamber (nice archaism there) it is the office of 'Vice Chancellor' that is addressed and colleagues (elsewhere referred to by all manner of sobriquets) are there addressed as 'The distinguished Professor of Obstetrics' or whatever

The Performers: Higher Education as Theatre

and, what is more, addressed not directly but 'through the Chair'. The rigmarole of procedure ('On a point of order, Vice Chancellor ... ') and the care taken over the sacred text – the Minutes – ('Is it your wish that I sign these as a true and correct record of our proceedings ... ?') – together with the constraint imposed by the balanced and often special seating, emphasize that in this setting, if nowhere else, performances must follow the appropriate and sanctioned pattern. And, note, they are rarely played 'tongue-in-cheek'; the script is followed and performed as if for the first time.

Malcolm Bradbury, Professor of American Studies at the University of East Anglia, captures the theatrical nature of the departmental meeting brilliantly in his novel 'The History Man'.[23] The extract reproduced below, taken out of context as it must be, hardly does justice to the depth of his insight but does, I believe, illuminate the point that I have been labouring to make.

> Professor Marvin ... says 'Can we now come to order, gentlemen?'. Immediately the silence breaks; many arms go up, all round the table; there is a jabber of voices. 'May I point out, Mr Chairperson, that of the persons in this room you are addressing as "gentlemen", seven are women?' says Melissa Todoroff. 'May I suggest the formulation "Can we come to order, persons?" or perhaps "Can we come to order, colleagues?"'. 'Doesn't the phrase itself suggest we're somehow normally in a state of *dis*order?' asks Roger Fundy. 'Can I ask whether under Standing Orders of Senate we are bound to terminate this meeting in three and a half hours? And if so, whether the Chairman thinks an agenda of thirty four items can be seriously discussed under these limitations, especially since my colleagues will presumably want to take tea?' 'On a point of information, Mr Chairman, may I point out that the tea interval is not included within the three and a half hours limitation, and also draw Dr Petworth's attention to the fact that we have concluded discussion of larger agendas in shorter times?' 'Here?' asks someone. 'May I ask if it is the wish of this meeting that we have a window open?' The meeting has started; and it is always so. It has often been remarked, by Benita Pream, who services such departmental meetings, that those in History are distinguished by their high rate of absenteeism, those in English by the amount of wine consumed afterwards, and those in Sociology by their contentiousness ...

The essence of the classic drama in universities however, as elsewhere, lies not in the rigid adherence to the words (the term script should not be taken literally) but in the predictable nature of the patterns of behaviour which are enacted. A script in the sense used here is a structure that describes appropriate sequences of events in a particular context; a predetermined, stereotyped sequence of actions that define a well-known situation. There are scripts for eating in restaurants, watching and playing cricket or football, participating in seminars and staff meetings, and so on. Both what Holmes and what Bradbury have to say is plausible because we can recognize, at least to some extent, the events which they describe; there is a classic element to the formal seminar just as there is a classic element in a departmental meeting; the metaphor drawn from drama highlights these features in a way which few other metaphors attempt.

Presentation of Self and Altercasting

Before concluding this chapter with some comments upon the improvization of order within institutions of higher education and upon the endemic tendency towards rehearsal they display, some comments upon the performers may be appropriate. One man in his time is called upon to play many parts, sometimes in the classic or ritual dramas of his particular setting, sometimes backstage. Success in his endeavours depends, in part at least, on histrionic ability; the capacity to present in a simple and charismatic fashion some side of oneself or one's policies such that the presentation draws the plaudits of one's supporters and silences the opposing claque. Self presentation, it will be recalled, is an attempt to structure encounters by suggesting or imposing a definition of the situation in such a way as to constrain others to perform in line with your wishes. Again novelists have presented us with a long and often humorous list of characters to be found performing in higher education but few can match the list of 'masks' provided by the political anthropologist, F.G. Bailey.[24] He notes ten self presentations – which read like a cast list for a Restoration play: Reason, Buck (the currency), Sermon, Stroke, Saint, Baron, Formula, Rational, Patron and Rock – some of which, as with Holmes, I have taken the liberty of recasting in my terminology in order to illustrate the utility of the metaphor I am advancing in this chapter.

Reason presents himself as one who believes that every problem has a solution and that this solution is discoverable through reasoned debate and reasoned argument. What is more, he implies in every phrase and gesture that, once discovered, the solution will be accepted and implemented, since everyone will be able to see the logic. His altercasting is obvious if somewhat crude: I am reasonable, therefore you must be. Bailey characterizes Reason as a 'technician of the intellect', who refuses to countenance the full sordidness of human nature: 'jealousy, motive, love, personal ambition, all other irrational things, which in fact fuel the thinking machine' are disregarded. He presents himself as somewhat aloof from the political fray, someone whose reasoned advice is obvious to those with eyes to see and who is thus not disposed to fight for his point of view since 'if one is casting pearls, one should not also be asked to blow them down the creature's throat'.

Another finely drawn performer in Bailey's cast list is that of Sermon. He presents himself as the guardian of our eternal verities. If Reason is expert at erecting fine chains of argument from first principle to action, Sermon is expert in first principles, and sees no need for their justification. He operates by simply asserting: 'The tradition of this University is and has always been ... '; 'Standards of scholarship long established in this community require ... '. Whereas Reason seeks to cast others as reasonable, Sermon seeks to obviate the need for argument; since it has been thus and thus and since all right minded people respect authority, then it follows ... and so forth. A windy fellow much given to platitudes.

One other from Bailey: Formula. He is a relation of Reason but differs from him in that he believes that solutions to all problems exist already in the Statutes, Regulations and Ordinances and need only to be applied. Thus he is also nephew to Sermon, since he too presents himself as one who believes in the ultimate wisdom of that which has been long established and he operates so as to cast others into similar moulds. He is never more delighted than when regulations are being bandied back and forth across the Senate Chamber.

A final couple from myself (it is an activity anyone may indulge in): Sneerwell or Backbite, truly Restoration characters. Their particular strength lies in allowing others such as Reason, Sermon or Formula to erect huge balloons replete with rational argument, precedent or principle which they then deflate with a well chosen phrase from the classics or the bible; if it can be done in Latin, Greek or Hebrew, so much the better because they thus reap the double benefit of disabling their targets and of causing their colleagues to laugh at allusions which, for the most part, they do not understand. Some have been known to make entire Senate careers from little else than a close study of the Oxford Book of Quotations.

One last character, although the temptation to continue is great: Bemused. This presentation consists of asking questions or making interjections which others regard as almost spectacularly inane or irrelevant. This demonstration of incompetence or, at best, unworldliness, is often sufficiently well done, however, to serve its perpetrator well since it often operates to save him from service on sub-committees, working parties and the like. Such interjections as are made from this character can occasionally promote the most splendid of bureaucratic tangles, as when innocent or naïve questions about, say, promotions, salaries or allocations are raised in what others deem as the wrong settings.

The Tendency to Improvization in Higher Education

The actions of Bemused may thus serve to challenge the rules which hitherto have prevailed; the drama is transformed from the predictable to the spontaneous, the closely scripted to the improvized. Such behaviour, as I have previously asserted, is not common; for the most part, organizations may be characterized by the boring little stories which constitute situational scripts with which all concerned are familiar and within which most are content to perform.

Rehearsal, as I have indicated, has a 'stop and think' quality to it which, for the most part, is not a characteristic of performance; indeed, to stop the graduation ceremony and debate its possible form, or to speculate in the middle of a seminar on its process to the neglect of the content of one's presentation could – at best – be regarded as somewhat eccentric behaviour. In many, many social situations in institutions of higher education as elsewhere, familiar and appropriate scripts are readily accessible and can be used to provide concise and coherent descriptions of what is going on.[25] In certain circumstances, however, actors can appear to be unsure of their parts, uncertain of the appropriate conventions or – in extreme cases – they may appear to be performing in completely different plays. In such situations, the process of rehearsal may readily be observed; for example, the beginnings of low structure events such as T-Groups or sensitivity training sessions are often characterized by numerous and often divergent attempts on the part of participants to structure the event as, indeed, are meetings of new committees with ill-defined objectives, though these tend to move quite rapidly into well defined committee scripts.

Public performances such as seminars, meetings of Senate and Council, Graduation ceremonies and the like are rarely likely to be characterized by processes of rehearsal; each of us has sufficient world knowledge as to what to expect and how to align ourselves with regard to others to enable us to put on a successful performance. Much of the rehearsal quality of social interaction may, however, be observed backstage, as it were, in the more private areas of the institution, although very occasionally the predictability of a public routine breaks down and uncertainty casts us all into rehearsal and improvization. Consider the following exchange which I witnessed (with barely concealed delight and no little embarrassment) in an interview for a post in a university. The session had followed the usual routine for establishing identity, credentials, job experience and the like, and was proceeding according to the fully expected if somewhat rambling script when the chairman, an eminent full professor, asked the candidate the standard polite question and received a somewhat non-standard response:

Chairman: Well, would you now like to tell us a little bit more about your research interests?

Candidate: No.

Chairman: Oh. (*Waits for candidate to relieve the tension created by his remark. No relief forthcoming. Assumes or pretends to assume that he may have been misunderstood.*) Research interests. Well ... we need to know ... Couldn't you just briefly indicate the areas which interest you?

Candidate: No. (*Long, long silence, during which members of the committee look at each other, shrug, smile, study the table, and so on. The candidate stares steadily at the Chairman.*)

The Performers: Higher Education as Theatre

Chairman: Do you mind telling me why not?

Candidate: I don't believe that you would be able to understand it. You and I are poles apart in our approaches to the subject, so it would be a waste of my time trying to get my ideas across to you.

Clearly we were faced in this usually predictable script with that which I have termed rehearsal – a 'stop-and-think' – before we could proceed or terminate the interview. For many scripts, we are aware of the more common 'what-ifs' (whiffs)[26] and have set routines to deal with them; in this circumstance, we had no whiff for an outright refusal to talk and had to improvize new roles and a new script. More often than not, as I have indicated, ambiguity and uncertainty is handled in private places, rehearsal and improvization takes place out of the public gaze. Thus Senate working parties, and small, often informal groupings, need to 'sort out' issues before they are given a public airing. Thus in universities, as elsewhere, one may readily observe social actors indulging in such dry runs: let us assume, the discussion may go, that I make the following proposal; how might you (your group, your school, your faculty or whatever) respond. Well, we might do such-and-such. How would you respond to that? Thus in offices and common rooms, small committee rooms and Vice Chancellor's lodges, the possible scripts are tested and the performances polished. Unlike other institutions, however, universities may be more likely to have recourse to more public rehearsal than many other institutions; failure to work hard at upholding the rules may, in the case of universities, lead to a rapid collapse of the rules and a fragmentation of the situational script. It is worth expending a sentence or two as to why this should be the case.

Cohen and March described institutions of higher education as examples of 'organized anarchies'; loose collections of professionals with highly ambiguous purposes, structures and criteria of performance.[27] Leaders of such institutions 'felt themselves to be the victims of the pressures upon them and the limitations of time and their own energies .... Too many "trivial" activities that had to be engaged in. No time for thinking or reading or initiating action'. Another study has suggested the relationship between lack of presidential self-direction and lack of institutional shared purpose: most presidents testified that they could not direct effect toward the area they themselves perceived as their greatest responsibility – providing purpose and direction for their institutions.[28] Such studies are valuable and just about half right; the point is not that the leaders do not know where they are going (which may or may not be the case), but that there is – and *given the nature* of institutions of higher education always may be – a lack of *institutional shared purpose*. Rice and Bishoprick provide a typology of organizations based on a single dimension – the right of members to determine an organization's goals – which may serve to advance the analysis a step or two further.[29]

They identify four types of organization: directive, consensual, democratic and collegial. The first three need not concern us except insofar as they may illuminate aspects of the fourth: the collegial. Colleges 'represent the opposite end of the spectrum from the directive organization' in which 'orders come from the central authority and are to be obeyed'. This is far from being the case in the collegial systems which, insofar as they recognize the need for direction, achieve agreement on it through the use of committees.

Drawing some of these ideas together, we have a situation in which an *association* of loosely organized souls seek to protect themselves, acquire and expend resources through a system based upon committees and lacking any widely shared *institutional* goal. Institutions of higher education are, for the most part, characterized by a lack of clear, agreed objectives and purposes. Many of the members look upon themselves as colleagues in a community of scholars, equals in the pursuit of knowledge and justifiably impatient with structures and procedures which, in their eyes, unnecessarily hamper this activity. My contention is that, since few can agree on the overriding purpose of the organization and few devote their energies to sustaining any such purpose but all reserve their right to comment upon or disagree with particular actions, no situational script is safe, all the meanings that underlie established and recurrent joint action are subject to dissatisfaction and challenge. Institutions of higher education can thus be seen as an ideal type of improvized order, the dyadic encounter writ large, whereby those party to it try to accommodate or at least align themselves with some part of the projected and interpreted reality. Order for professionals, but particularly for professionals who have but the weakest of associations, is always and inevitably improvised and frequently temporary. Institutions of higher education are peculiarly open to a shifting improvization of order; since all may have a hand in the formulation of the roles all – ultimately and theoretically – may have a hand in rewriting the scripts.

One man in his time plays many parts – some of them grossly under-rehearsed. Despite the ubiquity and provenance of the theatrical analogy, to paraphrase Sean O'Casey, it has been grossly under-utilized. This chapter has done little to redress that circumstance insofar as it, too, has but made light use of it although, I trust, it has rendered that which has been described and addressed sufficiently plausible to cause others to wish to pursue the metaphor in more depth. The time is ripe for such a development since, not to put too fine a point on it, few other analogies have proved useful. As Merton comments, 'We have many concepts but few confirmed theories; many points of view, but few theorems; many "approaches" but few arrivals. Perhaps a shift in emphasis would be all to the good'.[30]

Notes and References

1 This chapter has benefited from the comments of my colleagues Cyril Tomkins, Ian Colville and Michael Overington.

2 For further comment, see *On Metaphor* edited by Sheldon Sacks, University of Chicago Press, 1979.
3 PSATHAS, G. (1973) *Phenomenological Sociology: Issues and Application*, New York, Wiley Interscience, pp. 12–14.
4 There are, of course, problems with Psathas' criteria, not the least being the implication that the natives are the *prime* judges of the utility of a particular framework. For my present purposes, I have chosen not to enter this debate.
5 This section draws heavily upon the work of Elizabeth Burns (1972) *Theatricality*, New York, Harper Torchbooks.
6 See WEBER, M. (1921) *The Theory of Economic and Social Organization*, New York, Free Press (1947); and WOLFF, K. (Ed.), *The Sociology of Georg Simmel*, New York, Free Press.
7 MEAD, G.H. (1934) *Mind, Self and Society: From the Standpoint of a Social Behaviourist*, edited with an introduction by Charles W. Morris, Chicago, University of Chicago Press. For an interesting comment upon the philosopher's work see David L. Miller's (1973) *George Herbert Mead: Self, Language and the World*, University of Texas Press. Symbolic Interactionism in its various guises is covered in MELTZNER, B.N., PETRAS, J.W. and REYNOLDS, L.T. (1975) *Symbolic Interactionism: Genesis, varieties and criticism*, London, Routledge and Kegan Paul.
8 See, for example, OAKES, P. (1976) *A Cast of Thousands*, London, Gollancz.
9 GOFFMAN, E. (1959) *Presentation of Self in Everyday Life*, Garden City, New York, Anchor Books.
10 See the comments of GOULDNER and others (1975) in MELTZNER, B.N., PETRAS, J.W. and REYNOLDS, L.T. *op. cit.*
11 It is currently being expressed by myself and Michael Overington. See *Organizational Appearances and Theatrical Realities*, John Wiley (forthcoming); 'Dramatism and the theatrical metaphor: Really playing at critical distances', in MORGAN, G. (Ed.) (forthcoming) *Research Strategies: The Links Between Theory and Method*, Heinemann; 'Performance and rehearsal: Social order and organizational life', *Symbolic Interaction*, 5, Spring 1982.
12 GOFFMAN, E. (1959), *op. cit.* PERINBANAYAGAM, R.S. (1974), 'The definition of the situation: An analysis of the ethnomethodological and dramaturgical view', *Sociological Quarterly*, 15, pp. 521–541; MCCALL, G.J. and SIMMONS, J.L. (1966), *Identities and Interactions*, New York, Free Press.
13 The framework proposed draws upon my previous book (1978) *Interactions and Interventions in Organizations*, London, John Wiley and Sons, where a full acknowledgement of sources may be found.
14 Drawn from a very fine paper: PERINBANAYAGAM, R.S. (1974) *op. cit.*
15 For further comments upon altercasting, see WEINSTEIN, E.A. and DEUTSCHBERGER, P. (1964) 'Tasks, bargains and identities in social interaction', *Social Forces*, 42, 451–456.
16 The most comprehensive account of the negotiation of working agreements may be found in MCCALL, G.J. and SIMMONS, J.L. (1966) *op. cit.* A recent work by Anselm Strauss considerably extends the notion of negotiated order (1978) *Negotiations: Varieties, Contexts, Processes and Social Order*, San Francisco, Jossey Bass Inc.
17 For an interesting discussion of the notion of possession as applied to the stage, see COLE, D. (1975) *The Theatrical Event: a Mythos, a Vocabulary, a Perspective*, Connecticut, Wesleyan University Press.

18 See particularly my book *Interactions and Interventions in Organizations, op. cit.*
19 Source of the quote: BLUMER, H. (1969) *Symbolic Interactionism*, New Jersey, Prentice Hall. Blumer is essential reading, particularly as it was he who coined the term 'symbolic interactionism'.
20 Role theory is clearly closely related to much of what I have to say, although it has tended to be somewhat too deterministic for my taste. B.J. Biddle's latest work (1979) *Role Theory: Expectations, Identities and Behaviour*, New York, Academic Press, provides a comprehensive outline of the approach.
21 See MANGHAM, I.L. and OVERINGTON, M.A. 'Performance and rehearsal: social order and organizational life', *op. cit.*
22 HOLMES, R. (1967) 'The university seminar and the primal horde: A study of formal behaviour', *British Journal of Sociology*, 18(2).
23 BRADBURY, M. (1975) *The History Man*, London, Secker and Warburg.
24 During an idle moment in a Senate meeting, I developed a list of characters ranging from Lord High Principle through Sir Timothy Fixit to Sneerwell and Backbite, and was somewhat piqued to find that BAILEY, F.G. (1977) *Morality and Expediency*, Oxford, Blackwell, had beaten me to print with a similar list. Since his is the finer assembly, I have drawn upon it rather than upon my own save for two characters I include at the end of the section.
25 See MANGHAM, I.L. and OVERINGTON, M.A. 'Dramatism and the theatrical metaphor', (forthcoming), *op. cit.*
26 See MANGHAM, I.L. (1978) *op. cit.*
27 COHEN, M. and MARCH, J. (1974) *Leadership and Ambiguity: The American College President*, New York, McGraw Hill.
28 PERKINS, J. (1967) 'College and university presidents: Recommendations and report of a survey', Albany. New York State Regents' Advisory Committee on Educational Leadership.
29 RICE, G.H. and BISHOPRICK, D.W. (1971) *Conceptual Models of Organization*, New York, Appleton, Century-Crofts.
30 Robert K. Merton, quoted in BIDDLE, B.J. (1979) *op. cit.*

Mysticism, Management and Marx

Roger I. Simon
The Ontario Institute for Studies in Education

Mysticism and management: the very conjunction of these words strikes us as paradoxical. The claim that the study of mysticism might help clarify and inform what is at issue in the activities we call management seems acutely silly. The rational and reality-oriented world of management appears as remote as we might imagine from the realm of metaphysical, mystical speculation. Still, I wish to attend to the possibility of such a relation within an analogical mode of analysis so that perhaps the mystic may yet inform the manager.

My specific, concrete focus will be on those activities of management normally referred to as leadership and supervision, particularly leadership and supervision of teachers. I will begin this discussion with a synopsis of a previous effort to relate mysticism and leadership: an intriguing article by Eugene Borowitz which discusses the thought of the Jewish mystic Isaac Luria (1534–1572) and its application to the problems of contemporary leadership. Borowitz's discussion is not, however, without problems for it opens up several basic questions concerning the possibility and responsibility of educational leadership. These I shall define and discuss, showing how the concepts and thought of critical Marxist theory suggest directions for addressing these questions. The final result, I anticipate, will be a fresh examination of some basic issues in the management of educational institutions.

Editor's note: Much of the theory used in education management takes a simplified and even simplistic form. This is probably a consequence of the short history of education management as an area for academic study. But we are entering a period when theory is becoming much more sophisticated and several different streams of academic thought are being drawn upon. Roger Simon's chapter illustrates how ideas are being developed in order to deepen an understanding of organizational processes.

It is helpful to be reminded from time to time that educational organizations are about students and teachers and management raises substantial problems of order and control, freedom and authority. In his chapter, Simon argues for an exploration of individual perceptions of the world which organizational forms often obscure and he ponders a tentative theoretical basis for a dialectic or 'problematic' process for educational behaviour.

Isaac Luria and the Tzimtzum Concept of Creation

The following discussion is developed by Borowitz (1974) in his article: 'Tzimtzum: A mystic Model for Contemporary Leadership'. The premise for Borowitz's argument is the implicit assertion that central to any leadership activity is the intent of *creation*. That is, in exercising leadership one has a vision of what kind of situation would be desirable and one acts so as to enhance the possibility that this situation will occur. This is the basis on which Borowitz turns to examine that component of mystical, religious thought which concerns the processes of The Creation, the processes through which God created the universe. Thus, more explicitly, Borowitz is concerned with exploring the analogy between mystical versions of cosmic creation and the intention latent in all acts of leadership and supervision.[1]

Borowitz discusses two radically different versions of cosmic creation: that perhaps most clearly understood through an analysis of the conceptual dynamics implicit in Michelangelo's depiction of the creation of man in the Sistine Chapel, and that developed in the thought of Isaac Luria. I shall briefly recapitulate the contrast.

The Creation conceived as an act of God may be thought of in terms of the employment of God's power to bring others (organic and inorganic forms) into existence. Given this position as a point of departure, one may then enter the realm of speculation on the nature of God's creative power and processes of creation. Within Western religious thought the dominant conception of the Creation process is, in Borowtiz's terms, 'a movement of externalization; what was God's will is now turned ... into a reality "outside" him'. It is a process of emanation of the being of God. Borowitz clarifies the dynamics of the process by reference to the imagery of Michelangelo's depiction of the creation of man. 'The mighty God stretches forth the full length of his arm to one fingertip and thus brings man into being.' What is basic here is a process of extension and emanation. Analogously, we quite commonly think of human creative activity 'as an act in extension of ourselves, of producing something "there" that was previously only within us'.

This core dynamic, the movement of externalization, leaves unresolved however a major metaphysical question. Expressed in spatial terms it is: if God is initially everywhere, how can there be any place outside of him for him to create in? Ontologically, the question becomes: If God's being is perfect and fully realized, how can there be a secondary being, imperfectly realized, that emanates from and depends upon the primary perfect being? It was to concerns of this sort that Isaac Luria addressed himself, resolving such paradoxes in a process of cosmic creation radically different from the linear movement of externalization.

Luria was a rabbi, mystic and communal leader who lived in the town of Safed (now in northern Israel) in the 16th century. His conception of creation was so radical for its time that his disciples were quite circumspect about communicating his ideas to others. What is known of his thought today

Mysticism, Management and Marx

comes from the writing of his followers who, perhaps with a degree of editing, recorded Luria's teachings. What is expressed here about Luria's thought is a greatly simplified discussion of that explication of Luria by Gershom Scholem (1974).

Luria taught that the process of creation began with an act of contraction: what he termed 'tzimtzum'. That is, God purposefully contracted into himself to make room for something outside of himself to come into being. This was, according to the doctrine, the first and essential movement of creation. Hence, subsequent to the act of 'tzimtzum' was a void. This void was empty of any form of existence except for a residue of God's being, much as a jug of wine which has just been emptied contains a residue of wine which clings to the clay. At this point God then externalized his being, sending his 'light' into the void. It is this 'light' which is referred to as the light of creation. Thus, as Borowitz explains, 'there is a new twist here'. Previously we discussed creation as a pure act of extension. Luria, however, saw it as a twofold process of contraction and expansion. Exploring the analogy between cosmic and human creative activity, Borowitz deduces that under the 'tzimtzum model' one may think of creation as requiring power first applied to oneself in order to assure an independent existence of another. Further pursuing the analogy, Borowitz concludes that 'tzimtzum' implies a concept of leadership that requires an act of contraction of oneself to help others achieve independence. Such a stance is seen in contradistinction to a linear externalization of control as a device for ensuring the accomplishment of one's own plans.

To this point Borowitz's analogy begins to sound ominously like a metaphysical plea for a version of participative or human resources management.[2] Yet in Luria's concept of creation things are still not so simple. In Luria's thought, God's light combines with his residue to produce 'vessels' which come to completion when filled with the divine light. But here Luria introduces another radical dimension to his conception of creation. As the vessels fill, God's power proves too strong for the vessels and they shatter (what Luria calls 'shevirah'), sending 'husks' or 'shells' of what should have been in a random shower throughout creation. Thus Luria teaches that the creation was essentially imperfect. However, the perfection intended is still possible under Lurianic thought, for the final restitution of the intended divine order is to be made through human action which lifts the sparks from their enclosures and restores them to their proper place (the act of 'tikkun' or restoration). But not any form of action will do. Human action which accomplishes this task of restoration is the performance of 'mitzvot' – i.e., acts which fulfil God's will as specified in his commandments.[3] Thus the Messianic time, the time when perfect creation will be at hand, is to be brought nearer through the responsibility and actions of people. As Borowitz points out, 'such an estimate of human initiative was at its time unique and powerfully appealing, so much so that some scholars have argued that Luria's ideas, transmitted by Christian Cabbala and transformed by late Renaissance and early rationalist humanism, were influential in producing the heady confidence

65

in humankind of the 18th-century enlightenment'.

Returning to Borowitz's analogical application of the Lurianic model to the problems of contemporary leadership, he is quick to refute that such a model implies a *laissez-faire* orientation. Just as God sent forth his light after contraction, so a leader must know when to help and provide guidance. Yet, for Borowitz, the priority for the leader is not the perfect accomplishment of his will, but rather the creation of an independent agent. Following the analogy, this leads necessarily (from the leader's point of view) to an imperfect creation, yet it rests the responsibility for the completion of that creation with those toward whom the act of leadership is addressed.

Several of my colleagues, upon reading an earlier draft of this paper, have misunderstood my stance *vis-à-vis* Borowitz's application of Luria's concept of creation. Borowitz's intent is to advocate a particular form of leadership. My intent, however, is to probe unrecognized issues in that leadership form. Reversing cliché, I come to bury Caesar, not to praise him. For readers familiar with the literature on leadership and supervision, Borowitz's recommendations on leadership offer nothing new, it is only his justifications for them that are novel. My interest too is in his justifications, the dynamics of the 'tzimtzum model', for it is through a consideration of the application of Lurianic thought that essential questions can be raised concerning the basis of power and control in organizations.

Tzimtzum and Teacher Supervision – Where's the Link?

There is no all-encompassing, universally agreed-on statement that defines what constitutes teacher supervision. Most contemporary writers would agree that supervision is better discussed as a set of activities rather than a prescribed enumeration of role responsibilities. Such a set of activities may be quite diverse and thematically broad in scope. However, as Mosher and Purpel (1972) point out, any discussion of supervision has as its core intent, suggesting and articulating ways to ensure that another person does a good job. It is from this basic intent that all discussion of supervision methods ultimately springs.

Of course, as is well recognized in the context of the supervision of teachers, a comprehensive, objective work standard against which to check the adequacy of a person's job performance is lacking. There is agreement neither on precisely what should be taught nor on how teaching should be done. Despite this diversity of views, however, the thematic concerns of *improving* instruction and curriculum tend to dominate the practical orientation of what is labelled 'supervision'. Indeed, in recent years supervision in education has come to be defined increasingly as the improvement of student learning through the improvement in instruction (Cogan, 1973).

The implication of such an orientation is quite important, for 'improvement' as an active process suggests some standard against which a change may be assessed. How one conceives of what such a standard might be is a crucial question whose answer can determine the basic intentionality inherent in the act of supervision. Within the context of improvement of instruction, the standard against which improvement can be assessed is most often specified in terms of specific changes in teaching behavior and/or materials. Why this is so we shall leave aside for a moment. What is necessary to underscore at this point is that, if improvement is to be defined against some notion of behavior and materials, someone must have some vision of what 'better' methods and materials would be. Hence, when improvement is thought of in these terms, supervision *requires* an element of creative intent aimed at enhancing the possibility that one's vision of what should be will be actualized by someone else.

This perspective would be recognized as reasonable by most individuals pursuing activities with a supervisory intent. I have chosen to emphasize it, however, for two reasons. First, it establishes the link between discussions of a mystical creation process and supervision, thus giving the analogical application of mysticism to management a certain *prima facie* plausibility. Second, the perspective acknowledges that supervision cannot be seen as simply a technical problem devoid of the historical and cultural influences which, of necessity, impose an ideological cast to any act of supervision. If supervision were to be a purely technical concern, as was aspired toward by the early movement to put supervision on a 'scientific' footing, it would require not only a statement of the best methods to achieve one's objectives but a statement of the most desirable objectives as well. However, neither consensus on 'the most desirable objectives' nor agreement on 'best methods' is available. Therefore, whatever approach to supervision is taken, it demands an *a priori* value stance on the part of the supervisor. The importance of this issue will be discussed after the problems raised by Borowitz's analogy are articulated.

If the link between mystic conceptions of creation and the core creative intent of supervision is accepted, a critical contemplation of Borowitz's analogy raises some basic concerns. Foremost among these are the nature of the creative extension or externalization subsequent to the act of contraction as well as the requirements for conceiving of an act as restorative (tikkun) of the original intent. In the version of the creation process attributed to Luria one finds the following simplified sequence: contraction (tzimtzum) → externalization (light) → vessels → breaking of vessels → restoration (tikkun) → perfection of creation. If we continue with our analogical play on this theme: the creator, the one who is attempting to enhance the possibility of the fulfilment of one's operative vision, directly influences events first through the nature of externalization and the initial shaping of 'reality' (externalization → vessels). Additionally, the creator indirectly influences events by providing the *standard* which determines whether or not an act is restorative. Thus, while one may argue, as modern advocates of human resources supervision (e.g., Sergiovanni and Starratt) do, that supervision rests on the assumption that the task is one of helping others to the 'successful accomplishment of important and meaningful work' and that this requires giving subordinates opportunity to define, initiate and complete such work (experience the contraction of the supervisor's power), such a position does not exempt supervision from the issues of how an initial guiding vision is given and how the standard of acceptable work (what constitutes a restorative act) is communicated to subordinates. Thus even under the 'tzimtzum model' questions concerning the functional aspects of authority and power need to be addressed. As Borowitz has indicated, it is not simply a position that 'anything goes'. In this respect, the rest of this paper can be read as an exploration of forms of power that may be operative even when teachers are given the opportunity to define and initiate elements of their own practice.

The very parallel, between God and man in the Lurianic conception and between supervisor and teacher, is worth considering. Both relationships are complementary: that is, they may be seen as co-defining each other. The subordinate is seen as part of the superior, yet distinguished from the other. One is bound to the other by the intent and act of creation, yet each implies what the other is not. The subordinate is dependent on the superior and at the same time independent of him. By calling on the superior, the subordinate obtains a personal recognition and confirmation of his 'ego'. However, the subordinate is also required to transform a situation which he did not choose into one in which he himself chooses by exercising his given responsibility of action. Thus the basic question inherent in this form of relationship, both for theology and for supervision, is how will the subordinate choose to act?

Here mystic and theological questions must depart from our analysis. We have reached the limits of analogical play in the equation of the supervisor and God. The individual in the subordinate position to God is invited through *a relation of faith and revelation of God's will* to liberate himself from his ego through acts which conform to the ultimate authority. But the supervisor, of course, rests his invitation on a variety of *appeals to legitimacy and modes of specifying appropriate performance.* Our concern must now be with the nature of that legitimation and performance specification as a source of defining authority. Within the context of Borowitz's 'tzimtzum model', we have to ask how does a supervisory authority continue to assert itself under a condition where space has been made for the subordinate to choose.

Let us take up this question in a more concrete, educational context. Consider the act of teacher supervision which requires the supervisor to provide a teacher with the necessary conditions for responsible action. That is, we may ask what is required by a teacher who is to be given the opportunity to define, initiate and complete important and meaningful work? In my view, if a teacher is going to take an active, defining, reflective stance towards his or her own practice, what really counts is how the form and content of dialogue between teacher and supervisor is defined. As Grumet (1979) has indicated, such discourse is formed by the questions the supervisor and teacher each bring to the situation of supervision. Indeed, it is the questions that each asks of the other and oneself which define the very nature of the situation of

Mysticism, Management and Marx

supervision. Grumet suggests three types of questions which may be seen not only to address the specifics of a concrete situation but also as helping to determine that situation:

1. questions that dominate the 'theory' that the supervisor brings to the interpretation of classroom events;
2. questions that the individual teacher asks of his daily work;
3. questions that supervisor and teacher ask of their relationship.

These are questions that determine the nature of the topics that supervisors and teachers will discuss and the authority, trust and initiative that each will express in communication with the other.

It is this theme of the determinative power of the nature of the questions posed in a situation of supervision which must now become the central concern of this paper. Furthermore, if we are to attempt to clarify how a supervisory authority may continue to assert itself even under a form of supervisory relationship which gives teachers an opportunity to define, initiate and complete important and meaningful work, then a specific concern with *questions teachers ask of themselves and their supervisors must be singled out for close examination.* This specific concern is of primary importance for I intend to argue that supervisory authority manifests itself in the very nature of the questions teachers pose about their own practices and job situations. If we desire to explore the themes of power and control latent in the 'tzimtzum model' we must now begin to frame our concern in terms of how individuals come to choose the actions they engage in. It is within this arena of concern that concepts of critical Marxism can be shown to be an illuminative force.

Forms of Control and Human Choice

I want at this point to step back for a moment and consider the issue of how control is typically exercised in organized social settings. Drawing on Edwards (1979), Michael Apple (1980) has explicitly pointed to three forms of control in organizations and discussed their implications for certain trends in schooling (in particular, curriculum development). Apple's argument is the following. In corporate society, firms purchase labor power. That is, a firm buys one's capacity to do work and seeks to employ that capacity in ways that enhance its contribution to the productivity of the firm. As production as a process is increasingly seen as a technical problem, the legitimation for a particular mode of employment of labor power is dictated by supervisory recourse to the logic of technological rationality. Thus, under this form of social organization, when one sells one's labor power the buyer assumes the 'right' (within limits) to stipulate how that labor power will be used. This stipulation is the core intention of control in the workplace; control is a process of stipulating the employment of labor power.

Historically, according to Edwards, firms have used three forms of control:

simple, bureaucratic and technical. Simple control is telling someone that you have decided what should go on and that they should follow or else. This approach to control is, of course, not unknown to those performing supervision in schools. Whether employed by principals, superintendents or inspectors, in the parlance of the profession it is usually called 'the direct approach'. It is not a method consistent with the 'tzimtzum model' under discussion here. However, it remains the recourse of many supervisors 'when a teacher just can't get his or her "act" together'.

The second form of control – the bureaucratic – is embedded in the normative legitimacy ascribed to the hierarchical relations of the workplace. One is hired to a position and the position is allocated certain obligations, rules, criteria of successful role accomplishment, sanctions and rewards. Supervision of teachers in this mode of control has in the past been achieved through rather detailed specification of a 'course of study' detailing what a teacher should be teaching at what point in time and with what methods.[4] Recently other forms of bureaucratic control have supplanted the 'course of study'. For example, competency-based teacher evaluation may be seen as an attempt to develop a system of obligations tied to the achievement of specific learning objectives on the part of students. That is, one is free to teach in a manner one judges to be appropriate as long as such practice results in specified achievement within a specified time-frame. Given both a restriction on what is deemed legitimate 'learning' and a functional relationship between objectives and methods *within a given time-frame*, such a mode of control functions to stipulate the employment of labor-power. Thus the use of bureaucratic controls is, like simple control, not consistent with the 'tzimtzum model' requirement of according a teacher independence and responsibility.

Apple points out that teachers have had a relatively high degree of freedom in resisting forms of simple and bureaucratic control. Given the relative autonomy of teaching (one can close the door), the infrequency and artificiality of the supervisory visit, the ambiguous nature of modern curricula guidelines and the difficulty in reducing curricula aims to easily measurable learning outcomes, Apple's conclusion is not surprising. However, it is in the arena of the third form of control discussed by Edwards that Apple finds an increasingly powerful stipulative quality.

Technical control refers to the stipulation of the use of labour power which is embedded in the physical or material structure of one's job. Archetypical of this form of control is the assembly line where the very requirements of one's job are determined by both the task sequence of a machine or routinized process and the pace of the presentation of jobs to be done. The locus of control is in neither a person nor a position within a set of structured relationships, rather, it is centred in the requirements of the technique of production. Apple cites, as the best examples of technical control procedures in schools, the rapid growth in the use of prepackaged sets of curricular materials. Such materials (popular examples being 'DISTAR' or 'Science ... a Process Approach') are of the form that the goals, process, outcomes and evaluative criteria are defined as precisely as possible by people external to the situation in which such materials are to be used. Such materials are sometimes referred to as 'teacher-proof' materials: that is, they provide a task structure that is difficult or impossible for teachers to subvert. It is not just by chance that such a term is semantically similar to a blatantly racist expression I have heard from automotive assembly-plant designers in Detroit who talk of the need to make the assembly-line design 'nigger-proof'.

At first appearance technical control seems completely contradictory to supervision consistent with the 'tzimtzum model'. Certainly, if a tightly-defined curriculum package is given to a teacher with the instructions to 'use it', this would be the case. Yet such materials are as often chosen for use by teachers as they are dictated by supervisors. Why teachers gladly employ such curricula forms is an important question which I will return to later. However, for the moment consider what the use of such curricula packages implies relative to our concern with the requirements of the 'tzimtzum model' and the issues of authority and control. If, under the terms of teacher-based goal determination and curricula choice, a teacher opts for a prepackaged set of materials, the teacher implicitly assigns to the materials the legitimacy to define what questions teachers may ask of themselves relative to the adequacy and efficacy of their practice. Indeed, here is the first example of how a supervisor, without directly determining what a teacher should do, may be said to be still providing the vision and 'standard' of appropriate practice by providing a set of materials embodying a particular concept of teaching practice.

Technical control, then, is one form through which one's influence on a teacher's questions can be made manifest. However, there is another even more implicit form of control yet to be considered. Here is where we complete the alliterative conjunction of the title of this paper; enter Marx.

Problematics and Ideology: Contributions of Critical Marxism

It is with ambivalence that I present the concepts and argument that follow as emerging from a tradition of Marxist thought. The term 'Marxist' has acquired so many meanings and associations that, in employing the term, I risk either being misconstrued or charged with a failure to *really* understand what Marx said. However, there is a tradition in Western social theory of the last sixty years which deserves a clear delineation as an important, separate, theoretical perspective. This tradition, what is becoming known as critical Marxism,[5] is based upon a rejection of orthodox Marxism[6] and a support of the basic libertarian spirit of Marx's early work. It is a perspective, however, which takes Marx as showing a direction for analysis but not providing a fully-developed system of 'scientific' truth. As a form of both theorizing and praxis, critical Marxism is based on the premise that 'Marxism must be ... made possible for every generation'.

The Management of Educational Institutions: Theory, Research and Consultancy

In the following discussion, I borrow from the recent work of Henry Giroux (1981), who has developed a perspective drawn from the tradition of critical Marxism and has situated it explicitly in relation to educational inquiry. Giroux, when discussing what is central to his interpretation of critical Marxism, calls for theoretical demonstration in education of the

> ... need for educators to work for the development of an active critical consciousness among teachers and students. To work for modes of reflexivity that allow people to critically examine the taken-for-granted assumptions that shape their discourse, actions and consciousness. This does not mean that the world simply exists as we interpret it. Quite the contrary: the value of the nature of Marxian analysis is that it starts from the assumption that men and women are unfree in both objective and subjective terms, and that reality must not only be questioned but that its contradictions must be traced to the source and transformed through praxis.

The assertion that we are unfree in both objective and subjective terms is the key idea relative to what has now become the guiding question of this paper: i.e., how do teachers define and posit questions to themselves and their supervisors? An understanding of the way in which the critical Marxist perspective informs this question first requires a discussion of the interrelated concepts of rationality, problematic, and ideology.

In his discussion of rationality, Giroux defines it as 'a specific set of assumptions and social practices that mediate how an individual or group relates to a wider society. Furthermore, underlying any one mode of rationality is a set of interests that defines and qualifies how one reflects on the world'.[7] What is crucial to appreciate in Giroux's use of the term is that the concept of mediation is to be taken as a dialectical process. That is, the knowledge, beliefs, expectations and biases that define a given rationality both condition and are conditioned by the experiences into which we enter. In addition, it is important to stress that our experiences in the world only become meaningful within a mode of rationality, for it is that rationality which confers on them an intelligibility.

Drawing on Althusser (1970), Giroux continues: 'All modes of rationality contain a problematic. "Problematic", in this case, refers to a definite theoretical structure characterized by a dialectical interplay of structuring concepts that *serve to raise some questions while suppressing others*' (my emphasis).

This point is of major relevance to the theme of this paper. If our concern is with the questions teachers ask of themselves and others, it is important to introduce the concepts of rationality and problematic directly into our concern with the determinative consciousness of teachers. As Giroux elaborates, 'the problematic represents a conceptual structure whose meaning is to be found not only in the questions that command the range of answers provided, but also in the questions that are not asked'.

Consider for a moment the implications of the concept of 'problematic' and its relation to rationality. First of all, we should recognize a positive moment in the use of this concept, for it renders as topical the explicit and implicit messages in a conceptual structure. That which is not spoken or asked becomes as important as that which is. But there is something else at issue here which is far more basic to the issue of control and its operative form within a model of supervision which stresses teacher autonomy and goal-setting. The concept of 'problematic' also reveals in the logic of its relation to a specific mode of rationality the ideological source that lies beneath the choice of what is considered legitimate and important or illegitimate and irrelevant in a particular instance of practical deliberation.

What is meant here by the logic of the relation of a problematic to a specific mode of rationality? The relation of problematic to rationality must be understood as not only a derivative of the inner logic of a specific mode of rationality but as a response to the 'tensions, issues and struggles of the concrete historical situation in which that rationality becomes operative'. Giroux stresses that a problematic is, in part, the medium *and* the outcome of constituted and constituting social practices and as such must be viewed in relation to those organizations and cultural forms that serve to produce and maintain the existing social order'.[8]

It is here that ideology as a concept enters the discussion. For if we consider ideology as a mode of consciousness and practice that is related to specific social formations and movements, we begin to see how a problematic must be seen in relation to the specific order that both affects the constitution of that problematic but is, as well, maintained and produced by actions which respond to the questions and concerns of the same problematic. Following this line of thought ideology must be seen as related to issues of power and control. Social order, while a concept descriptive simply of the patterns of social behavior, is not neutral in its implications. Any order implies a set of personal and categorical interests that are being served by the pattern of relation that defines the order. Thus, a particular problematic, in the sense that it is dialectically interwoven into the fabric of a specific social order, is invested with power to preserve that order and serve the interests of those that are benefiting from the existing arrangements.

We have now come full circle back to our theme of control. What is the nature of control that remains central to a model of supervision or leadership that requires 'tzimtzum', the overt contraction of one's power? An answer lies in the above discussion of the concepts of critical Marxist thought. Following Giroux, power is not only a relation of constraint but also, in light of our concerns here, 'must as well be seen as a form of production which becomes a major force in the constitution of the subject. Ideology, as an element of power seen in this way, points to an interest-based constitutive relation that is formative in the development of a specifically limited perception of the world and, correspondingly, the taken-for-granted social practices that mold and shape as well the structure of dispositions and needs'.

Problematic and Ideology: Some Examples

This dialectical relation between problematic and ideology is a pivotal concept for our concern with the origin and nature of the questions teachers pose to themselves and others. Thus, it is important that this relation be illustrated concretely. I have provided below two very different examples. The first illustrates a relation which has served to frustrate curriculum reformers, the second illustrates a relation within which management control is enhanced.

In a paper written with John Wilinsky (Simon & Wilinsky, 1980) I examined the origins and development of a 'language policy' in an Ontario high school. In recent years in Ontario the Ministry of Education has been attempting to stimulate a serious re-examination of teaching practice through a focus on the relation of language and learning. The intent of this effort is to work out in teaching practice the implications of the view that knowledge acquisition is dependent on language as a vehicle for learning. This requires a concern with issues such as, for example, the amount of opportunity given students for multiple modes expression, rather than concerns of related to correct forms of language use. In the high school Wilinsky and I examined, the expectations regarding the content of the school's 'language policy' were left vague by the administration. Instead, the teachers, as a staff, initiated their own language review and produced a document calling for higher standards of correct usage. Why was this the result? In our view such an example cannot be explained simply by alluding to the staff's ignorance of the 'language and learning' perspective nor to the lack of curriculum leadership in this situation. The questions posed to themselves by that staff in regard to the goals and methods of their teaching must be dealt with and understood as arising from the concrete location of those teachers within a particular social order. Indeed, it is important to acknowledge this perspective as a determinative fact that will always be present no matter how much 'in-service' education is provided.

While the argument is more extensive than space here allows, the following suggests how what is seemingly a common-sense way of defining a problem is tied to a form of control embedded in the very structure of school organization and the place of the school within the larger social order. Consider this excerpt from our paper.

> It is our view that the current form of the language policy is no accident. It must be considered that the high school teachers themselves maintain a conception of schooling that supports an emphasis on language as a correct form, and that this view is at least indirectly linked to the economic and cultural stratification of the society of which the school is a part. We shall discuss such a proposition with reference to two dimensions: 1. the cultural value of correct form; and 2. the utility of a language as an imposed social convention for justifying and maintaining the existing social order of the school. . . .

Despite an increasing lack of confidence in the economic value of education, schools are still being promoted as vehicles of social mobility. Teachers, in part because they have attended university, claim membership in the educated class and see themselves as responsible for offering the same opportunities for social and economic success to their students. ... This view emphasizes the acquisition of the 'codes' of the educated class. ... University training certifies teachers as members of the educated community. This community speaks and defines standard, elaborated English as its official language.

Teachers, as they aspire to be part of that community or to maintain their place within it, must emphasize standard English as their official language. Thus when asked for a language policy, teachers concerned with their position within the social order will emphasize standard language use. Such a policy is a symbol of community membership and its supporters can justifiably consider themselves as defenders of a cultural heritage. ...

Furthermore, the language policy adopted ... reflects the contribution of the policy to the maintenance of the relative distribution of power and authority in the school. When linguistic competence is conceived of as the attainment of correct form and, it is assumed, teachers have already demonstrated attainment of such competence (while such demonstration by students remains in question), the authority for certifying legitimate linguistic expression lies with the teacher. In this frame of reference a teacher's job is defined as providing students with access to the demonstration of correct form and the opportunity to acquire such form as personal mode of linguistic expression. If this is the task, and since the teacher is the source of authority about correct form, the teacher logically sets and controls the opportunity for written and oral expression.

As the above example illustrates, the opportunity for exercising autonomy worked against those in leadership positions concerned with the 'correct' installation of a language policy.[9] Thus, the control that is operative in a specific problematic-ideology relation is not to be seen as always consistent with the agenda of a specific supervisor, especially when the supervisory vision runs counter to the structure of relationships which define a given social order. More to the point the above example shows how a particular ideology, rooted in a specific social formation, is intimately tied to a specific problematic regarding teaching and language competence. Indeed it is hard to imagine how any form of curriculum leadership concerning the relation of language and learning could be effective without finding a way for teachers to address the ideological bases of their own thought. I shall return to this theme in the next section of the paper. However, there is still a second example of the problematic-ideology relation to be given, one that illustrates its perhaps more overtly manipulative side.

The following excerpts are taken from a transcript of an interview with a teacher who recently has begun to participate in a supervisory system based on individual objective setting and self-determination of the means of accomplishment[10].

> *Interviewer:* Is this process much different than what went on before?
>
> *Teacher:* The process is very different. I have a lot of input. I can set goals for myself. And I can set the specific steps that I want to follow to obtain my goal. I sit down with my supervisor and we discuss these and if we are agreeable that they are within reason ... then I would start off. I would go through many of the steps, then we'd have another conference to discuss my progress. Maybe I'd decide I was barking up the wrong tree so the two of us would sit and discuss it and maybe come up with a different approach. ... There's a lot more input. I sort of have a great deal to say in what I want to do with my growth professionally as a teacher.

Contained in this teacher's statement is a brief summary of the intent and process of supervision under a 'tzimtzum model'. But where do the teacher's self-initiated goals come from? She continues:

> *Teacher:* It's not necessarily classroom growth. There are five areas that we focus on ... diagnosis in the classroom, how you instruct ... , how you evaluate children, how you communicate all your findings to yourself, your boss, to the children and their families, and a, what's the other? ... The other we added at our school ... basic thinking skills ... it's a new programme being introduced in the county. I would choose one of those areas as a category that I would work under. ...

In listing these five categories the teacher is indicating where her cue comes from as to what goals are to be set. These categories have been established at School Board level (through a process of consultation with teachers) and set the parameters for what legitimate goals might be. Is the teacher fooled into thinking she is being self directive? She is not.

> *Interviewer:* Are you saying that this new procedure gets at all the things that supervisors looked for before, but now under new names?
>
> *Teacher:* The same things are being observed. But the process

> itself is very different. The things that are being discussed have always been discussed, I would expect all the way back. However, the process is very clearly defined. The headings are very clearly set. All of the kinds of things that were inspected in the past that I felt were kind of foggy are very clearly stated in the document under the headings of diagnosis, prescription, and so on. So I think it's.... The old things that have always been inspected are still being inspected in a very different process ... I just think that they've clarified in no uncertain terms the kinds of things teachers should be doing.

The teacher in this interview is under no illusion about this particular supervisory system. She knows where and how the questions and goals of her practice are determined. Yet how then can her enthusiasm for the process and feelings of increased responsibility and autonomy be explained? She does indeed now have more control, but it is not over the grounds of her own practice. Rather the new system gives this teacher control of the focus and timing of her own supervision. By having a choice of which category or topic and associated objectives will be her concern 'for the year', she now 'knows where she stands'. But there is still more to be said in order to tie this example back to our concern with the concepts of problematic and ideology. For this teacher the basic problematic at issue here can be thematized as: 'What should I do?'. What is not usually asked, given a problematic of this order, are questions such as: 'How do I know what I should do?'. It is not because teachers are incapable of addressing such questions that they are often suppressed. Teachers work amid and through the concrete social relations of schools and these relations define and are defined by those whose interest is the purchase of teachers' labor power. Once a teacher legitimates this source of authority and its concomitant technological rationality, the problematic of 'what should I do?' becomes the most reasonable, operative stance (see my earlier reference to Apple's discussion of this issue). This is not just a matter of knowing one's place in the bureaucratic order.

Why should the locus of control in sources outside of one's judgment be seen as so reasonable? Whether in the case of the teacher quoted above or in the instance of the prestructured curriculum packages alluded to earlier, what is the source of legitimation that will cause people to accept forms of control and view them as a result of their own initiatives? To address such questions, theorists drawing on critical Marxist thought have relied upon the concept of ideological hegemony.[11] Giroux discusses ideological hegemony as a process within which 'one class has the ability to expropriate the interests of other social groups to its own'; that is, one class within a social order has the ability to universalize a set of interests that define the 'common good' through a principle that brings together common elements drawn from world views and interests of other allied groups.

An example of the process of hegemony is given by Apple in his discussion of why there has been a growing acceptance of technical control (in the form of curriculum packages) in schools. He argues:

> The strategic import of the logic of technical control in schools lies in its ability to integrate into one discourse what are often seen as competing ideological movements and, hence, to generate consent from each of them. The need for accountability and control by administrative managers, the real needs of teachers for something that is 'practical' to use with their students, the interests of the state in efficient production and cost savings, the concerns of parents for 'quality education' that 'works', industry's own requirements for efficient production and so on, can be joined. The fact that the form taken by these curricular systems is tightly controlled and more easily made 'accountable', that such systems do usually allow for individualization, and that they focus on 'basic skills', nearly guarantees their acceptability to a wide array of classes and interest groups.

The issue within the concept of hegemony is not that there are no common or universal interests among people in a specific social order; rather, the point is that hegemonic control attempts to simplify the complex of interests at stake within a specific order and negate the legitimacy of those aspects of an order which contain sets of antagonistic relations. Thus, if a problematic (fused with an ideology) is hegemonically offered the constituents of a social order, it is not difficult to see the implications: 'a definition of the limits of discourse, a setting of the ... agenda, a definition of the issues and terms of the debate, and an excluding of oppositional ideas' (Kellner, 1978). In reference to the teacher transcript above, hegemonic control is achieved by offering a supervisory method which addresses the interests of teachers, interests (clarifying and controlling the terms on which one is judged) which are defined by and act to maintain the very distribution of power that generates such interests in the first place.

On the Possibility of Autonomy in Social Organizations

The thread of the arguments of this paper presents a rather sombre view of the possibility of autonomy in social organizations. As I indicated previously, the key idea is the premise that we are 'unfree both in objective and subjective terms'. However, such a position must be counterposed with its liberative correlate. This is the assumption that by critically examining the basis of one's problematic and its locus in a web of ideological relations, the conditions of autonomous and responsible action can be achieved.[12] Indeed, it is my view that without such an examination of one's problematic and its ideological roots, teacher autonomy in relation to the determination of goals and means in one's own practice is a fraud. If we view as desirable the fostering of the conditions necessary for responsible, practical action what will be required is a conception of supervision that does not proceed from an external specification of what is required (e.g., appropriate behaviour or materials; see p. 67) but rather from a standard of what reasoned, responsible action might be. Such a conception of supervision requires methods of working with teachers that offer the possibility of critical, self-reflection of one's operative logic in the classroom and its ideological basis in existing social relations. What might such critical, reflexive methods look like? I will conclude this paper with two suggestions which offer directions for the development of such methods.

Supervisory leadership is often baldly transparent in its intention to impose the problematics of instruction. Consider my previous example of the development of a high school 'language policy'. As a case study in curriculum implementation the documentation of the 'failure' of the high school I referred to earlier to adopt a 'correct' version of a particular curriculum concept can be seen as commonplace. As a remedy for such failures what is often called for are better theories of 'planned change' along with their implications for clarifying expectations and provision of 'in-service' to both inform and provide the skills necessary for implementation.

But what is the essential idea behind this attempt to improve implementation? Stripped to the core, it is a concern with getting someone else to do what you want them to do. Connelly (1979) illustrates what it means to lay bare the intention.

> Psychologically, I believe the term [implementation] carries unpleasant authoritarian overtones; 'somebody is doing somebody else's bidding'. My discussions with teachers suggest that they sense this and they often resist efforts of implementors because of the feeling that the various implementation activities are designed to get them to do things the way the developer or administrator wants. Overall, I believe that 'implementation' is a poor term. It connotes undesirable relationships among people and it draws attention away from ... the curriculum.

Most often in-service designed to support implementation has as its goal providing teachers with at least an 'understanding' of the idea to be achieved. In terms used within this paper, such an 'understanding' is achieved by in-service that is minimally aimed at the establishment of a particular form of problematic relative to the curriculum idea in question. Curriculum supervisors, who at times despair of ever seeing a change at the level of classroom practice, have been heard more than once consoling themselves with the phrase 'well, at least we have them asking the right questions. The problem with such a method of improving instruction is that it intends that teachers acquire a problematic without knowing they've done so.

Connelly, however, suggests another view of the educational accompaniments of implementation. Instead of providing teachers with activities designed to overcome their resistance to a new programme he suggests engaging teachers in an analysis of the new programme itself. What is meant here is a detailed, deliberative examination of the curriculum concept leading to a responsibly achieved basis not just for 'doing' but, as well, for knowing the basis on which one is justified in doing something in particular. More specifically Connelly states,

> The teacher needs to understand the perspective itself and how it is reflected in the organization of ... content for learning purposes. Further, they need to understand that any one meta-level content perspective is one among several. *They need some sense of why it, rather than others, is the basis of the curriculum.* Without understanding such as this, the teacher is left to imagine that the new curriculum is merely an arbitrary rearrangement which will shift with the politics of the times and with the prejudices of those who control what curricula are taught.
>
> (my emphasis)

This approach is not to suggest that helping teachers acquire the 'tricks of the trade' is unimportant. Of course it is. But what is being suggested here is one definite approach to providing the conditions for autonomous and responsible professional action. For, in addition to his call for implementation as an occasion for 'teacher re-education' in its best and most profound sense, Connelly realizes that such a supervisory approach may lead to a teacher 'objecting to one's curricula ideas on reasoned grounds and hence failing to teach as his or her supervisor has intended they teach'. This is both the risk and the basis of supervision that seeks to promote serious, responsible practice.

However, Connelly's suggestions fall short of what is necessary as a basis for responsible, practical action. What is needed as well is an understanding of one's operative problematic that locates its roots within ideology. There is an approach that promises such an understanding. This is the autobiographic method as illustrated and developed by Grumet in her paper which I referenced earlier. Remember Grumet's basic concerns are how teachers come to pose questions to themselves about their own practice. While Connelly advocates focusing on the 'text' of a given curriculum, Grumet states that 'the concept of teacher effectiveness requires that the teacher learn to hear, formulate and articulate her own questions about her experience of teaching'. Thus to Grumet, 'the primary function of supervision is to establish a dialectical form of reflection upon experience that the teacher can adapt to her own pedagogical practice'. How such reflection might take place is the topic not only of Grumet's paper referred to here but much of her work on autobiographical methods (see also, Grumet, 1980). Here is a brief version of what such a method involves.

> The use of an autobiographical methodology permits questions to emerge that are the teacher's, questions that are embedded in the

assertions, illusions, contradictions of her own prose. The teacher is asked to write an essay that defines educational experience by presenting an account of specific experiences that fall under that rubric. The teachers tell stories, reminiscences of grade school, travel, family relationships, tales of humiliation, triumph, confusion, revelation. When the stories are very general and muted they bury their questions in clichés and happy endings, and the supervisor's response is to ask for more detail. When the stories are extremely detailed, they often exclude any reference to the writer's response to the event that are chronicled as well as the meanings that have been drawn from them, and then the supervisor's approach is to ask what these meanings might be. Often the interpretations that the teachers provide appear to contradict the stories to which they refer. *Ideas about educational experience are not limited to research paradigms. They permeate the culture, providing a mythology so pervasive and unconscious that it subsumes even those experiences in the history of the individual that contradict it. Here the supervisor's familiarity and understanding of the dominant themes of educational psychology, the history of schooling as well as the social and political norms that it perpetuates is crucial if he is to help the writer make the relationship of this mythology and his own experience of education explicit.* What these autobiographical pieces initiate is an examination of the teacher's own educational theory, as well as a study of its origins in both the received wisdom and the teacher's own experience. The questions that are drawn from these autobiographical pieces are the products of a collaboration of teacher and supervisor, and they provide the basis for their relationship.

(my emphasis)

It is not surprising that Grumet's version of supervision often strikes supervisors as unrealistic. Given our usual assumptions about the nature of the supervisory task, the time requirements necessary for adequate reflection and dialogue between a supervisor and those supervized would appear to be quite prohibitive. However, the key to this objection lies not in the 'constraints of the real world' but rather in the very definition of supervision as an activity one person *does* to another. As long as supervision is thought of in these terms,[13] any suggestion of an approach which might foster a genuine critique of one's problematic and ideological location is illusory. However, if we re-define the supervisory function as one whose goal is the creation of a form of teacher re-education based on an engagement of teachers in an analysis of new curricula or methods and their own forms of practice, new ways of thinking about supervision may result. Such a re-definition must broaden the sphere of responsibility for supervision beyond administrators and incorporate as well, anyone who is capable of helping in the analytical engagement referred to above. This would include teachers themselves, students, curriculum experts and consultants, and teacher education institutions.

The suggestion that supervision be re-defined as a form of teacher re-education is not simply a plea that teachers need be more thoughtful about their practice. The point here is that we are referring to a major re-deployment of money and energy into the development of a programme which has at its prerequisite the requirement that teachers be put into a position where they must be able to claim the responsibility for their own actions. This requires not just the opportunity to set one's own goals but, also, the discipline of questioning one's own problematic and the acceptance by others, that one may choose to reject our ideas on reasoned, defensible grounds.

The implication of such a position on supervision should not remain hidden. Every form of social life requires some form of order. While at times an anarchistic rejection of existing order is warranted, it can never be a solution to the establishment of a just and compassionate communal life. A form of re-education as suggested above may lead to the generation of productive conflict; conflict which defines itself in terms of affirmations of what is important and desirable in social affairs. In such a context, every person who aspires to the title 'educator', must work through an analysis of their own assumptions and practices to an affirmed position regarding a future social order. Administrators and teachers thus are not unalterably entwined in an oppositional, hierarchical relation. Rather the more fundamental concern is where groups of educators stand on issues that speak to either the reproduction or alteration of communal life. True conditions for autonomous and responsible action in social organizations inevitably engender critique, coalition, and struggle. If as Luria suggested, the imperfect world is to be repaired by human action, teachers and administrators will have to work out together what it is that God will judge as an act of restoration.

Notes

1. I am not here equating the creative processes of God and man. It is significant that in the Bible the Hebrew word for God's creative activity is different than that used to signify the creative actions of man. However, it is plausible to explore certain aspects of the conception of creation metaphorically. For an extended version of such an effort see Northrop Frye (1980) *Creation and Recreation*.
2. See, for example, Sergiovanni and Starratt (1979) for a discussion in the context of educational leadership. Note that the 'tzimtzum model' *requires* contraction for creation to take place.
3. The history of western religious thought might be considered as one of contention over what the nature of human action is that fulfils God's will.
4. Control through a detailed 'course of study' has rather rapidly become an historical relic. Why this is so is important to consider. As education has increasingly incorporated scientific research into its methods, the recognition that different methods might be needed for different subject matters and different categories of students has become widespread. Thus, with the increasing incorporation of a technological rationality into teaching, the administrative

stipulation of how one teacher should employ his or her labor power has become complex and unwieldy, thus according other forms of control (bureaucratic or otherwise) increasing legitimacy.
5 I am according Lukacs (1971) *History and Class Consciousness*, first published in 1922, seminal status. In this tradition would be included the writings of Antonio Gramsci; the Critical Theory of the Frankfurt School, in Britain theorists such as E.P. Thompson and Anthony Giddens; in North America theorists and educators such as Russell Jacoby, Stanley Aronowitz, Michael Apple, Philip Wexler and Henry Giroux; and in Australia, Rachel Sharp and R.W. Connell.
6 For a helpful discussion of the assumptions and problems of modern orthodox Marxism and its critical alternative see JACOBY, R. (1980) 'What is conformist Marxism?', *Telos*, Number 45, Fall.
7 Jurgen Habermas has provided perhaps the best known analysis of a set of varying interests that underlie specific forms of rationality. See his *Knowledge and Human Interests*, (1971) or better the exposition of Habermas' work by McCarthy (1978).
8 In orthodox Marxist analysis the concept of social order often becomes equivalent to a set of class relations defined in terms of one's position in the relations of production. However, the perspective of critical Marxism that I am discussing rejects the reduction of the complexities of a social order to simple economic class terms. Other forms of lived experience that define people's orientations to one another include gender, ethnicity and age. It is essential that any study of so-called class consciousness acknowledge each of these sets of relations as potentially primary in its relation to human consciousness.
9 For a version of what a 'correct' policy might be see Marland, (1977) *Language Across the Curriculum*.
10 I am indebted to Tom Ritchie for his permission to use this transcript.
11 Ideological hegemony is a concept first articulated by the Italian social theorist Antonio Gramsci.
12 I do not wish to imply that critical reflection is the only basis for autonomous action. As studies such as Willis (1978) have shown, resistance to forms of control is a feature of school life. However, what I am concerned with here are forms of pedagogy which may foster the rupture of the non-reflective, reflexive relation of a social order and its constituent members (Simon, 1980).
13 I am here calling into question the legitimacy of the common problematic of supervision.

References

ALTHUSSER, L. (1970) *For Marx*, New York, Vantage Books.
APPLE, M. (1980) 'Curricular form and the logic of technical control: Building the possessive individual', *The Journal of Economic and Industrial Democracy*.
BOROWITZ, E.B. (1974) 'Tzimtzum: A mystic model for contemporary leadership', *Religious Education*, November–December, 69(6): 687–700.
COGAN, M.L. (1973) *Clinical Supervision*, Boston, Houghton Mifflin Company.
CONNELLY, F.M. (1979) 'Curriculum implementation and teacher re-education', in TAMIR, P., BLUM, A., HOFSTEIN, A. and SABAR, N. (Eds.), *Curriculum Implementation and its Relationship to Curriculum Development in Science*, Jerusalem, Hebrew University, pp. 71–76.

EDWARDS, R. (1979) *Contested Terrain: The Transformation of the Workplace in the Twentieth Century*, New York, Basic Books.
FRYE, N. (1980) *Creation and Recreation*, Toronto, University of Toronto Press.
GIROUX, H. (1981) *Ideology, Culture and the Process of Schooling*, Lewes, England, The Falmer Press.
GRUMET, M. (1979) 'Supervision and situation: A methodology of self-report for teacher education', *Journal of Curriculum Theorizing*, Vol. 1, No. 2.
GRUMET, M. (1980) 'Autobiography and reconceptualization', *Journal of Curriculum Theorizing*, 2(2), Summer.
HABERMAS, J. (1971) *Knowledge and Human Interests*, Boston, Beacon Press.
JACOBY, R. (1980) 'What is conformist Marxism?', *Telos*, 45, Fall, pp. 19–43.
KELLNER, D. (1978) 'Ideology, Marxism and advanced capitalism', *Socialist Review*, 8(6), November–December, pp. 37–65.
LUKACS, G. (1971) *History and Class Consciousness*, Cambridge, Mass., MIT Press.
MARLAND, M. (1977) *Language Across the Curriculum: the Implementation of the Bullock Report in the Secondary School*, London, Heinemann.
MCCARTHY, T. (1978) *The Critical Theory of Jurgen Habermas*, Cambridge, Mass., MIT Press.
MOSHER, R. and PURPEL, D. (1972) *Supervision: The Reluctant Profession*, Boston, Houghton Mifflin.
SCHOLEM, G. (1974) *Kabbalah*, Jerusalem, Keter Publishing House.
SERGIOVANNI, T. and STARRATT, R. (1979) *Supervision: Human Perspectives*, (second edition), New York, McGraw-Hill.
SIMON, R. (1981) 'The concept of a critical reflective pedagogy', a paper presented at the Curriculum Theory Conference sponsored by the *Journal of Curriculum Theorizing*, October 29–November 1, Airlie, Vancouver.
SIMON, R. and WILLINSKY, J. (1980) 'Behind a high school literacy policy: The surfacing of a hidden curriculum', *Journal of Education*, 162(1), Winter, pp. 111–121.
WILLIS, P. (1978) *Learning to Labour: How Working Class Kids get Working Class Jobs*, England, Saxon House.

The Nature of Managerial Activities in Education*

Peter C. Webb, HMI, DES
Geoffrey Lyons
Anglian Regional Management Centre

In recent years various theories or precepts have emerged relating to the management needs of the large complex educational institution. Among the range of managerial needs and functions which have been postulated or identified, some have been specific to schools and colleges – staff development within an educational context, development and innovation in curriculum and assessment, development of pastoral or caring organization, and so on. Others which have been identified seem to share features in common with all organizations – examples are the maintenance of sound working relationships, incentives and communication, of effectiveness in planning and operational organization, and of cost effectiveness combined with flexibility and adaptability.

Underpinning this development of ideas has been the underlying premise that complex organizations in education demand enhanced managerial capacities and skills, particularly at a time when various forms of accountability, evaluation (e.g. cost-benefit), participation and consultation mechanisms, and

Editor's note: The chapter by Webb and Lyons is an account of empirical research into the managerial behaviour of senior staff of schools. It is the only straight research account in this book but its significance is that it points up the importance of behavioural approaches to understanding management. Because the behaviour of managers in education (but also elsewhere) is personal, idiosyncratic and highly contigent upon a perception of need and pressure rather than planned, systematic and logical, it can be best understood from a psychological standpoint. If we are to look for explanations of managerial behaviour and discover effective ways to help managers by consultancy and training, then we need more behavioural research and better behavioural theory.

The detailed analysis of behaviour that forms the basis of this chapter should be related to the approaches of analysis and training exemplified by OD in subsequent chapters. But there is always the question whether managers can be persuaded to undertake the training their actual behaviour demands. How can they be encouraged to seek the insights necessary to change and improve their own performance?

*Authors' note: The views expressed in this paper are entirely those of the authors. They do not and were never meant to represent the views of the Department of Education and Science.

The Management of Educational Institutions: Theory, Research and Consultancy

trends in employment relations, are emerging, or being imposed as elements in their management or governance. One might expect, therefore, that the actual activities of managerial figures in large schools and colleges would bear some relationship to their needs as complex organizations, and also to the various management theories which have been advanced.

A widely remarked criticism of management theory has been the lack of an effective basis of empirical observation, and this has been thought to have led to inadequate development of both theory and research and consequently also, to limitations in training design.

It seems crucial, therefore, to investigate what senior executives actually do within the educational setting in order to determine (for example):

> What high level managerial skills are actually deployed, and by whom; What specially educational elements appear in the managerial activities recorded; what changes in these executives' functions appear to be associated with changes in the size, complexity and educational/social function or role of the school;

> what responses senior school or college executives actually make to the pressures arising from consultative processes, educational change, professional concerns (with recent changes in employment legislation for example), educational and governmental 'politics' and so on;

> the degree to which corresponding perceptions of role and response have adjusted to these changes, and to the longer term problems produced by pressure and pace of work within increasingly restricted resource provision.

In the last twenty years or so, a wide variety of approaches to recording and analyzing what, in general context, managers and senior executives do, have been developed and tested. Such studies have been made in most countries, and in relation to a wide range of types of organization.[1] Case studies and incident studies, participant observation, simulations, surveys, etc., have all been used as ways of generating information and insights. Here we propose to concentrate on one approach, that of using diaries as an investigative technique. The diary approach has proved a rewarding investigative technique in many types of organization. The first reported use of a diary technique was developed in Sweden by Sune Carlson, who published a review of the activities of a selection of industrial managers.[2] In England, diary investigations of the activities of factory and other executives have been published by Burns,[3] by Horne and Lupton,[4] and by Stewart.[5] Mintzberg[6] also initiated investigations in the United States, including studies of senior executives in hospitals and a school system.

The results of most of these investigations tend to contradict the notion of managerial activity as a systematic ordering of activities and programmes based on a constructed strategy of corporate development. Instead, the manager presents himself in his activities as an individual working at a high

The Nature of Managerial Activities in Education

intensity of tasks rapidly dealt with on a personal basis, subject to a stream of short-term interruptions presented as problems to be resolved. He collects and uses large quantities of detailed, but unsorted, information of both internal and external origins, and the greater part of his time and information is used to keep the organization working effectively in the very short run; all this gives him only limited time or opportunity to consider longer term matters. Only the best organized managers seem able to combine longer term strategic considerations with short-term managerial activities, and at the same time to involve other senior figures, by task delegation or other means, in differentiated patterns of team working.

Some years ago a diary investigation was made by Lyons,[7] as part of a larger research project for the DES into the administrative duties of Head and Senior teachers in large secondary comprehensive schools. A substantial proportion of the Senior Staff of some sixteen large comprehensive schools recorded their activities on a pre-designed diary form over a sample of weekly periods, which taken together covered a complete academic year. This chapter reviews some of the initial analysis of the diary returns and then discusses the results of a re-classification of some of this diary material using a reformulation afforded by Mintzberg's[8] work, and then discusses the implications of this re-classification, particularly its comparability to other research undertaken in other employment sectors and the problems identified there by other researchers. The use of this approach as a research tool and its ramifications for training in the educational sector are discussed in a concluding section.

Figures 1a, 1b, 1c and *1d* present a typical sample of the diary entries which were made by the various Head Teachers, Deputy Heads and Senior Staff themselves. A careful inspection of these entries will reveal most of the major problems involved in undertaking diary investigations – problems of sampling and representativeness, of the clarification and definition (in standarized form) of the activities themselves, of their inclusiveness, and of the timing of the diary period (the school year does not contain an even flow of administrative events, for example).[9] Probably the most important requirement of the diary returns themselves is their credibility as descriptions of what is actually going on, to those whose activities are being recorded.

Figure 1a. Diary Entry of Headteacher

Anticipated Morning		Unanticipated Events			
Time	Event	Time	Mode	With	Event
8.15– 8.30	Preparation for Assembly	8.30– 8.35	Discuss	Senior Mistress	Various topics
		9.10– 9.20	Discuss	Youth Wing Leader	Staffing activities – school membership
			Discuss	Building Contractor's Foreman	Vandalism on building site
			Arrange interview	Applicant for post	Appointment
			Discuss	Hd. Maths	Temporary allowance for member of department

The Management of Educational Institutions: Theory, Research and Consultancy

Figure 1a. – continued

Anticipated Morning		Unanticipated Events			
Time	Event	Time	Mode	With	Event
			Discuss	5th form unattended	The work they were doing
			Discuss	Senior Mistress	Condition of girls' toilets yesterday
			Discuss	School Sec.	Delivery of H.M.'s report to Governors
		9.35–10.45	Tour of inspection		
			'Phone	H.M. Primary Sch.	Vandalism on new site after school hours
			'Phone	H.M. another Primary Sch.	Vandalism on new site after school hours
			Discuss	Senior Mistress	G.C.E. entries – refund for candidates withdrawn from exam. and alteration of date of Mock G.C.E. exam. next year
			Discuss	P.E. master	House cross-country competition
			Visit	3rd form Chem.	Lesson in progress
			Visit	3rd form Physics	Lesson in progress
			Visit	3rd form History	Lesson in progress
			Discuss	Graduate tchr.	On desirability of obtaining professnl. qualifications
			Discuss	Boy who had been put outside room	Reasons for this
			Discuss	Deputy Head	Parent not wanting son to do P.E.
			Discuss	Duty prefect	Locking of form room door of outlying form room
			Discuss	Boy	Who had just returned to school after yellow jaundice
			Discuss	Hd. Eng. Dept.	Application form for a teaching post
			Discuss	Pupil	Application form
			Discuss	Unqualified tchr.	Admission to Coll. of Educ.
			Discuss	Hd. Commerce	As above and new scheme of development
		10.45–10.55	Discuss	Hd. Commerce	Extension of Commerce in 4th & 6th years
			'Phone	L.E.A.	Grant for pupil given place at Stage Sch.
			'Phone	From a H.M.	A post advertised in this school
			Discuss	Hd. 4th year	Form staff for next year
			Discuss	Hd. 5th/6th year	Arrangements for meeting this p.m.
			Discuss	Hd. 5th/6th year	The new report form for 6th year
		11.20–11.30	Discuss	Hd. Science + applicant for Biology post	Appointment
			Discuss	Hd. Science	Enquiries re. further applications
			Discuss	2 6th formers	Teaching practice re. college for summer term
			Visit	6th form Chem.	A-level grades
			Discuss	Hd. P.E.	Complaint from parent
			Discuss	School Sec.	Advertisement of posts for next year
			Discuss	5th form girl	Course in 6th year
			Discuss	Teacher	Allowance approved by governors

The Nature of Managerial Activities in Education

Figure 1a. – continued

Anticipated Morning		Unanticipated Events			
Time	Event	Time	Mode	With	Event
			Discuss	Dep. Hd.	Staff meeting planned on Monday
			'Phone	From Hd. L.S.	Improper behaviour of 2nd year boy
		11.50–11.55	Discuss	Dep. Hd.	Governors' Meeting
12.05–13.05	Supervision of school dinner				

Figure 1b. Diary Entry of Deputy Headteacher

Anticipated Morning		Unanticipated Events			
Time	Event	Time	Mode	With	Event
8.30– 8.40	Staff substitutions	8.30– 8.40	Write	Self	Staff absences
			Discuss	Teacher	5th form Liberal Studies lesson
			Discuss	Snr. Mistress	Assembly organization
			Discuss	Snr. Mistress	Work done by an R.E. class
		8.45– 8.55	Discuss	Dep. Hd. L.S.	Staff meeting
8.55– 9.10	Lower School Assembly	8.55– 9.10			Morning Assembly
			Discuss	Dep. Hd. L.S.	Unsatisfactorily explained absence of 2nd year girl
			'Phone	Sec. U.S.	Staff absences
			Discuss	Teacher	Absent boy in his form
			Discuss	Hd. of 1st yr.	Boy temporarily removed from area
		9.25– 9.45	Discuss	2nd yr. girl	Truancy
			'Phone	Snr. Mistress	Staff substitution in exam. room
			Discuss	Hd. L.S.	2nd yr. girl truant
			Discuss	Hd. Science Dept.	Teacher to take charge of a class to free him for interview
			Discuss	Dep. Hd. L.S.	Staff available for substitution.
			Discuss	Teacher	To substitute with Science class
		10.10–10.20	Discuss	Teacher L.S.	Examination invigilation
			Discuss	Dep. Hd. L.S.	Letter from girl's parents re. lost meal tickets
		10.30–10.45	Discuss & 'Phone	Teacher/ parent	Organization of classes Loss of dinner tickets
			Discuss	Teacher	Reason for recent absence
			Discuss	Sec. L.S.	Papers for Upper School
			Discuss	Hd. L.S.	Time-tabling next year
			Write	Sec. U.S.	Signing certificates re. staff absences
			Discuss	Hd. French	Visit to bookshop
			Discuss	Hd. 5th/6th yrs.	Venue for Hd. to speak to 5th forms
			Discuss	Tech. Drawing Tchrs.	How exam arrangements had worked
			Discuss	Headmaster	Letter from parent re sons P.E.
			Discuss	Snr. Mistress	3rd yr. girl absentee
			Discuss/ write	Boy on behalf of Hd. Art	Comment on 5th yr. girl
			Discuss	Hd. Science	Candidate for interview for science post
10.50–11.40	Teaching	11.40–11.50	Write	Self	Continued absence of 3rd yr. girl
			Discuss	Hd. 3rd yr.	Sub. for science tchr.
			Discuss	Snr. Mistress	Next year's timetable
			Discuss	Headmaster	Governors' meeting
			Discuss	Hd. Science	Sub. of staff
		12.05	End of morning school		

89

The Management of Educational Institutions: Theory, Research and Consultancy

Figure 1c. Diary Entry of Senior Mistress

Anticipated Morning		Unanticipated Events			
Time	Event	Time	Mode	With	Event
8.15– 8.45	See H.M. gen. prep.				
8.45– 9.00	See pupils				
9.00– 9.10	Assembly				
9.10– 9.20	See a certain class				
9.20–10.30	Gen. administration	9.20– 9.53	Discuss	Youth Leader	Under-age pupils in Youth Wing
			Discuss	H.M.	Girls' lavatories
			Phone	Dep. Head	Invigilation for 'A' level exam.
		9.53–10.30	Clerical	Self	Filing & gen paper work.
			Discuss	Teacher	To invigilate mock 'A' level exam
			Discuss	Pupil	Message to exam room
			Discuss	H.M.	'O' level entries resulting from post
			Discuss	Pupil	Tummy pains
			Check	Self	Counted this week's Lent collection
			Phone	Prospective school cleaner	Took message for Caretaker
			Discuss	Teacher	To take over invigilation
			Care	Pupil	Sprained ankle
			Discuss	Pupil	Coffee to exam room
10.45–11.40	Gen. administration	10.40–11.12	Writing/ Checking	Self	'O' level results sheets
			Discuss	Pupil	Feeling sick – sore throat
			Discuss	2 pupils	Eye trouble
			Discuss	Pupil	Headache
			Discuss	Pupil	Dom. Science money owing.
			Discuss	Pupil	Feeling ill
		11.15–11.24	Writing	Self/ Dep. Hd. L.S.	Pupil's absence
			Discuss	Pupil	Headache
		11.25–11.32	Phone	P.T.A. member	Wine & cheese dance P.T.A.
			Discuss	Pupil	Headache
		11.45–12.20	Discuss	2 visitors	Liberal Studies for 5th form
			Discuss	Dep. Head	Lib. Studies for next year.
			Discuss	Pupil	Still ill
			Discuss	2nd pupil	Still ill
			Discuss	Pupils	Checking out
			Discuss	Pupil	Offering to fetch my milk
		12.24–12.35	Discuss	Pupil	Audition for Drama Sch.
			Discuss	H.M.	Pupil's success at audition
			Discuss	Playground supervisor	Girls' lavatories flooded. Collected sanitary towels
		12.36–12.55	Discuss	Leader of 5th form studies	5th year Liberal Studies next year
			Discuss	Pupils	Lavatories flooding
			Discuss	Pupil	Exam result sheet
			Discuss	Prefects	Putting certain lavatories out of bounds
			Discuss	Pupil	Exam result sheet
		1.00– 1.24	Discuss	Leaders of 4th & 5th yr. Lib. Studies	Summer Term programme
			Discuss	Pupils	Checking in
			Discuss	Pupil	Feeling ill
			Discuss	Pupil	Stamped, addressed result envelope
			Discuss	Prefect	Returning Biro

The Nature of Managerial Activities in Education

Figure 1d. Diary Entry of Head of Lower School

Anticipated Morning		Unanticipated Events			
Time	Event	Time	Mode	With	Event
8.20– 8.45	Discussion with Dep. Head L.S.	8.20– 8.45	Discuss	Dep. Hd. L.S.	Routine for the day
			Discuss	Teacher	Tchr. unwell and likely to need help
			Discuss	Hd. 1st yr.	Day ahead
			Phone	Youth Leader	Missing key
			Discuss	Hd. 1st yr.	1st yr. timetable problem.
8.45– 9.10	Prepare supervision lists etc. for the day	8.45– 8.55	Discuss	Various tchrs.	Missing key
			Discuss	Girl	Missing P.E. kit
			Discuss	Needlework t.	Access to room
			Phone	Dep. Head	Absent staff
			Discuss	Boy	Hospital treatment
		8.55– 9.15	Check	Self	Supervision for absent staff
			Discuss	Teacher	Absence enquiry note
			Discuss	2 teachers	Minor dispute over teaching base
			Ring bell for school to know all dinner money collected.		
			Check	Self	M.I. room equipment
			Discuss	Monitors	To take supervision lists to staff concerned
9.10– 9.20	Discussion with Youth Wing Ldr.	9.15– 9.27	Search	Youth Ldr. staff free	Key for Youth Wing
			Discuss	New boy	Family break-up
			Discuss	Girls	Lost property
			Discuss	3 boys	Broken lamp-shade
			Discuss	Dep. Hd.	Outcome of the morning
			notes	L.S.	Hds of Years meeting attended by Dep. L.S.
			Phone	Sec. U.S.	More forms
			Read	Self	Report on child for parent (10 a.m. mtg.)
10.00–10.30	Parent (by appt.) (Break)	10.30–10.50	Available in staff room at coffee break		
			Written report	Hd. Remedial Dept.	Letter from parent
			Discuss	Secretary	Staff lunches
			Discuss	Music t.	Music for assembly
			Discuss	Union Rep.	Levies
			Discuss	Rem. tchr.	Domestic problem
			Discuss	Student tchr.	Project
		10.50	Setting out in attempt to reach the loo!		
			Note	Messenger	Youth wing key
			Phone	Dep. Head	Youth wing key etc.
			Notice	Dep. Head	Assembly routine/format
			Mail	Self	Timetables etc. from US
			Discuss	Dep. Head	Absence notes etc.
			Notice	Dep. Hd. L.S.	Dem. of equipment
			Discuss	Lady tchr.	Girl's behaviour
			Discuss	Caretaker	Wiring fault on stage
			Discuss	Science tchr.	Wiring fault on stage
			Discuss	Secretary	Dinner money
			Discuss	Y.W. Staff	Wiring fault
			Discuss	Music tchr.	Choice of hymn tunes
			Discuss	Boy	Access to store with tchr.
			Discuss	Hd. 1st yr.	Staff meeting agenda
			Discuss	Playground helper	First aid plasters
			Discuss	Secretary	Banda materials etc.
			Writing	–	Banda master for staff bulletin
		12.35–12.50	Discuss	Music tchr.	Assemblies
			Care	Boy	First aid

Some analyses of these returns have already been published.[10] They show, among other things, that

> the average working week for Head teachers, Deputy Heads, Senior Mistresses and Heads of Sections was 44–45, 40, 42 and 41 hours

91

The Management of Educational Institutions: Theory, Research and Consultancy

respectively; the nature of work in a school setting demands intense activity at certain parts of the day, the week and the year – the Deputy Heads' work often involving very considerable pressure;

the average duration of individual activities was of the order of 5–25 minutes, with a range from less than 1 minute to over 2 hours; this is shown in Figure 2.

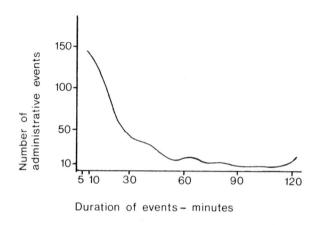

Figure 2. *The distribution and duration of administrative events undertaken by senior teachers.*

the range of contacts made in undertaking their managerial work and the proportion of time involved in these contacts is shown below in Table 1.

	Self	Head or Super-ordinates	Peers	Sub-Ordinates	Pupils	Other Internal	External	Other
Head	29%			19%	8%	6%	30%	8%
Deputy Head	36%	7%	3.5%	15%	12%	4%	15.5%	7%
Senior Mis.	28%	7%	3.5%	16.5%	18.5%	4%	16.5%	6%
Heads of Sections	28%	5.5%	Not Available	15%	27%	3%	16%	5.5%

Table 1. *Time spent by senior staff of schools in direct contact with various other figures* (This is shown as percentages of total time spent on administration.)

The Nature of Managerial Activities in Education

The above information shows some differentiation between the senior staff concerned; for example, the Head Teacher's concerns with external activities (although one of his principal characteristics is his involvement in more or less every aspect of the life of the school), and the more specifically pupil-centred activities of the Senior Mistress and Heads of Sections. For all of them, however, although they spend a certain amount of time working alone – usually in clerical activities, the dominant mode of work is through personal contacts. For teachers are the sort of managers who do their work largely through direct face-to-face contact with others – a characteristic shared by most managers in other employment sectors. Most senior staff do some teaching (there is considerable variation found between schools in the amount of time allocated to teaching amongst the most senior staff). By contrast, heads of departments, although having a defined managerial role often find that such is the commitment of their time to teaching duties that very little time is available for their managerial role – the school, in other words, tends to perceive and use them mainly as classroom teachers.

> The latter sort of issue is among the many that lead to a sense of frustration and exhaustion among staff, for it seems that the work at certain parts of a day, or week, or the school year, is undertaken at considerable pressure or intensity. It follows that a school's resources, at certain periods of the day, week or year, may be totally committed – perhaps over-committed – and that a typical day would show considerable disruption and interruption to anticipated (planned) activities. Consequently, work which requires uninterrupted periods of time for its completion tends to take place after school hours, at weekends, and in holidays.

> As with managers generally, heads and senior staff in schools spend a minority of their time working alone. The average in Lyons' analysis were, as can be seen in Table 1 above, head teachers 29 per cent, deputy heads 36 per cent, senior mistresses 28 per cent, section leaders 28 per cent; these may be compared with the Rosemary Stewart analysis of 160 managers across various business and industrial organizations which produced an average of 32 per cent of their time spent alone.[11] The remaining 70 per cent or so of management time is spent in the company of one or more other people. Of these, immediate colleagues in senior management take up approximately 10 per cent of the total time devoted to administration, and impressionistic analysis of the substance of these relatively limited contacts indicates that the topics covered may be little different in terms of administrative level or strategic significance from those with other individuals in the organization. Between 50 per cent and 60 per cent of the total administration time of senior staff in schools, therefore, is spent on the day-to-day contact with pupils, teachers, non-teaching staff and visitors (officials, governors, parents); much

of this contact seems to be at these others' instigation. Detailed analyses of the diaries of the senior staff themselves reveal that whatever their job specification or descriptions, the pattern of events duplicate each other to a remarkable extent. Evidence of team working, either in terms of continuous contact or of a differentiation of functions, suggests only limited development. Clearly, regular meetings of heads of academic departments, of pastoral departments, or of faculties, with the members of the senior management group, regular meetings at a departmental level between heads and members of departments, and so on, do feature in schools. Similarly, although working parties, committees, and open door management styles on the part of some heads are evidence of the involvement of others, the style of leadership adopted does not necessarily imply shared decision-making, collaboration or a functional differentiation of tasks. What is however becoming apparent in a number of schools is the emergence of a managerial group composed of its most senior members of staff – often the head and deputies – who meet regularly, over lunch or coffee in some cases, to review and discuss aspects of the school's work. Various labels are used to describe them, the management, the hierarchy, and so forth. However, little has been documented or evidence presented in relation to the numbers or types of schools having such groups, the level of discussion which is entered into, the authority or force of any decisions reached, the differentiation of task and interlocking nature of the associated activities, the degree to which such teams are able to plan ahead systematically, their impact on the styles of management adopted throughout the school, and the differences in effectiveness of teaching and care which are characteristic of such schools in comparison with others.[12]

One further feature apparent from the diary analyses is the impact of the school's working conventions on the roles accepted by senior staff. This appears most strongly in the mix or balance of teaching as against managerial and administrative and pastoral activities recorded. Quite considerable variations occur; at one extreme in a small number of schools, the senior echelon of staff do virtually no teaching at all, whilst at the other extreme, in schools of similar size, senior staff may average 10 to 15 hours teaching a week, still apparently coping with similar patterns of contact, and administrative, personal and professional demands. Some of these conventions may well be responses to external pressures of an administrative or political kind; but in many cases it is possible that they have become accepted features of the school's pattern of custom or precedent. As illustration, the amount of non teaching work in terms of hours and in terms of the volume of activities handled, for a three week period, is given below in Table 2 for a sample of Head and Deputy Head Teachers.

The Nature of Managerial Activities in Education

Table 2. *Non-teaching work of heads and deputy heads at 16 comprehensive schools in a sampled three-week period*

School Number	1	2	3	4	5	6	7	8	9	10	11	12	13	14	15	16
Head Teachers																
No. of non-teaching events	234	306	222	232	254	302	242	232	284	278	222	194	104	130	202	74
Number of hours	174	166	150	146	126	122	120	116	108	106	104	90	86	86	84	44
Deputy Heads																
No. of non-teaching events	172	168	234	172	174	344	256	62	252	206	196	176	124	196	138	62
Number of hours	70	66	114	110	72	108	90	34	98	76	98	38	86	68	54	34
Number of pupils on roll	1593	809	1170	733	1502	2070	1600	830	1189	1720	1575	989	1099	1050	1551	1006
State of development	D	D	D	D	D	D	FD	D	D	FD	D	FD	D	D	D	FD
Internal Divisions	U/L	None	U/M/L	None	U/L	U/L	U/M/L	None	U/L	None	U/M/L	None	U/M/L	None	U/L	U/L

State of development: D = developing FD = fully developed
U = upper school M = middle school L = lower school
Internal Divisions:

95

Other conclusions, tested by the authors in various teaching situations (short courses on school management, etc.), are that in general, Head Teachers and Senior Staff accept the accuracy of the diary returns as indicators of real working patterns (though some say that in more recent years they have been able to establish better control of the various activities and interventions); that such patterns are a major ingredient in the sense of frustration often expressed by senior staff – the pace and pressure of a host of relatively minor, even clerical, matters, which effectively prevent sustained attention being given to more professional matters of longer term significance; and that they illustrate a need to reconsider the organization of the work of schools' senior executives in that the diaries seem to indicate a duplication of activities and an insufficient differentiation of function at senior levels.

Such feelings are often accompanied by a sense of disturbance on the part of these senior staff at their lack of control, the low level of administrative skills which seem to be demanded, the excessive involvement in personal/verbal interchanges, the elementary levels of information used, and the non-discriminating patterns of involvement in problems. But these reactions are often followed by a questioning of the diary approach, seemingly contradicting its earlier initial acceptance. Are all the events being recorded, or is the sampling biased towards those activities which can be recorded as simple, timed events?[13] Is not something of greater professional significance and continuity going on in parallel – for example, retaining a grip on the 'tone' of the school as a community; a continuous professional assessment of the quality and effectiveness of the staff, corporately and as individuals; a continuous monitoring of what goes on inside the school to affect its immediate and future performance?

These are very real questions. Continuous personal contact with the day to day events which make up the life of any organization is essential to its good management, in no case more so than for schools. The style of school management is people-oriented and hence the head and his senior staff must be accessible, to each other, to the pupils and their parents, and to the wider community. They must therefore be open to approaches and demands from all levels. Perhaps this 'person' orientated approach and accessibility are to some extent counter-productive? It might well be argued that the patterns revealed in the diary returns are in some way inevitable, given the specific nature of the school as an organization, and of the roles of its senior staff. Alternatively, it may be argued that this is exactly how schools should be, and that they should be resourced with this philosophy in mind. The kinds of questions asked in the original analysis and in the various management courses, often by the school teachers themselves, indicate their own perceived need to seek more effective patterns of both organization and contact/access for senior staff. Some examples of such questions will illustrate:

> Could it be that the roles of senior staff are insufficiently differentiated; would a more functional organization be a better response?

The Nature of Managerial Activities in Education

> Do the diary patterns indicate a failure to train middle management staff to undertake some of these functions? How should 'middle management' staff in schools be trained?
>
> Should not senior staff become more oriented to long term decision making and to more creative approaches to such matters as curriculum and staff development? If so what mechanisms can be devised to free them to do this?
>
> Should not senior staff seek to exercise a more educative and creative influence over their colleagues and the school in general than through the elementary personal problem-solving which appear as the most frequent diary entries?

The contradictory nature of such questions when set alongside the earlier arguments that the diary approach may tend to be biased, further illustrates a degree of confusion which may actually have been aggravated by management teaching precepts about system and organization, coordinated decision-making, reflective planning and longer term thinking and so on. Ideally, it might be thought that the activities of managers should be such; but the researches of Carlson, Stewart and Mintzberg show that it is otherwise in practice. Perhaps the most interesting thing about the diary returns produced for Lyons by the Heads and Senior Teachers is that they were so typical of such returns from managers generally.

The following summary of the various researchers' conclusions about managers in general illustrates this point:

> Most managers work at a high intensity of tasks rapidly dealt with on a face-to-face or telephone basis. 'Their activities are characterized by brevity, variety and discontinuity', and when they need to undertake a task calling for systematic and reflective consideration of a complex situation, they tend to have to shut themselves away somewhere to do it.
>
> Most managers become conditioned to giving higher priority to live rather than delayed needs, and appear to respond to real-time stimuli demanding action in preference to abstracted or planned systematic work concerned with the future.
>
> Diary studies have shown that the time span of many managers' activities varies between 2 and 20 minutes or so, with an average between 5 and 10 minutes; and that many of these activities are of an apparently trivial nature, often involving only minimal skills – clerical, communicative, technical or ceremonial.
>
> Small-scale routines are often carried out by managers when subordinates who could handle them are not momentarily available. This helps them 'to keep a line on what is happening'. They prefer

to handle information, even about strategically important matters, on a verbal rather than a written basis, and tend to discuss the implications of written information with peers or subordinates, often giving them instructions how to make written responses or take follow-up action. In their reading, it appears that many managers screen or scan papers, memoranda or letters for matters on which they can do something; this often becomes the main trigger for action or decision.

Most managers prefer to keep themselves open to both internal and external contacts and demands for the solution of problems, hence they work under sustained pressure and interruption to ensure that their organization is free from minor disturbances or unpredictable short-term stresses. Their roles in this are not simple, but in fact both complex and diverse; although the standard precepts of management training are to set up systematic procedures and to share out the broad range of responsibilities by delegating functions or sectors of control to subordinates, few managers seem able to do so in a consistant and reliable manner. The way many managers work in itself may tend to inhibit such sharing of work or responsibility, and members of a management group or 'team' often duplicate each others' activities and contacts rather than sharing them out; really effective team working is probably comparatively rare. Indeed the development of 'democratic' or participative norms in modern management may further inhibit the creation of functionally organized top management teams and increase the pressures on the senior management figure.

If indeed the Lyons diaries are typical of descriptions of the activities of managerial figures generally, then some of the more fundamental questions posed by such analysts as Carlson, Burns, Stewart and Mintzberg may very well apply to the educational institution. The following are some examples. Is there a natural managerial tendency of the kind outlined above in all complex organizational situations? If so, what is really happening, what roles are being played out, and what are the real levels at which the manager is responding to organizational complexity through these apparently elementary but general practices? What are the important fundamental skills which a manager needs to learn and apply if he is to handle the sustained pressures, and develop his organization's capacities for effectiveness and creative growth? What strategies does he need to employ to free himself from day to day pressures in order to gain a longer-term perspective?

Most of the analysts who have made their investigations of the actual activities of managers using diary or other forms of recording techniques, agree that the apparently simple or elementary activities and skills recorded tend to conceal deeper and more fundamental processes, or roles, being played out. The entries appear to record single discrete activities, but the analysts, and the managers themselves to some extent, recognize them as more complex or multi-faceted. One, for example, Wrapp,[14] sees these managerial activities as a simultaneous process of monitoring the 'stream of events and operating decisions' for significant opportunities and relationships. Others have seen the process as the creation and maintenance of a network of understanding, information and relationships, the managers themselves using words like 'getting a grip' or 'setting a tone' or 'maintaining contact'.

Possibly the most explicit assessment of the underlying structure and purpose of this apparently fragmentary stream of managerial activities recorded in diary investigations has been made by Mintzberg. As a figure accepting responsibilities in relation to the organization as an organization, Mintzberg[15] sees the manager as having to accept an array of roles fanning out from the formal facts of authority and accountability. The term 'role' is used here in the sense of a set of behaviours defined according to a range of expectancies and reciprocal relationships set up by the nature of the organization and its internal 'culture' patterns. Mintzberg postulates a set of interpersonal roles arising from authority, giving rise to, and interacting with, a set of informational roles and a consequent set of decision roles. The essence of this postulated system is the simultaneous playing out of roles from some or all of the three groups when a particular managerial activity is being undertaken, and it thus represents, *prima facie*, an experimental, interpretive, yet workable approach to the analysis of diary returns, which could give a much more complete and informative evaluation of the manager's activities recorded. It thus lends itself to the production of a more refined set of conceptual tools for both research and training.

The authors of the present article have therefore reassessed a large selection from the original diary returns provided for Lyons, using a variant of the Mintzberg model, combined with some assessment of the types and levels of the managerial skills deployed. The very full descriptions of the activities actually recorded in the original diaries fortunately allowed a satisfyingly detailed assessment of both roles and skills. The representation of the results below are meant to do no more than indicate the degree to which this form of analysis provides a satisfactory basis to account for the managerial behaviour of senior staff in schools. The data are available for examination and the authors would recommend application, replication and comparisons with the findings of other studies.

Transferring Mintzberg's role system into the sphere of educational organizations allowed some illustrative definitions, which are set out below:

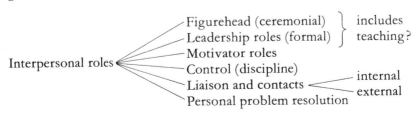

Some of these roles clearly overlap, some may be little more than repetition of the same role between different major groupings. In practice, however, the authors found relatively little difficulty in assigning most of the recorded activities to one or other role in each group.

A range of managerial and administrative skills was additionally postulated and each entry was judged to demand a major or minor level of these skills; occasionally more than one type of skill was evidently brought into play, and it was possible to record these together. The specification of skills was set out as follows:

Executive Skills Code

Description	Code Major	Code Minor
1. *Bureaucratic and clerical skills* – concerned with running or controlling a section or unit and achieving a good flow of information and bureaucratic response reliably: at lower levels, clerical skills.	B	b
2. *Administrative skills* – involved with establishing norms and allocations for resources and regulation of the work of the organization; relationships with external administrators.	A	a
3. *Resources planning and strategical skills* – concerned with establishment of planned development, including logistics, with capacity to generate and implement long term solutions	R	r
4. *Leadership skills* – exercise of authority, credibility,	L	l

arbitration, use of dependence, ceremonial.

5. *Counselling skills* – personal/professional problem-solving.	C	c
6. *Peer skills* – establishment of contacts for external information: skills in setting up and maintaining professional affiliations.	P	p
7. *Negotiating skills* – dealing with people, systems, groups, interests – aligned with need to induce cooperation and control.	N	n
8. *Decision-making skills:* conflict resolution, in conditions of uncertainty; strategy development.	D	d
9. *Evaluatory and critical objectivity skills* – concerned with diagnostics of people, resources, situations, trends.	E	e

Some examples of the reassessed diary material are given below. They show, among other things, that it is possible to evaluate diary returns as multi-faceted activities, in terms of

(a) several roles being played at the same time, and
(b) a combination of executive skills being deployed in any single situation.

Whilst it is true that the actual activities or events depicted are often low-level, or even trivial in some cases, the picture nevertheless emerges as a good deal more complex than the initial analysis of the returns implied. Perhaps it should be stressed again at this point that this new classification is entirely based on the authors' subjective evaluation of the original diary material.

To illustrate, in the most elementary kind of situation, a Head Teacher or Deputy Head who is approached by a Teacher or Head of Department on a disciplinary matter, and deals with it by having the miscreants brought to him, is operating as a manager on several levels at once. He has to relate his judgments and actions to the needs of the school as a whole, as well as to the teacher and pupils directly concerned. As an educationalist he has to judge the value of any punishment he metes out as a matter affecting the personal development and reactions of the pupil but as a manager he has to judge the impact of his decisions and actions on the whole system of relationships and professional confidence, character and style of the school and its staff as a whole, this is how he will be judged. In this, his position is not the same as that of the teacher, the parent or the social worker; it is a matter of his responsibility as a manager. In Mintzberg's terms, he is simultaneously acting out a set of interpersonal (leadership etc.), informational and decisional roles.

The Management of Educational Institutions: Theory, Research and Consultancy

All this, to experienced senior staff in schools, will be a statement of the obvious. But it illustrates well the complexity of the extended role of a manager in education – and it is surprising how little appreciated and understood the significance of these extended roles is, sometimes, among experienced staff in other than the more obvious fields such as discipline. It is common, for example, for Senior Staff and Heads to be 'forgiven' a whole range of lapses of a professional and even of an interpersonal kind, provided they meet certain managerial and decision demands which are recognized by a staff as having higher priority – among these might be achieving a strength and a consistency in professional support, a capacity to get things done or decided (organizing and enabling skills plus influence wielded on behalf of the school in negotiation with external agencies – LEA, elected members, governors, social workers, examining boards), and access to resources for the work of the school. These features, plus a capacity to solve individual problems, often appear to have the highest priority, and represent the major managerial roles, as seen by a school staff. An example of the recoding of one of the original diary returns to illustrate these points is found below in Figure 3.

What then are some of the implications of this analysis? It seems self evident to assert that managerial roles enacted in schools and colleges are complex, as are those enacted by managers in other employment sectors. The similarities between the managerial behaviour of those in schools and other sectors are probably greater than have hitherto been recognized. For both, the interlocking nature of the roles adopted seems to imply a personally oriented and self conscious adoption of sets of role configurations, or perhaps partly stereotyped and partly pragmatically determined behaviour, which hard won experience has shown to be appropriate and which enables the manager to see his way towards survival with effectiveness. This choice of role configurations has to be undertaken in the knowledge, typically for those with management responsibilities, that the positions and actions taken at any moment will not be appropriate to all situations, and are likely to be rejected or misunderstood by significant sections of the populations the manager regularly deals with. It would seem that a degree of role confusion and ambivalence is a principal characteristic of the manager's lot, given the disparate nature of the personal and professional values and interests of a large school or college staff. These ambivalences are the products of many contemporary circumstances present within their environments: growing uncertainties of the pluralistic goals their organizations are expected to achieve; an increasingly articulate and organized workforce with divergent interests; external pressure groups of many sorts, and competition for scarce resources within an LEA tending to make the head teacher more of a 'politician' or a 'fixer; the complexities of recent legislation on employment and other aspects of work, having direct impact on the organization; the growing conflict between the manager's authority and his responsibility; and the ever increasing difficulty in an increasingly specialized technological world of preserving his credibility.

The Nature of Managerial Activities in Education

Figure 3. Recoded Headteacher Diary Entry

CODING	SKILLS		INTER-PERSONAL							INFORMATION					DECISION-ASPECTS						
Week No. School No. Teacher	Duration (to nearest 5 minutes)	Deployed (by implication)	Figurehead (ceremonial)	Leadership	Motivator role	Control	Problem Solving (for people)	Internal Contacts	External Liaison Contacts	Spokesman	Consultation	Focus and Filter	Monitor ('soft' information)	Disseminate—share information	Disturbance—Fire-fighting	System Maintenance activities	Negotiating activities	Resource allocation	Organising major tasks	Development project—initiative and review	Longer term planning
Monday	10	b																			
	10	I/i						6th Form	corres-pondence			advice on UCCA form filling									
	15	b						prefects teacher on duty						various letters after discussions							
	10	I/c						S.T. S.M.								misbehaviour of pupils					
	20	c												bullying by another boy							
	20	?		round school					parents			careers advice re girl									
	10	c							telephone parent												
	5	I/c						New Teacher								modification of T.T.					
	30	r						D.H.M. & S.M.								dates of future events —decisions					
	45	c						Various pupils interviews				counselling etc advice				behaviour problems					
	10	I/c						D.H.M.								behaviour problems					
Tuesday	30	b						Self								relief T.T.					
	5	b						S.M. discuss								t. table mods.					
	15	c/d/n	Prep. ppr. for morning assembly					various interviews								decision					

103

The Management of Educational Institutions: Theory, Research and Consultancy

HEAD TEACHER	SKILLS	INTER-PERSONAL			INFORMATION		DECISION-ASPECTS
20	I	morning assembly					
10	i				morning post—read		
10	b						sign invoices
15	b	organizing tests of attainment	discussion with H.L.S.				organizing attainment tests
15	b						relief T.T.
30	I/b/d	discussion	Various staff				decision
25	I/n/b	problem— showers	S.M. & P.E. staff				decision
25	b/d		S.M				new entrants to school
45	Teaching—relief time table						
15	Coffee						
45	I/b	timetable	3 students				timetables
25	c	UCCA Applics.	Sixth Formers				
15	b				read incoming correspondence		
10	b						prepare for history lecture
45	Teaching						
15	b		3 staff				sort out room t.t. problems
15	b/n		S.M.				various admin. problems in l. school
10	Supervising pupils moving and in classroom						
20	n		Chief Education Officer		letter to CEO re-advert	Staff appt.	
20	b		Sec.			correspondence	
15		UCCA Applics.	6th Form				

104

The Nature of Managerial Activities in Education

The manager becomes the man who copes with countervailing pressures. The skills necessary to do this and to survive with effectiveness appear in the Mintzberg based formulation adapted here, to be increasingly sophisticated.

Whilst the traditional role of the authoritarian or paternalistic head teacher would appear inappropriate in the present circumstances, sufficient vestiges of the earlier system are probably still present in enough schools and colleges, or found particularly in expectations of staff, parents, education committee members, and so forth, to encourage its performance. The circumstances which encourage this behaviour are however changing, and the extent and nature of these changes are by now well enough rehearsed not to need stating here. It seems likely that effective managerial role performance in schools will call for an extended repertoire of skills and greater sensitivity, sophistication and adroitness in their selection and use.

Interestingly, Stewart[16] has recently drawn attention to the possibility of determining the effectiveness with which the manager undertakes his job through an evaluation of the contact patterns he makes. Whilst postulating different typologies and indicating their appropriateness to distinct managerial roles, Dr Stewart indicates that managers in the contacts they make, appear to differ quite markedly from these 'expected' patterns. Here, therefore, apparently lies an opportunity of choice, a freedom of action. It becomes a possibility that the manager who departs from an expected profile in a positive way, is making a more creative use of his opportunities than the manager who appears to be unnecessarily constrained by factors within his environment or by the intentions of those with whom he regularly works.

These statements are not uniquely applicable to schools in Britain. The findings of a recent major survey in the USA by McCleary[17] comparing the Senior High School Principalship now with twelve years ago, found that

> The nature of the high school, in terms of almost every factor, has changed substantially in the last twelve years. Given the nature of that change, the time, responsibility, and expertise expected of the principal has increased substantially. This leads to a basic conclusion of the study: that the principalship needs to be redefined if it is to retain a significant viability. A redefinition needs to be undertaken on both conceptual and operational grounds.

Volume 2 of the same survey[18] which looks at the performance of a sub-group of effective Principals restated these conclusions, and went on to assert the major need that exists for role clarification due to the 'ambiguity of expectations on the Principal'. The key attribute of the effective Principal is the 'skill he displays in personal relationships, the effectiveness of his human relations'. Thus the capacity to work with and through others, already clearly indicated above by earlier studies,[19] assumes paramount importance.[20]

It seems likely therefore that the findings of this major American study have relevance to us as we attempt to gain insights into the managerial activities of Head and senior staff in schools and colleges: additionally, the findings of research conducted into many industrial and commercial sectors, and a reclassification of diary material collected earlier from schools, equally point in the one direction, indicating the complexity and ambivalence of roles, the breadth of the repertoire, and the real level of skills necessary for successful managerial performance. The implications of this analysis are manifold, the following are merely provided as exemplars of the issues which need a much more searching investigation:

> (i) Which of the available roles and skills are deployed most often (or the least often for that matter) and what factors would account for this behaviour, more specifically:
>
> > (a) what predisposes a senior executive in a school or college to adopt a restricted set of role configurations and skills, his personal signature? For example, the reasons may lie within the needs of the educational system, within the executive himself, within the culture of his work place, and so on, and
> >
> > (b) are there then uniquely executive educational roles and can these be associated with discernible educational tasks?
>
> (ii) the problems of communication which the educational manager faces in trying to get those he works with to appreciate the complex roots of his actions and decisions, especially given the 'incremental' nature of their reactions and perceptions;
>
> (iii) the diagnostic skills he can bring to bear on complex situations often involving considerable uncertainties, in order to perceive the issues significant to his own and others' interests and to the teasing out of longer-term strategies;
>
> (iv) the availability of an acceptable 'language' – for arbitration or negotiation, for example – which will help in clarification of issues without distorting the various interest groups' perceptions of realities and priorities;
>
> (v) the perceptions and 'clues' he uses in order to match his own abilities, attitudes and temperament as a manager to a pattern of behaviour and decisions which will stand the best chance of being accepted by a majority of those he has to work with;
>
> (vi) the 'survival', or political, skills he needs in order to retain the allegiance of the widely differing (and fluctuating) interest groups which make up his school and its workers and clients;
>
> (vii) from these and other factors, the development of a general basis for training for educational management, in skills and competences as well as in professional knowledge.

Much of the discussion has clearly extended well beyond the direct implications of the diary material, and the revised approach to its analysis suggested here. What has made this seem feasible, and to an extent credible, are the parallels between the diary returns from schools' senior staff and their counterparts in a wide range of other sectors of organization, administrative, commercial and industrial; their suggestion that managerial behaviour and activities – and the basis on which they are judged by those with whom managers work closely – are similar in schools to what they seem to be in hospitals, administrative organizations, and a range of industrial and commercial organizations.

Whilst the diary analyses certainly suggest all this, it is evident that a good deal more research and development are needed before direct application to training programmes, and to the development of useful hypotheses in relation to the specific managerial needs of complex institutions, or application to assessment of their effectiveness can be envisaged. We are not suggesting here that diary based investigations are the only useful mode of enquiry, a direct study of managerial behaviour can be approached by a wide range of methods, as Mintzberg and others have suggested. What seems important to us is that this is one avenue of research likely to yield dividends in terms of applicability – and that the results should be tested and further developed in these same terms by exposure to the educational executives themselves in the context of their own training programmes. Working alongside practitioners and offering them the findings of research as conceptual tools or insights capable of helping them with their work may both sharpen the work itself and lead practitioners and researchers to operate in dialogue with each other. In this the context of in-service LEA-, school-, or college-based training programmes provide very suitable opportunities for profitable interaction.

Working in this way it would seem possible to use the formulation derived from Mintzberg's earlier work and outlined above, to test a number of different and factually based hypotheses which should have tentative implications for the conduct of further research, for the articulation of training requirements, for assessment of performance, and for future recruitment and executive replacement, and for help with those problems which consistently appear to cause the greatest difficulties.

It seems likely also that quick short-term gains in both research and training programme development could be derived from a careful examination of research into, and managerial training in, sectors other than schools and colleges. If major thrusts of current activity in such sectors can be shown to have some relevance to the education sector, then diagnosed and tested training requirements and procedures might also have applicability. Such an approach whilst probably producing some rapid short term gains, should not be allowed to divert attention totally from the more fundamental problems of the analysis of the 'nature of management' or of 'managerial behaviour'.

Notes and References

1. A useful survey of investigations of this type appears in MINTZBERG, H. (1973) *The Nature of Managerial Work*, New York, Harper and Row. See also MINTZBERG, H. (1974) 'The manager's job: Folklore and fact', *Harvard Business Review*, pp. 49–61.
2. CARLSON, S. (1951) *Executive Behaviour*, Stockholm, Strombergs.
3. BURNS, T. (1957) 'Management in action', *Operational Research Quarterly*, Vol. VIII, No. 2, June.
4. HORNE, J.H. and LUPTON, T. (1965) 'The work activities of middle managers', *The Journal of Management Studies*, Vol. 1, No. 2, February.
5. STEWART, R. (1967) *Managers and Their Jobs*, London, Macmillan.
6. MINTZBERG, H. (1973, 1974) *op. cit.*
7. LYONS, G. (1974) *The Administrative Tasks of Head and Senior Teachers in Large Secondary Schools*, University of Bristol, and also LYONS, G. (1976) *Heads' Tasks: A Handbook of Secondary School Administration*, National Foundation of Educational Research.
8. MINTZBERG, H. (1973, 1974) *op. cit.*
9. The practical difficulties of coding and analyzing diary returns are discussed in Appendix 2, LYONS, G. (1974) *op. cit.*
10. LYONS, G. (1974) *op. cit.*, see also LYONS, G. (1976) *op. cit.*
11. STEWART R. (1967) *op. cit.*
12. See, however, the recently published research results in RUTTER, M., MAUGHAN, B., MORTIMORE, P. and OUSTON, J. (1979) *15,000 hours*, London, Open Books.
13. The findings of the larger sample in the survey were confirmed by results from a more intensive sampling of a sub group of the respondents using portable tape recorders as an aid to diary compilation. See LYONS, G. (1974) *op. cit.*
14. WRAPP, H.E. (1967) 'Good managers don't make policy decisions', *Harvard Business Review* 45, September–October.
15. MINTZBERG, H. (1973) *op. cit.*
16. STEWART, R. (1979) 'The managers contacts: Demand or choice', *Journal of European Industrial Training*, 3(4), 3 March.
17. BYRNE, D.R., HINES, S. and MCCLEARY, L.E. (1978) *The Senior High School Principalship, Vol. 1, The National Survey*, National Association of Secondary School Principals.
18. GORTON, R.A. and MCINTYRE, R.E. (1978) *The Senior High School Principalship. Vol. 2, The Effective Principal*, National Association of Secondary School Principals.
19. See BURNS, T. (1957), HORNE, J.H. and LUPTON, T. (1965), STEWART, R. (1967, 1979), LYONS, G. (1974, 1976) *op. cit.*
20. GORTON, B.A. and MCINTYRE, R.E. (1978) *op. cit.* Gorton and McIntyre additionally draw attention to the need for technical competence in such areas as curriculum development, school community relationships, time management, staff development... and so forth.

The Emergence of the Politics of Education as a Field of Study

Donald H. Layton
State University of New York at Albany

This essay will examine recent developments in the field commonly known as the politics of education. By necessity, the perspective will be that of a North American and, more specifically, that of a United States resident. Nevertheless, there are many commonalities in the political milieus in which school administrators on both sides of the Atlantic currently find themselves. These commonalities were confirmed to the writer during a recent year's intensive study of one south east England local education authority. English education officers were grappling with many of the political issues – diminished resources, parental concerns, enrolment decline, standards – that characterize the daily agendas of their American counterparts. In short, it is hoped that this essay will have broader relevance than for an American audience.

As a focus of scholarly inquiry, the politics of education is a late arrival to the field of educational administration. In the USA even the usage of the term 'politics of education' was long resisted by practitioners and academicians alike. The former preferred to speak of their political roles in the language of 'community relations' or 'public relations' or similar wording. In the UK, the term 'politics of education' never has had much currency even though, in

---

Editor's note: The management of educational institutions cannot proceed without an understanding of the context in which they function. Yet the ways in which institution and environment are related are by no means clear cut even with the simplest and crudest open systems model. Many management practitioners lack the discipline to examine and analyze precise aspects of their job and swing too easily from one set of perspectives to another with the result that management ideas have become nebulous and whimsical.

In his chapter on the politics of education, Layton reminds us that a consideration of education in its widest context is still a matter for intellectual discipline. The problems of making the politics of education a legitimate area for study are the same as for other areas of educational concern. There must be frameworks for analysis and description that lead to valid and practical insights; the basis for research and making conclusions must be subject to agreed processes and criteria.

Layton's chapter is a reminder that there is still a very long way to go in the theories of education management but it also illustrates how the essential intellectual skills for investigation and communication may be used.

actuality, education has been more overtly enmeshed with the political processes of local and central governments than in the United States. In both countries, expressions like 'educational policy making' have been more acceptable to refer to processes by which resources are determined and allocated for education.

The phrase 'politics of education' began to achieve greater usage in the USA beginning in the early 1960s. These increased references to the 'politics of education' were attributable largely to the attention political and other social scientists began to direct toward educational politics at that time. For decades political scientists had had scant interest in educational issues, preferring to direct their energies toward more exotic policy areas or possibly not to specialize in any particular policy area at all. Education's unique governmental status (largely autonomous from other units of local government) also proved to be a strong deterrent to scholarly study by American political scientists. Education was perceived to be 'peculiar' compared to other governmental services.

The burgeoning interest of American political scientists and other scholars in the politics of education in the past two decades is due to several factors. First, education itself moved from a routine, low priority interest of politicians (and society as well) to the center of their concerns. In post-World War II years, elected officials have had to tackle a number of vexing educational problems, including the fiscal pressures arising from expanded services, student protests, concern over standards and achievement, and many other issues. Second, government-sponsored funding of educational research grew by almost geometric proportions in the past three decades. Much of the research effort focused upon the classroom and learning processes concerning which political science had few insights to offer. But significant amounts of monies went to studies of policy development and implementation, educational finance, and optimal administrative arrangements where the skills of the political scientists were likely to be more relevant. And educational practitioners and scholars, journalists, and others also contributed to the mounting literature on the politics of education. The politics of education was too important to leave only to political scientists (or for that matter, to educators!).

Politics of Education: Definitions

Every school administrator develops an operational definition of the politics of education, and many scholars find it necessary to establish working definitions of the politics of education as a field of study. Scholars, however, have not arrived at consensus as to what is or should be encompassed by the study of 'politics of education'. Both the words 'politics' and 'education' are somewhat nebulous, and in their broader interpretations encompass a vast assortment of activities. Scribner and Englert (1977)[1] have dealt with interpretations of politics. They point out that, in an earlier era, politics was

The Emergence of the Politics of Education as a Field of Study

applied largely to the activities of formal government, but that in later years the term 'politics' came to include many other related concepts.

> The trouble was that as the concepts proliferated, the politics of education became more and more inclusive. When politics is found under every bed and in every closet, the distinction between the politics of education and other areas of study becomes quite blurred.[2]

As this quotation suggests, the word 'politics' may be applied to everything from two or more individuals bargaining about private matters to a narrower range of phenomena, including activities and behaviours, associated with organized government.

In seeking to establish some boundaries regarding their field, most American researchers into the politics of education have identified with one of the prevailing definitions of politics or the political system. The work of David Easton, a University of Chicago political scientist, has been by far the most influential, and his taxonomy of politics (the political system) has been widely applied in the politics of education. Easton (1965) defines politics (political system) as 'the authoritative allocation of values'.[3] In Easton's framework authoritative is approximately equivalent to governmental, which thus excludes the decision processes of private agencies. Allocation is equated with distribution. Perhaps the most ambiguity surrounds Easton's meaning of values, due principally to the common usages of that word. In Easton's schema values may be material (e.g. money or physical assets) or symbolic (e.g. status or deference). Thus, Easton's definition of politics can be rephrased as government's distribution of things valued by members of the larger society.

Easton's writings, while not theoretically oriented, have been useful in providing a heuristic tool for researchers into educational politics. Easton has provided the framework for at least two of the most popular texts in the field[4] as well as many individual studies, including numerous dissertations.

Other researchers have utilized other definitions of 'politics' in their politics of education investigations. One of the more popular definitions of 'politics' was suggested by the late Professor Harold Lasswell of Yale University. Lasswell's definition of politics is contained in the title of his (1936) book, *Politics: Who Gets What, When, How*.[5] In Lasswell's characterization of politics, the 'who' directs attention toward the recipients of the benefits which government bestows; the 'what' focuses upon that which is bestowed; and the 'how' upon the means of delivery. Scribner and Englert,[6] embarking from an essentially Eastonian definition of politics, identify four operational concepts relevant to politics (and the politics of education) which help to identify and define the researcher's territory. These operational concepts are government, power, conflict, and policy. Each of these concepts suggests certain issues, problems, and lines of inquiry of potential value to the politics of education investigator.

In spite of many attempts to 'carve out' or delimit its domain, the politics of education as an identifiable field of study remains diffuse. A few scholars have questioned whether or not the politics of education can even be called a scholarly field. For example, Iannaccone and Cistone (1974)[7] provide a telling criticism in their 1974 politics of education review:

> The politics of education is presently without an integrative intellectual identity. Its scope is not well defined or its boundaries firmly fixed. Researchers in the field have shown differing conceptions of the essential core of their studies, whether it be the governance of education, education and the political system, or the policy process in education. Moreover, they have indicated little interest in designing analytical classification schemes or mapping systems that might lend form and direction to their collective effort. A diversity in purposes and priorities and a wide range of approaches and methods are symptomatic of the lack of a coherent conception of the field.

Paul Peterson[8] voiced some related concerns in a review of the 1977 yearbook on the politics of education of the National Society for the Study of Education:

> The politics of education is a new field, but so far it has very little discipline to it. As practiced by those wearing the label, it reaches across the very breadth of political science and education. What's more, no methodological approach is peculiar to or excluded from this field. Significantly, neither political science nor education, as fields, are disciplines with distinctive conceptual categories and/or methodological orientations. In contrast to other of the social sciences, their unity lies in the social sector serviced by the research and teaching – schools and government – not in constructs or approaches internal to the field. The offspring of such polyglot parents is not likely to have a very predictable shape.

Finally Grant Harman,[9] an Australian political scientist and politics of education specialist, in reviewing politics of education research from 1973–79 in several countries, concluded that

> ... there was little writing and debate concerning what the focus and scope of the politics of education as a research field should be, comparatively few detailed comparative studies, a neglect of work in many countries on the role of central government (as opposed to state or local government) in education governance, and a lack of emphasis on detailed studies on policy implementation and the impact of policies. Further, there were relatively few studies summarizing, interpreting and synthesizing research findings on particular topics, and attempting to convey conclusions and explain implications to the wide educational community.

All of the scholars cited above have been among the most productive politics of education researchers in the past decade and a half. Their indictments of the state of the art in politics of education research must be taken seriously; the criticisms contain much truth. Such concerns, however, mirror the laments of many political scientists concerning the status of their discipline; recent meetings of the American Political Science Association have been replete with these self-criticisms. Accordingly it is important, in reading recent critiques of the politics of education literature, to keep some of the concerns expressed in proper perspective, and to recognize that many of the deficiencies supposedly endemic to politics of education research are true of many other social science fields. In a provocative piece entitled 'The Study of Educational Policy and Politics: Much Ado about Nothing?' William L. Boyd[10] reviews several of the criticisms of politics of education research and finds many of the concerns

> to be overstated or misleading. The study of educational policy and politics in fact remains worthwhile, although the status of the enterprise unquestionably leaves much to be desired. However, the status of this field is probably no worse than that of most other phases of the social sciences, all of which suffer when compared to *ideal* conceptions of science. Indeed, this actually is an exciting time for those interested in the study of educational policy and politics, for there is much that is promising about recent developments.

Selected Issues

Since many, if not most, of the conceptual and methodological problems in studying the politics of education are not likely to be resolved soon, it is perhaps more profitable to examine a few substantive issues which have been studied by politics of education researchers in recent years. Research problems dealing with methodologies and conceptualizations are perhaps best left to the researchers to quibble about. In the meantime school administrators have to deal with the substance of political problems not in terms of esoteric research issues but in terms of the here and now. Today's school administrators, whether heads of schools or colleges or with central office responsibilities, constantly tread upon shifting political sands whose contours are hard to discern.

Three issues – parent and community involvement in education, teacher power and bargaining, and increased centralization of educational policy making – have been selected for further elaboration in this essay. While the substance of the following discussion is extracted largely from American experience, all three topics have a far wider applicability. At the present time an explication of these issues would appear to be relevant, in part, to British, Canadian, Australian, and other national experiences. Conceptually none of the three issues to be discussed is unique or distinctive. All three are interrelated, and some crucial governance concerns such as accountability, responsiveness, and control permeate an analysis and understanding of each issue.

Parental and Community Involvement

In the United States, the control of schools lies in the hands of legislators, state education departments, local boards of education, and other instrumentalities charged with specific governance responsibilities. For governance purposes schools are grouped together into districts. Earlier in this century, there were more than 100,000 school districts in the United States, each with its lay board and other governing arrangements but, through consolidations and reorganizations, only 16,000 districts remain intact today. The governance of schools, however, is somewhat chaotic and uneven in the United States. In the case of New York City, one million students are served by the city's school district but, in other sections of the country, school districts abound with only a handful of students under their charge.

When every hamlet had its own school and its school board, the schools were subject to direct community and parental control. If a problem arose, it was not difficult for a taxpayer or parent to get at the root of the matter and in many cases to bring about desired changes. With the growth and bureaucratization of schools, parents and other community members found it more difficult to gain access to school decision makers. This occurrence was especially notable in large cities, such as New York and Los Angeles, where large groups of ethnic minorities could be found. In several urban school districts, the 1960s saw a number of efforts toward decentralizing school decision-making and arriving at greater community control of schools within parts of the larger city.

From a school governance standpoint, the central issue always has been and remains: 'Who shall rule the schools?'. Americans have always had a strong loyalty to localism, a point mentioned later, and they have liked to feel they were in control of their local institutions. Historically, in education, the local school board has been the instrumentality through which the accountability of schools to their communities has been achieved, but in large school districts such as New York or Chicago the board mechanism alone has proved incapable of performing the representative function. Therein has been the source of much controversy and debate in recent years.

There have been some significant trends in the past fifteen years. For example, a number of mechanisms are now available (theoretically at least) for parents and others in the community to be more involved in school decisions. Don Davies (1975)[11] of the Institute for Responsive Education has identified the following means of participation utilized by schools and school systems in recent years:

>   Decentralization
>   Community-Controlled Schools

Advisory Committees
School Councils
Councils for Federally Supported Programs
Parents Organizations
Community Surveys and Goal Setting
Individual Participation in School Programs
'Exit' Models of Parent Influence (includes vouchers)
'Outside' Organizations

A number of these forms of participation were evolved in response to parental and community discontent in the 1960s. In large urban districts minority parents and their interest groups complained bitterly about the lack of achievement of their youngsters, and they protested their concerns to school administrators and boards of education. New York City actually created local districts and boards within its highly centralized governance structure to accommodate criticisms of unresponsiveness. In New York City and elsewhere, the increased vocalness of the community and parents in school affairs could be traced to ethnic awakenings, a more highly educated and articulate citizenry, the impermeability of bureaucratic school systems, and the relationships of educational achievement to the life chances of individuals exposed to the educational process. The movements toward decentralization, however, soon ran foul of strongly organized teacher and other professional interests, and in some instances efforts at greater community participation and control were strongly resisted.

Accordingly it is difficult today to assess the overall impact of the 1960s and 1970s upon school governance in the United States. Much of the momentum for community and parental involvement slowed in the mid-1970s as a more conservative mood swept over education and the nation as a whole. Education officials, teachers, and lay board members opposed changes in governance arrangements and, by the late 1970s, not a great deal had changed in the educational governance in the United States. So little had things changed that two scholars made this overall assessment:

> ... in spite of all the potential for lay control of education, the reality of local school district governance suggests a different picture. The quantity and quality of citizen participation are low, perhaps lower than in any other unit of American government. Only a small minority takes advantage of the opportunity to vote in school district elections, to attend public meetings, to speak at public meetings, or to communicate in private with school district officials ... [12]

The same researchers noted further that 'when laymen do participate, they are not often successful or influential'.[13]

Community (and parental) participation and control of education have produced a voluminous literature in the United States, much of it specific to the circumstances in New York City. Further, much of the research into patterns of community involvement in education has had a strong advocacy bent; a great deal of it was prepared to convince, not just to illuminate. More recently, a support of voucher plans has overtaken interest in less drastic restructuring of the schools, and 'community participation' and 'community control' have lost some of their saliency. The American people (and perhaps other nationals as well) might well benefit from a dispassionate analysis of the drive in the 1960s for more community control of schools. It would be useful, for example, not only to document what reforms were instituted by parental and community pressures but also to determine how durable these reforms have been.

Teacher Power and Bargaining

In the United States as well as other countries, recent years have seen a rise in teacher militancy, as demonstrated by a growth in union membership, greater demands upon local officials, and occasional strikes. The growth in unions has increased the power of the teaching profession to control essential elements of the educational process ranging from conditions of work (such as hours and salary) to curricular matters dealing with what shall be taught. At local, state, and national levels of government, teachers are well organized, teacher interests are well represented in most cases, and teachers are recognized as a potent force in the political process. Beyond a doubt, the new US Department of Education, established in 1979, would never have been created if it had not been for the persistent lobbying activities of one large teacher organization, the National Education Association.

Not too many years ago, teachers were only ineffectively organized into a labour movement. Their professional associations were dominated by school administrators who, while sharing many interests in common with teachers, still had other interests distinctive from those of rank-and-file teachers. Many writers have documented the reasons why teacher militancy increased in the US in recent years. One factor was the impact of demonstrations for civil rights as well as against the Viet Nam War; these demonstrated that 'peaceful marches can be an effective force and that picketing need not be confined to working class groups'.[14] Other factors were the increase in numbers of males entering the teaching profession, the concentration of teachers (but their separation from administrators) due to school district consolidation, competition between the two teacher groups, and the gains achieved in early teacher actions in communities like New York City.[15]

In earlier years school boards and school administrators often acted unilaterally on behalf of teacher interests, but in the 1960s and 1970s teachers demanded to speak for themselves. Structurally the principal consequence of teacher unrest and militant action has been collective bargaining; teachers and their employers sit down together to determine the details of their contracts, including matters of great import to the teachers. Grant (1975)[16] states the impact of these negotiations as follows:

Teacher bargaining has revolutionized education in many ways. It has forced dramatic increases in the pay of teachers and an overhaul of the administration of public schools. In areas where they have won the right to collective bargaining, teachers now have the power to help shape every major educational decision from curriculum to school design.

Some sceptics have questioned the actual economic gains teachers have achieved through their new activism. On the one hand, teachers are among the lowest paid professionals in the USA – their remuneration is far below that of most other professions – and there is little evidence that teachers have enhanced their position relative to other groups in recent years. Second, highly organized teachers (in terms of unionization) have not always fared that much better, if at all, in economic settlements than teachers who have been less well organized. Of course, such comparisons are tricky since without some teachers being highly organized and activated, it is not possible to know how any of the teachers would fare in their settlements. On balance, it would appear that teacher militancy has enabled all teachers to fall less behind other groups than would have been the case had teachers remained inactive politically.

Few would quarrel with the fact teachers ought to be active participants in the formation of educational programs and policies. The 'rub' arises with precisely how much control the teachers should have and the extent to which, as a group, they should be permitted to veto policies adopted for schools through legally sanctioned channels. Several scholars have pointed out that, with the rise of compulsory public education, schools have become increasingly captivated by professional interests, and some cynics have even suggested that schools seem to exist today for the benefit of professional educators, not for the students or their parents. Teachers tend to define what is good for them (higher salaries) with the public good (improved education for children), and there is not necessarily a correlation between these two things.

Ultimately the issue of teacher power revolves around that of public accountability: the right of the public to control those citizens who labour on behalf of all. Powerful unions, whether in the public or private sector, can achieve a monopolistic position in their service area which renders them largely unaccountable to the citizenry at large and to political control. The problem is that of balance between professional prerogatives and the interests of the public.

Centralization of Decision Making

Throughout much of history, there appear to have been alternating periods of centralization and decentralization of governmental decision making. Certain nations, including some of the democracies, have stronger centralist traditions while countries influenced by Anglo-Saxon jurisprudence tend to have strong traditions of localism. In the US localism or local control is rooted more in custom than hard law, but localism is deeply embedded in the national character. The aphorism that 'that government is best that is closest to the people' is nearly universally accepted in the US, and these 'close' governments include local school boards.

The localized, or decentralized, governmental approach has been well suited to a country as diverse and geographically scattered as the United States. The opportunity to develop local responses to community needs makes sense in the American context; the results are more likely to represent a 'closeness of fit' between the policies evolved and the conditions they seek to address. Localism can also make those entrusted with public responsibilities more accountable to the persons they serve. Since local control is based more upon tradition than upon law in the US, local education figures must generally defer to state officials when the two are in conflict. Legal power over education is lodged with state bodies, and the latter can recall powers delegated to local officers whenever they please.

While local control of education has long been a fervently held value of many Americans and may be defensible pragmatically, the drift in the US, and one suspects elsewhere, has been toward increased centralization of educational decision making. Both state and national governments have retrieved or usurped part of the decision-making power which formerly was exercised by laymen, local school administrators, and teachers. This usurpation (perhaps too strong a word) of powers of local officials has been gradual, sometimes episodic, and in a manner that frequently has not aroused strong protest. To a major extent, the control has come through funding of programs which, in theory, have been optional for local school districts but in reality were not optional since the districts have felt pressured to go after the funds. Further, the present drift away from local control has arisen due to the failure of localities to meet many of their needs on a performance level satisfactory to some groups within the community. When needs are unmet at the local level, those in support of changes and new directions are likely to address their concerns to higher levels of government. When unsatisfied persons can link up with likeminded citizens in other communities, they are often able to exercise considerable leverage at higher governmental echelons, particularly if they can state their individual and group interests in terms of state or national imperatives. Wise (1979)[17] states it this way:

> As other and higher levels of government seek to promote equity and increase productivity in our educational institutions, important educational decisions are increasingly being determined centrally. The discretion of local officials is limited by their need to conform to policy decisions.

It is not just parents or other disaffected lay persons who are shifting decisions to higher councils of government. Wise (1979)[18] and many other writers have documented that teacher organizations have sought to have many decisions made centrally by state and national governments. Teacher groups, for example, have sought legislation in several states to have statewide collective bargaining. For the teachers and their unions, this means that time and energy are not dissipated in an effort to achieve contract settlements on a district-by-district basis. Possibly, also, it would enhance pressure upon the employer to come to terms more quickly than would otherwise be the case. Ironically, school administrators and even school board members contribute to centralization by attempting to secure protections for their interests at higher governmental levels.

The establishment of a federal Department of Education in 1979 was perhaps the most recent evidence of the centralization trend. Since the first small education unit was established in the US government in 1867, the federal role in education has been a controversial topic. For most of the years since 1867, US officials have attempted to downplay the federal involvement in education, and even many educators were unwilling to elevate education to cabinet-level status. But a friendly President Carter, combined with a strong lobbying effort by the National Education Association, brought the Department of Education to a reality in the late 1970s. The strengthened presence of education in Washington is bound to further centralized decision making in future years.

Other examples could be cited about the powerful drift upwards of educational decision making. At the same time it is necessary to put recent events into historical perspective and to realize that critics have charged a loss of local control for more than a century. If all the fears about the end of local control had been valid over the years, local school officials would have been stripped of all their discretionary authority and would be automatons. There is clearly still 'tug' and 'pull' left, and adjustments in favour of decentralized control of education may yet be made if citizens and their local representatives are willing to argue forcefully for their convictions.

Future Directions

The concluding portion of this essay will address some possible implications of recent politics of education research for administrative practice, for training school administrators, for policy makers, and for future research efforts. Rarely, if ever, do research endeavors provide a clear direction to human conduct, and politics of education research has been far from conclusive. Thus, the following comments should be seen as observations and as highly speculative observations at that.

For Administrative Practice

Politics of education research, whatever its limitations, has relevance for administrative practice. Among other things, politics of education research examines the relationship of educational institutions to their external worlds and identifies the supports the larger society provides for education and the constraints those charged with administering educational entities must face. The successful school administrator has to be able to draw upon societal supports for education and either overcome or manoeuvre around its constraints.

Since a significant strain of its literature has focused upon the nexus between the institutional administrator and his environment, politics of education research has helped to inform educational administrators of community needs and expectations concerning education. The community power studies, although often simplistic in their design, did confirm some truths to school administrators, namely, schools do not operate independently of community power structure and school administrators need to understand the power configurations within their communities if they are to maximize their effectiveness. Characteristically, economic élites predominate in local power structures, and while school administrators may choose to operate independently of such élites they may do so at their peril.

Other strains of politics of education research provide insights into the real world of the educational administrator. In the US, there is a voluminous literature on the politics of school desegregation, one of the country's most urgent social problems. There are individual case studies, comparative case analyses, legal studies, and other research reports which furnish insights about factors related to successful integration of schools, their students and their faculties. A few years ago school decentralization efforts, notably in New York City, were researched and extensively reported on, and some of these studies have been of practical value.

While politics of education research has utility for the practitioner, it rarely provides many of the 'do's' and 'don'ts' that school administrators might desire to guide their administrative behaviour. To be worthy of its name, politics of education research must deal with many complex variables and, by its nature and design, the research is less reducible to simple guides for action than other types of research. Those who generate politics of education research should not oversell its utility.

For Administrative Training

Politics of education research also has implications for training educational administrators. Research findings in the politics of education provide a legitimate content for training programs of those who are already practising administrators or aspire to be so. In the US, many, if not most, university courses of study in educational administration currently incorporate some content in the politics of education, and curricula at British training institutions such as the Anglian Regional Management Centre include extensive use of political and policy frameworks.

The Emergence of the Politics of Education as a Field of Study

In the US, the response by academic units in educational administration to the politics of education has run the gamut from piecemeal curricular efforts to rather complete reorganizations of their courses of study. At the one extreme, several universities in the US have restructured their total educational leadership programs around politics and policy themes. Such a radical reorganization of courses and training activities was discernible by the early to mid-1970s and has continued to the present time. Among the programs that have undergone transformation are those at UCLA, UC-Berkeley, Stanford, and Harvard (the author's institution, the State University of New York at Albany, is in the throes of such a reorganization at present).

The new curricula usually featured politics and policy analysis at or near its core. Policy-oriented programs also placed a greater emphasis upon data collection and manipulation, quantitative skills, strategic planning, operations research, as well as theories and concepts from the social and behavioural sciences. De-emphasized were role-based courses (e.g. the principalship) and other coursework which drew heavily upon the practical experiences of active or retired administrators. These policy-oriented programs attracted many young, inexperienced persons whose career aspirations departed drastically from the traditional student in educational administration. The universities rationalized these drastic curricular changes in terms of the need for broader-based skills by future educational leaders, but the new orientation was sometimes resented by alumni who had completed traditional, role-based training programs.

The more common curricular response to the growth of interest in the politics of education was the addition of a course on the subject in educational administration departments. In the late 1960s the politics of education was the fastest growing component of educational administration curricula in the US, and many departments of educational administration and other academic units added politics of education specialists to their faculties or existing faculty were asked to develop competence in the field. In a few instances, the personnel who were recruited to teach politics of education courses lacked systematic training in political science and this deficiency limited their research contributions to the emergent area of study.

How and to what extent the incorporation of politics and policy-oriented content has benefited the training programs (and ultimately the skills of those subjected to them) is still difficult to assess at this time. For a few prestigious universities, the policy orientation has appeared to be a way out of training institutionally-based practitioners and toward training decision-makers for state, federal, or even international positions. Indeed, the deep concerns expressed by alumni at some institutions seem to be based upon a sense that their universities are forsaking their traditional missions. While the writer would argue that politics and policy content has made a contribution to the education of institutionally oriented administrators, politics or policy probably provides an insufficient basis on which to organize major training programs for these individuals. There appears to be a lack of congruence and relevance between so-called policy-related skills and the on-the-job requirements of the institutional administrator. Such conceptual frameworks and intellectual skills useful to the college or school head are still more likely to be found in the organizational and management sciences.

For Policy Makers

Politics of education research, if it is good, is relevant to policy makers in government – legislators, executives, and even jurists. Indeed, much research on educational politics and policy making may have more implications for governmental policy makers than for administrators of local educational institutions. This is because much politics of education research is macro in its focus, examining how policies are formulated and implemented in the state or the nation, and it often dissects legislative actions, judicial opinions, and executive decisions of state and national governments. These policies and decisions often impact eventually upon the institutional administrator, but he is placed in a reactive, not proactive, stance toward them.

Literally dozens of studies completed in the past decades contain important findings which governmental decision makers should take into account. Several studies have examined the structure of education at the state and national levels: the nationwide examination of state governance by Campbell and Mazzoni (1976)[19] is a noteworthy example. A research and information project by the National Committee for Citizens in Education (1975)[20] contained several recommendations for the reform of local school governance. Many policy issues in education have been thoughtfully researched and conclusions presented for public debate, including the issues of school desegregation, decentralization, vouchers, sex equity, and education for handicapped children.

The usages of social science research (of which politics of education is but one example) have been the focus of much recent writing in the US. A few years ago, researchers had not grasped adequately that the quality of their research efforts may have little to do with the use of the research in the policy process. Now it is recognized that both format and timing (how and when materials are presented) play an integral part in research utilization. Wirt (1980)[21] has pointed out that 'there is not one but numerous meanings to the "use of social research" or "research utilization"'.

This is a central point made by Carol Weiss (1977) in an introductory essay in her book, *Using Social Research in Public Policy Making*.[22] Weiss identifies a half-dozen meanings of the use of social research. These include: instrumental or problem solving, knowledge-driven, interactive, political ammunition, miscellaneous, and conceptualizing and redefining issues. The first meaning or model, instrumental or problem solving, is the one with which researchers tend to identify. It is linear: 'A problem exists; information or understanding is lacking either to generate a solution to the problem or to select among alternative solutions; research provides the missing knowledge;

a solution is reached'.[23] Weiss points out that 'the direct application of research findings to solve a specific problem is not the common pattern.... The ways that most social research is "used" are much more diffuse and circuitous...'.[24]

For Research

The future of politics of education as a field of study and as a potential frame of reference for school administrators is linked to future research efforts in the field. If politics of education researchers are able to generate more theoretical constructs and to apply existing theories more creatively to their field, the omens are good for the continuing vitality of the politics of education as a focus of study. If researchers can find ways to describe, categorize, and explain the often inchoate incidents and events in their field, they will perform a useful function for the practitioner, the policy maker, and the citizen at large. If researchers and scholars fail to do this, then the opposite is likely to hold true. Researchers from other disciplines and with other agendas will move into the field, and courses in the politics of education will fade from university curricula and be supplanted by current fads and exotic offerings.

This latter scenario suggests that researchers in the politics of education need to assess and reassess the substance and quality of their efforts on a continuing basis. In the past two or three years, the Politics of Education Association has launched both retrospective and prospective examinations of the field. Some of the recommendations for politics of education researchers follow.[25]

More comparative studies. Most serious researchers agree that the field is now ripe for more trans-national studies on politics of education phenomena. The propensity of most researchers to limit themselves to one (their own) nation is generally seen as a handicap in establishing propositions about the field which are likely to be valid in broader applications. The difficulties with launching multinational studies are largely financial (they are expensive) but efforts have been made through OECD, the Ford Foundation, and other bodies to fund such research.

At least two political scientists, Wirt in the United States and Harman in Australia, have identified several fruitful areas for trans-national research in the politics of education. Wirt (1980),[26] for example, states that most nations are facing serious problems with the education of their cultural minorities, with the generation of sufficient finances to educate their young in light of faltering economies, and with a decline in the birthrate and its attendant reductions of school populations. Problems such as these might constitute some of the agendas for collaborative research efforts focused on several countries.

More studies utilizing aggregate data. There seems to be a near-consensus that case studies have dominated too long the study of the politics of education. There are, of course, inadequate case studies, and there are excellent ones that are rich in insights about the politics of education. One problem with many current case studies on educational politics is the lack of a theoretical base. Further, many case studies examine an institution or process within a narrow time frame and prohibit generalizations that are less time bound. Case studies ought to be supplemented by research designs which look at selected phenomena in many settings, not just one. With the development of advanced statistical techniques, including sampling, it is possible to examine selected variables across large numbers of local authorities and school districts or states and provinces. When based upon sound theoretical constructs, such studies have the potential for adding more to our knowledge about the politics of education than a series of noncumulative case studies.

More studies with a multiple-perspective theoretical framework. In general, political science has failed to develop distinctive theoretical and conceptual frameworks, and much research on educational politics has reflected some of the consequences of this failure. In the short term, one appropriate strategy for politics of education researchers is to utilize a variety of theoretical constructs and paradigms drawn from disciplines in addition to political science, and in this regard, the multiple-perspectives approach seems to hold promise. As popularized by Graham Allison (1971),[27] this approach would subject a set of research findings to examination through differing conceptual lenses. Paul E. Peterson (1976)[28] has utilized the multiple perspectives approach in a study of the politics of the Chicago school board. Wirt (1980)[29] is among those who have argued for the use of more than one frame of reference by which to examine politics of education phenomena. He has asserted that, in the United States, 'We lack voices from neo-Marxist and conservative thought about the political process of schools . . . ', and he feels these perspectives and others might be usefully employed in politics of education research.

More historical and longitudinal studies. Survey research and descriptive case studies in the politics of education have suffered from a lack of a time dimension in their designs, and thus many research findings in the politics of education are not placed sufficiently within their historical context. Fortunately the politics of education has been greatly enriched by the work of historians who have examined school governance concerns over longer time periods and have provided valuable insights to the student of educational politics. Issues such as 'Who shall control the schools?' and 'What should be the role of central government in local school affairs?' are not new to our present age; they have been present since the establishment of the first publicly supported schools. Politics of education research, employing historical methods, should be encouraged, and historians themselves should be enticed to examine perennial concerns in the nexus between school and the political order.

More synthesis studies. There is a need for greater efforts to draw together and synthesize extant research findings on the politics of education. Research synthesis is an art, requiring great skill and talent, and unfortunately relatively few scholars are willing to devote their energies to this craft. In part, this reluctance is attributable to the high value society accords to the discovery of new information; 'original' research is thus seen to have greater pay-off. Further, much politics of education research in the US continues to be done by doctoral students and their research projects are normally expected to represent original investigations. There have been some periodic efforts to synthesize politics of education knowledge; the 1977 NSEE yearbook on the politics of education[30] is the most recent example. One book, however, is an insufficient response to existing needs, and hopefully further efforts will follow. When synthesis of research findings is skilfully done, our understanding of the politics of education (as in any field) is greatly enhanced, and is a necessary first-step toward theory development.

This list of desirable research agendas and approaches in the politics of education could be expanded *ad infinitum*. In this discussion there has been insufficient attention to the 'what' that should be studied by politics of education scholars. Research endeavors always require selectivity in terms of what is or is not included within the agendas for investigation. Hopefully more careful analysis and synthesis of completed research studies should help identify some profitable *foci* for future research efforts. And perhaps the concern in the future should not be just with 'what' but as Harman (1980)[31] and others have pointed out, 'So what?'. What outcomes can be attributed to inputs into the educational policy system? What is the difference if one policy is adopted rather than another?

Notes and References

1 SCRIBNER, J.D. and ENGLERT, R.M. (1977) 'The politics of education: An introduction', in SCRIBNER, J.D. (Ed.), *The Politics of Education: The Seventy-Sixth Yearbook of the National Society for the Study of Education*, Chicago, University of Chicago Press.
2 *Ibid.*, pp. 21-22.
3 EASTON, D. (1965) *A Framework for Political Analysis*, Englewood Cliffs, New Jersey, Prentice-Hall.
4 For example, WIRT, F.M. and KIRST, M.W. (1972) *The Political Web of American Schools*, Boston, Little, Brown and Co.; and THOMPSON, J.T. (1976) *Policymaking in American Public Education: A Framework for Analysis*, Englewood Cliffs, New Jersey, Prentice-Hall.
5 LASSWELL, H. (1936) *Politics: Who Gets What, When, How*, New York, McGraw Hill.
6 SCRIBNER, J.D. and ENGLERT, R.M. (1977) *op. cit.*, p. 23.
7 IANNACCONE, L. and CISTONE, P.J. (1974) *The Politics of Education*, Eugene, Oregon, ERIC Clearinghouse on Educational Management, University of Oregon, p. 8.
8 PETERSON, P.E. (1978) 'Review of Jay D. Scribner, "The Politics of Education"', *American Educational Research Journal*, 15(2), Spring, quoted in Harman (see below note 9).
9 HARMAN, G. (1980) 'Reassessing Research in the Politics of Education', Paper

presented at the American Political Science Association meeting, Washington, D.C., August 30, p. 7.
10 BOYD, W.L. (1978) 'The study of educational policy and politics: Much ado about nothing?', *Teachers College Record*, 80, December, p. 251.
11 DAVIES, D. (1975) 'New patterns of participation in educational decision making', in SANDOW, S. and APKER, W. (Eds.), *The Politics of Education: Challenges to State Board Leadership*, Bloomington, Indiana, Phi Delta Kappa, pp. 33–42.
12 TUCKER, H.J. and ZEIGLER, L.H. (1980) *Professionals Versus the Public: Attitudes, Communication and Response in School Districts*, New York, Longman, p. 229.
13 *Ibid.*, p. 230.
14 PIERCE, L. (1975) 'Teachers' organizations and bargaining: Power imbalance in the public sphere', in NATIONAL COMMITTEE FOR CITIZENS IN EDUCATION, *Public Testimony on Public Schools*, Berkeley, California, McCutchan, p. 130.
15 *Ibid.*, pp. 130–131.
16 GRANT, W.R. (1975) 'School desegregation and teacher bargaining: Forces for change in American schools', in SANDOW, S. and APKER, W. (1975) *op. cit.*, p. 28.
17 WISE, A.E. (1979) *Legislated Learning: The Bureaucratization of the American Classroom*, Berkeley, California, University of California Press, p. 47.
18 *Ibid.*, p. 105.
19 CAMPBELL, R.F. and MAZZONI, T.L. (1976) *State Policy Making for the Public Schools* Berkeley, California, McCutchan.
20 NATIONAL COMMITTEE FOR CITIZENS IN EDUCATION (1975) *op. cit.*
21 WIRT, F.M. (1980) *Is the Prince Listening? Politics of Education and the Policy Maker*, Paper presented at the American Political Science Association annual meeting, Washington, D.C. August, 30, p. 5.
22 WEISS, C.H. (1977) 'Introduction', in *Using Social Research in Public Policy Making*, Lexington, Mass., D.C. Heath, quoted in WIRT, F.M. (1980) *op. cit.*
23 *Ibid.*, pp. 11–16.
24 *Ibid.*, p. 16.
25 The following list has been influenced by the writings of Grant Harman, an Australian political scientist at the University of Melbourne.
26 WIRT, F.M. (1980) *op. cit.*, p. 26.
27 ALLISON, G.T. (1971) *Essence of Decision: Explaining the Cuban Missile Crisis*, Boston, Little, Brown and Co.
28 PETERSON, P.E. (1976) *School Politics, Chicago Style*, Chicago, University of Chicago Press.
29 WIRT, F.M. (1980) *op. cit.*, p. 11.
30 SCRIBNER, J.D. (1977) *op. cit.*
31 HARMAN, G. (1980) *op. cit.*

What Business Management can Teach Schools

C. Brooklyn Derr
University of Utah
Thomas J. DeLong
Brigham Young University

Introduction

In the mid 1960s, US schools picked up Organization Development (OD) from work done in industry a decade or so before. Like many approaches to school management, the initial theories and methods of organization development were transposed directly from business to schools, not always successfully. As one of the prominent OD consultants of the day proclaimed, 'I used to be Mr OD in industry and I now want to be Mr OD in education. There's challenging problems, interesting people and lots of government money to be had in schools'.

Now fifteen years later, most of the pioneers of OD in education have left the scene – many to work in industrial settings and on business school faculties. Government funding for education has dropped, public support has eroded, and many diagnose educational institutions as 'at best stable but probably declining'. The OD movement as a fad has come and gone in American education, though there are some indications that it may be just beginning in

---

Editor's note: On the whole, educationists (teachers and administrators) are not well informed about business – nor for that matter is the business world well informed about education. But teachers who first become interested in management often get hold of the wrong end of the stick and create their own imaginary ideas about 'good business management practices'.

In fact, before one can properly understand what business has to offer education, one must have a good theory of education. Sadly, many teachers have theories which are just not adequate and so it is impossible for them to understand what is useful and what is not useful in industrial practice. Certainly, industrial ideas must be considered with extreme caution.

Derr and DeLong, with an experience of education and also business, attempt to point up some of the problems that arise from considering management as relevant to both industry and education. The USA has a comparatively long involvement in attempts to apply management ideas to education (hence the references to OD) and other countries should observe carefully what has been achieved so that too many mistakes are not repeated but that there is effective building on the undoubted achievement in American educational administration.

other parts of the world, and organizational improvement efforts in schools persist.

In business and industry, OD has been transformed by current emphases into human resource management and deals broadly with how to enhance overall human productivity yet preserve the quality of working life; how best to use scarce human resources under conditions of slow growth; how to integrate OD, personnel, labor relations, manpower planning, and information systems into a more integrated human resource management system; how to extract better performance appraisal and accountability programs – in short, how to work smarter, not harder.

The general historical development of OD raises three important questions. First is it useful for education to continue following business management practices or do schools require a unique approach to management? Second, can school systems and other educational enterprises overcome the stagnation caused by little public support, restricted advancement opportunities for staff members, and declining enrolments complicated by aging staffs who are tired and cynical and whose ranks are not rejuvenated by optimistic new members? Many staff members have psychologically retired; mere survival is their goal. If these conditions continue, chances for any organizational improvement in schools may be small.

The third question, linked to the second, is: 'Will organizations of the future, educational enterprises included, somehow adapt to the enormous social and economic changes imposed from the outside by such events as the women's movement and the energy crisis?'. The increase of new workers (mostly women) reentering the work force at a time of slow growth requires massive work redesign. The pervasive change towards dual-career families has obvious implications: less transfers and travel, less availability as workers share home responsibilities, and more requirements for flexible work scheduling. Younger workers find the job less central to life than self/family development and lifestyle. Inflation, high-priced transportation and recession could set many workers moonlighting. All of these considerations affect productivity.

Business and Education Compared

How do schools compare to business? Education, of course, includes more than public schools and businesses cannot be summed up by a single image either. Still, there are some fruitful comparisons to be made.

1. Schools often have unclear goals; businesses usually have a very clear shared objective – making a profit.

    For the most part, schools socialize, instruct, and control the students, but toward what end? And with what means? Diffuse goals make it difficult to analyze the effectiveness of a given organizational system or pursue a central direction.

2. Schools are controlled by their environment.
    They must interface successfully with the community. Much of what a school does is public relations work, creating an image of smooth-running efficiency (Bidwell, 1965). Because schools must depend on community support and cannot take risks with public funds, they typically make short-term plans designed to enhance their image but are otherwise restrained in their long-term options and plans.
3. Schools, unlike business, attract people who have high needs for autonomy. Although teachers may work together on committees, research suggests that their required collaboration is quite low compared to that in other organizational settings (Derr, 1971; Schmuck and Miles, 1971).
4. Schools produce inbreeding and offer a refuge to the security oriented. There exists in the public school arena a guaranteed clientele and many security-oriented individuals prefer this 'public sector' advantage – something often loathed by business types. The ideas of tenure, good benefits, and geographic stability are frequently cited as incentives for employment in education. Schools are also inbred organizations. Since much of the staffing is done from within the organization, most administrations are typically inbred. Some studies suggest that it is virtually impossible to become an administrator in a school district without first having taught in the district for several years. Furthermore, few people with noneducational backgrounds become administrators, even when 'fresh blood' would be desirable.
5. Schools exist in a decreasing market and generally have few economic resources. They are unable to 'diversify' their markets because of their legal mandates. There is, thus, a real question whether school systems can support long-term organizational plans.

These qualities of educational systems mean that adapting business management practices to traditional schools would be a difficult assignment. Basic management training for principals and superintendents, restructuring school organizations, improved management information systems, and long-range planning could serve as a starting place for such interventions. However, the basic issues are still the nature of schools and schooling versus business and the political/educational role of school administrators versus business managers. Are school administrators managers in the business sense? Are they more than managers? How is their managerial world different?

Educational Survival

As we have already pointed out, the internal structure of most schools may work against innovation. Yet as we look to the future for both business and education, we recognize that external forces will cause many internal changes. A systems orientation to change has always underscored the importance of the external environment, but it now appears as if world economic, political, and judicial forces are more directly affecting internal organizational affairs than ever before. This seems especially true in public education which is, by its nature, vulnerable to external demands. Some of the special external forces now facing educational institutions are:

1. Declining enrolments that create a need to close many schools, to lay off staff, to retrain senior teachers and administrators for new roles and responsibilities, and to re-allocate human resources without jeopardizing the quality of existing programs.
2. Competency-based learning involving a thorough overhaul of teaching approaches and creating the need for new systems of evaluating students, teachers, and administrators.
3. The new emphasis on accountability that stimulates new approaches for evaluating teacher and administrative performance and assessing educational outcomes – the results of which are usually open to full public disclosure.
4. The rising importance of parent and community groups as forces that collaborate with (or sometimes dictate to) the schools – as well as the ever-powerful influence of teachers' unions.
5. Court decisions to equalize educational opportunities and their far-reaching organizational implications.
6. The long-term implications of new laws mandating multicultural education and requiring the mainstreaming of handicapped children within the school districts.
7. The financial cut backs both locally and nationally which burden the school district at every turn.

In such a world, one key to effective educational change and survival in the future may be for school administrators to become more efficient and 'tougher' managers, for decisions to be more centralized and autocratic. This is often the mode of business in adapting to a competitive and turbulent arena. Yet, such a response sets up a paradox. The business of education is teaching, nurturing, stimulating and otherwise providing a healthy and supportive learning climate for children. Can educators afford to become ruthless and overly rational?

We maintain that in the future, principals and teachers at the school level may need to become experts in motivation to counter the survival orientation of central administrators. The effective use of motivational theories and methods may play a significant role in student-teacher, teacher-principal relations – to the end that the loosely coupled school building becomes somewhat protected from the tough-minded behaviours at the central office.

Motivational theories fall typically into three major categories: need, incentive and cognitive.

The cognitive theories describe how different individuals respond to internal and external motivations. These theories also probe the relationships among such ends as behavior, rewards, satisfaction, and productivity – a helpful guide to teachers in setting up motivational programs for the classroom.

Need theories analyze internal states of disequilibrium – physical as well and psychological – causing individuals to pursue certain courses of action aimed at regaining equilibrium (Steers and Porter, 1974). Maslow (1954), McGregor (1960), and McClelland (1961) used the concept of need as the basic unit of motivational analysis. The study of needs helps explain and predict what goals or outcomes will become important to an individual – and when.

For example, students like certain teachers, the theory goes, because they provide various means for the student to satisfy their needs. Existence needs (biological, physical, and security) can be met with physical conditions in the classroom, while affiliative needs (companionship, belonging, and affection) can be met with opportunities for socialization and participation, and growth needs (achievement, recognition, and advancement) can be met through student-teacher interactions.

Incentive motivation describes a classroom stimulus which can influence student behaviour – usually a reward. These incentives can be intrinsically and extrinsically mediated to satisfy the student's needs.

Individuals respond very differently to the same incentive depending on how they perceive its value, whether they believe that their past performance will be rewarded, and whether they believe that their efforts on the present task will be rewarded. According to expectancy theories (Atkinson, 1964; Lawler, 1974; and Vroom, 1964), a student will feel most motivated to perform a task when he/she finds the incentive attractive, his/her performance is the means of attaining the reward, and he/she has a good chance to accomplish the required task.

The modern teacher and principal will be most successful if he/she can integrate all three theories – cognitive, incentive, and needs – to motivate students, mixing and balancing them to match classroom incentives to each student. Obviously the incentive will thus become more valuable and the students will be more satisfied. The sensitive teacher and principal must know how these various motivations interact and how to use them most effectively.

In recent years, many educators have also felt that the teacher's personality is extremely important. There are many who argue that in addition to sensitivity a teacher needs humour, empathy, and enthusiasm. According to Fuller (1969) a teacher's classroom behaviour grows at least partly from his/her concerns – for instance, self-image, expertise, compassion, etc. Fuller also indicated that individual teachers have unique sets of concerns and that concerns develop at different rates in different people. Although Fuller feels that all these concerns are present throughout the career, he asserts that the beginning teacher's primary concerns are about him/herself, next the task of teaching, and finally the impact on the students. See Figure 1 for an illustration of how these concerns develop.

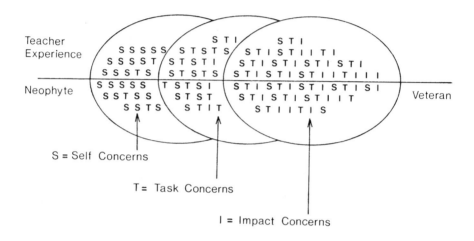

Figure 1. *Three-Phase Developmental Model of Teacher Concerns*

Fuller suggests that a teacher must have time and experience to create the final impact on students, even though this model does not show the teacher's need for continual feedback as he/she struggles to motivate students but also to keep his/her own enthusiasm.

The critical issues here are: can school systems, employing methods from business and other settings, adapt to a fast-changing and even hostile external environment? At the same time, can the classroom remain somewhat protected from this struggle? Can it remain, by employing motivational theories and methods, a supportive and stimulating environment for learning? The former problems, those of environmental coping, are certainly in the realm of business and much can be borrowed from years of business experience. The latter issues, maintaining classroom climate in the face of environmental adaptation, are unique problems for educators to resolve.

Organizational Adaptation and the Future

Of relevance to this paper, even if it might seem somewhat beyond its scope, is the significant issue of future organizational effectiveness in all settings. While business and education alike will struggle with these problems, it may be that the business sector has taken more of a lead in attempting to cope with the impact of a myriad of social issues.

First, younger workers have different values. Research shows that young women are fearful of success, but also that young men are rejecting the success ethic as a central value (Rapoport, 1976; Safilios-Rothschild, 1977). One author has declared that men are starting to behave at work more like women used to, favouring shorter and more flexible hours so they can have more time for leisure and household responsibilities (Crittendon, 1977).

Moreover, men of all ages are reevaluating their priorities. Studs Terkel's *Working* (1974) includes several portraits of high-ranking executives who dropped out of the corporate scene. There is a significant trend towards career switching (usually from a managerial or professional position to one which has greater lifestyle potential) among middle-aged men (Walker, 1976).

One of the central themes of today's lifestyle is that people everywhere are trying new ways of living, from changing careers to changing marriage partners (Van Maanen, Schein, and Bailyn, 1977). Lotte Bailyn and associates (1977) contend that in the future more and more people will want different things from their work and career. This idea of 'pluralism' suggests that some workers of the future will be very career-oriented; others will want substantial time with their families; others will seek job security above all; others will need creative and autonomous work, where they, not the organization, can define their role (Schein, 1978).

How will organizations of the future deal with this employee orientation towards more self-development and family life? Related issues include greater development of human capacities at work, adequate and fair compensation, more employee rights, and more socially relevant work.

A problem emerging from these new values is our national lack of productivity. Former President Jimmy Carter, for one, in his carefully prepared 22 June 1979 energy address to the nation, accused us of basic selfishness and laziness at work. The so-called 'new economists' see the decline of the work ethic as a key reason for our economic woes. Workers used to put their jobs and the company's interests ahead of leisure/lifestyle needs. Such recent books as *The Seven Deadly Sins of Today* (Fairlie, 1978) and *The Culture of Narcissism: American Life In An Age of Diminishing Returns* (Lash, 1978) illustrate similar points. *Time Magazine* (10 September 1979) attacked the American 'Fascination With Decadence'. The 1970s are labeled already as the 'me decade'.

Clearly, both quality of work life and productivity must be addressed simultaneously. And this requires that effective human resource managers administer programs that consider quality, not just quantity.

Business is already aware of and concerned about the problem. *The Wall Street Journal* reported, 16 October 1979, a survey of 2,000 executives of top business and financial firms, about 40% of whom said they spend about twenty hours a week on personnel matters (up from only 25% who reported that much involvement five years ago). Moreover, a majority reported that their chief human resource executive was paid as well as other top-level executives, a significant change.

Business is also coping with the problem of many senior executives who are keeping their positions longer than originally anticipated while 'baby boom' executives are now at midcareer, ready for promotions but with no place to go. Education shares the problem; as the economy stagnates, fewer 'burned-out' teachers are leaving for other fields.

Corporations have started to experiment with nontraditional career development options such as, more lateral moves to slow the aspiring executive's advancement; more sabbaticals, leaves of absence, and part-time options at mid-career; making senior executives consultants or shifting them to lower positions; and trying to provide high potential administrators with experiences central to the basic purposes of the organization. Schools have long struggled with stagnation at the top and the lack of career opportunities. Perhaps they could benefit from studying industry's career development programs.

Since education has traditionally employed as many or more women than men, government regulation would not necessarily be the same problem for schools as it currently is for business. However, the lack of women in top management positions may certainly be subject to investigation in some districts.

More important than industry's answer to any specific problem, however, may be its methodology. First, there is an effort to broaden the role of human resource specialists from the limited role of their predecessors, the OD specialists. Second, there is an attempt to require human resource managers (HRM) to work more closely with related personnel such as planners, strategists, information processors, and marketing people. Third, companies often require HRM specialists to learn the core aspects of the business and relate all of their materials to the core function. Some companies prefer training line managers to perform HRM activities.

In contrast, education has traditionally appointed teachers as principals and principals as central office administrators. Whatever the gains from this approach, many educational administrators seem outdated or untrained for some of their functions. Schools should consider requiring greater specialization in the future.

Certainly business organizations can learn how to deal with the public and consumers from educational enterprises; but both schools and businesses must become better at environmental scanning and planning, less crisis-oriented and more improvement-centered. They both must learn to manage fewer resources better, to shrink, to aim for quality rather than quantity. They also need to emphasize efficiency, high performance, and better ways of learning from experience to provide better services faster and with fewer employees.

This is indeed a tall order. More sophisticated technology will help, but the real challenge facing both the educational and business sectors is the process of managing human resources more effectively.

Conclusion

What can business teach schools? One response might be, 'Precious little! Schools are unique organizations'. Some might even add that schools have done themselves a disservice by blindly following, without adequate adaptation and rethinking, some of the business managerial practices. We feel that schools have distinctive needs but are not unique. They can profit from borrowed techniques as long as they tailor new programs to their own setting. We have suggested several management techniques and practices that school administrators might find useful in attacking their problems.

By the late 1970s, schools had contributed relatively little to management thought and practice in the USA compared to business, health care, and the military. Retrenchment and survival had taken precedence over innovation. By contrast, educators played a leading role in the mid-sixties and early 1970s. However, schools are currently struggling with many of the social, political, and economic problems other areas will inevitably encounter. Thus, the 1980s may be the decade for schools to point the way for businesses.

An ultimate question is whether school districts will continue to exist in their present form. In the meantime, all organizations must confront some of the managerial problems we have pointed out.

The energy crisis has taught us all that the world is getting smaller. Nations feel increased interdependence which might serve as a new basis for world collaboration. So do organizations. As managers, similar problems confront all of us across the differences of our separate institutions. We must all deal with the social, political, and economic forces confronting us.

We recognize that much of this discussion has used American examples, but we hope that some of the issues dealt with by US schools have counterparts in other countries. Sharing management theory and practice can only help us, both between sectors (education, business, health care, public administration, arts administration, social work, etc.) and across national boundaries and cultures.

References

ATKINSON, J.W. (1964) *An Introduction to Motivation*, Princeton, N.J., Van Nostrand.
BECKHARD, R. (1969) *Organization Development: Strategies and Models*, Reading, Mass., Addison-Wesley.
BERMAN, PAUL and MCLAUGHIN, M. (1974–75) *Federal Programs Supporting Educational Change*, Chicago, Rand Corporation.
BIDWELL, C.E. (1965) 'The school as a formal organization', in MARCH, J.G., *Handbook of Organizations*, Chicago, Rand-McNally.
BLAKE, R.R. and MOUTON, J.S. (1968) *Grid Organization Development*, Houston, Texas, Gulf.
CHUNG, H.H. (1977) *Motivational Theories and Practices*, Columbus, Ohio, Grid, Inc.
CRITTENDON, A. (1977) 'Women work and men change', *New York Times*, January 9.

DERR, C.B. (1971) 'An organizational analysis of the Boston school department', Dissertation, Graduate School of Education, Harvard University.

DERR, C.B. (1974) 'OD in schools: Some questions, some alternatives', *Thrust for Educational Leadership*, November 4.

FAIRLIE, H. (1978) *Seven Deadly Sins of Today*, New York, New Republic Books.

FRENCH, W.L. and BELL, C.H. (1973) *Organization Development*, Englewood Cliffs, N.J., Prentice-Hall.

FULLER, F.F. (1969) 'Concerns of teachers: A developmental conceptualization', *American Educational Research Journal*, 6, pp. 207–226.

GALBRAITH, J. (1973) *Designing Complex Organizations*, Reading, Mass, Addison-Wesley.

GROSS, N., GIAQUINTIN, J.B. and BERNSTEIN, M. (1975) 'Failure to implement a major organizational innovation', in BALDRIDGE J.V. and DEAL, T.E., *Managing Change in Educational Organizations*, Berkeley, Ca., McCutchan Publishing Corporation.

LASH, C. (1978) *Culture of Narcissism: American Life in An Age of Diminishing Expectations*, New York, Norton Publishers.

LAWLER, E.E. (1974) *Motivation in Work Organizations*, Brookes Cole.

MASLOW, A.H. (1954) *Motivation and Personality*, New York, Harper.

MCGREGOR, D. (1960) *The Human Side of Enterprise*, New York, McGraw-Hill.

MCCLELLAND, D.C. (1961) *The Achieving Society*, Princeton, N.J., Von Nostrand Reinhold.

PACKARD, J. (1975) 'Changing to a multi-unit school', in BALDRIDGE J.V. and DEAL, T.E., *Managing Change in Educational Organizations*, Berkeley, Ca.: McCutchan Publishing Corporation.

RAPOPORT, R. and RAPOPORT, R.N. (1976) *Dual-Career Families Re-Examined*, London, Martin Robertson and Co.

ROEBER, R.J.C. (1973) *Organization in a Changing Environment*, Reading, Mass., Addison-Wesley.

SAFILIOS-ROTHCHILD, (1977) 'Dual lineages between occupational and family systems', in ARLENE, S. and SKOLNICK, J.H. (Eds.), *Family in Transition*, Boston: Little, Brown and Company.

SCHEIN, E. (1969) *Process Consultation: Its Role in Organization Development*, Reading, Mass., Addison-Wesley.

SCHEIN, E.H. (1969) *Career Dynamics: Matching Individual and Organizational Needs*, Reading, Mass., Addison-Wesley.

SCHEIN, E.H. (1977) *The Role of the Consultant: Content Expert or Process Facilitator*, Paper from Sloan School of Management, MIT.

SCHMUCK, R.A. and MILES, M.B. (1971) *Organizational Development in Schools*, National Press, 1971.

SMITH, L.M. and KEITH, P.M. (1971) *The Anatomy of Educational Innovations: An Organizational Analysis of an Elementary School*, New York, Wiley.

SPADY, W.G. (1974) 'The authority system of the school and student unrest: A theoretical explanation', in GORDON, C.W., *Uses of the Sociology of Education*, Chicago, National Society for the Study of Education.

STEERS, R.M. and PORTER, L.W. (1974) 'The role of task-role attributes in employee performance', *Psychological Bulletin*, 81, pp. 434–452.

TERKEL, S. (1974) *Working*, New York, Pantheon Books.

TYACK, D. (1976) *Conversation with the Authors*, Stanford University.

VROOM, V.H. (1964) *Work and Motivation*, New York, Wiley.
WALKER, J.W. (1976) 'Will early retirement retire people', *Personnel*, 53, January–February, pp. 33–39.

Organization Development for the 1980s

Richard A. Schmuck
University of Oregon

It is important to think of the consultative strategy of Organization Development (OD) as a complex cluster of concepts, values, skills, procedures, and techniques. It is not a consultancy that is simply conceived nor can it be very simply implemented. OD is as much a philosophy or a way of life as it is a design and technology for school improvement. As such, it is more than a method of consultation; OD is also a theory and technology of management.

Organization Development involves the organizational members themselves in the diagnosis, transformation, and evaluation of their own social system. Rather than simply accepting the diagnoses and prescriptions of outside technocratic experts, the participants involved in OD, with the aid of process-oriented facilitators, examine current organizational problems and their causes and participate actively in the reformation of goals, the development of stronger group problem-solving skills, the redesign of structures and procedures for achieving the goals, the improvement of the working climate of the school, and the evaluation of results.

Editor's note: The chapter by Schmuck on Organization Development (OD) is an important account of the history, development and current state of affairs. The development of Organization Development in America has been much fuller than anywhere else and there are reasons for believing that cultural factors have been an important condition for this. It seems unlikely that OD will follow the same pattern elsewhere though there are parallel movements such as school focused INSET (In-Service Education and Training) in the UK. The situation in Australia is indicated in the chapter in this book by Mulford and in the UK by Gray and Heller. In the UK the influence of school counselling and personal development is much stronger, for example, than the 'organizational' aspects of development.

An additional important quality in Schmuck's chapter is that it raises questions about all forms of management applied to education and the insistence on full participation by all the members of the school – including especially students – is important. However OD develops, the wide experience in the USA will be very significant because of the application to implementation that has occurred there. As an approach to managing schools it is one of the most thoroughly thought out and theoretically coherent to have been applied to date. It provides an ideal model for research and consultancy in educational institutions.

The value position undergirding educational OD is that schools, perhaps more than most organizations, should embody democratic values in their norms, structures, and procedures. Moreover, it is assumed that OD consultants and educational managers using OD methods should be inspired by democratic values, not only according to their preferred outcomes, but in the very change strategies they employ. This means that whenever it is feasible the OD design directly engages teachers, students, and parents. OD involves the grassroots of the school in diagnosis, training, and evaluation. Indeed it is the cherished hope within the 'OD establishment' that the strategies of OD will offer viable, democratic alternatives to the traditional élitist or hierarchical methods of change typically used by educational consultants and managers.

OD contrasts with such traditional change strategies as 1. recruiting new people with innovative ideas and special skills into the school; 2. sending faculty members to special workshops and seminars with the objective that they will bring new information and skills back to the job; and 3. hiring experts for their advice on how to modify the *status quo* within the school. OD focuses on the system rather than the individual faculty member as the target of change. The emphasis is on improving both the ability of the entire faculty to cope with its relationships within, and on its relationships with the student body and the community. While individuals gain insights and new attitudes during OD, the primary concern of OD is with such systemic matters as adequate communication, the integration of personal and organizational goals, the development of a climate of trust in decision making, and the effect of the culture of the school on staff and student morale.

Theory and Technology

The theoretical foundations of consultation in organization development are in social psychology and in particular in the Field Theory of Kurt Lewin (1948). The OD perspective commences by conceiving of schools not as clusters of individuals working at separate tasks, but as interdependent subsystems made up of students, teachers, and administrators working at particular tasks and moving into coordination with one another as they move from task to task. The system nature of a school lies in the coordinated interdependence (or lack of it) of subsystems of persons who work together in pursuit of educational goals. A starting point for school improvement calls for a diagnosis of how skilfully teachers, administrators, and students interact with one another.

Interpersonal Skills

The interpersonal skills of processing information, conceiving problems, and taking collective action are the fundamental ingredients of effective organizational problem solving in schools. As such they also represent the building blocks of effective school management. Collaborative problem solving involving teachers and administrators requires at a minimum the gathering of diagnostic information, sharing and clarifying that information, agreeing on the selection of a specific problem, conceiving and analyzing the problem, and having the ability to respond with experimental trials.

Giving relevant information about one's role and task, and eliciting task-related information from others constitute the two sides of processing diagnostic information. They offer the paths through which staff members can create the common reality prerequisite to collaborative action and experimental change. However, when feelings run deep, as they frequently do in schools, particularly as anxiety or disagreement surface, teachers and administrators tend to close off channels of communication that are ordinarily open when things are going smoothly. In those circumstances, the people who withhold information about their skills, ideas, preferences and other resources might deprive others of useful information and their colleagues the potential means of solving problems. Thus, communication about relevant information and constraints, particularly during high emotion, represents a basic interpersonal skill for improving the way schools function.

Conceiving problems entails the search for available information about what is known of the present situation and the goals that are valued or preferred. In particular, it requires specifying a discrepancy between current aspects of a situation and an ideal target, and referring to that gap as the problem. Locating such gaps, acknowledging them, and accepting them as challenges requires time, energy, creativity, and discipline. Above all, successful problem solving requires norms that support taking risks in uncovering problems heretofore unknown or ignored. While there is no positive way for all participants at all times to conceive of the steps of problem solving, the OD perspective assumes that a school staff will be stronger to the extent that it has norms, structures, and procedures that are supportive of conscious and continuous collaborative problem solving.

Norms and Roles

The organizational processes of a school may be conceived as the complex interplay of norms and roles. Norms are shared expectations that a range of behaviour within a specific context will either be approved, disapproved, or ignored. Roles are the sets of norms that specify how a staff member in a particular status position should behave. Norms when collected into a gestalt constitute the subsystem's culture, while an interrelated set of roles make up the subsystem's structure. Every school has a culture and a structure. Along with a focus on interpersonal skills, OD looks to modifications in the school's culture and structure that will enhance problem solving and effective change.

The social psychological character of norms is relevant to OD in several ways. They help to coordinate the school's structure by guiding behaviour through common expectations, attitudes, and understandings. Norms can also facilitate both the school's viability and the individual staff member's sense of well-being. Moreover, norms can promote a clear division of labour by helping to specify the appropriate behaviours for each task. Finally, for the staff member, norms provide a basis for social reality, especially when objective reality is ambiguous, as it so often is for administrators and teachers.

Although norms may act to resist school change, they can be gradually modified to facilitate changes in tasks, roles, and classroom procedures in the school. Therein lies an important part of the theory of OD. The OD perspective argues that norms can be altered when staff members conjointly and simultaneously experiment with innovative ways of doing things, and sustain those actions long enough until each staff member can see that his or her colleagues will accept and continue with the new patterns of role behaviour. This sort of sustained, conjoint action is particularly important when the norms to be changed are integrally associated with the competencies of individuals. Many interpersonal patterns and features of a school can be modified if staff members make explicit formal agreements conjointly (and this is always a basic tenet of OD), but many patterns of interaction featured by strong ego involvement might, at the same time, require time-consuming one-to-one agreements reached through private discussions. In whatever manner agreements about new norms and roles are reached, they must be finally supported by other staff members and legitimized through formal, staff agreements.

School Capacity for Problem Solving

In the monograph, *Transforming The School's Capacity for Problem Solving*, Runkel, Schmuck, Arends, and Francisco offer four clusters of staff activities that characterize a school's capacity for problem solving. When functioning in a robust manner, those clusters of staff actions are legitimized and guided by appropriate norms, accomplished as a formal aspect of the structure, and acted out through regularly executed procedures.

First is the systematic diagnosis of discrepancies between actual and ideal states that exist within the school's environment, between its subsystems, within the school's subsystems, and between particular staff members. Second is proactive retrieval of appropriate resources from within and outside the school for the purpose of reducing the discrepancies specified during the diagnosis. Third is the rapid formation of *ad hoc* groups, frequently with staff members from diverse subsystems of the school, that can efficiently and effectively use available resources to reduce the diagnosed discrepancies. Fourth is the self-analytic, formative evaluation of the above three clusters of activities. The technology of OD aims to help school staffs take a periodic look at themselves, and in particular to look at their problem-solving effectiveness.

Focal Techniques of OD

The specific activities that constitute a typical OD project make primary use of experiential learning. Just as John Dewey and Kurt Lewin recommended, learning by doing is emphasized over listening to lectures. The approach to intervention is intended to help staff members translate what is learned into the real-life work situations of the school.

Because organization development makes use of experiential learning in the group setting and because OD sessions frequently are emotional, some critics of OD confuse it with sensitivity training. The OD perspective argues that sensitivity training typically convenes people who are strangers and who agree to focus on individual development by helping each group member to become more aware of themselves and of their impact on others. In distinct contrast the technology of OD works chiefly through intact, task groups, and the major foci are group effectiveness and organizational problem solving. There are indications now that a new reintegration of OD and of personal development may occur during the 1980s, but more about this possibility later in the paper.

OD as it has been practised deals specifically with increasing the effectiveness of group members' job-related interaction and their satisfaction in the work. Skills in effective communication, managing conflict, problem solving, decision making, and in giving and receiving constructive feedback provide participants with tools that will enhance their ability to work more effectively toward achieving group objectives.

The OD consultant and the school administrators with an OD perspective assume that by making opportunities for staff members to learn interpersonal skills and to use them in relation to improving subsystem effectiveness within the school, any school can set in motion a design for change through which collaboration and subgroup problem solving can establish the school's capacity in solving its own problems. The following categories of techniques are those focused upon in OD projects:

Clarifying communication. Because skill in communication opens channels within the subsystem, as well as between it and other subsystems or segments of the environment, clarity of communication is essential to school effectiveness. By developing more precision in the transmission and reception of information, ambiguity and conflict about norms and roles can be alleviated and interpersonal trust can be built, which can, in turn, reinforce a climate of openness and authenticity. The skills most used in OD include paraphrasing, describing behaviour objectively, describing one's own feelings, checking one's impressions of others' feelings, and inquiring about the thoughts of others in relation to a specific point. (See Schmuck, Runkel, Arends, and Arends, 1977, Chapter 3).

Establishing clear goals. Since educational goals tend to be diffuse and ambiguous, sharpening goal definitions can lead to exploring the differentiation

The Management of Educational Institutions: Theory, Research and Consultancy

and integration of effort needed to achieve them. Recognizing the pluralism of goals within the organization and the environment can be a vital step toward acceptance of differences and greater ownership of common goals. Frequently employed techniques include instrumented methods involving questionnaires and interviews, the Delphi Method, the Phi Delta Kappa Survey of Educational Goals, and various unobtrusive methods including content analyses of memos, reports of meetings, and speeches given by administrators, or board members. (See Schmuck, Runkel, Arends, and Arends, 1977, Chapter 4.)

Uncovering and working with conflict. Just as clarifying communication and goals will lead to increased awareness of areas of conflict, so can confronting conflict help to clarify the norms and roles that will aid the organization in accomplishing its tasks. Norms for collaboration can replace norms for avoiding conflict. Individualized roles can satisfy diverse abilities and value systems as well. Techniques for managing conflict include checking expectations, various conflict resolution scales, the Imaging activity, interpersonal feedback, role negotiation, and third party intervention. (See Schmuck, Runkel, Arends, and Arends, 1977, Chapter 5.)

Improving group procedures in meetings. The face-to-face group meetings in which most organizational activity occurs in schools need not be frustrating or unproductive. Procedures aimed at facilitating task productivity and group maintenance can make such meetings more satisfying. Meetings can serve as integrating devices if group members were using problem-solving procedures to maximize the use of available human resources. Techniques used in OD to improve meetings include diagnostic questionnaires for feedback, observation tools for process consultation, exercises for helping members plan, conduct, and evaluate meetings, and the like. (See Schmuck, Runkel, Arends, and Arends, 1977, Chapter 6.)

Solving problems. A school's adaptability implies continual active engagement in problem-solving cycles for specifying, analyzing, and acting on goals that are not being reached. A problem is any discrepancy between an actual state of affairs and some ideal status to be achieved. Since both the current situation and a preferred target are in flux, problem solving must be a continuous process. Techniques for problem solving include questionnaires and interviews to specify problems, and the S-T-P sequence, including force field analysis, systematic planning, and methods for forecasting consequences of intended actions. (See Schmuck, Runkel, Arends, and Arends, 1977, Chapter 7.)

Making decisions. Effective faculties must be capable of moving decisions into action. This can be done effectively only when staff members clearly understand a decision and are committed to it. Although it is not necessary for some to have less influence for others to have more, it is sometimes helpful to reduce authority if it is not based on knowledge and competence. Techniques used during OD projects in relation to decision making include hand mirroring, card discovery problems, consensus exercises, intergroup exercises, and several procedures for helping staff define their roles and functions during decision making. (See Schmuck, Runkel, Arends, and Arends, 1977, Chapter 8.)

A Historical Snapshot

Organization Development was being used rather widely in industrial and governmental settings during the 1950s. It was formed, at least embryonically, in 1947 when a group of social psychologists and educators, stimulated by the leadership of Kurt Lewin, commenced summer training conferences at Bethel, Maine and formed the National Training Laboratories. The conception that Lewin brought to Bethel was that of action research – wherein the members of a group or organization would collect data about their own functioning so as to carry out collaborative problem solving to improve their own functioning.

During its infancy the field of what was then called human relations training at Bethel centered on the intensively self-analytic experience of the Training group (the T-group). T-groups did action research on their own group dynamics. The original T-group experiences were set up with groups of strangers. The sessions set off in the countryside of Western Maine constituted a 'cultural island' wherein participants met with strangers away from their homes and places of work. It was just a few years after the first T-group met at Bethel that another generation of trainers involved more directly in management development began to experiment with the use of T-groups in their own organizations.

The initial uses of T-groups within industrial organizations followed the Bethel approach of forming such groups from pools of relative strangers. In the late 1950s, a major innovation occurred when the ESSO Company launched a large-scale program involving not only T-groups for persons drawn from diverse parts of the organization, but also training in problem-solving for intact teams of superiors and subordinates to help them to be more trusting, collaborative, and productive in their work. The ESSO Company also experimented with intergroup workshops, during the '50s, for clarifying and managing conflicts between departments and between management and labour. In those experiments in organizational improvement the first designs in organizational training, survey data feedback, and intergroup confrontation were being tested. From then on, organization development in industry grew leaps and bounds, in particular coming into its own during the 1960s.

In 1961, the National Training Laboratories began offering annual T-group laboratories specially designed for educators. About the same time the first systematic effort to carry out and conduct research on OD for school districts was launched by Miles (1963). That three-year project at Teachers College, Columbia involved collaboration with two suburban districts. The interventions tested included survey data feedback, problem-solving workshops, and the training of teams through process consultation (see McElvaney and Miles, 1971).

Beginning in the fall of 1965, a collection of university-based specialists and researchers launched a large-scale, comparative OD project labeled COPED (Cooperative Project for Educational Development). Unfortunately COPED did not produce any longitudinal studies on the impact of OD because funding was terminated even before the first year of OD consultation. Nevertheless, since data had been collected in over 80 schools on a wide variety of organizational and educational variables, research was possible on the interrelationships among the variables at a single point in time. Those findings (COPED, 1968 and 1970) tended to confirm the hypothesis that a school's educational effectiveness was associated with high staff morale, power-sharing between administrators and teachers, the adequacy of problem-solving in faculty meetings, and the degree of trust among colleagues.

Then in 1967 Schmuck and Runkel commenced the most active and sustained program of research and development on OD in schools at the University of Oregon. Over the decade of the '70s more than 100 people worked on OD in schools with Schmuck and Runkel and more than 100 publications were produced within their program of research and development. The most important publication was *The Second Handbook of Organization Development in Schools* by Schmuck, Runkel, Arends, and Arends which was cited above in the discussion on the focal techniques of OD.

For historical significance the very first project executed by Schmuck and Runkel (1970) probably had the most to do with raising the consciousness of educators about the potentiality of OD for school improvement. In that project, Schmuck and Runkel set out to test whether a comprehensive design for training an entire faculty in OD could strengthen the problem-solving capacity of the school. It was the first attempt of its kind; it was the first time an entire staff was trained in process skills together. The consultant-researchers spent the equivalent of 12 days, with a concentrated 5 days before school in August, 1967 and the equivalent of 7 days spread throughout the '67–'68 school years, training the whole staff – including janitors and cooks – of a junior high school.

The attempt was to train the staff to establish norms and procedures in support of publicly describing school goals clearly, to help the staff diagnose its present functioning in relation to its goals, to facilitate the generation of action plans to move the staff closer to its goals, to help staff members make decisions of a consensual nature to carry out particular action plans, and to train staff in methods of checking whether movement toward the goals was truly taking place. The use of an organizational training design for those purposes resulted in school problem-solving processes more sophisticated and exemplary than had been imagined by the consultants.

The training design started with the development of skills in interpersonal communication. It aimed to build increased openness and ease of communication among staff members by having them practice the basic skills of paraphrasing, describing behaviour objectively, describing one's own feelings, checking one's impressions of another's feelings, and giving or receiving feedback. Those communication skills were practiced within the context of serious simulations. Once the communication skills had been practiced, staff members were encouraged to state frustrations or confusions they were experiencing and were taught to use a sequence of problem-solving steps, which were as follows: identifying the problem, analyzing the problem, generating multiple solutions, designing plans for action, forecasting consequences of intended actions, taking action, and evaluating those actions.

The amounts of communication and collaboration required to complete the problem-solving sequence reduced some of the staff member's frustrations and confusions, and also brought the satisfaction to many of them that they had participated in viable solutions. The problem solving also helped with the development of skills of group interaction and with the establishment of constructive norms in the school's intact work groups. The design culminated with the creation of new structures for communication and problem solving among the staff, the students, and members of the community. Follow-up summative evaluation, as well as a research design implemented successfully, raised staff morale, improved the organizational climate of the school, and facilitated the use of a number of innovative instructional strategies in the classrooms.

This project became the basis for a research report that was honoured in 1969 as the outstanding work of that year delineating a connection between behavioural science theory and the practice of organizational improvement. The award known as the Douglas McGregor Memorial Award had never before been given to a school-based project. OD in schools had now been recognized as an important domain of applied behavioural science (see Schmuck, Runkel, and Langmeyer, 1969).

The program at Oregon continued to make contributions on OD in schools through the '70s. Working in five districts (urban and suburban) and in 20 schools (elementary and secondary), the Oregon program developed and tested designs other than its initial organizational training format. Along with training, the other types of OD designs tested were data feedback, confrontation, and process observation and feedback.

In training the OD consultant determines the learning goals for a particular period of time, initiates structure, and directs activities. Thus, training involves highly planned teaching and experience-based learning in structured formats that often feature lecturettes and assigned readings. Data feedback, in contrast, involves collecting questionnaire or interview data from faculty so that problems might be pinpointed and an agenda for problem solving and change might be generated. Confrontation aims at identifying the character of the social relationships between two or more role takers or groups, as well as at identifying the problems that are contributing to conflicts among them. The OD consultant brings two or more bodies together to interact and to share the perceptions that each has of the other; to identify areas where each is viewed as helpful or unhelpful to the other; to establish clear communication channels between the two groups; to introduce a problem-solving procedure that may facilitate collaborative inquiry into mutual problems; and finally to identify the common concerns that cut across all parties involved in the confrontation. In carrying out process observation and feedback, the purpose of which is to help group members become more aware of how they are working together, the consultant sits with the client group during its work sessions, observes the ongoing processes, and occasionally offers personal comments or observations. This last type of OD consultation aims to involve the participants in talking about their working relationships themselves, and in making group agreements to modify the ways in which they will work together in the future.

When Miles and Schmuck surveyed the state of the art in educational OD in 1970 they could uncover only ten researchers, perhaps 40–50 consultants, and just a handful of school districts that were involved in OD (see Schmuck and Miles, 1971). Furthermore, only a couple of those researchers were doing sustained research on OD in schools, just a very few of the consultants regularly worked with schools in OD, and hardly a school district could be found in which OD procedures and structures had been institutionalized. By the end of the decade the picture was significantly different.

During the '70s there were replications of the Oregon training design in Alabama and Norway. A major program on school renewal in New York City was established. Having consulted in 14 New York City secondary schools, Bassin, Gross, and Jordan (1979) applied data feedback and process observation and feedback to the problem of organizing secondary faculties to execute their own problem-solving procedures. During the same period Keys (1979) was testing OD methods in urban parochial schools, Milstein (1979) was exploring ways of using OD to facilitate school desegregation, and Scheinfeld (1979) was developing comprehensive OD designs for linking faculty problem solving to classroom teaching. There also emerged a European project in the '70s called IMTEC (International Movement Toward Educational Change) in which data feedback was employed as the vehicle for facilitating local problem solving in Norwegian schools (see Dalin, 1978 for details). And the Oregon program, the New York City Renewal groups, IMTEC, and Milstein were all exploring ways to institutionalize OD in schools through various internal and external networks of OD consultants.

However, even while there were a number of very active OD researchers and developmenters spread through North America and Europe, there was no systematic knowledge on just how much OD was being practised by school people. Moreover, there were no general literature reviews and very few in depth analyses of what actually happens during an OD project. In the late '70s the time was right for a comprehensive state of the art study on OD in schools.

A State of the Art Study

In 1978, Fullan, Miles, and Taylor carried out the first large-scale analysis of OD in schools in North America. Their study consisted of a comprehensive assessment of the state of knowledge of educational OD and the nature and extent of its use in school districts in the United States and Canada. The full report is divided into five volumes, all under the title, *Organization Development in Schools: The State of the Art*. The five volumes are: Introduction and Overview, Review of Reviews, Consultants and Programs in School Districts, Case Studies, and Implications for Policy, Research, and Practice. (See Fullan, Miles, and Taylor, 1980, for a summary of the study.)

The Introduction and Overview has a summary of the main findings and the principal conclusions of the different components of the study. The Review of Reviews summarizes knowledge of OD in schools by reviewing over 50 recent sources in the research literature, including some major case studies. The report on Consultants and Programs consists of two surveys – the first, a survey of OD consultants and the second, a survey of districts. The Case Studies contain three on-site analyses in which different types of OD projects are discussed in detail. The report on Implications for Policy, Research, and Practice formulates a series of recommendations for educational organizations as diverse as local school districts, intermediate units, universities, and state, provincial, and federal-government agencies.

While the report is too large to summarize in an article of this length, it might be useful to point out some of the more significant findings and conclusions of the study.

What is OD?

The researchers found a plethora of definitions and theoretical statements about OD in general and in relation to educational OD specifically. From the diverse literature they gleaned what they considered to be an 'aggregate definition' of OD. Fullan, Miles, and Taylor conclude the best definition of OD to be as follows: 'OD in school districts is a coherent, systematically-planned, sustained effort at system self-study and improvement, focusing explicitly on change in formal and informal procedures, processes, norms, or structures, using behavioural science concepts. The goals of OD include improving both the quality of life of individuals as well as organizational functioning and performance with a direct or indirect focus on educational issues'. The researchers go on to emphasize the planned and sustained nature of OD, the centrality of self study and reflexive procedures, the relevance of both the formal and the informal, and the values of quality of life and organizational performance.

How Much OD is There?

The most surprising finding to people integrally involved in research and development on OD in schools was the considerable number of consultants and programs uncovered. For example, the researchers located 308 consultants who have been doing extensive OD consultation with schools in the United States and Canada during the last five years. This number is more than double those that were located in 1971 by Schmuck and Miles (1971). Moreover, the researchers amassed a sample of 76 school districts where OD had gone on for at least 18 months. And surprisingly more than 50 per cent of the consultants involved in those projects were insiders in school districts with little or no linkage to experts in OD. The study also indicated that approximately half the districts with OD had district-level coordinators, a steering group for school improvement, and released time available to support the effort. On the other hand, specially trained networks of OD consultants within districts – made prominent in the Oregon and New York programs described above – were very rare. Apparently, a considerable amount of OD is being carried out by district specialists who have received only minimal amounts of formal education in OD.

What is the Impact of OD?

Fullan, Miles, and Taylor report that virtually no systematic evaluation has been carried out in the 76 districts, aside from the work in Oregon and New York and that of Keys and Milstein reviewed above. The results from a self-report questionnaire, however, indicated OD to be frequently associated with the implementation of instructional innovations, such as team teaching, individualization, and alternative schools. Some administrators also associated OD with negative effects, such as increased resistance to change or increased work load, but most of the annoyances did not result in termination of the OD effort.

The self-reported retrospective perceptions of OD were largely favourable. Indeed, two thirds of the districts consistently reported that OD should 'definitely' be used more widely in the schools, and that they were sponsoring extensions of OD to other schools in their own district. Many of the favourably-oriented school administrators reported having attended workshops and conferences in which they informed others about how OD had helped their district. About a third of the districts reported having visited other districts to explain their work. Apparently, the users of OD tend to proselytize. And, it is also important to note that three-quarters of the districts predicted that OD would become institutionalized in their district.

What Does It Take For OD to Work?

Fullan, Miles, and Taylor – in both their two questionnaire studies and their three case studies – tried to uncover the factors associated with successful OD efforts in schools. The most consistent findings were the support required from top management to get OD initiated, the need for a task focus and emphasis, the importance of sustained consultation from consultants within the district, and the high time costs that are involved. Other important findings were that: 1. careful, early planning of an internal, steering committee is important, 2. OD efforts are easier to launch when the school environment is not turbulent, 3. while time costs are considerable, successful OD projects did not require large budgets, 4. success is frequently accompanied by a close partnership between consultants inside the district and experts in OD outside the district, 5. the view that OD is not a special add-on, but a central way-of-life in the district, and 6. the probability that true institutionalization will take up to 5 years for a moderately-large school district.

Emerging Interest in OD Worldwide

While the study by Fullan, Miles, and Taylor focused entirely on educational OD in the United States and Canada, they also described rapidly emerging interest in OD in Australia, England, Norway, Sweden, Holland, and Germany. The most analytic and data-based contributions to date have come from Mulford (1977) in Australia and from Dalin (1978) in Norway. The work of Bolam (1978) and others in England on 'school-based inservice' makes contact with the theory and technology of OD and promises an interesting extension of OD. The journal *Educational Change and Development* edited by Gray in England offers an outlet for publications on OD and related subjects such as school-based inservice. Unfortunately, there is no counterpart study to Fullan, Miles, and Taylor on the European context. A significant need exists for a state of the art study on OD in schools not only on the European continent but in England and Australia as well.

An Agenda-Building Conference

Seventeen behavioural scientists gathered in New York City on May 12 and 13, 1980 to generate a research agenda on organization development in schools. The conference used as its starting point the state of the art study by Fullan, Miles, and Taylor. The objectives of the conference were to summarize the knowledge on the state of OD in schools, to suggest research that should be done on OD in schools during the '80s, and to commence planning activities to put the research agenda into motion.

The participants, chosen because of their involvement in OD research, were: Clayton Alderfer, Yale University; Marc Bassin, New York City Schools; Terry Deal, Harvard University; Richard Francisco, University of Oregon; Michael Fullan, Ontario Institute for Studies in Education; Lynn Gray, Urban Coalition of New York; Tom Gross, New York City Schools; Patricia Jordan, New York City Schools; Christopher Keys, University of Illinois at Chicago; Daniel Langmeyer, University of Cincinnati; Matthew Miles, Center for Policy Research; Michael Milstein, State University of New York at Buffalo; Fritz Mulhauser, National Institute of Education; Philip Runkel, University of Oregon; Dan Scheinfeld, Institute of Juvenile Research;

The Management of Educational Institutions: Theory, Research and Consultancy

Richard Schmuck, University of Oregon; and Ernie Turner, Urban Coalition of New York.

Before the conference, nine conferees prepared brief written reactions to Fullan, Miles, and Taylor. During the conference, those written reactions were summarized and discussed. The various points brought out during the conference were recorded in a round robin fashion by the two chairs, Schmuck and Jordan, and by all but four of the other conferees. After all of the presentations, four small work groups were formed to discuss a tentative research agenda on OD. During the afternoon of the second day each of those work groups reported in a plenary session; the co-chairs led the entire group during this time toward a research agenda. A paraphrased summary of the themes and topics of that jointly reached agenda follows.

Theme A: Clarifying the Theoretical Bases of OD in Schools

1. Coherence. Increased consistency and more logical integration would be desirable in the theory of OD in schools, particularly in the interrelationships of existential, behavioural, sociological, political, and economic perspectives.

2. Complexity. An extension of the conferees concern with coherence was to establish conceptual contingencies and relationships not only among those above-listed perspectives but also between them and OD technology, school characteristics, and educational problems.

3. Causal mapping. A useful exercise in theory development would involve creating alternative conceptual scenarios to describe the sequential events of OD from startup to institutionalization. This would contribute to an increased understanding of how and why OD works.

4. Calibrating. Another contribution to theory would involve developing and refining methods for quantifying OD variables more precisely to estimate how much of a particular variable or of a cluster of variables is 'enough' to obtain the desirable effect.

5. Effect. Further conceptualization is needed on the success or failure of OD efforts, particularly in relation to the multiple levels of impact that are possible in the complex human systems of schools. For example, there should be more explications of system-wide effects and of student outcomes.

Theme B: Studying Specific Issues Related to the Practice of OD

1. Readiness. Critiques of previous research on a school's readiness to benefit from OD are needed. Conceptual work should be increased to redefine or to clarify those characteristics of schools that act as important preconditions to successful or unsuccessful OD efforts. These might include attempts to match school characteristics with different startup strategies and with different consultative designs. Empirical studies might include: (a) surveys of OD consultants to codify what readiness conditions they consider to be important, (b) retrospective in-depth analyses of successful and unsuccessful

OD efforts, and (c) longitudinal studies that commence prior to start-up and which last through institutionalization or until the OD project is given up. Studies might also focus on what consultants do to increase a school's readiness for OD and how consultants go about tailoring their designs to fit a variety of school characteristics.

2. Power. Not enough is known about the exercise and impact of power in OD projects. For example, can we usefully conceptualize interventions in terms of French and Raven's (1959) base of power? How do OD interventions affect existing power structures? Is there backlash from the centers of power that should be expected in OD? What are the mechanisms through which OD designs change the distributions of influence in a school?

The data of the Fullan, Miles, and Taylor study indicate that there are numerous instances of OD being delivered by personnel in line positions. We should have more information on how the strategies and techniques of line personnel compare and contrast with those of staff personnel. What about the administration's mandating aspects of OD? In what ways might classical OD be integrated with the methods of Management-By-Objectives, etc.?

3. Imagery and symbolism. Little systematic knowledge has been amassed on the images and myths that constitute a part of the thought processes of OD consultants, that appear implicitly in the OD literature or in the dialogues between consultants, and that are associated with OD in the minds of the clients. What poetic images or literary symbols guide the conceptual schemes, the intervention designs, and the consultative techniques of OD? How might we describe the 'existential underbelly' of the OD enterprise? How do the images held by consultants facilitate or hinder their relationships with clients, their communication with evaluators and policy makers, and their collaboration with colleagues? What might be learned from viewing OD as drama and OD events as theatre?

4. Educational problems. More conceptual development is needed to compare the appropriateness of OD with other non-OD strategies for coping with important educational problems such as low student achievement, low staff morale, high community alienation, extensive racism and sexism, and inadequate funding. It would be useful to have a series of parallel case studies in which OD and non-OD procedures are compared across different educational problems in different school environments.

5. Pupils. More conceptualizations and data are needed on ways in which OD projects influence pupil achievement, pupil motivation, peer group interaction, and teacher behaviour during instruction. Also, some further experimental attempts are needed on bringing pupils directly into OD designs with administrators and teachers. Under what circumstances and through what mechanisms do OD interventions have impact on pupils? What happens to staff relationships when pupils are brought into OD projects? How does teacher-pupil problem solving about school-wide issues relate to the teaching and learning processes that take place between them?

6. Reflections. During OD, systemic information is typically gathered that reflects the system members' functioning. This data-based reflection is analogous to an organizational mirror. But what does the self-reflection process look like concretely? What are consultants, administrators, and teachers doing when self-reflection is taking place? How does such reflection differ from OD project to OD project? What about the functions of formal reflection versus informal reflection? How does the reflection get converted into ownership, into commitment, or into problem solving?

7. Consultants. Whereas the Fullan, Miles, and Taylor research offers some data on school-based OD consultants, more systematic knowledge is needed about them. Who are they? How are they trained? What are their favourite concepts, designs, and techniques? What do they actually do when they execute a design? What sociological circumstances might explain the rise or fall of OD consultants in school districts? What about issues of stress and burnout for consultants? How can OD consultants be encouraged to carry out research on what they are doing? What structures or mechanisms might be created to induce communication among educational OD consultants?

8. Politics. Knowledge is needed on how OD relates to the politics of a school district. What are the political functions of the board, the superintendent, or the teachers' union during start-up, diagnosis, reflection, problem solving, taking action, evaluation, or institutionalization? What sorts of acceptance or protection does the OD consultant need at each of those stages? What are the skills that an OD consultant needs to cope effectively with the political realities of the district? What are the ethical issues that typically arise for the OD consultant who attempts to deal with those political realities?

9. Institutionalization. Whereas there is a literature on the institutionalization of OD in school districts, we need still more data on both concrete aspects of the capacity for problem solving and how the internal OD role gets shaped and sustained in districts. In particular, what are the advantages or disadvantages of having counsellors assume support roles in OD? What about the benefits or debits of line vs. staff personnel? What about cadres of OD specialists? What sustains them? What causes them to go down hill? What sorts of negative effect do they have on school districts?

10. Diffusion. The Fullan, Miles, and Taylor study is the first on the growth of OD in North America, but more in-depth information is needed on how much OD theory and technology has penetrated school districts. We need more conceptualization on why OD in schools is developing at this time, particularly in England, Australia, and Europe, and on what its prospects are for the future. If OD is to spread, clearer explanations of what it is and how it works will be necessary for school administrators. It would be useful to have survey data from superintendents and principals on their ideas and attitudes about OD. Moreover, it would be helpful to have OD consultants testing various strategies for changing the *status quo* and for championing OD in schools, and to have OD researchers attempting to speak about their results both to educators and to educational policy makers.

Theme C: Studying OD in Combination with Other Change Strategies

1. Additive. Studies need to be done on the events that take place when OD techniques are added to ongoing planned change projects in schools, such as desegregation, busing, mainstreaming, school closings or mergers, alternative schools, and the like. Such studies could be done under varying conditions of crisis and stability in the district and of authoritarian and democratic leadership in the district administration. In what ways does the addition of an OD component facilitate or hinder the change process? What are the ethical and existential dilemmas that the OD consultant confronts in such projects?

2. Integrative. More research and development are needed on the integration of OD theory and technology with top-down, directive change strategies such as management-by-objectives. How can centralized thrusts for improvement in planning, problem solving, and accountability be enhanced by integrating them with OD methods? What are some alternative ways in which OD and MBO might be combined into a single design for school improvement? What are the ethical problems for the OD consultant doing such mixing?

Theme D: Enlarging the Scope of Research Designs

1. Surveys. Whereas Fullan, Miles, and Taylor's research makes a substantial start in locating consultants and districts involved in educational OD more surveys should be done to study: (a) the designs and techniques of school-based specialists who label their consultative activities as OD, (b) the cognitive and attitudinal reactions of teachers, administrators, parents, students, and board members towards OD projects, (c) the unintended consequences of OD, (d) change projects not labeled OD but which fall within our definition of OD, and (e) the reactions of educational specialists toward adding or integrating OD techniques into their activities. Also, it would be useful to have a regular updating of the surveys taken by Fullan, Miles, and Taylor, and to extend them to England, Australia, and Europe.

2. Documents. Very little research on OD has been done with the records that often exist in school districts. For example, efforts should be made to locate evaluation reports of school-based OD projects. Also administrative memos about OD projects could be a useful resource for understanding how school administrators think about OD.

3. Cases. Whereas there are only a few cases of OD in the literature, there is a need for considerably more in-depth descriptions of several levels of events during OD projects such as: (a) the behaviours of consultants and their immediate impact on the clients, (b) the behaviour of principals and teachers during formal OD meetings and between them, (c) the differences and similarities between the formal and the informal behaviours of the clients during the OD project, and (d) the thoughts and feelings that the consultants and clients are experiencing at different points in the developmental sequence of the OD project. There is also a need for more detailed descriptions of OD successes and of autopsies of OD failures, particularly from the diverse vantage points of the consultants and of the participants. Particular cases could be useful such as: (a) OD and mainstreaming, (b) OD and professional retrenchment, (c) OD and team teaching or Individually-Guided-Instruction, (d) OD and staff morale; and (e) OD and student retention.

In-depth cases of OD in schools, could also help with an understanding of the causal and sequential aspects of OD efforts. For example, it would be useful to trace the ups and downs of the OD process, both from the points of view of the consultants and the participants. Or we might ask: what are the satisfactions that consultants and participants obtain from OD? What are the functions of conflict during the OD process? How does the make up of the consulting team influence the execution and the impact of the design? In what ways do internal consultants differ from external consultants in what they do and in the impact they have? How might we assess the potency of key elements in the OD design? How might we assess the impact of the charisma of the consultant?

4. Comparisons. There is a substantial need in OD for a series of strategic comparative studies. The usefulness of surveys, documents, and cases, moreover, will be enhanced when they are executed within a comparative perspective. For example, we need to compare: (a) OD in schools with OD in other organizations, (b) OD with non-OD strategies in similar schools with similar educational problems, (c) OD delivered by internal consultants and OD delivered by external consultants, (d) the same sort of OD design used in very different schools, (e) OD in schools with different levels of readiness, (f) OD in healthy and unhealthy systems, (g) different OD designs matched with different school problems; and (i) high and low impact schools as defined in the Fullan, Miles, and Taylor study.

Case studies can help achieve the strength of a comparative perspective if they employ a standard format. They might all include descriptions of the values and goals of the project, the organizational and educational conditions at outset, the design along with what went on during implementation, the inner lives of the participants in terms of their thoughts and feelings during the project, the impact of the intervention in terms of changes in structure, norms, and procedures, and the policy implications that were derived from the project. Information might also be included on changes in the school's capacity for problem solving, the staff climate, student alienation, and student achievement.

OD Clearinghouse and Exchange

The agenda for educational OD raises many questions that require increased communication and interdependence among OD researchers and consultants worldwide if we are to obtain valid answers during the '80s. The Center for Educational Policy and Management of the University of Oregon is currently considering the establishment of an international clearinghouse and exchange for OD in schools. The objective of this endeavour would be used effectively for further research, development, and dissemination. The OD Clearinghouse and Exchange would store a collection of annotations and abstracts, develop an international repository of data, and maintain networks of researchers, practitioners, and school districts involved in OD.

Annotations and Abstracts

This activity will call for the continual monitoring of literature on OD in schools. Whereas Schmuck and Miles summarized the literature in 1971 and 1975, and Runkel and Burr produced a large number of annotations on research done before 1977, there is now a need for another updating of the relevant literature. A major activity of the OD Clearinghouse and Exchange would be to prepare up-to-date annotated bibliographies of research and practice on OD in schools worldwide, and to add to those bibliographies annually. The objective is that researchers and practitioners would be able to use the information much in the style of ERIC. Also, topical reviews would be prepared periodically by the staff using the bibliography as a resource.

Repository of Data

This activity will call for assembling data on the conduct and evaluation of OD-in-schools projects worldwide, organizing the data so that they would be available in useful forms to researchers and practitioners, and supporting the use of the data by researchers and practitioners throughout the world. Each OD project included in the repository would be described thoroughly, including both qualitative and quantitative data. Examples of information that could be included are: 1. identifying information about the schools, consultants, dates, etc.; 2. demographic, sociological, and psychological information about schools and consultants; 3. information about the OD training or consultation itself, including goals, designs, exercises, procedures, budget, etc.; and information about the impact of the OD consultation, including data about structural and normative shifts of staffs, and about effects on students.

Network of Researchers

Networks of people doing research on OD in schools would be a useful accompaniment to the data repository. By exchanging information researchers would be stimulated to conduct more informed research that builds cumulatively on the previous work of other researchers. The behavioural scientists who met during May, 1980 in New York City could form the initial core of such a network.

The Management of Educational Institutions: Theory, Research and Consultancy

Network of Practitioners

Several informal networks of OD consultants already have begun to form; with minor effort the staff of the proposed clearinghouse and exchange could establish formal networks of OD consultants to support further development of experienced consultants and to encourage the startup development of new OD practitioners. Annual conferences of OD consultants in North America have already taken place, three times in Eugene, Oregon and twice in New York City. Using those conferences along with the lists of consultants in the Fullan, Miles, Taylor study and the lists maintained by IMTEC in Europe, the Clearinghouse and Exchange would have a nucleus of OD consultants from which to form international and national networks. An initial activity could be to have those consultants complete a questionnaire on their characteristics as professionals and about the sorts of OD designs they are implementing. The Clearinghouse and Exchange would share those data with all those interested and arrange conferences, newsletters, and workshops to encourage useful exchange among OD practitioners.

Network of Schools

The schools that have been doing OD for 18 months or more that were uncovered by Fullan, Miles, and Taylor in North America along with other schools we know of in Australia, England and other Europe countries would form the initial population out of which a network of schools would be constituted. From this population, the Clearinghouse and Exchange would gather information about the OD designs and techniques that are being used to strengthen the quality of life in schools. Data about perceived needs would also be collected to determine the sorts of resources needed by those districts to make their OD efforts more effective.

A Personal View of the Future

In this chapter I have tried to look toward the future of OD in schools. To orientate the reader, I first summarized educational OD theory, technology, and research, but I deliberately dealt with those topics briefly. I assumed most readers to have knowledge and background in the topics. Those who feel the need for additional information can be brought up to date, at least about educational OD in North America, by reading Fullan, Miles, and Taylor (1980). I went on, in the bulk of the chapter, to describe an important conference in New York City for building an agenda for educational OD in the '80s, and to explain how a Clearinghouse and Exchange on OD in schools could offer a useful integrating structure for stimulating both research and dissemination.

My intention has been to present a picture of the directions that OD in schools is likely to take during the '80s; the picture that I have drawn is based on the information about the state of educational OD that exists today. It is difficult, of course, to estimate what actually will happen with educational OD. Will the movement to employ OD techniques, which has gained steadily during the last decade, continue to grow among educators during the next decade? It now certainly looks as though the momentum will continue. Will the agenda that was created at the New York conference during May, 1980 get implemented? There are signs that at least parts of it will get worked on, but it is of course too long an agenda to complete in a decade. Will the Clearinghouse and Exchange get off the ground at Oregon? That too looks promising; however, one cannot be sure of how effective it would be. Will there be counterparts to the Fullan, Miles, and Taylor studies in Australia, England and elsewhere in Europe? I certainly hope so.

In this context of uncertainty, I would like to describe a few of my own hopes for educational OD in the future. First, as I have already indicated, I hope that the experiences with educational OD in Australia, England and Europe will be analyzed, published, and widely disseminated. There is need, for example, for a better articulation and integration between School-Based Inservice created in England (see Keast and Carr, 1979) and our North American version of OD in schools. Moreover, it would be useful to have additional articles from Australia of the sort by Mulford (1977), and to have more information published on the IMTEC program in Europe (see Dalin, 1978 and Schmuck, 1980).

Second, I hope that more and more educational managers world wide will come to view OD as a viable alternative to the traditional methods of planned change in schools. For those responsible for managing the schools to gain a new consciousness about OD, it would be important for them to see that: 1. teachers become more committed to organizational and program changes which they help to create; 2. the quality of solutions to educational problems improves when those who are a part of the problem and have relevant information are allowed to influence the solutions; 3. responsibility for professional growth and improvement can be developed if teachers are given responsibility for creating school-wide changes themselves; and 4. school renewal on a continuous basis will be unlikely to obtain without open discussion of the staff on educational goals, methods, and program. In summary, the intellectual magnet which draws OD people together – and which I hope more and more educational managers will be drawn toward – is the belief that change in the complex way of doing things in schools will occur most effectively when the people who must change participate in the processes of identifying the need for, and the definition of, change.

Third, I hope that there will be many new experiments in educational OD wherein not only teachers become engaged in collaborative problem solving with school managers, but in which students and parents also act as integral parts of the OD design. Many schools now require parent participation on advisory committees; still there has been little use of OD methods to create cohesive educator-parent committees. Many schools now openly hope to reduce student alienation and to increase teacher-student collaboration; still there have been very few published studies on OD applied to enhancing collaborative teacher-student problem solving on school-wide matters. The concept of student participation in school renewal continues to be viewed as radical and impractical by many educational managers. But viewing students as organizational participants is not obtuse, and bringing students into school-wide problem solving and decision making can work (see Arends, Schmuck, and Arends, 1980).

Fourth, I hope that OD concepts and techniques will more and more become integral parts of the repertoires of educational managers. The most important aspect of educational OD for the managers to master involves the skills of running effective meetings. They need to attend more systematically to arranging appropriate preconditions for their meetings, to developing clear and reasonable agenda, to integrating communication skills into their chairperson roles, to arranging for effective recording of the meeting's important points, to using problem-solving concepts to guide discussions, and to implementing appropriate and clear decision-making procedures. Educational managers could also improve their understanding about goal-setting, about using conflicts productively, about collaborative problem-solving, and about participatory decision-making. In the spirit of the self-reflection of OD, I hope that more and more educational managers will choose to ask teachers for feedback about their performance, and will at appropriate times ask OD consultants to observe them in action and to coach them on possible improvements.

Fifth, I hope that educational OD will gradually expand toward a more holistic, multiple-systems level perspective. At the moment, OD in schools emphasizes improved interpersonal relations, strengthened group processes, and an enhanced capacity for organizational problem solving. I would like to see OD projects expand to include both a focus on individual-educator development and on strengthening the school-community interface. In relation to the former, I hope that OD projects will more and more include designs for coping with teacher stress and burnout, for helping teachers set and carry out personal-growth agenda, for stimulating managers and teachers to develop designs for their own professional growth, and for assisting individual teachers to deal more effectively with classroom group processes. In relation to the latter, I hope that OD projects will more and more emphasize the school's relationship to its economic and political communities. Such an ecological perspective, incorporated into an OD design, could not only benefit the problem-solving capacities of the faculty, but could also become a strong pedagogical component in the practical socialization of youth.

Finally, I hope that we will continue to seek ways in which the concepts and methods of OD can be integrated with other pedagogical and change strategies. OD in schools does not offer a remedy for all educational ills; it is not a panacea. Educational problems and the human dynamics of schools are much too complex to be ameliorated by one theory or a single technological repertoire. I hope for a future zeitgeist in education wherein educational OD takes its proper, but modest, place in relation to the myriad of other applications that are being addressed in this book.

References

ARENDS, J., SCHMUCK, R. and ARENDS, R. (1980) 'Students as organizational participants', in MILSTEIN, M. (Ed.), *Schools, Conflict, and Change*, New York, Teachers College Press, pp. 96–113.

BASSIN, M., GROSS, T. and JORDAN, P. (1979) 'Developing renewal processes in urban high schools', *Theory Into Practice*, 18(2), April, pp. 73–81.

BOLAM, R. (1978) 'School focussed INSET and consultancy', *Educational Change and Development*, 1(1).

COOPERATIVE PROJECT FOR EDUCATIONAL DEVELOPMENT (COPED) (1968) Final Report, Project No. OE6-10-205. Grant No. 3-6-062802-1527. Washington, D.C., United States Office of Education.

COOPERATIVE PROJECT FOR EDUCATIONAL DEVELOPMENT (COPED) (1970) Final Report. Data Analysis Project. Project No. 8-0069. Grant No. OEG-3-8-080069-0043 (010). Washington, D.C., U.S. Office of Education (Vol. 1, Research Outcomes, Vol. II. Case Studies, Vol. III. Diagnosing the Professional Climate of Your School. Appendix, Instruments and Code Manual).

DALIN, P. (1978) *Limits to Educational Change*, London, The Macmillan Press, Ltd.

DEWEY, J. (1916) *Democracy and Education*, Macmillan.

FRENCH, J., and RAVEN, B. 'The bases of social power' (1959) in CARTWRIGHT, D. (Ed.), *Studies in Social Power*, Ann Arbor, Michigan, Institute for Social Research.

FULLAN, M., MILES, M. and TAYLOR, G. (1980) 'Organization development in schools: The state of the art', *Review of Educational Research*, 50(1), Spring, pp. 121–183.

GRAY, H.L. (Ed.) (1978 et seq) *Educational Change and Development*, Vol. 1, et seq, Department of Education Management, Sheffield City Polytechnic, UK.

KEAST, D. and CARR, V. (1979) 'School-based inservice: Interim evaluation', *British Journal of Inservice Education*, Summer, pp. 25–31.

KEYS, C. (1979) 'Renewal processes in urban parochial schools', *Theory Into Practice*, 18(2), April, pp. 97–105.

LEWIN, K. (1948) *Resolving Social Conflicts*, New York, Harper's.

MCELVANEY, C. and MILES, M. (1971) 'Using survey feedback and consultation', in SCHMUCK, R., and MILES, M. (Eds.), *Organization Development in Schools*, La Jolla, CA., University Associates, Inc., pp. 113–138.

MILSTEIN, M. (1979) 'Developing a renewal team in an urban school district', *Theory Into Practice*, 18(2), April, pp. 106–113.

MULFORD, W.R. (1977) 'Organization development in schools: An octet of dilemmas', Lecture presented at A.C.E.A. Conference, Brisbane, Australia, August.

RUNKEL, P. and BURR, A. (1977) *Bibliography on Organizational Change in Schools: Selected, Annotated, and Indexed*, Eugene, Oregon, Center for Educational Policy and Management.

RUNKEL, P., SCHMUCK, R., ARENDS, J. and FRANCISCO, R. (1979) *Transforming the*

School's Capacity for Problem Solving, Eugene, Oregon, Center for Educational Policy and Management.

SCHEINFELD, D. (1979) 'A design for renewing urban elementary schools', *Theory Into Practice*, 18(2), April, pp. 114–125.

SCHMUCK, R. (1980) 'Conceptualizing innovation comprehensively', (and essay review of DALIN, P. *Limits to Educational Change*) *Review of Education*, 6(1), Winter, pp. 1–9.

SCHMUCK, R. and MILES, M. (1971) *Organization Development in Schools*, La Jolla, Ca., University Associates.

SCHMUCK, R. and RUNKEL, R. (1970) *Organizational Training for a School Faculty*, Eugene, Oregon, Center for Educational Policy and Management.

SCHMUCK, R., RUNKEL, P., ARENDS, J. and ARENDS, R. (1977) *The Second Handbook of Organization Development in Schools*, Palo Alto, Ca., Mayfield Publishing Company.

SCHMUCK, R., RUNKEL, P. and LANGMEYER, D. (1969) 'Improving organizational problem solving in a school faculty', *Journal of Applied Behavioral Science*, 5(4), pp. 455–482.

Training Internal Change Agents for Schools

Mike M. Milstein
State University of New York at Buffalo

The past two decades have witnessed unprecedented efforts to change schools. In the United States the drive toward innovation has been particularly rampant. The federal government has provided incentives to stimulate educational innovations, many states have increased their sponsorship of special aid programs, and innumerable school districts have mounted their own 'grass roots' plans.

Evaluations of these efforts thus far tend to point toward a picture of much effort but relatively little long-term impact. For example, a review of the results of the Rand studies (Rand Corporation, 1975), which attempted to ascertain outcomes of federal aid programs, points out that 'the net return to the federal investment was the adoption of many innovations, the successful implementation of few, and the long-run continuation of still fewer' (Berman and McLaughlin, 1980, p. 58).

Why has it been so difficult to have a substantial impact on educational organizations? Three explanatory notions seem particularly relevant for the purposes of this discussion. First, some argue that we must look to the properties of schools to understand the low implementation rate. In this view, because schools are 'loosely coupled' organizations (Bidwell, 1965; Weick, 1976) it is difficult to disseminate major innovations. Schools are decentralized organizations with very little formal control apparatus to bind them, or even

Editor's note: It is very difficult to get the flavour of an OD programme or intervention partly because each case is unique and probably significantly unlike any other and partly because traditions and practices vary considerably, especially between the UK and USA. Milstein's account of a training and consultancy programme based on OD principles gives a good idea of an American approach.

Readers should look carefully for cultural indicators in the account, such as method of funding and support and the value systems of the supporting organizations and individuals. There is much controversy in OD over value systems and in the industrial context they vary widely and sometimes wildly. But the important element in OD that crosses national and cultural boundaries is that it must be embedded in the value system of the organization(s) where it is applied because it must be owned by the membership at large in the organization. Milstein illustrates how this may be possible in an American setting.

individual classrooms, together. Given the relative independence of operating units, it becomes difficult for distant policy centers, such as federal and state policy bodies and regulatory agencies, to have a direct impact upon them.

Second, it has been noted that those attempting to encourage innovation often lack the skill needed to develop political linkages that enhance institutionalization of change programs (Tye, 1980). It is one thing to have the substantive and technical know-how to introduce educational changes. It is quite another thing to have the ability to work effectively with power centers, such as school boards, mayors' offices and labor unions.

Finally, the context of education has changed radically over the past several decades. Given such phenomena as the advent of collective negotiations, increased interest group activities, and demands for accountability by funding agencies, it is more difficult to implement change strategies. For the most part these strategies, which were developed during the 1950s and 1960s, assume good will and cooperation. These are commodities that are available less frequently today than they were twenty years ago (Milstein, 1978).

No longer can we expect that changes identified at distant policy centers, and which leave only minimal room for 'fine tuning' at the school district level, will have the potential for significant impact. This rather linear arrangement, which assumes that those who must operate the programs will accept the purposes of policy makers while having little or no say in the development of programs, is unworkable. Given the changing context of education, along with the 'loosely coupled' nature of educational organizations and the lack of political sophistication of innovators, it is not surprising that so little has been accomplished in the way of long-term implementation of innovations.

New strategies will have to be designed that 1. put less reliance on distant policy centers having great influence over expectations; 2. encourage involvement of those from within educational systems who are knowledgeable about the political connections that must be forged; and 3. enhance the probability of cooperation of interest groups since this cannot be assumed in ways that it was in the past.

There is a popular simulation used in laboratory training and organizationally-based interventions, called Planners and Operators (Schmuck and Runkel *et al*, 1977, pp. 355–359), that requires a small group (planners) to design a task that will be carried out by another group (operators). The planners work in closed session while the operators try to anticipate what is expected of them. The task is then given over to the operators, after a brief instruction period, and the planners withdraw from the activity.

As might be guessed, the results typically include frustration for both groups. Planners are frustrated because they are not allowed to carry out the task while operators are frustrated because they are asked to carry out an unknown task, one for which they have had little or no opportunity to develop a commitment. Often antagonism and a sense of competition develops between the groups.

When conducted with school staffs planners and operators frequently leads to a debriefing discussion that centers on the frustrations that teachers and administrators experience when they are required to carry out tasks that are designed by central office personnel or officials from the state or federal governments.

The point is that involvement, commitment and ownership are important considerations in the process of implementing change. As Berman and McLaughlin concluded from the Rand research, implementation of an innovation 'ultimately depends on local choices about how the money should be spent and how the new ideas should be implemented and sustained. From the beginning to the final stages of a project, a supportive institutional environment was necessary for a project to be effectively implemented and to take root' (Berman and McLaughlin, 1980, p. 71). In short, a basic flaw in attempts to bring about change in educational settings is that those who are expected to manage the innovations are not often consulted about their views or asked to participate in the setting of purposes and/or the design of delivery systems. Innovation designers, operating from distant plateaus, have been so busy planning that they have rarely thought much about the commitment needs of those who have to operate the innovations.

Strategies for Involving the Operators

The concern for improving the impact of change efforts has led me to experiment with strategies that increase the level of involvement of those who will be responsible for implementation. In this respect I have worked toward the development of a pre-service graduate training program at SUNY/Buffalo which encourages present and would-be school leaders to develop and sharpen their skills in involving school staffs in planning for and implementing educational innovations. In addition, I have helped the Buffalo Public Schools to develop an internal change team composed of professionals from all levels within the district to assure that it will have a continuing capacity to respond to innovation requirements.

These programs have been built upon Organization Development (OD) values and strategies. [The reader interested in further details about OD is encouraged to refer to such basic introductions as Bennis (1969); Lawrence and Lorsch (1969); French and Bell (1973); Schmuck and Runkel *et al* (1977)]. A comprehensive definition of OD as it relates to educational organizations holds that OD 'in school districts is a coherent, systematically-planned, sustained effort at system self-study and improvement, focusing explicitly on change in formal and informal procedures, processes, norms or structures, using behavioral science concepts' (Fullan, Miles, and Taylor, 1980, p. 135).

This notion of OD lends itself well to the values of the writer; that is, those expected to implement an innovation should be involved in the planning of that innovation. What follows are descriptions of the programs, which are founded on these values, at SUNY/Buffalo and in the Buffalo Public School District.

SUNY at Buffalo's Graduate Program in Educational Administration

Buffalo's pre-service educational administration program has been undergoing constant modification since 1970. Faculty and students have worked together to institute a program that includes three optional tracks or 'concentrations': policy, operations analysis, and organizations (cf. Gibson and Stetar, 1976, and Milstein and Conway, 1976). The organizations concentration, employing OD as a central focus, has been designed to enrich students' skills in helping work groups cope with change. Students become deeply involved in learning groups as we attempt to approximate work setting conditions. One concern that we had about this design is that research indicates that learnings mastered in temporary groups do not tend to last when learners return to their own work setting (cf. Dalton, Lawrence and Greiner, 1970, pp. 357-361). In large part this is because others in the learners' home organizations tend to reject the newly acquired skills and behaviors. Not having participated, other organizational members do not understand the bases of the changed behavior and feel threatened when their own behaviors and skills are challenged by the returning member.

This concern led us to design a program with two critical features to minimize the rejection effect. First, we limit membership in the program to those who are in, or soon will be in, key leadership positions; e.g., assistant principals, principals and central office personnel. This enhances the probability of positive impact because the individuals involved are already recognized as organizational leaders so they can apply new skills as they learn them. Being in leadership roles they have opportunities to test their learnings because they are expected to lead. The potential for impact is thus enhanced by a careful selection of participants.

Second, we build field-based activities as well as laboratory activities into the program. We feel that readings, lectures, and participation in a wide variety of group exercises in laboratory settings should be complemented by a good deal of experience with real organizations undergoing changes. These field efforts confront students with the many complexities of managing change efforts; gaining entry, doing diagnoses, developing prescriptions, conducting activities associated with the prescription, and evaluating outcomes. This experience increases the confidence of those involved in the program that they can carry out such activities in their own organizational settings.

In short, by purposefully including experienced leaders who are exposed to group-based learning and then confronted with challenging change efforts in organizational setting, we have been able to compound the long-term effects of our pre-service program.

What has evolved over time is a program that is several years in duration and which prepares students for improved leadership capacities in their own organizational settings. The 'core' of the concentration includes, sequentially, a comprehensive exposure to organizational theory; role analysis experiences which help members to assess the impact of their leadership styles; diagnostic experiences that require students to develop and apply instrumentation to real school-based situations; and, finally, an intensive exposure to 'intervention' activities in which individuals and/or small teams contract with a school organization to carry out a diagnosis, develop prescriptions, conduct 'interventions' based upon the prescriptions, and evaluate outcomes. [Initially students worked in large groups contracting with a single field site. However, we soon found that role specialization developed, and students did not gain on overall sense of the whole process. Therefore over the past several years we have required students to work as individuals or on small teams so that each student will have a better notion of the entire flow of change efforts.]

Field projects have been conducted in a variety of public and private settings, including work with entire school faculties, teaching teams, and administrative teams. They have been district-wide and in-school, and have included such diverse populations as teachers, administrators, support staff, parent groups, and student organizations. There have even been some projects conducted outside of the school sector, e.g., in an army reserve unit, with a church governing body, and with the staff of a home for girls who are wards of the court. Students are responsible for conducting the project from initial contact to evaluation and exiting from the field site. However, projects are closely supervised; each succeeding phase is reviewed and must be approved before it is set into practice. Tutorials are conducted to provide needed information, guide students to appropriate resources, and improve field project designs.

As might be expected field project outcomes vary widely. In a few cases projects never proceeded beyond the initial contact stage because potential clients decided that the proposed activity did not meet their needs. At the other extreme some projects expanded in scope and continued for two or more years. Overall evaluation data indicate that there have been demonstrable and positive results for the efforts made. Outcomes have included clarification of over-all organizational goals, refinement of decision making and problem solving processes and structures, development of functioning management teams, improvement of meetings and resolution of interpersonal, group and intergroup conflicts. Specific 'product' outcomes include increased attendance, role specifications, and the development of planning documents, organizational charts and policy handbooks. In short, organizations that have served as field sites generally feel that they have come away from the effort better off than when they went into it.

More important for present purposes, is whether there is a positive impact upon the students who conduct the field projects. Does the program improve their ability to help organizations change? This question was explored in some depth in an earlier article (Buergenthal and Milstein, 1978). In that paper, participants ($N = 62$) who had completed the activities noted above between 1971 and 1976 were asked to respond to several instruments that focused on shifts in attitudes, leadership styles, and leadership effectiveness that could be traced to their involvement in the organization concentration.

The design of the study called for documentation of short-term effects (i.e., shifts that occurred from entry to exit in the preparatory program) and long-term effects (i.e., several years after completion of the preparatory program). Responses to the instruments show strong and consistent shifts in attitudes as well as perceived shifts in leadership behavior and leadership effectiveness.

Short-term outcomes were established using Wallen's Group Expectation Survey (NWRL, 1972). The instrument, which was administered at the outset of the diagnosis and intervention experience and immediately after it was completed, probes individuals' perceptions regarding their own and others' openness in group situations about giving and receiving feedback within the group. Items vary from relatively low risk – focusing on whether participants understand each other, to relatively high risk – focusing on whether participants 'feel hurt, rejected, embarrassed, or put down' by each other. Results show consistent outcomes for each of the groups included in the analysis. In brief, attitudinal changes include the following:

1. A consistent increase in belief that self and other members of the group would provide honest feedback, at the cognitive level (e.g., 'when he does not understand') and at the emotive level (e.g., 'when he feels hurt').
2. A reduction in the perception that self will be more open and sharing than other members of the group. In other words, members became more positive about the participation of other group members.
3. In the pre-test members indicated low willingness to take emotive risks in the group, but in the post-test there was a marked increase in willingness to participate in these important maintainence issue areas.

In short, group members were able to internalize concepts and experiences. In the process they altered their attitudes regarding groups and group processes. The question remained: would these changed attitudes prolong and transfer to behaviors once group members left the program and concentrated their efforts on leading their own organization?

A follow-up survey was then sent to all participants who had completed the program. Items on the survey probed for participants' perceptions of long-term modifications in their views of leadership and of their own leadership effectiveness as a result of their involvement in the program. Anecdotal comments were, with few exceptions, positive: 'I am more sensitive to the needs of my colleagues ...', 'I am more open to ideas and able to communicate; a skill that has been helpful in dealing with others ...', 'I now attempt to help a group help itself to accomplish tasks ...', and 'I see the complexity of inter-human relations in a different light and my role as a facilitator of good relations'.

Ninety-five percent of those responding to the questionnaire felt that they continue to employ the skills learned in the program. High on the list of specific skills retained are communications, decision making, problem solving, diagnostic and evaluation techniques, consensus seeking, observation, and planning. Respondents were able to cite a variety of ways they have been able to employ these skills in school settings, including in-service workshops, administrative team meetings, advisory committee work, staff meetings, departmental reorganizations, curriculum development projects, and classroom organization assistance for teachers. Participants tended to feel that they have 'become more effective...' are 'more approachable...', 'less dogmatic ...', 'more open with superiors...', and more concerned about 'making others an integral part of change'.

Many respondents felt that others in their organizations have responded positively to these changed behaviors. They report 'greater understanding among group members' of the need for organizational improvement, 'more productive participation by members...', 'improved school climate...', 'clarification of program goals...', 'improved communications...', 'improved meetings...', and 'a more stable school and improved learning for students'. To the extent that these self-perceptions are accurate, there are strong indications that participants in the training program have been able to influence the behavior of others.

The evidence suggests that preparatory programs which emphasize basic concepts of organizational dynamics, are experiential and group based in focus and include field-based experiences, can have significant and positive effects on the subsequent performance of educational leaders who participate in them.

The School Improvement Resource Team (SIRT)

The impetus for an internal change team in the Buffalo Public School District was a 1976 federal court order to racially desegregate all schools. The district's leaders were concerned about community, staff and student responses to the major changes that would be required to comply with the court order. Magnet schools were designed as the center-piece of the district's desegregation plan. This minimized community unrest, but there was still much concern about the ability and willingness of school staffs to design alternative educational programs and to adapt to changing conditions. What was anticipated was a need to modify basic value orientations as well as the need to develop improved human relations skills and conflict resolution skills. The district's leaders recognized their own skill and time limitations to provide this support for school personnel. However, given the long-term changes that would be called for, they were also skeptical about employing outside change agents to conduct the necessary in-service activities.

My own experience in the university's preparatory program, described above, supported the district officials' view that an internal capacity to respond over the long-haul should be developed. That is, the probability of institutionalizing the mandated change would probably be increased if those responsible for implementation activities could be involved in the development of required values, norms, goals, skills and structures.

I advised the district's leaders to consider adapting the model initially developed by Schmuck and Runkel (1977, pp. 524-545) in Kent, Washington and Eugene, Oregon. In both districts Schmuck and Runkel were able to help teachers and administrators develop a basic understanding of OD values and sufficient skills to apply OD strategies. Those trained then formed district-wide teams to help school staffs as they confronted problems. The Kent Cadre has since disbanded, but the Eugene Cadre has persisted. In fact, after a full decade of activity, the experiment in Eugene has proven that the concept of internal change agents making effective contributions in schools is feasible. If anything, the Cadre's contribution to the Eugene schools, as reported in an evaluation by Callan and Kentta (1980), has grown in importance as well as in stature over time.

The question was, could the strategies pioneered in small and medium sized school systems in western settings be applied elsewhere? Specifically, could the notions of self-renewal be applied in a complex eastern metropolitan setting? Further, could it be applied where the focus of attention would be much more specific and problem-oriented rather than on the general upgrading of organizational performance?

The district applied for and received funds under ESEA Title IV-C to establish the team. The full account of the early development of SIRT (Milstein, 1979) and exploration of the major events over the first three years of SIRT's existence (Milstein and Lafornara, 1980) have been detailed elsewhere. The basic events in the growth and institutionalization of the team are explored here to support the contention that an internal change team can be viable and, probably, superior to the more traditional route of employing external change agents in its potential for enhancing the implementation of change programs.

SIRT was initially formed in the summer of 1977, on the eve of the desegregation of the district's secondary schools. Members of the team (16 in total) were chosen from among 65 applicants on the basis of their communications skills, commitment to desegregation, past achievements in the district, ability to lead groups, and desire to serve the district. In addition, the team includes teachers and administrators, elementary and secondary personnel, majority and minority representatives, and males and females, to insure that the various constituencies of the professional staff are represented.

Table I summarizes critical events over the first three years of SIRT's existence. The table indicates a shifting set of priorities over time. Initially the major issue was self-development for individuals and the team as a whole, and the gaining of legitimacy within the central office and over the school district as a whole. During this developmental phase some members dropped out. Those who remained had to take up the slack that was created while creating a viable scheme for group maintenance and providing services to the district.

In addition the team had to grope towards independence from myself as external consultant. This was a painful process at first because the team did not yet have the confidence that was required to become self-directing. Over time this stress dissipated as the team became more skilful and I could gradually withdraw from the central leadership role. When the group was also able to confront disciplining a member whose performance was judged inadequate, by taking the painful decision of removing her from SIRT's roles, it was clear that 'ownership' of its activities and continuation was transferred from the consultant to the team. In a real sense, this phase, which led to team self-responsibility, provided a model for the kind of efforts that SIRT was preparing itself to conduct with school-based groups.

As Table I depicts, outside of some short-term activities at the conclusion of the first summer's training, SIRT did not provide direct services for school sites until the Spring of 1978. As noted, the team was initially pre-occupied with internal maintenance issues. It took a full six months for SIRT to work through these issues before it was able to turn to the tasks for which it was initially formed. There was a sense of urgency on the part of the team to become more visible and perform as expected.

This concern was even greater for those central office officials who had initially agreed to support the project. Given hindsight, one should have expected a period of group development before SIRT became a viable mechanism for change in the district. However, central office administrators, perhaps understandably but certainly unrealistically, were counting on immediate performance and were not interested in hearing about team maintenance needs. Thus the stresses for the team were compounded by lack of early support by key authority figures.

By the end of the first year of its implementation the team did begin to perform, conducting interventions in two school-sites and giving additional assistance to the 'liaison teams'. [Liaison teams were composed of approximately six teachers and administrators from each of eight schools that were significantly affected by the court order. These teams received a week of training from SIRT and then devised and ran in-service programs for their own schools]. During the second year the team began to work in the three high schools that were most affected by racial desegregation and, two years later, are still continuing long-term projects in each of these sites. The outcomes are substantial, including the development of 1. plans for maintaining discipline, 2. faculty groups to advise the administration in each school, 3. alternative curricula and 4. improved relationships between and among students, teachers and administrators. SIRT has also launched long-term projects as diverse as developing and assuring an ongoing problem-oriented

Table 1. Major SIRT Events 1977-80

TOPICS	SPRING 1977	SUMMER 1977	FALL 1977	SPRING 1978	SUMMER 1978	FALL 1978	SPRING 1979	SUMMER 1979	FALL 1979	SPRING 1980
SIRT membership selection	Selection process. 16 of 65 applicants			Second generation team selected. 10 of 45 applicants						SRC Teacher advisers assume responsibility for planning and operation of SRC, but do not become members of SIRT. Exploration of alternatives for team expansion being discussed.
SIRT training		Two weeks on processes, one week on microdesigning, facilitated by outside consultant.	Monthly in-service meetings. A portion of each meeting normally devoted to further training facilitated by outside consultant.		Three weeks. Outside consultant facilitated original team's training. Original team facilitated second generation team's training.	Monthly in-service meetings. Time for training cut back as press of ongoing activities requires more time for 'business' discussions.		Two weeks. Facilitation responsibility divided among SIRT members.	Monthly in-service meetings become even more 'business' oriented and training opportunities decrease further.	
Maintenance Issues, Internal		Five of the original 16 members resigned within first week of training.	Establishment of internal working relationships. One member asked to resign by the team. Shift in leadership from consultant to team.			Identification of two team members to act as co-ordinators. Shift from leadership of consultant to the team is completed. Weaving of the two 'generations' into one team is accomplished. Some members sense work overload.			Work overload syndrome continues to be a problem: new approaches are being devised. SIRT members are beginning to share the work more equitably	
Maintenance Issues, External		Press by central office (CO) for team to take on tasks before it is fully prepared.	Need to gain visibility within the district. Lack of CO understanding of OD. SIRT members' principals complain about them being out of the buildings. Demands for achievement by CO. Need to identify alternative sources of funding because the district is under increasing budgetary constraints.			Rules are laid down for SIRT activities by the CO (e.g. budget reports and time sheets). Improvement of liaison function with the CO continues to be necessary and time consuming. SIRT writes several grant proposals which are approved and becomes the best funded in-service arm in the district.				
SIRT intervention activities		One day workshops in three desegregated high schools. One week training for school-based in-service groups (liaison teams).	Additional training for liaison teams. Problem based intervention for faculty of a special education school. In-service training for one of the magnet schools.			Issue-identification sessions for two district community groups. Problem-based intervention for two high school. Student Relations Committee (SRC) from 3 high schools formed by SIRT. Focus on skill development, problem identification and problem resolutions. In-service sessions for two elementary schools.	Problem-based intervention in a third high school.		Continuation of the three high school projects. Continuation of SRC project. Goal setting and needs assessment for ESAA advisory committee.	Problem-based intervention in four elementary schools. Conference for high school teachers, school board and CO administrators.

group of student leaders (fifty in total) from the above-mentioned three high schools; working with several community-based groups; assisting the staffs of several elementary schools that are being confronted with school closings; and taking responsibility for its own continued training during the summer months. SIRT has also conducted a variety of short-term projects, including the development and implementation of conferences between the school board, administrators and teachers, and running in-service programs for the teachers' union and for district sponsored teachers' conference days.

To move so rapidly from inactivity to a high level of service to the district is an impressive achievement. In part the team's success is related to its willingness and ability to modify traditional OD assumptions in order to meet the needs of the local situation.

Two of these OD tenets in particular have been compromised in order to achieve SIRT's intended purposes. The first assumption is that OD consultants should be invited to assist an organization. However, it was not long before it became clear that most schools were not going to invite SIRT to provide assistance. In part this was because there were many innovations being initiated at the time and, in the flood of new activities, it is likely that a majority of the district's school-level administrators were not even aware of the team's existence. Further, those administrators who did know about SIRT were reluctant to admit to having difficulties that they could not resolve themselves. The team dealt with this dilemma by requesting key central office administrators to identify the district's most needy school sites and encourage these schools' leaders to give SIRT a fair hearing. This has been a most effective strategy, establishing the initial openings that the team needed to start a dialogue with prospective clients who might not otherwise have made themselves available to SIRT.

The second assumption is that OD consultants should urge all members of organizations to participate in intervention activities. SIRT's experience has been that many teachers either cannot find the extra time required to become involved or simply do not care to participate. The team's response has been to focus on real problems so that teachers will see the value in becoming involved and, rather than insisting on faculty-wide involvement, to rely on enlisting volunteers who are highly interested in participating. Sometimes this means that only a handful of teachers are actively engaged in a project, but more often as many as 25 percent of a school's faculty choose to become involved. Further, involvement tends to grow as projects progress, useful outcomes are put into effect, and teachers come to believe that they can really have an impact on their school's destiny.

SIRT found one OD assumption to be critically important but difficult to fulfil. This assumption is that OD consultants should encourage organizational leaders to provide resources for compensation if staff members have to put in extra time, as a recognition of their efforts. This is particularly relevant in urban schools today, where teachers' unions have insisted that their members be compensated for any and all additional work that is performed beyond a contract's specifications. Unfortunately, urban school districts are confronted with decreasing resources. SIRT soon found that it would have to create a funding base if it was going to entice many teachers to participate in the improvement of their school situations. SIRT's initial, and predictable, response was to petition the central office for supplementary funding. This was forthcoming on a short-term basis, but it was made clear that alternative resources would have to be secured over the long-haul. SIRT's strategy has been to write a number of grant proposals, several of which have been funded. In fact, at this time SIRT is the district's best funded in-service unit.

What are the costs associated with the development and implementation of an internal change team? The fiscal costs are surprisingly low; maintenance costs for SIRT over the first three years has hovered at about $25,000 annually. When one considers that Buffalo's 1979–1980 budget was about $126,000,000, this cost appears miniscule. Actually it represented .0002 percent of the district's budget that year! It is difficult to calculate comparable costs for outside consultants carrying out such work but, given the many man-hours involved, a conservative estimate is that it would be at least ten times the actual costs involved.

More important, look at the benefits accrued. These benefits, in the form of long-term school-based self-renewal, cannot be easily measured in dollars and cents, but it seems fair to say that the returns for investments made are great. In fact, it is unlikely that such returns could have been achieved with outside consultants. Many teachers have told SIRT members that they would not have participated if the projects were run by outsiders who, by definition, could not be familiar with the complexities of their situations and who probably would not remain to see activities through over the long term.

Spill-over benefits also seem to be associated with SIRT's efforts. For example, learnings acquired by both school-based staff members and SIRT members are being applied in the classroom. We have received frequent feedback to the effect that organizational self-renewal skills and techniques are directly applicable to the improvement of classroom organization. It should also be noted that some SIRT members have confided that they might have left education if they had not had the opportunity to participate in this exciting and challenging activity.

In Summary: Key Design Features for Training Internal Change Agents

The substantial evidence that those who have participated in SUNY/Buffalo's graduate program and in Buffalo Public School's SIRT effort have had important impacts in a variety of educational organizations supports the contention that internal change agents can contribute meaningfully to implementation of innovations in schools. Further, the training of internal change agents can be quite cost-efficient. In the present instance the pre-service program was already in place so it was basically a problem of curricular modification, while the SIRT effort, as noted, attracted external funding and has required only a modest amount of support on an annual basis.

Generalizing from the two settings there are several key design features that seem particularly relevant to the ultimate success of an internal change agent effort:

1. Those selected to be internal change agents should be recognized beforehand as leaders within their organization. That is, focus on the careful selection of individuals who already have formal and/or informal leadership roles if you expect them to be able to influence their organization's future direction. Those selected could be in administrative roles or they could be recognized leaders from among the teachers' ranks. The point is that they should be viewed as having legitimate rights to act as leaders by others in the organization. Without this perception by others, their efforts will be rejected and they will become highly frustrated because they will not be able to apply the learnings they have acquired.

2. Internal change agents should be knowledgeable about all aspects of the change process. Training should assure that they have a basic understanding of the complex interactions of the parts of schools and school districts; an understanding of the importance of problem specification and the mastery of the diagnostic skills required to get this specification; the ability to devise alternative prescriptions to respond to problems identified; the ability to conduct activities required to carry out agreed-upon prescriptions; and the ability to conduct formative and summative evaluations to ascertain the impact of change efforts. This is an ambitious set of expectations, but experience shows that change is a complex process and that those who are responsible for its conduct must be competent in all phases of that process. If a team is developed it may be possible to modify these expectations by assuring that all participants have the basic knowledge to perform these functions and then dividing responsibility for the several aspects of change among different individuals.

3. Learnings for participants can be compounded and more fully internalized if concepts and skills are tested in laboratory settings before being applied to 'real-life' situations. Since participants will ultimately be responsible for moving groups to implement change programs, it makes sense that they should test out newly acquired concepts and techniques in group settings as they learn them. Further, this scheme allows individuals to develop skills in a relatively secure environment before having to perform in high risk situations. Testing learnings within laboratory group settings enables participants to explore the impact of their efforts and incorporate appropriate modifications before attempting to deal with groups in their own organizational settings. For some it may also offer an opportunity to reassess their potential for taking on internal change agent roles.

4. Substantial guidance and support should be provided during the early stages of the training. For most participants the experience will be new and will likely challenge some of their earlier professional training as well as some of their established behaviors and attitudes. If the trainers exhibit support and empathy as participants stumble through the initial days and weeks, it is more likely that the learners will gradually be more willing to try out new behaviors and take greater risks. With the passage of time and the accumulation of experiences the need for support will diminish rapidly. This modeling behavior of the trainers will have further payoff when, in turn, the newly trained internal change agents will have to exhibit the same supportive traits in their work with school-based groups.

5. It must be recognized that it requires a significant amount of time to have a noticeable impact on an individual's values, leadership potential, skill development, and confidence to be a change agent. Time is required to provide opportunities for learning, introspection, testing, modifying, experiencing, etc. Thus training designs should incorporate opportunities for continuous skill development rather than rely solely on a heavy concentration of knowledge and skill inputs at the initial stage.

6. Textbook approaches should be de-emphasized. Experience indicates that adaptability is a vital ingredient because of the abilities and limitations of individual change agents as well as the idiosyncracies of particular school situations and the purposes of specific innovations. As they grow in confidence internal change agents should be encouraged to tailor-make designs to match the realities of particular situations.

There is much potential for improving our ability to change educational organizations through the deployment of internal change agents. Further, as evidenced in Buffalo, this is possible in urban school districts as well as in suburban and rural school systems. The major advantage of the use of internal change agents as opposed to external change agents is the increased likelihood that those who will ultimately be responsible for institutionalizing innovations will be involved in the process much earlier and in more meaningful ways. Outside change agents have little commitment to the long-term survival of the organization; are not readily available when, inevitably, problems arise, because they are only retained for short periods of time; and rarely take the time and effort to develop 'ownership' of the innovation on the part of group members. Internal change agents, on the other hand, are organizational members so they have a great stake in the future of the organization; are on-site to be called upon as needs arise; and, due to the nature of their training, have an intimate understanding of the relevance of involving those who will have to carry out change programs.

In short, my experience strongly supports the contention of the Rand researchers that 'a supportive institutional environment' is 'necessary for a project to be effectively implemented and to take root'. This environment can be greatly enhanced if highly skilled individuals in key leadership positions from within educational organizations are available to help organizational members over the difficult path to the implementation of educational innovations.

References

BENNIS, W.C. (1969) *Organization Development: Its Nature, Origins and Prospects*, Reading, Mass. Addison-Wesley.
BERMAN, P. and McLAUGHLIN, M.W. (1980) 'Factors affecting the process of change', in MILSTEIN, M.M. (Ed.), *Schools, Conflict and Change*, New York, Teachers College Press, pp. 57–71.
BIDWELL, C.E. (1965) 'The school as a formal organization', in MARCH, J.G. (Ed.), *Handbook of Organizations*, Chicago, Rand McNally and Company, pp. 972–1022.
BUERGENTHAL, D.A. and MILSTEIN, M. (1978) 'Bridging the impact gap between stranger based and ongoing work group organization development training: A case study', *Educational Change and Development*, 1(2): 28–40, Sheffield, UK.
CALLAN, M.F. and KENTTA, W.P. (1980) 'A backward glance over traveled roads: An evaluation of the Eugene Cadre', Available through the Center for Educational Policy and Management, University of Oregon, Eugene, Oregon.
DALTON, G.W., LAWRENCE, P.R. and GREINER, L.E. (1970) *Organizational Change and Development*, Homewood, Illinois, Richard D. Irwin Inc.
FRENCH, W.L. and BELL, C.H. (1973) *Organization Development*, Englewood Cliffs, New Jersey, Prentice-Hall.
FULLAN, M., MILES, M.B. and TAYLOR, G. (1980) 'Organization development in schools: The state of the art', *Review of Educational Research*, 50, spring, pp. 121–183.
GIBSON, O. and STETAR, M. (1976) 'Preparatory program at SUNY Buffalo: A report of experience', *UCEA Review*, XVII, May, pp. 12–17.
LAWRENCE, P.R. and LORSCH, J.W. (1969) *Developing Organizations: Diagnosis and Action*, Reading, Mass., Addison, Wesley.
MILSTEIN, M.M. (1978) 'Analyzing the impact of adversarial relations on the management of educational systems', in MOSHER, E.K. and WAGONER, J.L. (Eds.), *The Changing Politics of Education*, Berkeley, California: McCutchan Publishing Corporation.
MILSTEIN, M.M. (1979) 'Developing a renewal team in an urban school district', *Theory Into Practice*, XVIII, April, pp. 106–113.
MILSTEIN, M.M. and CONWAY, J.A. (1976) 'Redesign of an educational administration program: SUNY at Buffalo', *Education and Urban Society*, 9, November, pp. 5–26.
MILSTEIN, M.M. and LAFORNARA, P.A. (1980) 'The institutionalization of an internal change team: The Buffalo experience', Paper presented at the American Educational Research Association Annual Meeting, April.
RAND CORPORATION (1975) *Federal Programs Supporting Educational Change*, Vols. I–VIII, (R-1589-3-HEW) Santa Monica, California: Rand Corporation.

SCHMUCK, R.A., RUNKEL, P.J., ARENDS, J.H. and ARENDS, R.I. (1977) *The Second Handbook of Organization Development in Schools*, Palo Alto, California, Mayfield Publishing Company.

NWRL (1972) *Trainers' Manual: Systematic and Objective Analysis of Instruction*, Portland, Oregon: Northwest Regional Educational Laboratory.

TYE, K.A. (1980) 'Politics and organization development', pp. 215–227, in MILSTEIN, M.M. (Ed.), *Schools, Conflict and Change*, New York, Teachers College Press.

WEICK, K.E. (1976) 'Educational organizations as loosely coupled systems', *Administrative Science Quarterly*, 12(1): 1–19.

Consulting with Education Systems is about the Facilitation of Coordinated Effort

Bill Mulford
Canberra College of Advanced Education

Introduction

Writing in confessional vein, Reddin (1977; 36) explains that as a change agent he has been attached to different organizations as, 'servant, master, captive behavioural scientist, visiting professor, tame seal and resident magician'. He adds, 'I sometimes have to remind clients that I have not walked on water recently. Sometimes I have to remind myself'. While Reddin's self analysis raises the question of the different roles external consultants can have in working with education systems, they also point to some of the important issues that need to be resolved by consultants in their relationship with those systems. These issues include the over-dependence of clients on consultants and the over-confidence of consultants in their own abilities or importance.

It is my intention in this chapter to mention some of the different roles consultants can take when working with systems and to illustrate the particular importance, but difficulty, in the facilitation of coordinated effort role in their contact with *education* systems. The focus will be on the area of school evaluation. I propose to raise and to examine in more detail at least five of the factors that need to be considered to ensure an effective carrying out of this role.

Editor's note: Writing from his experience and researches in Organization Development (OD), Mulford discusses the problems of the consultant. The implications for all types of consultancy are clear, whatever the idealogical focus, though in some cases (e.g. OD) the value system of the consultant himself presents problems of authority and collaboration.

The intractable problem of research is that the researcher always interferes in some way with that which he is researching. When the researcher role is also part of the consultant role (as it invariably is in some measure) only an acknowledgement of researcher/consultant behaviour is helpful, and this acknowledgement can be used as a positive advantage.

With much consultancy the problems of implementation remain unresolved. Changes are not taken into the organization once the consultancy period is over. Even when all the members of an institution have been 'trained', once the consultant leaves, the situation may remain virtually unchanged. Comparatively little is known about implementation though Mulford, and Fullan in his chapter, raise many of the pertinent questions.

Consultant Roles

Consultants will take one or more roles in their attachment to education systems. Sometimes the consultant may take a very active role in initiating or carrying out an intervention. At other times within the same or a different situation, the consultant role may be passive or indirect, but still important to the success of the intervention. In facilitating an intervention, the consultant may include among his or her roles that of referrer to other courses, linker to a trainer to be brought in, manager of a sequence of activities conducted by others, process observer, trainer, and analyzer of data about the system.

It seems obvious that it is critical for consultants to maintain clarity between role switches as they work with a client. Some would go further and suggest that because of the role expectations the client builds up for the consultant, a situation could arise when it would be better to bring in a different consultant to help the client with particular needs, even when the original consultant has the requisite skills and knowledge.

Later in this chapter it will be argued that *one* particular consultant role makes the most sense when working with *education* systems, and that to step outside this role would be to negate the role itself. But for now let us seek clarification of the possible differences in the roles consultants may hold when working with education systems.

Bennis (1973) identified three roles for a change agent: training, consultancy, and applied research. While not focusing solely on the consulting role, he emphasizes the roles of educator and fact-finder. Lawrence and Lorsch (1969) propose a three-fold role for an OD specialist: diagnostician (to identify organization problems and analyze their causes), educator (to train organization members in the use of concepts to conduct diagnoses and to plan action), and consultant (to provide action proposals for consideration by an organization). Havelock (1973) in seeing consultancy in a problem-solving context, has a similar classification, although he uses the terms Catalyst, Process Helper, and Solution Giver. Both he and Menzel (1975), however, add a fourth role of Linker, effecting the linking of the best resources with the correctly identified needs. Eraut (1977), in analyzing the relationships between teachers and significant others outside the school but within the education profession, has identified a preliminary typology consisting of eleven consultant roles. The eleven roles are:

> The Expert
> The Resource Provider
> The Promoter
> The Career Agent (a role, rarely made explicit, of assisting promotional opportunities)
> The Link Agent (to resources of information and advice, or to other teachers and schools)
> The Inspector/Evaluator

The Legitimator
The Ideas Man (providing ideas for consideration rather than for adoption, without claiming any special authority)
The Process Helper
The Counsellor
The Change Agent

Jung (1977) goes further and lists the following nineteen different major roles a consultant can take:

Expert	Counsellor
Instructor	Adviser
Trainer	Observer
Retriever	Data Collector
Referrer	Analyzer
Linker	Diagnostician
Demonstrator	Designer
Model	Manager
Advocate	Evaluator
Confronter	

Some writers have sought to group these burgeoning lists of consultant roles. Margulies and Raia (1972) divide what the consultant does into 'task oriented' and 'process oriented'. In considering the consultant in schools, Schmuck (1973) differentiates among three approaches: *Consultative Assistance* – which brings technical expertise to a problem situation, but does not change the skill levels of organizational members, nor affect the inter-personal relations among them; *Content Consultation* – which aims at educating members in a substantive area and seeks to bring about individual changes in understanding, attitude or skill, but does not focus on the organization; and *Process Consultation* – which focuses on such organizational phenomena as communication patterns, planning, decision-making and interpersonal relationships.

Lippitt and Lippitt (1978) have developed a descriptive model that presents the consultant's role along a directive and non-directive continuum. The nine points they identify along this continuum range from Advocate, Informational Expert, Trainer, Educator, Joint Problem Solver, Alternative Identifier and Linker, Fact Finder, Process Counsellor, through to Objective Observer/Reflector (the least directive).

Clearly, an awareness of the different consultant roles or of the grouping of roles according to various criteria (such as task/process; directiveness/non-directiveness) might be of value for the individual consultant in understanding how he or she operates. However, of more practical significance would be the approaches that seek to link specific types of intervention to particular types of organizational problem or which describe the roles that consultants adopt during the intervention process. The OD Cube developed by Schmuck and

Miles (1971) classifies OD interventions for organization development, namely, training, data feedback, confrontation, and process observation and feedback. Each of these interventions calls for unique behaviours on the part of the consultant. Schmuck and Miles (1971) include four other intervention modes that are especially applicable to large-scale OD efforts. These comprise a sequence of problem solving, plan making, establishment of a task force for continuing consultation, and some modification in the technostructural activities of the client system.

Blake and Mouton (1976) have produced a Diagnosis/Development Matrix which categorizes interventions into five types. These they name Acceptant, Catalytic, Confrontation, Prescriptive and the Application of Principles, Models and Theories of Human Change.

Hersey et al (1979) classify leadership style in relationship to the maturity of the group and to appropriate bases of power. Their four-fold classification could also be interpreted as an attempt to match situations with appropriate consultative behaviour. The links can be summarized as follows:

Leadership (Consultant) Style	Role Emphasis Task	Role Emphasis Relationship	Maturity of Group*	Appropriate Bases of Power
Delegating	Low	Low	High	Expert, Information
Participating	Low	High	↑	Information, Referent, Legitimate
Selling	High	High	↓	Legitimate, Reward, Connection
Telling	High	Low	Low	Connection, Coercive

* Defined as the *ability* (skill, knowledge, experience) and *willingness* (motivation, commitment, self-confidence) of individuals or groups to take responsibility for directing their own behaviour.

Cameron (1978), in building on the work of Jones' (1973) *Helping Relations Inventory* and Cohen and Smith's (1976) *Intervention Cube*, has developed a Consultant Intervention Analysis model consisting of the following intervention categories and sub-categories:

Level	Group, Sub-Group, Individual
Type	Structured, Unstructured
Content	Task, Interpersonal
Intensity (of Confrontation)	Low, Medium, High
Function	Reflective, Supportive, Probing, Interpretive, Informative, Advocacy, Evaluative
Position (of Consultant)	Foreground, Background

Cameron believes that the first subcategory in each of the six basic categories is a 'safe' behaviour from which a consultant might start. It is, however, not necessarily an appropriate behaviour as progress is made through the stages of process consultation outlined by Schein, (1969) i.e.:

>Initial contact with the client organization
>Defining the relationship, formal contact, and psychological contract
>Selecting a setting and a method of work
>Data gathering and diagnosis
>Interventions
>Reducing involvement
>Termination

Unfortunately, Cameron does not elaborate on how his different categories would or should apply at the different stages of consultation. It may be that consultants tend to operate in a certain way no matter what the situation. In this respect Tichy's work is of interest. (Tichy, 1974; Tichy, 1975; Tichy and Nisberg, 1976; Tichy, 1978). He has classified change agents by the way they themselves say they operate with clients. His resultant groupings were:

>Outside Pressure
>Organization Development (OD)
>People Change
>Analysis for the Top

Tichy discovered however that in the time between his original study in 1972 and a follow-up study in 1977, each of these groupings *had* changed its approach and attitude towards its role. These changes can be summarized as follows:

	1972	1977
Outside Pressure	From outside, through application of pressure using mass demonstrations, civil disobedience, etc.	Split into two i.e.; 'Establishment Types' who use evolutionary approach, and 'Anti-establishment Types' who are more convinced of the need for revolution.
OD	Change individual functioning in organization. Use of clarification, confrontation, etc.	Less use of counselling, sensitivity. Greater emphasis on structure, power and political processes.
People Change	Emphasis on individual and psychological factors.	Greater concern with structure, power, etc.
Analysis-for-the-Top	Operates within structures to improve organization, using analytical procedures to generate expert advice.	More emphasis on timing and implementation (e.g., psychological factors). Less interest in long range planning, technical innovations, changes in reward structure.

As Tichy found, the situation in which a consultant works is of prime importance. In fact, the situation may be so important that it precludes many, if not most, of the consultant roles outlined earlier. Working with *education* systems, it could be argued, provides such a situation.

A Unique Role?

What is so special about the educational situation that it should dictate the role to be taken by consultants working with education systems? At a very broad level of analysis, it is clear that educational establishments, as human systems, are among the most complex kind of organization found in our social system. Their product is the vastly complex phenomena of change in human behaviour. At a more specific level, it has been suggested by Miles *et al* (1978) that the special properties of school organizations include goal diffuseness, a technical capacity that is often sub-optimal, problems of coordination, problems of boundary management. They are owned by their environment, their survival is guaranteed, they are not competitive for resources, and they form a constrained and decentralized system.

We might expect then that schools would seek assistance with problems generated by one or more of these properties, for example, help with goal setting, coordination of attempts to buffer the environment. Unfortunately, it has been the experience of many that schools avoid seeking help because of these very properties; for example, if goals are diffuse and survival is guaranteed, why aim to change anything?

It may be, as Miles (1974) argues, that permanent systems find it difficult to change themselves. Schools, it could be claimed, are by nature stable or homeostatic systems, in which most of the available energy is expended in carrying out routine operations and maintenance of existing relationships. Such a system carries within itself characteristics that inhibit change. Havelock (1973) divides these characteristics into input factors, which inhibit change from entering into the school system; output factors, which prevent the genesis of change from within; and, throughput factors which limit the spread of new ideas and practices through the school system. Change inhibitors that fall into one of these three categories would include:

Input   Resistance to change from the environment
Incompetence of outside agents (to judge value of an innovation)
Overcentralization
Teacher defensiveness
Absence of Change agent or Linking-pin
Incomplete linkage between theory and practice
Underdeveloped scientific base
Conservatism
Professional invisibility

Output Confused goals
No rewards for innovation
Uniformity of approach
School as a monopoly
Low knowledge component – low investment in research and development
Low technological and financial investment
Difficulty in diagnosing weaknesses
Product measurement problems
Focus on present commitment: accountability
Low personnel development investment
Lack of entrepreneurial models
Passivity

Throughput Separation of members and units
Hierarchy and differential status
Lack of procedure and training for change

These characteristics of schools certainly suggest the inappropriateness of a rational or, to use Wise's (1977) term, 'hyperrational' model of consultation with education systems. Closer to reality may be what Lindblom (Lindblom, 1959; Lindblom, 1968; Braybrook and Lindblom, 1963) calls 'disjointed incrementalism' or 'the science of muddling through'. Awareness of the following specifications derived from this body of theory could, with profit, be deeply ingrained in every consultant working with schools:

1. *Let a thousand wheels be reinvented* ... Each site seems compelled ... to a drudging rediscovery of the inadequacy of sleds and rollers and then to a discovery of the usefulness of an axle stuck through a disc ... [Mann, 1978:405]

2. *Marginal Change* ... Changes are ... always incremental, they are calculated from the existing, unchanged base, and they are calculated in millimetres, not kilometres [Mann, 1978:406]

3. *Limited Calculation* ... People use that information which is most convenient – chronologically, geographically, psychically, politically, and economically [Mann, 1978:406]

4. *Goals to Means Adjustments* ... stated goals will be tailored to available means and not ... the other way around [Mann, 1978:406]

5. *A Remedial Orientation* ... Despite rhetoric, very few programs aspire to do much more than make rotten situations somewhat better [Mann, 1978:406–407]

6. *Successive Approximations* ... the design ... will need to incorporate many cycles, many iterative stop-and-start attempts to reach a goal [Mann, 1978:407]

7. *Social Fragmentation* ... The multiplicity of roles that contribute even to schooling (let alone education) is extraordinary. A ... system will need to accomodate and arrange these multiple inputs [Mann, 1978:407]

It is not that school people simply behave irrationally. The point, Mann suggests, 'is that they use a sort of rationality that is over-arching or architectonic; that rationality is much more subtle, it reflects more vectors, and it is necessarily more obscure than we have assumed' [Mann, 1978:407]. He continues, 'It has been called a sort of rough-and-ready guidance rationality that is not yet adequately captured either in the descriptive models of academics or in the prescriptive models of practitioners' [Mann, 1978:407].

The crux of the argument in this chapter is that for more successful consultation with education systems there is a need to give greater emphasis to *implementation* and that the most important aspect of effective implementation is obtaining *cooperation among teachers*. Unfortunately, as the above lists of special properties of education systems imply, there are strong and predictable reasons why effective cooperation in schools is already poor and will continue to be difficult to achieve. It is proposed to illustrate this last argument through a detailed examination of a more recent move in education systems: consultation for school evaluation.

An Example: Consultation for Educational Evaluation

Many of the unsuccessful attempts to effect change that consultants working with education systems have made in the past may have had potential. The problem has been, however, that those involved in championing these changes basically had a content role orientation. In other words, their underlying assumption has been that if we could agree on new goals in terms of curriculum, teacher inputs, and more recently, evaluation – that is, if we could develop superior content – somehow the education system would respond positively. They have tended to develop their ideas from research designed to understand and predict – not to make events come about. However, discovery of the problems and concepts in order to help those in schools understand and predict them ignores the problems of developing skills. Not the least of these are the skills of implementation (Dalin, 1978).

All the knowledge that their methods produce remains at the level of espoused theory of invention. A great many evaluation models, for example, emphasize multiple measurable factors. The complexity, rationality and beauty of these models are what lead school people to admire them – like paintings in a museum – but not to imitate them in their work (Dunn and Swierczek, 1977). Planning and developing educational changes are not the same as implementing them.

That implementation is difficult should not deter us. For example, one writer

Consulting with Education Systems is about the Facilitation of Coordinated Effort

(Glaser, 1977) has likened attempted change at the interface in schools to the punching of warm jelly: if you hit it hard and often enough, you can splatter some of it, but it soon takes the form of the bowl as it cools and then congeals. The argument here is that while effort needs to be made to overcome technical and methodological barriers to change or evaluation, the major obstacles arise from the organizational context, structural constraints and the interpersonal relationships which characterize the change or evaluation endeavour. It is paradoxical that influences which are in many respects somewhat irrational should assume so important a role in a venture which, in origin and intent, represents the height of rationality (Gurel, 1975).

It could be argued, in fact, that there are no techniques available to the contemporary evaluator that do not depend heavily for their validity on the cooperation of those persons being evaluated. It is noteworthy, perhaps, that an endeavour – evaluation – which depends so thoroughly on the cooperation of its clients has thought so little about what cooperation means (Glass, 1975). A common interpretation is that consultants should help a school tackle its problems immediately and directly and that effective group functioning and cooperation will somehow result from the spirit of working together for what is generally agreed to be the best for the school. This does not make very much sense. One cannot assume that group effectiveness is just a matter of pushing people in at the deep end of what I have termed the 'profusely propounded pool of participation'. This is especially true of those schools where interpersonal interaction between and among teachers and administrators is poor. *We must learn how to lose time in order to gain time.* Awareness of, and skill development in, group and organization processes must be a *first* step in any change, particularly one as difficult and potentially threatening as evaluation (Mulford, 1979). It is the role of the consultant working with education systems to facilitate this step.

Unfortunately it would appear that poor interpersonal relationships are characteristic of many schools. For example, Ogilvie (1977:43), commenting on the high schools he studied, stated that there 'was little evidence of openness and honesty in interpersonal relationships'. Two other Australian studies underscore this argument. The first, a description and evaluation of a partial organization development project, in a primary school, includes in the discussion of results the statements that 'the principal and teachers had had no preparation for the collaborative problem solving approach' and that these 'are skills and attitudes that need to be developed' (Hearn and Ogilvie, 1973:4). The second was a study of some consequences of the Radford scheme in Queensland which replaced external examinations at the end of high school with a system of internal assessment. The study found that while some teachers in all schools reported satisfaction from the increase in common involvement, help and encouragement since 1971, this was a minority opinion. In the latter study, the consensus with respect to concern and affection was quite clearly 'no change'. As one teacher quipped: 'We confer a lot, but haven't really changed. We're still rude to one another' (Campbell, 1976:270).

Australian studies using the 'Criteria for a Good School Questionnaire' (Mulford, 1976; Mulford and Zinkel, 1977) have indicated very clearly the isolation of the Australian teacher. He or she is isolated from parents, students, informed practitioners, resource-persons, professional educational material and other schools in educational discussions and decisions. Moreover, he or she is isolated from other schools, classrooms and other teachers in teaching; and is isolated from the evaluation of the goals and action of teaching.

Both Pusey (1976) and Ogilvie (1975) have found in different states of Australia (Tasmania and Queensland) a strong tendency for 'isolation between strata' in schools. A recent report on a team development program for Queensland Class I (601+ students) primary school administrators suggests that this situation arises because those at the top of the school simply do not sit down together to discuss their relationships, philosophies and roles 'in spite of the fact that many of the teams had worked together for some time' (Hampstead, et al, 1980:6).

Studies from Denmark and USA also support the contention that interpersonal interaction among school personnel is rare and often poor. The results of an evaluation of a Danish Teacher Course (Gregersen, 1978) involving study groups, which received books, study guides, access to advisory help and radio and TV broadcasts, indicated that the 'opportunity for discussions with colleagues was [found to be] a rare experience for many teachers'.

Sarason (n.d.: 200) has tagged teaching in USA the 'lonely profession' and noted two important consequences of the tag:

> Those of us who received our psychological training in clinics were brought up in the tradition of case conferences. One of the first things that hit me about the loneliness of school teachers was that the concept of the case conference does not exist in the school culture. People don't talk to each other. And it is even worse in the high school. Teachers feel alone: we don't. Now there are some consequences to this difference. (a) Over time, the loneliness has effects on the phenomenology of the teacher. (b) It means that teachers can't use each other in terms of one another's knowledge and talents.

Miles' (1974) research in the area of educational innovations and their adoption in USA schools, highlights the fact that anti-collaborative norms may permeate teaching. He states (Miles, 1974: 205):

> ... we collected data showing that up to 75 per cent of teachers had thought of innovations that might improve education in their districts outside of their own classrooms, but only half of the 75 per cent had in fact talked with *anyone* else about the innovations, and that only 5 per cent reported that any action had ensued. Anti-collaborative norms can be inferred.

Bredo's (1977:307) study of all the teachers from sixteen San Francisco Bay elementary schools, found that, on the whole, interdependence in teaching teams is limited and that this results from a number of characteristics of teaching itself:

> interdependences that evolve among teachers appear to be both limited and relatively non-binding, and to have no direct consequences for collegial control over individual teachers' instructional activities.... Compared to ... [work groups in other organizational settings], teaching is highly individualistic.... Four characteristics of teaching make collaboration comparatively unrewarding or difficult: 1. lack of external rewards for task accomplishment; 2. immediacy of the task and resultant pressures; 3. likelihood of disagreement over standards of procedures; and, 4. complexity of problems of organization and coordination.

Surely, given the special properties of education systems, as found by Bredo and as delineated earlier in this section, this difficulty with coordinated effort, with participation, with effective interdependence and thus with effective consultation in the evaluation of schools is highly predictable. Let me briefly discuss eight possible reasons for this predictability and then indicate how these reasons help determine the nature of any consultation in the area.

1. Cooperation has Few Rewards

At the point of give-and-take, of institutional problem solving, of a commitment to real interdependence, which participation and collaboration imply, people back down. They back down because there are few penalties in education systems for holding on to the old and no discernible reward for embracing the new. Interdependence is a psychologically risky business. Indeed, it can be downright inconvenient if the people you need to cooperate with are also the ones who disagree with you. It takes strong bonds [such as found in some marriages] before people will admit or accept their responsibilities in a relationship. Where in the world of the school do such bonds exist? What creates them?

2. School Structures reinforce Independence

A low level of colleagueship for teachers is supported by the physical layout of schools into separate classrooms, low task interdependence among teachers, constraints of timetables which discourage mutual association, and a reward structure which places heavy emphasis on rewards gained with students in isolation from other adults, and few rewards for mutual association. Collaboration is possible, but not essential. These conditions have existed, of course, for many decades and may have attracted persons who find them compatible with their predispositions.

3. Conflict is Avoided

In such a situation differences are rarely discussed, and whatever differences occasionally surface are quickly smothered 'for the good of the organization'. There is a strong norm that conflict is 'bad' and that professionals ought to be able to 'get along'. In practice, this means that differences between people and groups rarely surface, and conflict is managed by denial and compromise rather than by confrontation or the acceptance and working out of differences. One of the most important reasons that this style of managing differences is not more damaging than it is stems from the low interdependence itself. Issues that require real collaboration – such as long-term planning – are either poorly handled or not even attempted. Sweeping differences 'under the rug' seems to have little impact on the day-to-day effectiveness of schools.

4. Professionals Seek Autonomy

The high percentage of professional personnel involved with schools may help reinforce the lack of interaction. These professionals maintain a dual loyalty – to their direct employers and to their professions. They are bound by their specialized training, their code of ethics, their guilds and associations. This often means that professionals are less dependent on the support of the employing organization and are less threatened by the sanctions that can be used by that organization. Their professional identification shields them against intrusions on their autonomy.

People who work in schools can separate their functions, can feel that each has done a competent and effective job without worrying about what anyone else in the system is doing. Indeed, since many, if not most, of the others are equally well-trained and autonomous professionals, it would not be appropriate to inquire about their activities. In addition, given that concrete goals rarely exist in schools, their is little or no organizational reward for participation in joint exercises with others to negotiate so many value-laden matters.

5. Goals and Processes are Multiple and/or Vague and Result in the Use of Procedural Illusions of Effectiveness

Educational goals are often general in nature, often characterized by ambiguity and vagueness. This is probably a reflection of a political process since education is supposed to serve the whole population and therefore a number of compromises about the functioning of schooling will have to be made. Since, however, expectations about what schools ought to be are not clear, one cannot expect outcomes which are acceptable to all. Indeed, it is extremely hard to know the results of education unless one takes the easy route of measuring some narrow cognitive aspects of the teaching-learning process, such as reading scores.

James Thompson's conceptualization (Thompson, 1967; Thompson and

Tuden, 1959) is useful here. He argues that if the two variables, preferences about *outcomes* and beliefs about *causation*, i.e., methods for achieving outcomes, are considered in conjunction with the question of whether there is certainty, agreement or consensus within the decision unit (school) about these two matters, it is possible to construct a four-fold typology of decision issues.

		Preferences about Possible Outcomes	
		Agreement	Non-Agreement
Beliefs about Causation	Agreement	Computation (in bureaucratic structure)	Compromise (bargaining in representative structure)
	Non-Agreement	Judgement (majority in collegial structure)	Inspiration (in 'anomic structure')

The labels in the four cells are descriptive of four strategies (Computation, Judgement, Compromise and Inspiration) and four structures (Bureaucratic, Collegial, Representative, Anomic) which Thompson believes are appropriate for the four types of decision issues. The inference to be drawn, and one which has relevance to the point of view being presented in this chapter, is that unless those in schools are willing to argue that they are agreed on outcomes and methods for achieving outcomes, then the decision strategy and structure will require that people get together.

Decision-making in schools tends to be in the hands of educators who either do not have explicit goal systems or preferences about how to achieve outcomes, or who are insufficiently clear about the alternatives and their consequences. Rather than try to get together to decide on and then maximize objectives, those in schools merely try to satisfy constraints. The *modus operandi* is unprogrammed and reactive, trying to avoid uncertainty and conflict. The decision criterion is simply survival. Once one is locked into such a routine it is extremely difficult to break out.

Two reactions of administrators caught up in forces which are not understood are imitation of more prestigious and successful organizations or importation of prestigious and authoritative management consultants to tell them what they want and how to go after it. The effect is to convert the 'anomic' situation suggested by Thompson into something resembling a 'computational' situation and to rely upon a decision unit composed of one individual. It is in this situation that the consultant must be careful to remind clients – and themselves – that they cannot walk on water!

Those in schools may also have been encouraged in this act of survival by the unobtrusive acceptance of procedural illusions of effectiveness. This is a point that will be further pursued after consideration of the remaining three reasons behind lack of effective interdependence in schools.

6. *There is a Possible Assess/Assist Dilemma in Operation*

What I have called the 'assess/assist dilemma' may be behind the lack of cooperation found in many of today's educational organizations (Mulford and Zinkel, 1977:130). In a climate of ever louder calls for educational accountability through increased evaluation we must be careful to be aware of the possible dilemma or conflict between evaluating for assessment and evaluating for assistance. The first is related to such issues as public accountability, promotion, allocation of resources among competing programs and schools. It is summative in nature and is vulnerable to those procedural illusions of effectiveness mentioned earlier. The second is related to such issues as professional accountability, personal development, program and school development and is formative in nature. It may have a close connection with what actually happens in schools.

Abraham Maslow (1965:177) has highlighted this dilemma in the following way:

> In my early years in teaching I certainly looked at my students and felt very close to them. I learned only slowly that while *I* could keep my smiles and friendliness and so on separated from the grades, i.e. I could certainly love somebody who wasn't a very good student of psychology, *they* rarely could accept and understand this. Normally, when I was friends with students they felt I had betrayed them if they got bad grades. They thought of me as a hypocrite, as a turncoat. . . . Slowly I had to give up, until now, especially in large classes, I keep my distance and maintain English-style relationships rather than getting very close and buddy-like.

Current forms of school-based student assessment, particularly at the end of high school, have encountered the assess/assist dilemma. When teachers are seen as assessors by their students their relationship with him or her changes. The 'withdrawal' game is likely to be played. This should be cause for great concern given that the major satisfactions are intrinsic to the work that goes on in the classroom, e.g. helping pupils grow and open, friendly interaction with pupils (Campbell, 1975).

But the dilemma applies equally well to relationships between any set of superiors and subordinates, e.g. principal and teachers, inspector and principals, consultant and education personnel. The result is the same – the playing of the 'withdrawal game'. This game will be discussed in what follows. However, what is important for the position being argued is that the playing of the withdrawal game results in less cooperative effort in schools.

7. There are Predictable Levels of Use and Stages of Concern about any New Venture

Gene Hall's (Hall, 1976; Hall and Loucks, 1976) work on the Concerns Based Adoption of Innovations Model is helpful both in explaining the difficulty of promoting cooperation in schools and in offering some clues to effective implementation.

Two of the concepts Hall has developed for assessing people involved in change are Levels of Use (LoU) and Stages of Concern (SoC).

i. Levels of Use

LoU focus on the individual teacher's *behaviour* and performance with an innovation (such as an evaluation project). Eight different Levels of Use have been identified and operationally defined. The major Levels begin with the individual *'Orienting'* him/herself to the innovation. The individual is actively engaged in looking over and reviewing materials, attending orientation workshops, examining the innovation and considering its use. Usually, initial use of the innovation begins at a *'Mechanical'* Level of Use. At this time, use of the innovation is somewhat disjointed, with the user hanging on to the user's guide. A great deal of time is spent on logistical-management kinds of activities. Focus is on the short-term, day-to-day use of the innovation with little time for reflection.

Later on, there is a move to a *'Routine'* kind of use, where the user has the systems worked out and has a way to work with the innovation. Few, if any, changes are being made. Little preparation or thought is given to improving the use of an innovation or its consequences. Other users, however, move onto various types of *'Refining'* of their use of the innovation with the intention of increasing impact on clients.

ii. Stages of Concern

SoC focus on the individual teacher's perceptions, feelings and motivations about the innovation. It appears that a person's Stages of Concern about an innovation move through the progression from self, to task, to impact. During implementation of an innovation the *'Personal'* concerns (adequacy to meet demands of innovation, role in relation to the reward structure of the organization, decision-making or personal commitment) will initially be most intense. As the implementation progresses, *'Management'* concerns (efficiency, organizing, managing, timetabling and time demands) become more intense with *'Personal'* concerns decreasing.

With time, the impact concerns of *'Consequences'* (impact on students in his/her immediate sphere of influence) then *'Collaboration'* (co-ordination and cooperation with other teachers regarding use of the innovation) and then *'Refocusing'* (exploration of more universal benefits from the innovation, including the possibility of major

The Management of Educational Institutions: Theory, Research and Consultancy

changes or replacement with a more powerful alternative) became most relevant.

An important implication that arises from the LoU and SoC data is that teachers involved in using an innovation, e.g., school-based evaluation, are not able to work collaboratively until they have their 'own house in order'. Each individual teacher, it would seem, must master use of the innovation personally, in his or her own context before becoming active in collaborating with colleagues.

8. *There are Predictable Stages of Group Development*

My own work (Mulford, 1977; Mulford *et al*, 1980) suggests that a group, whether it be classroom, department or total school staff, progress through a number of clearly identifiable and sequential stages of development and that much can be done to assist the group through to a more effective later stage of *'Performing'*. If left to their own devices some groups may not progress beyond the early, less productive, stages of *'Forming'*, *'Storming'* and *'Norming'*.

The stages and their major emphases in the personal/interpersonal, task and behavioural areas and the major requirements for advancement to the next stage can be summarized as follows:

Stage of Group Development	Major Emphasis Personal/ Interpersonal	Task	Behaviour	For Advancement to Next Stage Need to
1. *Forming*	belonging	orientation	polite	risk possible conflict
2. *Storming*	power	organization	conflict	· establish roles · listen
3. *Norming*	groupness	data flows	open-mindedness	trust self and others
4. *Performing*	inter-and-independence	problem-solving	adaptive	
5. *Mourning* (can occur after *any* of the four stages)	re-assert independence	superficial rush to finish task or task de-emphasized for social-emotional	dis-engagement	

The implications of this stage of group development data seem clear. Effective collaboration will only be achieved at the *'Norming'* and, more particularly, *'Performing'* stages of group development and *after* the staff has been through the *'Forming'* and *'Storming'* stages.

Consulting with Education Systems is about the Facilitation of Coordinated Effort

The eight debilitating factors just presented help determine the nature of education evaluation in schools. At least eight directions can be discerned:

1. Evaluation Focus at Input End

Educational organizations do their main systematic, clearly understood, highly proceduralized evaluations at the input end, e.g., evaluating admission to the system. Once a person is admitted, uniting with others to create an institutional output is a very low priority. The output focus moves to the individual professional level. Organizational goal setting, evaluation and action are seen as restrictive and punitive and as undermining innovation.

2. Evaluation Seen as an Individual Constraint or Threat that may result in the Playing of the Withdrawal Game

Professionals (teachers) wish to be left alone. At best they wish to be critics. On the one hand, few show enthusiasm for sharing the risks and responsibilities inherent in making policies that constrain their own behaviour, even when such constraints may be based on rational analysis. On the other hand, continued goal diffuseness can lead to a high personal involvement in the task of reporting by teachers thus making evaluation of others more threatening since they are likely to be taken as evaluations of oneself as a person.

The truly debilitating effects of evaluation derive from the fear which it may excite in the person evaluated. In a situation where there is a goal diffuseness and vagueness and there are several constituencies to which schools must respond, e.g., elected officials, the Department, professional associations (including their own), media, clients, etc., extreme caution and a strong norm to protect oneself quickly become necessary defenses.

In school education, risk is involved for an administrator relying solely on his legal authority when a problem arises that demands intellectual skills beyond his capacity or where, as so often happens, it involves both emotional and technical factors. He may be shown to have no other power base than his legal authority. Of course, a similar argument applies to all promotional position holders and to the incompetent teacher who is placed in a situation where he has to interact with the rest of the staff. It is too easy to hide behind the lack of interaction that currently exists.

Defence mechanisms, those perplexing coats of mail we carry around that make us such fascinating and frustrating creatures, are rooted in fear of knowing ourselves objectively, the fear of really knowing what we are doing, why and with what consequences – fear of the feedback earnestly proferred by the evaluator. As one consequence, the 'withdrawal game' is played.

At all levels in schools or school systems it would appear to be highly predictable that people will play the 'withdrawal game'. This game involves putting as much social distance between oneself and a superior, scrupulously avoiding any kind of genuine personal or expressive behaviour. In other words, one tries to remain as faceless as possible. Having established this social distance, one then tries to reduce uncertainty by making the superior provide as much structure and/or rules as possible.

An illustration of the 'withdrawal game' in operation might run as follows. The consultant's preference for a measure of distance between him or herself and the school staff is granted in full measure. They will not discuss with him or her the essential personal details of what is going on in their classroom or school. To do so would, from their point of view, involve too high a risk. Since he or she does not know them socially as whole people, any open discussion of the school and its problems might well result in a summary judgement which the teacher or school administrator would not feel free to challenge. The consultant has defined his or her role in hierarchical rather than functional process or social terms and so he or she unavoidably and unconsciously takes unto him or herself the right to define the terms of conversation. Even if he or she does not assume this right the school staff will impute it to him or her and so the result will be the same.

Only the senior staff will drop into the consultant's office for a chat. Most of the junior staff will keep their distance. If the consultant enters one of their staff rooms the conversation will either close down altogether or turn to some inconsequential or non-school-related topic. In general, most of the teachers at staff meetings will hold back. They carefully maintain a spirit of formalistic impersonality.

Since there is little genuine dialogue the consultant is quite unable to lead or train the staff and so he has to go on 'running' them instead. The second aspect of the withdrawal game would ensure that he or she does so.

The trick is again to get him or her to reduce the uncertainties of their situation by structuring their environment. Since they feel threatened by his authority they must at least know where they stand. In meetings the school staff force the consultant to make every aspect of his or her policy explicit and to make pronouncements on every issue both major and minor. Sometimes the consultant understands what is happening and will try to keep the options open with a non-commital response. But then the staff will subtly throw him or her back into the logic of the first dimension with the echo of his or her own language: 'after all it is your responsibility' or 'you are getting paid to give us the answers'.

The dilemma between evaluation for assessment and evaluation for assistance is also one that must be faced. We must be careful not to take the easy way out in these times of increased pressure for public accountability by choosing only to assess. Some would argue that an excellent state of affairs is most likely to emerge in schools when those with most responsibility feel that they are being assessed, and that their failures are understood and they are able to feel that their worth is unconditional. And yet others argue that schools move more certainly toward excellence when the people in them clarify their purposes, measure the impact of action, judge it and move on (Glass, 1975). Can we have it both ways? Is it really a dilemma?

Consulting with Education Systems is about the Facilitation of Coordinated Effort

3. Evaluation Will Result in the Use of Procedural Illusions of Effectiveness

The 'loose-coupling' view of schools sees the activities of its members as only marginally related. Although we may agree that the work of schools is loosely coordinated, we may also argue that there are aspects of the organization that are tightly controlled. These aspects are concerned with what could be termed procedural illusions of effectiveness. Procedural illusions or ritual categories maintain the myth of education and function to legitimize it to the outside world (Meyer and Rowan, 1978).

In the absence of clear-cut output measures educators turn to processes as outputs. For example, there are precise rules to classify (and credential) types of teachers, types of students, and sets of topics. All these rules and regulations give confidence to the outside (and to many of those inside) that the schools know what they are doing. The structure of the school is the functioning myth of the organization that operates not necessarily to regulate intra-organizational activity, but to explain it, account for it, and to legitimate it to the members outside the organization and to the wider society. The transactions in educational organizations are concerned with legitimacy. Structures are offered that are congruent with the social expectations and understandings about what education should be doing, e.g. process goals explicitly stated by an education department to help maintain or develop this legitimacy may influence the use of consultants or the creation of organizational sub-units such as an evaluation section or office, or, at the national level, by the setting up of projects based in tertiary institutions. While such actions may have little effect on what goes on in the classroom, they do, at the time of their creation, demonstrate congruence with the goals and expectations of the wider society as perceived by the department or authority. It is interesting to note that such consultancies and units are usually maintained for some time after their funding agency changes its foci.

4. Evaluation will tend to involve 'Garbage'

Given the absence of clear-cut output measures some argue that we should force schools to set concrete goals and performance measures. But as we all know, these would provide but another illusion of structure, which, like beauty, is only skin deep.

Others argue that we should force schools to evaluate with or without concrete goals. Increasingly we find this to be the case with the moralistic accountability, or 'right to know'[1] argument employed as the 'forcer'.

But it is doubtful whether this approach will work either. Schools embark on an evaluation with a plethora of mechanisms such as staff meetings, report and memo distribution and formal and informal get-togethers with and without consultants. However, there is usually little cohesive organization. Rather there appears a blizzard of paper, a surfeit of staff meetings and mandatory and highly structured interactions. There is little in these activities to give participants a sense of really sharing in the shaping of the organization.

Huge resources, particularly of time, are mobilized within a school when the threat of evaluation is raised. The energies of the organization can be drained off into defensive posturing and play-acting for the accreditation team or the site visitors. Or, elaborate plans are laid out for things that never quite will be or glossy reports are produced of things that never quite were (Glass, 1975). Not only do we find ourselves in a situation, to use computer jargon, of 'garbage in–garbage out' but also we are, at best, ensuring the perpetuation of another procedural illusion or ritual category that may have minimal effect on the school or, at worst, that the results are regarded simply as garbage – to be disposed of and forgotten about as quickly as possible. The real pity could be that there may be little energy left for the real work of the organization when it is gripped by evaluation anxiety.

5. Evaluation will be Initially used in a Mechanical or Routine Way

Hall's research has shown that sixty to seventy per cent of first year users of an innovation are likely to be at the 'Mechanical' Level of Use and that most individuals who implement an innovation reach the 'Routine' Level and remain there. Once the 'Routine' Level of Use is reached it appears that movement is more dependent on factors beyond the control of the individual. The organizational context appears to play a greater part, as does the role of the unit administrator or principal.

Analysis of the Levels of Use data would suggest that a consultant attempting to implement an innovation (such as encouraging teachers as evaluators) should expect the incidence of 'Mechanical' and 'Routine' Level users to be relatively high and the incidence of 'Refining' users to be very low or non-existent for first year use.

6. Evaluation will require a Shift of Focus from the Individual Teacher to the Principal and the Total School for Refinement to take place

Hall's data also raise another important question. Is 'Routine' use an acceptable Level at which to end implementation support (i.e., individual teacher training in evaluation)? Surely it is more desirable to have a higher quality situation where materials and approaches are refined; where the teacher varies the use to increase the impact of his or her own pupils; where teachers combine their own efforts of use with related activities of colleagues to achieve collective impact on pupils within their common sphere of influence; and where the teachers re-evaluate the quality of use, seek major modifications of or alternatives to present use to achieve increased impact on all pupils in the school.

If this is the case, then it appears that the unit of intervention will need to shift from the individual teacher. The unit manager, i.e., the principal, now plays a key role and the school staff as a whole must be the unit of intervention.

7. Implementation of Evaluation will need to address Information and Personal Concerns, then Management Concerns and only then, Consequence Concerns

Analysis of Hall's States of Concern would suggest that attempts to implement an innovation (such as an evaluation project in a school) with those who have had little experience in the area should provide for their initial informational needs and personal concerns, perhaps by presenting general descriptive information about the proposed evaluation and by describing how it will affect them personally. For instance, potential users should be told the time the innovation will take and what they will have to give up if they are going to be involved.

It further suggests that those wanting the evaluation to proceed should downplay such things as the consequences for students. Non-users though naturally somewhat concerned about the implications of an evaluation for students are more concerned about what it means for them. Thus the often heard admonition that 'you should do this because it's good for students' is not addressing the concerns the typical non-user has.

The teacher at the 'Mechanical' level of use of an innovation has the greatest need for the 'how to do its' of getting the logistics and coordination of the innovation under control. He or she is probably not going to be interested in philosophical discussions or workshops dealing with more esoteric topics, such as criterion-referenced and norm-referenced tests or summative and formative evaluation.

8. Evaluation will need to take into Account the Stage of Development of the Staff, the Skills Required for Progression to a More Effective Stage and the Techniques Available to Assist in this Progression

If matters are not to remain at the early, less effective stages of group development, particularly with an area such as evaluation that has high potential threat for participants, then approaches to implementation would benefit greatly from taking into account not only the need to identify clearly the stage to which a particular school staff has developed but also the skills required for them to progress and the techniques available to help in this progression.

The Facilitation of Coordinated Effort

How then are consultants to facilitate the necessary prerequisites for change in our education systems?

Previously published material (Mulford et al, 1977; Mulford, 1976) about one particular form of Organization Development has clearly demonstrated that it facilitates many of the prerequisites in Australian schools. Nowhere is this more evident than in OD's ability to promote cooperation among

The Management of Educational Institutions: Theory, Research and Consultancy

teachers: the variable suggested in this chapter as most important for effective implementation.

A recent and very comprehensive North American study (Fullan *et al*, 1978) also found that OD can help overcome some of the debilitating factors discussed earlier. But the study is clear that this situation will only happen if OD 'is done right' – a point that has been argued with increasing fervour in Australia as well.

The Fullan, Miles and Taylor 1978 study for the National Institute of Education on the state-of-the-art with regard to OD in schools in North America had four objectives:

> a review of approximately seventy courses in the literature including some twenty-five critiques or commentaries on OD, a similar number of overviews, empirical or theoretical reviews of the field, and about fifteen case studies of OD efforts in school districts;

> the locating and questioning of 308 consultants who had been doing OD with schools in the United States and Canada;

> the locating and study through questionnaire responses of seventy-six school districts where OD work had gone on for at least eighteen months;

> the carrying out of three detailed case studies.

When, as a result of their research, Fullen *et al* (1978:14–15) discuss the future of OD in schools they state (emphasis in original):

> OD appears to be a good way to increase instructional innovation, to increase participation by all levels of personnel, and to improve various aspects of task and socio-emotional functioning, *if it is done right*, if the program meets the requirements in the definition of OD, and if it is implemented in a way which includes the key operating characteristics identified in our review of the literature, and in our school district sample.

The Fullan *et al* (1978:14) definition of OD is as follows:

> Organization development in school districts is a coherent, systematically-planned, sustained effort at system self-study and improvement, focusing explicitly on change in formal and informal procedures, processes, norms or structures, using behavioural science concepts. The goals of OD include *both* the quality of life of individuals as well as improving organizational functioning and performance.

The implications of this definition and Fullan *et al*'s (1978) key operating characteristics for what is meant by 'done right' can be summarized as follows.

Conclusions from the North American survey are consistent with earlier Australian material in stressing the importance of these factors for successful OD.

> coherence and systematic planning;
>
> sustained effort;
>
> a primary focus on self-study of structures and educational tasks by the organization (school) and the individual in it (as opposed to a personnel development of skill training for individuals emphasis);
>
> have or develop commitment (reflected in such things as support and active involvement of top management and use of the organization's own resources, particularly time and money);
>
> establish and increasingly use strong internal consultants.

So far this chapter has argued that the most relevant and successful consultation with education systems requires a greater attention to the role of implementation and that a most important aspect of effective implementation is the facilitation of coordinated effort by those in schools. However, it was pointed out that there are strong and predictable reasons why effective cooperation in schools is already poor and will continue to be difficult to achieve.

Recent evidence from Australian and North American studies was referred to because it supports the position that if 'done right' OD can help facilitate the necessary organizational prerequisites for effective change, particularly its ability to encourage involvement and cooperation among those on a school staff. It remains now to raise and examine some of the other issues that need to be considered in effectively carrying out this particular role.

Some Issues for Consideration

Steele (1969: 200) suggests that consultant roles are similar to those of fictional British detectives. Both roles share several attributes, as follows:

> The temporary nature of involvement in a system; the focus on gathering evidence and trying to solve the puzzles which it represents; the potential for 'dramatics'; the potential action orientation and excitement it contains; the stance of 'expert' in behavioural science; the stimulation of working on several 'cases' at once.

As was the case with Reddin's reminder to himself about his inability to 'walk on water', so Steele points out several responsibilities that must be taken by the consultant in order to prevent the complications that might arise from these attributes getting out of hand. He mentions five responsibilities: promoting consciousness of self; avoiding incorporation into the client system; arranging for some 'sounding board' with whom to check perceptions, ideas and feelings; using intuition as one means of generating ways to understand the situation; being wary of the tendency to lump people into the over-simplified categories of 'good' and 'bad'.

Reddin (1977:33-41) warns consultants against nine situations: relying on 'bottom-up' change; creating change overload; raising expectations beyond what is possible; inappropriate attachment (ground rules 'might range from not eating with the client – a rule Tavistock once used – to never talking to any one individual alone'); becoming trapped in one part of the organization; inappropriate use of behavioural versus structured interventions; losing professional detachment ('Does the client really have the right not to get well?'); assuming a change is needed; failing to seek help for themselves.

My own consultant work with school systems in Australia has led me to identify an 'octet of dilemmas' facing OD consultants (Mulford, 1979). These dilemmas centred around an obscure definition; on whether emphasis should be given to the total organization or one or more of its departments; the obstacle to development of an organization not being 'OD ready'; on an over-dependence on 'experts'; the danger of an 'Omphalos Dynasty' being established with a resultant over-estimation of OD's effectiveness; possible difficulties in obtaining a demand for OD that is consistent with 'the OD way of doing things'; the running of the Omnibus of Development or Workshop stage of an OD Project; and the difficulties in evaluating whether OD provides obvious deliverance from current school problems. Using some of this and other (Mulford, 1980) material as a base it is intended to complete the chapter with a more detailed discussion of five of the issues that need to be considered in effectively carrying out the role of a facilitator of coordinated effort: organization or department, awareness of andragogy, obtaining a demand, over-dependence, and Omphalos Dynasty.

1. Organization or Department?

Taking individual teachers out of schools and into courses run by consultants is very much like taking out one piece of a jig-saw (school organization), changing its shape and then finding it will not fit when you try to put it back. Not only will the piece not fit but it then has to suffer the anguish and frustration of being 'knocked' back into its original shape so as to fit in with the total jig-saw. This suggests that for effective change the total school (all the pieces of the jig-saw) needs to be involved. But is this really so? Can approaches be effective with a department or any other smaller group within a school or education system? Are some organizations just too large for total and simultaneous involvement?

A body of research evidence has accumulated over the past decade and it all points toward a very clear message: school improvement cannot be accomplished without attention to the fabric of the school's culture and organization.

Consulting with Education Systems is about the Facilitation of Coordinated Effort

It is clear that schools need to be developed *as organizations*. Hall's (1978) research provides recent support. He has argued as a result of his studies that for the adoption of an innovation that involved moving from a goal of 'all teachers teaching science and all kids receiving science' to a goal of 'having high quality configurations of science teaching', it would be necessary to have a second round of in-service training where the unit of intervention would need to shift from the individual teacher to the school building and its principal (Hall, 1978:32).

2. Awareness of Andragogy[2]

It is important to realise that the principles employed by consultants working with education systems need to be based on adult learning and not child learning. It is the difference between andragogy and pedagogy. Knowles (1974:116–117) was one of the first to make this distinction clear:

> The andragogical model is a *process* model, in contrast to the content models employed by most traditional educators. The difference is this: in traditional education the teacher (or trainer or curriculum committee or somebody) decides in advance what knowledge or skill needs to be transmitted, arranges this body of content into logical units, selects the most efficient means for transmitting this content (lectures, readings, laboratory exercises, films, tapes, etc.) and then develops a plan for presenting these content units in some sort of sequence. This is a *content model* (or design). The andragogical teacher (facilitator, consultant, change agent) prepares in advance a set of procedures for involving the learning (and other relevant parties) in a process involving these elements: 1. establishing a climate conducive to learning; 2. creating a mechanism for mutual planning; 3. diagnosing the needs for learning; 4. formulating program objectives (which is content) that will satisfy these needs; 5. designing a pattern of learning experiences with suitable techniques and materials; and, 6. evaluating the learning outcomes and re-diagnosing learning needs. This is a *process model*. The difference is *not* that one deals with content and the other does not; the difference is that the content model is concerned with providing procedures and resources for helping learners acquire information, understanding, skills, attitudes and values.

Huberman (1974:51) writing for the Council of Europe suggests that the implications of andragogy for education are obvious:

> The implications for education are obvious. We might best summarize them by advising adult educators to spend as much time studying the rhythm of mental, physical and emotional development of their students as do child psychologists and pedagogues in the primary

school. An adult psychology is as necessary for continuing education as is an adolescent psychology for education at the secondary level. . . .
A very important and recent field of research in continuing education is one which looks into the relationship between personality characteristics and teaching methods . . . . We need far more precise clinical portraits of both our learners and teachers, particularly in adult audiences where fear of failure tends to be great and the breaking of former learning habits is hard to bring about without chasing away the students.

A highly speculative and tentative attempt to make the relationship between adult personality characteristics and teaching methods has been made elsewhere (Mulford, 1979a). Four of Loevinger's (1976) stages of ego development were used as a base in an effort to link each stage to a number of areas such as motive for education, use of knowledge, origin of knowledge, teaching practices, student-teacher relationships, and evaluation. These data are summarized in Table 1 (for 'teacher' read 'consultant' and for 'student' read 'education system personnel').

The data concerning developmental stages can help us think more clearly about both content and process. They clarify the larger motives behind the investments of time, money and energy behind the personal sacrifices made by many educational personnel. They show us the more fundamental purposes that underlie degree aspirations, the pursuit of promotion or a career change, the desire to meet new persons, read more widely, explore new ideas and interests. They remind us that the existential questions of meaning, purpose, vocation, and social responsibility, dependence, human relationships which so many adolescents face with difficulty, are reconfronted by many thirty, forty and sixty year olds.

With such information in our working knowledge we can more effectively distinguish between those whose aim is simply professional training and those for whom professional concerns are clarification of the major expectations of a job and the career patterns associated with it. We can better recognize that the thirty-five year old who comes to courses run by consultants for clearly specified professional knowledge or competence needed for a promotion or a new opportunity will define a programme and approach it very differently from the forty-five year old who wonders whether all those long hours, family sacrifices, short-changed human relationships and atrophied interests were really worth it. Both of these teachers as students will be different from the twenty-five year old eagerly exploring the potentials of a first career choice.

Prevalent cognitive-developmental theories of adult growth operate from the premise that the core of human development is change in an individual's cognitive structure or organized patterns of thinking about himself and his world. This is *not* an easy matter. This developmental change should be directed to purposeful behaviour emanating from the consideration of moral-

Table 1. *Adult personality characteristics, education and teaching methods*

Four of Loevinger's Ego Development Stages	Motive for Education	What Use is Knowledge?	Where does Knowledge come from?	Teaching Practices	Student-Teacher Relationships	Evaluation
Self-protective opportunitistic	Instrumental: satisfy immediate needs	Education *to get*: means to concrete ends; used by self to obtain effects in world	From external authority from asking how to get things	Lecture-exam	Teacher is authority, transmitter, judge; student is receiver, judged	By teacher only
Conformist	Impress significant others; gain social acceptance; obtain credentials and recognition	Education *to be*: social approval, appearance, status used by self to achieve according to expectations and standards of significant others	From external authority from asking what others expect and how to do it	Teacher-led dialogue or discussion Open 'leaderless', 'learner centred' discussion	Teacher is a 'model' for student identification	By teacher only By teacher and peers
Conscientious	Achieve competence regarding competitive or normative standards; increase capacity to meet social responsibilities	Education *to do*: competence in work and social roles; used to achieve internalized standards of excellence and to serve society	Personal integration of information based on rational inquiry from setting goals; from asking what is needed, how things work, and why	Programmed learning, correspondence study, televised interaction	'Teaching' is an abstraction behind system; student a recipient	By system

Table 1. – continued

Four of Loevinger's Ego Development Stages	Motive for Education	What Use is Knowledge?	Where does Knowledge come from?	Teaching Practices	Student-Teacher Relationships	Evaluation
Autonomous	Deepen understanding of self, world and life cycle; develop increasing capacity to manage own destiny	Education *to become*: self-knowledge; self development; used to transform self and the world	Personal experience and reflection; personally generated paradigms, insights, judgements	Contract learning 1: Time, objectives activities, evaluation negotiated between student and teacher at the outset and held throughout	Student defines purposes in collegial relationship with teacher	By teacher, peers, system, self; teacher final judge
				Contract learning, 2: Time, objectives activities, evaluation defined generally by student, modifiable with experience	Teacher is resource, contributes to planning and evaluation	By teacher, peers, system, self; self final judge

ethical responsibilities, empathic insights into the feelings and ideas of others, and recognition of a widening range of explanations and solutions to classroom and school conditions and problems.

It would appear that few adults – including teachers – *naturally* progress to developmental 'levels' or 'stages' consistently reflecting the above characteristics. Movement from one developmental stage to the next occurs through cycles of challenge and response, cognitive dissonance, cultural discontinuity, differentiation and integration. It occurs when a person confronts situations for which old ways are not adequate, which require new ways of thinking and acting. The experience may be upsetting and uncomfortable; coping with disequilibrium, learning new skills, assimilating new knowledge, resolving value conflicts, does not always happen simply and smoothly.

The job of those responsible for the education of teachers and consultation with education systems seems to be the creation of challenge, dissonance and discontinuity which fosters increased differentiation. It is also necessary to help teachers as students learn effective responses, resolve dissonance and discontinuities so that integration can occur at a higher level of development. The difficulty is achieving that optimal distance between where the teacher is and what the new situations require so that the teacher is challenged but not 'bowled over'; so that change is possible without provoking trauma, entrenchment, or flight.

The developmental nature of the work on adult stages, as well as the material presented earlier in this chapter on stages of group development and Levels of Use of an innovation, pose a number of questions for consultants working with education systems. Perhaps the most important question is: Does the consultant have a *responsibility* to develop his or her clients through the stages or levels? If the consultant agrees with the tenor of the material in this chapter and accepts the position that it *is* his or her responsibility to develop education systems, and individuals in those systems, through the stages or levels, then extreme care must be taken to ensure that action by, or demanded of, the consultant at the early stages does not negate development to later stages.

3. Obtaining a Demand

The seeds of successful consultation with education systems are planted during the introductory phase of a project, (the approach and gaining of commitment). The consultant must know and clearly communicate his values to a school. It will be easy for him to take 'cheap shots' at the school's norms and processes and equally easy for him to be seen as an administration spy, pawn or dupe. Yet, to be effective, he cannot allow this to happen.

There is a dilemma here: on the one hand, the consultant must not be seen as the lackey of one person or group, yet, on the other hand, it is equally important, particularly in a setting with a history of necessary centralized decision-making such as that found in many Australian school systems, that early support be gained from the top administration.

Franklin's (1976) study in USA comparing eleven organizations with successful OD efforts and fourteen with unsuccessful OD efforts is clear in its finding that top management extended greater support to the efforts in the successful organization than in the unsuccessful organization.

Morgan (1976:53) succinctly summarizes the change required of many formal leaders under OD:

> Under OD the formal leader changes the basis of his authority from that of power, patronage and sponsorship legitimized by position, to one of authority based on skill in facilitating members' participation and in energizing members to solve problems and resolve conflict.

Fullan (in Morgan 1976:45–46) underscores the importance of this change to a facilitative mode in the top level occurring *during* the Workshop stage of an OD Project. If there is no change, then subordinates may find themselves at great disadvantage:

> Skills promoted OD ... heavily favour the most literate and articulate members of the organization. ... verbal facility is also probably related to the authority of the school ... those lower in the hierarchy may find themselves at a disadvantage in pursuing their own interests ...

There is also a possible dilemma between the method of obtaining the commitment of staff to consultations such as OD and the values of OD itself. Fullan (in Morgan, 1976:45) highlights this dilemma:

> ... it is problematic whether the conditions under which people asked to indicate acceptance are conducive to 'free' acceptance. For example, since OD has been initially endorsed by authority figures and introduced by outside OD 'experts' it is at least questionable whether these structured conditions allow for two-way communication from subordinates about their concerns.

How shall clients be induced to step across into the new non-manipulative world of more open communication represented by OD without manipulating the client? The dilemma for the consultant is that he may feel that there are many schools which could benefit from OD, yet he cannot, if he is consistent with the values of OD, impose himself upon them. He can make his work known via conferences and articles, but initiation of an OD Project lies with the school itself.

My own work has tried to recognize this dilemma, for example (Mulford *et al*, 1977:221):

> Teacher and support staff commitment at Wesley was also not well handled, and was, in fact, antithetical to many of the values implicit in OD. A formal staff meeting involving an explanation of OD,

question answering and then voting does not result in a consensus type of commitment. Preferable is the method (employed at Pearce) where a consultant visits the school informally on a number of occasions prior to speaking briefly at a staff meeting and then remaining at the school for at least one full day for informal individual or small group explanations and discussions. Commitment is made at a later staff meeting not attended by the consultant. It may even be desirable to extend the gaining of commitment stage over one or two months so that all participants are clear on what will be involved in an OD Project.

A move to institutionalize process oriented consultation such as OD in Departments of Education rather than to absorb its technology into the culture of schools also creates problems. By becoming independent such programs make themselves competitive with other programs within the Department. A dilemma arises because the politics of survival, of obtaining scarce resources, may not be conducive to, or consistent with, OD values. How, for example, do 'internal' OD consultants obtain a demand for their services? Are the methods used the 'OD way'?

4. Over-Dependence

There are many educational systems that hold unrealistic expectations for the consultants they employ. Consultations are looked on by some as a panacea or cure-all. This situation is perhaps understandable in those schools which require relief from immediate pain. Here administrators have a tendency to buy almost anything that seems to offer a way out. They become particularly susceptible to faddish packages that offer high promise of symptom relief. Consultation is seen very much as a strategy for survival.

Unfortunately, there will be consultants who will pander to these demands. Good consultation, that is consultation that focuses on implementation and developing cooperative effort among a school's staff, is hard work and takes time. Quick, flash interventions are not going to induce major, permanent changes and will often be detrimental to an education system. Wyant (1974), for example, after studying a large number of schools that had received various amounts of OD consultation, found that those receiving less than twenty-four hours actually declined in their communication adequacy.

Unrealistic expectations usually stem from a belief that good consultation is a product when, as this chapter has argued, it is a process. An assumption is that all we need to know is more and more facts (usually from being told by 'experts') when what is needed is knowledge of values. The latter requires the involvement and intervention of the participants themselves. The consultant's job is to facilitate this interaction. *What* the school decides to do is its business.

It is worth remembering the fable of Dumbo, the baby circus elephant

(Bentzen, 1974). A little mouse convinced Dumbo to use his large ears as wings by giving him a feather, a magic feather, that would enable him to fly. Dumbo trusted his friend and so could fly, even without the feather, as he soon discovered. At last he had self-confidence.

This fable tells something important about education personnel as well, and it suggests a critical question for consultants working with education systems. How can outside resources and stimulation be provided for schools which will encourage and enable them to try something different, to fly on their own? The answer suggested by the fable is to try the principle of the magic feather, help schools help themselves; help them to realize that their success was due to their own efforts and abilities and not to outside expertise.

Good consultation with education systems attempts to establish *self-renewing organization*. Dependence on consultants is the opposite of this aim. In fact, it is in this area that one could express doubts about the usefulness of education systems employing outside consultants who are dependent upon their work with schools for their livelihood. The temptation to prolong dependency on the consultant is strong in this situation, yet, if he or she believes one of the major aims of effective consultation is to promote a self-renewing organization, then obviously he or she should be *working to 'do himself or herself out of a job' at any school as quickly as possible.*

This stance poses a dilemma that my own work has yet to resolve: to what extent can one continue to be involved in follow-up consultation with school and still be developing a self-renewing organization. The point at which a course, workshop or consultation becomes self-directed and where additional direction by the consultant would detract from the development process is a very delicate, important, yet little discussed topic.

5. Omphalos Dynasty

Care must be taken by consultants *not* to assume that they stand at the central point of the earth and that *everything* revolves around them when they work with education systems. Consultants need to rid themselves of the 'chutzpa' tag recently given to OD practitioners by Hornstein (1974).

In fact a UK case study on inservice education and training of teachers (INSET) points out that school personnel do not always take kindly to outsiders, particularly those from tertiary institutions (Bolam and Porter, 1976:111).

> One of the main reasons for the appeal of school-focussed INSET is because outside experts frequently lack credibility with classroom teachers and school-focussed INSET appears to provide the ideal opportunity for excluding them and including other teachers as course lecturers, etc. This credibility gap exists to a greater or lesser extent with all external trainers, including LEA advisers, but it is widest of all between teachers and college lecturers. The latter are invariably

labelled as 'remote' and 'theoreticians' with little practical knowledge of contemporary school situations.

Schmuck's (1978:139-140) work in USA supports this position. His recent analysis of evidence for OD effectiveness, collected over more than ten years, stresses the importance of the following factors: during the start-up phase of an OD project the consultant should establish 'clear, supportive, and collaborative relationships with the key authorities of the school'; the consultants and their clients should reflect 'on their interpersonal perceptions and feelings about working together'; and there should be a belief on the part of consultants that they 'are able to help and when the clients recognize their own needs are willing to be helped to improve the situation'. Schmuck (1978:140) adds that 'unfortunately such mutual understanding between consultants and clients has been rare, especially when the consultants have been experts from universities'.

Any communication may be complicated by a situation where there is both a *power/authority* and an *epistemological* gap between educational personnel and consultants. Results of a Danish case study (Gregersen, 1978) on School-Based In-Service Training for Teachers are clear on the point that 'it is very time-consuming to clarify the *expectations* and to establish roles among consultants and teachers'. The reason for this situation was that they 'do not have the same position in the system'. The case study is equally clear in its finding that 'this social or professional perception is not changed simply by moving into a school and meeting the staff'. A case study on teacher-tutors and induction within the school from the UK (Bolam and Porter, 1976) found that tutors were more pastoral than training in their approach partly because of a fear of assessment and status differences. If nothing is done in situations such as these we will have a classic case of the real or perceived authority gap between school personnel and consultants resulting in the playing of the 'withdrawal game'.

Eraut (1977:99) elaborates on the little researched but obviously important epistemological gap in the following way:

> Because the teacher has to act, his language has to contain a strong prescriptive element which those who do not have to teach willingly avoid. Moreover he has to particularize his thought and action, whereas those outside the school are expected to generalize. He also has to learn to talk about his actions in a way that protects himself from blame and maximizes his autonomy. His epistemological world is bound to be different from that of the consultant and this can be a major barrier to communication. Both talk to each other in the way that they have learned to talk and neither will literally mean what he says.

The presence of this epistemological gap may help explain why those involved in a Swedish school leader education project (Elkland *et al*, 1978) 'had a serious backslide into the classical role of the student' and why other evidence has underlined the negative attitude teachers may have to external consultants.

Often this lack of understanding arises from a consultant's qualities involving presumption and arrogance (the 'Chutzpa' tag), which results in the consultant 'doing his or her own thing' no matter what the circumstances. Coad (1976:13) provides an example. He writes that among the important reasons for the modest impact of one OD program on satisfaction, group processes, climate, leadership or student achievement in a school he studied was that 'even with six days to build themselves into an OD team, the consultants practised their own strengths (sensitivity training and confrontation, for example) rather than implementing the pre-planned OD workshop design'.

To make the first phases of consultation non-threatening it is necessary to *avoid* having high-powered, high status consultants giving a 'proper' introduction. Similarly, over-use of jargon would limit communication with the client and reinforce dependence on 'expertise'. If the consultant believes in *self-renewing* organization then an increasingly low profile is highly desirable.

An 'increasingly low profile' will be difficult to achieve given educators' obsession with experts. It would seem that expertise increases with the distance travelled. A local expert cannot hope to compete with the interstate expert, let alone the almost divine worship accorded to someone from overseas. If overseas experts are brought in they may not only lack the necessary knowledge of the local education scene, but may also find it extremely difficult to cast off the shackles of the tag 'expert' and adopt the low profile necessary for self-renewing schools.

The technology of good consultation is the proper province of school personnel. Individuals who are now called consultants might better consider themselves to be essentially educators, preparing school personnel to utilize this technology along with other technologies. As indicated in an earlier section, their major job is to work themselves out of a job by educating school staffs in processes involving coordinated effort.

'Working oneself out of a job' in any particular school certainly poses a difficult dilemma not only for consultants dependent on projects such as OD for their livelihood, but also for 'internal' consultants (e.g., curriculum consultants, regional personnel or other members of education systems). Can a curriculum consultant be involved in an OD project, that is, emphasizing processes and working to 'do himself out of a job', and still consult in content (e.g., Maths, English, Social Sciences, etc.)? Can regional office personnel be involved when they may also have an assessment function (of teachers or curricula) as part of their role? It is the argument of this chapter that for effective consultation these roles are mutually exclusive. It is vital for effective consultation that school facilitators emerge who can take over from the external consultant before the end of the attachment to an education system.

There is a possible dilemma here: When should the training of in-school facilitators commence? Some argue that they should be trained prior to the workshop or consultation. This position does not make sense. Apart from the need to select in-school facilitators as a result of judging their performance during the consultation there is the danger of pre-selecting those who have had previous OD or similar type in-service experiences. As Franklin (1976) has shown in his study of successful and unsuccessful OD Projects, the unsuccessful organizations tend to have internal change agents who receive more change agent training prior to a workshop and have more previous work experience in personnel departments. Internal change agents in unsuccessful OD efforts tended to do little or nothing at all after the workshop or draw on their previous training and experience as a basis for action. This previous training and experience can be with process techniques, but, as discussed earlier in the section five of this chapter, this is not OD. For example, discussing the process and implications of a consensus decision making structured experience with a group of principals from twelve different schools is vastly different to the same discussion with twelve of a principal's own staff.

Conclusion

In conclusion, it is important to point out that the most important issue facing consultants working with education systems, and particularly those consultants who accept the role argued for in this chapter, is the one relating to the charge of manipulation.

One must exercise care with a 'human relations' as opposed to 'human resources' (Miles, 1965) attitude on the part of those in the school system administration responsible for the initiation of consultations. With such potentially powerful techniques the attitude that they can be used to pressure recalcitrant individuals into conforming with the administration's thinking must be avoided at all costs. Because of its avowed humanistic value basis, OD, for example, is open to the charge that it is even more deceptive than other change methods and even more capable of increasing power differences between administration and teachers (Huck, 1976). In a recent article Singer and Wooton (1976) gave a keen analysis of Albert Speer's method of participative management in Nazi Germany and showed how OD techniques could be applied to a system whose values are seemingly antagonistic to the values of OD.

As effective behaviour change inevitably involves manipulation and control and since manipulation of human behaviour inherently violates a fundamental value of freedom of choice, this places the facilitative consultant in a dilemma. The dilemma cannot be resolved completely. This, however, is no argument for avoiding discussion of the issue and spending a great deal of time ensuring and/or developing a consistency between school system and consultant values.

One of the problems is that the glory in relation to change usually comes at the start of a long run. But in the middle, where all the struggle is, there is

The Management of Educational Institutions: Theory, Research and Consultancy

a great deal of hard work with little immediate payoff. Hall (1978:34) in relating this situation to his Stages of Concern and Levels of Use conceptualizations, puts it as follows:

> The glamour usually comes with the front-end flag waving, announcements and proclamations. Attempting to resolve Personal and Management concerns and to facilitate each individual's move into a beyond a Mechanical Level of Use requires a great deal of time and energy. Individual consultation, hand holding, cajoling, answering the same questions over and over while keeping in mind where it is all supposed to be going is a hard and highly skilled job. The pay-off from these implementation efforts does not come until the point, down the road, when one can observe an individual or an entire staff that has developed a new capacity and has fully internalized use of the innovation. Unfortunately, it appears that for all too many, the front-end flag waving is all that they have time for.

Perhaps consultants working with education systems would do well to remember the words of a wise Chinese gentleman who in 640BC wrote the following about the best leaders (consultants):

> As for the best leaders,
>   people do not notice their existence.
> The next best,
>   the people honour and praise.
> The next,
>   the people fear;
> and the next
>   the people hate.
> When the best leader's work is done,
>   the people say we did it ourselves.

Notes

1 As Glass (1975) points out: To sanction all evaluations as the public's or the department's, 'right to know' is to forget that all rights are qualified. Even freedom of speech is qualified, namely by the principle that what is said must not place the social order in 'clear and present danger'. Does the public have an unqualified right to know about Miss Jones' educational values, feelings about her pupils, her impact on the cognitions, character, will, etc.? Or is this right qualified by a much less apparent – but insidious – jeopardy to her growth as a teacher and as a person, caused by judging her publicly?

2 This section relies heavily on unpublished material cited in OECD (CERI) files during 1978 and in particular background papers prepared by Kenneth Howey from the University of Minnesota and Dean Corrigan from the University of Vermont. It would appear that both have been greatly stimulated by the pioneering work in applying the theories of adult development to a college

setting by A.W. Chickering (see, 'A Conceptual Framework for Educational Alternatives at Empire States College', Saratoga Springs, New York, April 1976).

References

BENNIS, W.G. (1973) 'Theory and method in applying behavioural science to planned organizational change', in BARTLETT, A. and KAYSER, T., *Changing Organizational Behaviour*, Englewood Cliffs, N.J., Prentice-Hall, pp. 73-75.

BENTZEN, M.M. (1974) *Changing Schools: The Magic Feather Principle*, New York, McGraw-Hill.

BLAKE, R.R. and MOUTON, J.S. (1976) 'Strategies of consultation', in BENNIS, W.G. et al, *The Planning of Change*, New York, Holt, Rinehart and Winston, pp. 46-68.

BOLAM, R. and PORTER, J. (1976) *Innovation and In-Service Education and Training of Teachers in United Kingdom*, Paris, OECD.

BRAYBROOK, D. and LINDBLOM, C. (1963) *A Strategy of Decision: Policy Evaluation as a Social Process*, London, Collier-Macmillan, Free Press.

BREDO, E. (1977) 'Collaborative relations among elementary school teachers', *Sociology of Education*, 50(4).

CAMERON, W.G. (1978) 'O.D. consultancy: A model for analysis', *Educational Change and Development*, 1(2): 17-27.

CAMPBELL, W. (1975) *Being A Teacher in Australian State Government Schools*, Australian Government Printer.

CAMPBELL, W. (1976) *Some Consequences of the Radford Scheme for Schools, Teachers and Students in Queensland*, Australian Government Printer, AACRDE Report Number 7.

CHICKERING, A.W. (1976) 'A conceptual framework for educational alternatives at Empire State College', Saratoga Springs, New York, April.

COAD, R. (1976) *The Effects of an Organization Development Program on Satisfaction, Group Process, Climate, Leadership and Student Achievement*, ERIC Document ED-120-937.

COHEN, A.M. and SMITH, R.D. (1976) 'The critical incident in growth groups: Theory and technique', *1976 Annual Handbook for Group Facilitators*, La Jolla, California, University Associates, pp. 87-113.

DALIN, P. (1978) *Limits to Educational Change*, London, The Macmillan Press.

DUNN, W. and SWIERCZEK F. (1977) 'Planned organizational change: Toward grounded theory', *Journal of Applied Behavioural Science*, 13(2): 135-156.

EKLAND, H. (1978) *The Evaluation of INSET Programmes in Sweden*, Paris; OECD.

ERAUT, M. (1977) 'Some perspectives on consultancy in in-service education', *British Journal of In-Service Education*, 4(1) and (2).

FRANKLIN, J.L. (1976) 'Characteristics of successful and unsuccessful organization development', *The Journal of Applied Behavioural Science*, 12(4): 471-492.

FULLAN, M., MILES, M. and TAYLOR, G. (1978) *OD in Schools: The State of the Art*, Final Report to National Institute of Education, Contract Numbers 400-77-0051, 0052.

GLASER, E. (1977) 'Facilitation of knowledge utilisation by institutions for child development', *Journal of Applied Behavioural Science*, 13(2): 89-109.

GLASS, G. (1975) 'A Paradox about excellence of schools and the people in them', *Educational Researcher*, 4(3).
GREGERSEN, J. (Ed.) (1978) *Danish Case Study on Evaluation of INSET Programmes for Teachers*, Paris, OECD.
GUREL, L. (1975) 'The human side of evaluating human service programs: Problems and prospects', in GUTTENTAG M. and STRUENING, E. (Eds.), *Handbook of Evaluation Research*, SAGE Publications, 2: 17–28.
HALL, G. (1976) 'The study of individual teacher and professor concerns about innovations', *The Journal of Teacher Education*, 27(1): 22–23.
HALL, G. (1978) 'Concerns-based in-service teacher training: An overview of the concepts, research and practice', A background paper for the CERI International Workshop on School-Focused In-Service Education and Training of Teachers, Bournemouth, UK, 1–3 March.
HALL, G. and LOUCKS, S. (1976) 'A developmental model for determining whether the treatment is actually implemented', *American Educational Research Journal*, 27(1).
HAMPSTEAD, T.F., FORD, J.E. and HIRD, W.N. (1980) 'An administrative team development program', *Commonwealth Council for Educational Administration Studies in Educational Administration*, 18 May.
HAVELOCK, R.G. (1973) *The Change Agents' Guide to Innovation in Education*, Englewood Cliffs, N.J., Educational Technology Publications.
HEARN, P. and OGILVIE, D. (1973) 'Operation stocktake', *Administrator's Bulletin*, 4(3).
HERSEY, P., BLANCHARD, K.H. and NATEMEYER, W.E. (1979) *Situational Leadership, Perception and the Impact of Power*, La Jolla, California, Learning Resources Corporation.
HORNSTEIN, H.A. (1974) 'Chutzpa: A critical review of the preceding papers', *Education and Urban Society*, 6(2): 239–248.
HUBERMAN, A.M. (1976) *Permanent Education: Some Models of Adult Learning and Adult Change*, Council of Europe.
HUCK, J.R. (1976) 'Organization development: Manipulation or self-determination?', A paper presented to the Fifth International Training and Development Conference, Canberra, 29 August.
JONES, J.E. (1973) 'Helping relationship inventory', in PFEIFFER, J.W. and JONES, J.E. (Eds.), *Annual Handbook for Group Facilitators*, La Jolla, California, University Associates, pp. 53–70.
JUNG, C.C. (1977) *Organizational Development in Education*, Portland, Oregon, Northwest Regional Educational Laboratory.
KNOWLES, M. (1974) 'Human resource development on OD', *Public Administration Review*, 34(2).
LAWRENCE, P.R. and LORSCH, J.D. (1969) *Developing Organizations: Diagnosis and Action*, Reading, MA, Addison-Wesley.
LINDBLOM, C. (1959) 'The science of muddling through', *Public Administration Review*, 19(79).
LINDBLOM, C. (1968) *The Policy-Making Process*, Englewood Cliffs, N.J., Prentice-Hall.
LIPPITT, G. and LIPPITT, R. (1978) *The Consulting Process in Action*, La Jolla, California, University Associates.
LOEVINGER, J. (1976) *Ego Development*, San Francisco, Jossey-Bass, Inc.

MANN, D. (1978) 'The user-driven system and a modest proposal', *Teachers College Record*, 79(3).

MARGULIES, N. and RAIA, A. (1972) *Organization Development: Values Process and Technology*, New York, McGraw-Hill.

MASLOW, A. (1965) *Eupsychian Management: A Journal*, Irwin and Dorsey.

MENZEL, R.K. (1975) 'A taxonomy of change-agent skills', *Journal of European Training*, 4(5): 287-288.

MEYER, J. and ROWAN, B. (1975) 'Notes on the structure of educational organizations: Revised version', Paper prepared for the annual meeting of the American Sociological Association. Reported in HANNAWAY, J. (1978) 'Administrative structures: Why do they grow?', *Teachers College Record*, 79(3): 416-417.

MILES, R. (1965) 'Human relations or human resources', *Harvard Business Review*, Summer, pp. 340-347.

MILES, M. (1974) 'A matter of linkage: How can innovation research and practice influence each other?', in TEMPKIN, S. and BROWN, M. (Eds.), *What Does Research Say about Getting Innovations into the Schools: A Symposium*, Philadelphia, Research for Better Schools.

MILES, M.B., FULLAN, M. and TAYLOR, G. (1978) 'OD in schools: The state of the art', A paper presented at the American Educational Research Association Annual Meeting, Toronto, March 27-31.

MORGAN, C. (1973) *Organization Development (OD): The Case of Sheldon High School*, The Open University Press.

MULFORD, W. (1976) 'Two ACT high schools and their responses to the criteria for a good school questionnaire', in, *ACT Papers on Education 1957-76*, Canberra College of Advanced Education: 7-10.

MULFORD, W. (1977) *Structured Experiences for Use in the Classroom*, Australian National University, Centre for Continuing Education.

MULFORD, W. (1979) 'Organization development in schools: An octet of dilemmas', *Educational Change and Development*, 1(3): 13-25.

MULFORD, W. (1979a) 'Andragogy and some implications for teacher educators', in MULFORD, W. *ACT Papers on Education 1978-9*, Canberra, Canberra College of Advanced Education: 153-171.

MULFORD, W. (In press) *The Role and Training of Inservice Trainers*, Paris, OECD.

MULFORD, W., CONABERE, A.B. and KELLER, J.A. (1977) 'Organization development in schools: Early data on the Australian experience', *The Journal of Educational Administration*, 15(2): 210-237.

MULFORD, W., WATSON, H.J. and VALLEE, J. (1980) *Structured Experiences and Group Development*, Canberra, Curriculum Development Centre.

MULFORD, W. and ZINKEL, C. (1977) 'Assisting school evaluation: Four ACT primary schools and their responses to the criteria for a good school questionnaire', *ACT Papers on Education 1976-77*, Canberra College of Advanced Education: 130-137.

OGILVIE, D. (1975) 'Organizational climate in six high schools', *Administrators Bulletin*, 6(3): 1-4.

OGILVIE, D. (1977) 'Survey feedback in four high schools', *Australian Council for Educational Administration Bulletin*, 8.

PUSEY, M. (1976) *Dynamics of Bureaucracy: A Case Study in Education*, Sydney, Wiley.

REDDIN, W.J. (1977) 'Confessions of an organization change agent', *Group and Organization Studies*, 2(1): 33-41.

SARASON, S. (n.d.) in REYNOLDS, M. (Ed.), *Proceedings of the Conference on Psychology and the Process of Schooling in the Next Decade: Alternative Conceptions*, Bureau of Educational Personal Development, US Office of Education, DHEW.

SCHEIN, E.H. (1969) *Process Consultation: Its Role in Organization Development*, Reading, Mass, Addison-Wesley.

SCHMUCK, R.A. (1973) 'Consultation in organization development: Report of a research program at the university of Oregon, USA', A paper prepared for E321 Management in Education in the Faculty of Educational Studies of the Open University, England.

SCHMUCK, R. (1978) 'Peer consultation for school improvement', in COOPER, C. and ALDERFER, C. (Eds.), *Advances in Experiental Social Processes*, London, Wiley.

SCHMUCK, R. and MILES, M. (Eds.) (1971) *Organization Development in Schools*, Palo Alto, California, National Press Books.

SCHMUCK, R., RUNKEL, P., ARENDS, J. and ARENDS, P. (1977) *The Second Handbook of Organization Development in Schools*, Palo Alto, California, Mayfield.

SINGER, E.A. and WOOTON, M. (1976) 'The triumph and failure of Albert Speer's administrative genius: Implications for current management theory and practice', *Journal of Applied Behavioural Science*, 12(1): 79–103.

STEELE, F. (1969) 'Consultants and detectives', *Journal of Applied Behavioural Science*, 5(2): 193–194, 200.

THOMPSON, J. (1967) *Organizations in Action*, New York, McGraw-Hill.

THOMPSON, J. and TUDEN, A. (1959) 'Strategies and processes of organizational decisions', in *Comparative Studies in Education*, University of Pittsburgh Press.

TICHY, N. (1974) 'Agents of planned social change: Congruence of values, cognitions and actions', *Administrative Science Quarterly*, 19(2): 164–182.

TICHY, N. (1975) 'How different types of change agents diagnose organizations, *Human Relations*, 28(9): 771–779.

TICHY, N. (1978) 'Current and future trends for change agentry', *Group and Organization Studies*, 3(4): 467–482.

TICHY, N. and NISBERG, J.N. (1976) 'Change agent bias: What they view determines what they do', *Group and Organization Studies*, 1(3): 286–301.

WISE, A.E. (1977) 'Why educational policies often fail: The hyperrationalization hypothesis', *Curriculum Studies*, 9(1).

WYANT, S.H. (1974) 'The effects of OD training on communications in elementary schools', Unpublished doctoral dissertation, University of Oregon.

Management Development for Headteachers

Harold Heller
Cleveland LEA

Introduction and Argument

The opening 'disclaimer' is a traditional device among educational administrators in local or central Government in the UK, a ritual invoked whenever an individual emerges from the penumbra of corporate identity to venture a declaration of personal values. While this preamble will be recognized as my own somewhat inelegant apology for resorting to this device, it may also serve to advertize one of the central themes of my argument.

Whenever one of Her Majesty's Inspectors, say, or a Senior Officer of a Local Education Authority feels constrained to introduce an account of their most central beliefs or work-activities with some such formula as 'the views which follow are those of the author alone and do not necessarily reflect Departmental policy', a major discontinuity is betrayed which is perhaps characteristic of the management of British educational institutions, particularly in periods of crisis.

Since the policies of an Education Department find their formal expression

---

Editor's note: There are few accounts of extended programmes of management training for education in the UK and what does exist is cryptic and idealized. In this account of several years work in one UK LEA, Heller appears remarkably honest. Management training is much more difficult than we like to believe not only because we still do not have a good theory of educational organizations but because we do not have a very good practice of training. There is just too much yet to be learned about changing behaviour in large social areas. Although we know a good deal about counselling and group sensitivity, we have not yet learned to apply our skills well enough to people who do not choose willingly to be counselled and trained.

But in many ways Heller's chapter undersells the achievement. Few LEAs have attempted management training for heads with such thoroughness and with such resources. Heller hints at the risks in using techniques which deal with the heart of the problems. The climate for risk-taking in training in the UK is not favourable but there are signs of a change. The chapter has a very English 'feel' about it and a British diffidence but it indicates quite fully an important direction of development that will hopefully be taken up elsewhere.

in Ministry circulars or Council Minutes it is not surprising that these tend either to reflect administrative caution through an impersonality of language and commitment, or in the spirit of 'Realpolitik' to advocate the imposition of wholesale or monolithic change.[1]

Yet such overtly bureaucratic behaviour may in fact originate from those actively engaged in innovation and in the nurturing of tentative new mechanisms of change, whose outcomes cannot be accurately planned or foreseen.[2] One of the more comfortable ways of damping down such dissonance is to 'hive-off' innovation into a separate research or experimental function, whether this is located within the sponsoring Department (as a research unit which may be tolerated but given no significant role or authority), or by the establishment of countrywide endeavours (such as the National Foundation for Educational Research, the Schools Council, or special University projects). From the perspective of the individual school or local authority, it is evident that this latter group – despite the skills and resources deployed – have failed to make their anticipated impact on the practice of education in the UK over the last 10 years, a recognition that is now leading to a healthy self-appraisal.[3] This process of re-evaluation already suggests that global attempts to disseminate change from the centre need to give way to initiatives arising from and focused on the individual – whether the teacher or the institution.[4]

This lengthy digression aptly returns me to my opening disclaimer, since it is true that what I am to describe represents not so much the formally adopted policies of the Cleveland Local Education Authority, but rather the slow development of practice which has been facilitated by a climate in which innovation (both of a 'top-down' and 'bottom-up' variety) has been either implicitly tolerated or positively encouraged. The view I will present will be idiosyncratic and certainly not an official statement of Cleveland policy; it will be subjective and involved; as a piece of evaluation it will be 'formative' not 'summative', evolutionary rather than terminal.[5]

As with an earlier paper on a similar theme written for the NODE Journal[6], I welcome the opportunity to tease out a process with which I have been closely involved (at various levels of commitment) over some five years, but which has deeper and longer roots. These imperfections of methodology suggest that what emerges cannot be seen as a model capable of replication in any scientific sense. Yet the paradigm of how a local authority can define and pursue innovation amid the turmoil of political change, economic constraints, professional accountability and pragmatic management, may have relevance to others.

It would be tempting to anticipate the argument at this stage with the facile synopsis:

> Each local Education Authority should have an overall plan for institutional and organizational development, mediated primarily through its headteachers.

The premature promise and latest frustration of widely accepted planning

Management Development for Headteachers

instruments such as MBO and PPB[7] during the 1960s and 1970s suggest caution in the face of such universal nostrums. If my reflections on Cleveland serve, however, as a case-study (idiographic rather than normative) of what kinds of conditions inhibit or promote the development of desired institutional change, it may be that some wider principles will emerge. At this stage of my argument I would formulate these principles within broad questions of the following kind:

> Does 'planning' imply resort to structural techniques or instruments?
> How far can the appetite for change be stimulated from outside?
> Can personal and institutional growth be harmonized?
> What are the individual effects on 'managers' of facilitating change?
> How can the 'theory/practice' gap be made tolerable?

Such questions tend, of course, to generate others, but this sample may serve to indicate the general issues which seem to me relevant to the current position in Cleveland.

Cleveland – A Profile

It may be useful to frame a quick sketch of the area in which the work described has taken place. The emergence of this new County, arising from the 1974 reorganization of local government, would itself repay a separate study of political contrivance, vacillation and expediency. The County was formed substantially from the Teesside County Borough, which itself had only been created, after many decades of aspiration, in 1968. The inception of Teesside had represented, certainly in industrial and planning terms, a broadly rational step towards the management of a densely occupied conurbation of townships, with separate, but similar heritage and needs. Six years later it was dismantled, (although its presence – 70 per cent of Cleveland's population – remains a robust cuckoo in the County nest). The creation of new entities – however unwelcome or hybrid – is often best legitimized by name-change, and the new County was christened after a tract of land (Cleveland) which lies mainly outside its eponymous county. In order to fit the Procrustean bed of a nationally imposed re-organization, the Single Teesside Unit was divided into four districts, each with its own multiplication of departments and offices for certain functions. Education, however, is administered at County level, where a larger than average child population (approximately 125,000) is served by some 350 schools and 6,000 teachers. While classified as a 'Shire' County, Cleveland comprises a dense conurbation on either side of the industrial River Tees, with a relatively small coastal and rural hinterland. The Tees, is, however, its *'raison-d'être'*; the magnet for vast capital-intensive developments in the steel and petro-chemical industries; service, light, or white-collar industries are scarce, and local government with ICI and the British Steel Corporation are the major employers of labour. The area might be caricatured as marrying 21st century technology with 19th century social conditions – a travesty which carries disturbing echoes of truth. In its overall social priorities it seems to deviate from general trends by its traditional blend of public munificence and private squalor. Levels of unemployment and outward migration are high – but so too are wage-rates (particularly in the skilled manual sectors).

An interesting set of statistics, and one relevant to the tasks of education is provided in Table 1.

Table 1. Socio-Economic Status of Head of Household (% 1979)[8]

	Cleveland	England & Wales
1. Employers, Managers and Professionals	14.7	19.6
2. Other Non-Manual	16.9	22.0
3. Skilled Manual	40.2	33.0
4. Semi-Skilled Manual	21.6	18.9
5. Unskilled Manual	6.6	6.5

Cleveland's variation from National norms in SES classes 1, 2 and 3 has had major consequences for the education service. Staying-on rates after compulsory schooling have been low; performance in public examinations tends to be significantly higher in Mathematics, the Sciences and Craft subjects than in the Arts and Humanities areas; in common with other traditionally 'depressed' areas, the North-East sends more 18 year olds into the teacher training sector of Higher Education than into traditional degree areas, and the region has been broadly self-supporting in the output of teachers, leading sometimes to a static and inward-looking regionalism of approach. It should also be noted that the Teesside area is said to be the largest conurbation in Europe without its own University.

A further implication has been a local view of schooling as a means of providing technically skilled and numerate labour for an innovating and demanding industrial sector. Contrasting views of the education service as a vehicle for regenerating the local community and providing new skills, attitudes and opportunities, tend to be associated with 'professionals' who (like myself) have come to the area from a different background of experience and perspective.

The dependence of the area on a small number of well-entrenched employers has further bearing on the education system. While this nexus has been broadly benevolent in its outcomes, permitting rapid and easy liaison and mutual understanding, it may be argued that something akin to a patron-client relationship has been fostered between local industry and the education system. Such paternalism, however, has itself facilitated some of the interesting development described later in this chapter. When a company like ICI actively embraces a 'social conscience' policy towards the local community it can promote radical and progressive collaboration between its senior staff and

'Managers' within the education service.

As a further historical footnote, it should be stated that the Teesside Education Authority had set out to develop an Advisory and Inspectorate Service which would play a dynamic role in school development. Although this became standard in the new post-1974 LEAs, Teesside had moved away from the notion of School Advisers as narrow specialists in particular subject disciplines whose role was largely one of inspecting and organizing provision in such areas. (These traditional subjects dating from the early part of this century were largely identified with Physical Education, Music, and Home Economics.)[9] The 'generalist' role can be said to have been precipitated by secondary reorganization, as well as the development of new building design and curricula in primary schools; and these changes thrust the Adviser – whatever his or her original specialism – into the wider problem-solving areas of school organization and management. In this trend, education's own 'Peter Principle' soon became apparent; Advisers were traditionally recruited from the ranks of successful and enthusiastic practitioners of the separate subject specialisms (at least 12 different disciplines will be represented in an Advisory team that hopes to offer a comprehensive service to schools). Yet their day-to-day tasks tended to draw them away from their authentic areas of experience, into a consultancy role, with an increasing focus on general issues of management such as the use of resources, the recruitment and pastoral needs of staff, and, latterly, familiarity with a blizzard of employment legislation – areas where the Adviser had no prior claim to expertise. A clear account of this transition and the conflicts, tensions and anomalies it produced can be found in the study by Bolam *et al* of Advisory Services in the early 1970s.[10]

The Teesside Advisory Service which formed the central core of personnel and practice in Cleveland had, however, been recruited on this newer 'generalist' basis, had formulated appropriate policies and had, by 1974, experience in working on school development lines. This can be said to have eased the transition towards the kind of consultancy role described by Bolam and intimated in the later sections of this chapter.

To fill out this brief background portrait of the Authority, it should also be stated that secondary reorganization in Cleveland was effectively completed by 1975, and that most secondary schools were in modern and well-equipped buildings, while the building stock of primary schools had been largely replaced or updated. The twin effects of general structural reorganization and population expansion were to introduce in the middle 1970s a very high proportion of new and often 'young' headteachers (i.e. below forty by the criteria then current).

The next section will examine the consequences of such a background on the training and development of Heads in Cleveland.

Advisers, Headteachers and In-Service Education

The Teesside Advisory service had inaugurated a vigorous and enterprizing programme of in-service education, based largely on three full-time Teachers' Centres, each one with its own Warden (to become five full-time Centres and Wardens in Cleveland). This programme had largely followed the Curriculum Development movement of the 1960s and '70s, with its focus on specialist curriculum areas (the origins of the UK Teachers' Centres movement in the Nuffield Maths in-service workshops of the 1960s will be a familiar story). The establishment of a group of Heads and Advisers (1972–74) to consider the implications of new building philosophy (The 'Open-plan' development) on curriculum and practice in the Primary School, was an early indication that ways of developing schools other than by the traditional subject training of individual teachers were available and relevant.

The rapidly expanding child population of the early 1970s, bringing with it major programmes of new school building together with the wholesale reorganization of secondary schools, led to a sudden expansion of promotion opportunities in the schools. The task of managing and co-ordinating this wide promotion market fell to the Advisers who, through their subject expertise and their in-service activities, were deemed to be in a good position to appraise both the quality of existing manpower and the demands of the newly emerging posts. The powerful influence of the Advisory Service in these areas of career development meant that, for many teachers, perceptions of the Advisers' work were (and still remain) ambivalent. What are, often unconsciously, seen as the patronage or disciplinary aspects of the role, may sit uneasily with the pastoral or counselling stance which most Advisers would adopt as a preferred self-image.

The role-confusions which surround these areas of an Adviser's activity are touched upon in Bolam's work (see note 10) and in other descriptive accounts of the Advisory function;[11] they were also dramatically illustrated throughout the 'William Tyndale affair'[12] which can be said to mark the mid-1970s disenchantment with 'progressive' educational approaches – often associated with the work of LEA Advisers – and to usher in the 'Great Debate'[13] with its often unsubtle advocacy of a 'back to basics' approach. The impact of the Tyndale affair with its close scrutiny of the Advisers' activity can be illustrated by an extract from a contemporary editorial appearing in *The Guardian* – a newspaper with a 'liberal' pedigree on social issues.

> ... It is important, too, to insist that inspectors play both an advisory and an admonishing role. Supporting teachers may be more pleasant than criticizing them, but by refusing to speak out at the beginning of the Tyndale dispute, the inspectors only delayed judgement, not avoided it.[14]

Around the time of the inception of Cleveland (1974) the Advisory Service was closely involved with the appointment of considerable numbers of new Headteachers (more than 150 in the four years period from 1973 to 1977); a phenomenon with the following consequences:

Management Development for Headteachers

(i) A trend towards a norm, clustering around common sets of values or experience, in the newly appointed Heads;
(ii) A system of mutual dependence between the new Heads and the Advisers and Officers associated with their appointment;
(iii) A sudden 'leavening', by age and attitude, of the pool of Headteachers.

The 'symbiosis' suggested above has significant impact on the management of innovation within and across schools since, while the initial 'contract' between the new Heads and the appointing LEA (in the person of its Officers and Advisers) may facilitate certain approved lines of development, areas requiring new solutions or carrying a risk of conflict may be sensed as dangerous, thus conducing to a conservatism of action. It may be claimed that any such system of 'patronage', with life-tenure, is productive of immobility in the face of unexpected problems, however radical the slogans of Heads or Advisers. The inherent risk, however, that the success and effective development of schools is judged by and within a closed and self-reinforcing system, must be kept in mind, not least when reading this chapter.

Interest in the leadership qualities of Heads of schools has a long history, and examples of its implications are found widely in the literature of educational administration. It may, however, be asserted that the English tradition of headship has certain distinguishing characteristics, which have persisted across the period of mass public education. Apart from minor stylistic variants the following passage, describing paragons of excellence among Heads, might have occured anywhere over the past 150 years:

> ... without exception, the most important single factor in the success of these schools is the quality of leadership of the Head. Without exception, the Heads have qualities of imagination and vision, tempered by realism, which have enabled them to sum up not only their present situation but also attainable future goals. They appreciate the need for specific educational aims, both social and intellectual, and have the capacity to communicate these to staff, pupils and parents, to win their assent and to put their own policies into practice. Their sympathetic understanding of staff and pupils, their accessibility, good humour and sense of proportion and their dedication to their task has won them the respect of parents, teachers and taught. They are conscious of the corruption of power and though ready to take final responsibility they have made power-sharing the keynote of their organization and administration. Such leadership is crucial for success and these schools are what their Heads and staffs have made them.[15]

While there may be little doubt that the ten schools described are, in fact, examples of the best contemporary practice, the balance of the argument is presented in a style laced with rhetoric, assertion and anecdote, rather than in the language of social analysis or behavioural science which characterizes discussion of educational leadership in North America or Scandinavia. It may be that Britain's imperial traditions characterized by a complex interplay of Church, Army, Law and Politics with the emerging education system, have produced a climate in which certain styles of Headship are tolerated, if necessary, in defiance of the changing needs of schools.[16] I have caricatured these styles in the following four 'archetypes' of Headteacher.

> *Mr Major* (Head as Military Leader)
> 'Runs a tight ship'; leads from the front; is respected but not loved; relationships are distant; crises are handled with efficiency; staff feel guilt and discomfort if they sense the need to innovate or to challenge the system.
>
> *Mr Bishop* (Head as Missionary)
> Inspirational and charismatic; staff wish to do things for him; he can be thrown into disarray if facts contradict his principles; there is a tendency for his staff to fragment; some complain that they 'can't keep up with him'.
>
> *Mr Proctor-Gamble* (Head as Entrepreneur)
> Creates a very favourable image; never out of the public eye (a fact resented by his Headteacher colleagues); staff can be upset by the launch of sudden new initiatives; they often complain that 'he doesn't seem to care what actually goes on in the classroom'.
>
> *Mr Lowry* (Head as Artist)
> Sees the personal development of staff and pupils as the only worthwhile goal, in which aesthetics are the liberating force. Sometimes presents an anti-intellectual bias; fiercely defends his pupils. Untidiness of organization can infuriate staff.

It may be recalled that the Victorian patriarchy envisaged certain vocational destinations for their sons, among which the Army, the Church, Commerce and the Arts, might figure (probably in that order of preference). If the contemporary English school system is the heir of its Victorian progenitors,[17] it may not surprise us to find these four archetypes of Headship still dominant and cherished.

It must be said that this very concentration on 'leadership' as critical for schools, argues for a 'top-down' model of organization development, which much of the English tradition serves to reinforce. This is however not without challenge, particularly from those who have espoused a more participative or democratic style of management.[18]

The conflicts between a 'top-down' or 'bottom-up' style of OD came vividly to focus in Cleveland in the wake of pressures to review curriculum practice as part of the 'Great Debate' of the late 1970s. After considerable reflection (and some internal misgiving), the view was taken that such a major review of the curriculum would need to be widely based, focused on the local schools and concerned as much with process as with end-product.

The resulting review programme was open-ended, interactive, widely disseminated to all levels of the service and, in a way that sometimes proved threatening both to Heads and to members of the Advisory service, unpredictable in its outcomes.[19]

At this point careful negotiations took place with the Heads' organizations to ensure that full control of the whole programme was not lost to them, and a worthwhile set of compromises was struck. What these incidents in retrospect seem to underline may seem commonplace in OD theory and practice; namely that commitment to change by leadership is a necessary but not sufficient condition for innovation and that democratic participation has to be structured within a realistic and agreed framework of power-sharing. This corrective needs emphasis at this stage, if the apparent concentration of my account on the crucial role of the Head is not to be misinterpreted.

The Beginnings

The act of writing a retrospective account in which one element of many pressing activities is isolated, tends to attach to that particular thread a design or purpose which may misrepresent the shifting and casual nature of decision-making. In short, the group of Advisers who, in 1975, initiated the activities here described had before them no model of staff or organization development; were themselves restricted by experience and learning; and were often naive as to the demands and difficulties such a programme might entail. What was relevant in their motivation was an insight (often uncertain) that initiatives in these fields were opportune and consistent both with the needs of schools and the trend of historical development. I have already outlined the major organizational changes which schools were undergoing; the rapid promotion to senior management posts in schools; the clamant demand of curriculum change and development; the growing complexity and openness of schools, and the imminent signs (through the Tyndale affair, the 'Great Debate', and the Taylor Committee),[20] of greater public scrutiny of school performance. The recent accretion of staff from four different Authorities, in the 1974 Local Government Reorganization, sharpened the need to take action towards some unity of approach. (It may be argued that the in-service and staff development strategies which will be described were far more effective in fostering a sense of shared identity, than the often costly attempts to equalize schemes of provision, resources or policy which occupied considerable amounts of Officer and Member time over that period.)

At the very outset of Cleveland, the former Chief Adviser had organized 'Management Seminars' for Heads which were devoted exclusively to a sharing of management information and a personal introduction to the major decisions, policies and functions of the County bureaucracy. This was, in effect, seen as a passive, updating process, although much appreciated at the time.

The Management of Educational Institutions: Theory, Research and Consultancy

A year earlier the consortium of Local Education Authorities in the North of England had decided to establish a regionally supported series of three-week courses designed for Heads and Deputies of secondary schools, largely in the context of the comprehensive reorganization of Secondary Education. This course was contracted out to Sunderland Polytechnic's Department of Curriculum Studies and, unlike the National COSMOS courses (run by HMI since the late sixties and largely directed to mechanistic considerations of secondary schools' curricula and timetabling), examined 'process issues' in school management (staff relationships; counselling and interviewing skills; models of leadership and group behaviour) as well as the management of resources. While this course has been positively supported by Cleveland Heads and Deputies, it has always proved individualistic to participants rather than organic to a school's development. Without follow-up or 'back-home' reinforcement it has offered a speculative management package of uncertain effectiveness (in this as so much else, I suspect, mimicking the earlier history of management development within industry and commerce and stumbling over the same kinds of error).

It was, in part, to explore the possible transfer of learning from industrial to educational models that a small support group (The Norton-Hardwick group) began meeting in 1973–74, based on ICI's management training centre and composed of secondary Headteachers, Advisers, ICI personnel and Training Officers and the Coordinator of the Teesside Industrial Mission. This group was to prove influential in shaping the early progress of training efforts within Cleveland and inevitably imparted an Industrial flavour which has intermittently produced resistance whenever the Group's ideas or personnel have become especially active.

One of the tensions which Advisers have to face in their in-service training work is the fact that they have a 'line-management' relationship with teachers; in crude terms, they have (within formal safeguards) 'hire-fire' and disciplinary powers which must co-exist with the more creative, developmental aspects of their role. While this must impose certain limits to their personal OD involvement with schools it can, by contrast, often facilitate interventions which may prove productive of innovation. One such 'happenstance' can be quoted from this formative stage of Cleveland's development.

I have already described the plethora of new Headship appointments made during this period, arising from which the County Head Teachers' Association formally approached the LEA suggesting that a policy of exotic youthfulness was being pursued to the detriment of more mature and local candidates. One simple riposte was to tabulate the ages and origins of appointees over the challenged period – a device which exploded the charge by showing the alleged bias to be illusory. The more worrying residue of myth and suspicion could not, however, be dissipated merely by statistical argument, and we decided that a more profitable route would be to meet Heads, in local groups, to talk through the criteria used in making appointments; writing and evaluating confidential references; giving career advice and training to staff –

in short, to explore the whole concept of promotion and staff development. Not only did these seminars lead to greater mutual understanding, but they also gave some positive management tools to Heads in the key areas of staff management. Yet while this outcome had been unplanned and adventitious, it served to reinforce other developing initiatives and to argue for greater coherence and design in our approach to the management of schools. One small experiment, at this stage, was the mounting of 'induction' courses, for newly appointed Heads, which embraced not only the familiarization procedures already described, but explored issues of human relations training in the Headship role. These courses were led by the Senior Adviser for Primary Education and myself, and I can now recognize the transitional nature of their goals and content, with a firm grounding in the 'safe' areas of administrative or managerial competence, allied to a consideration of the more dynamic and challenging areas of leadership skills.

If we bear in mind that this period was characterized by the rapid promotion of relatively young teachers to senior posts in new and reorganized schools, it is not surprising that on both Primary and Secondary fronts major 'promotion' courses in the organization and management of schools were now devised by the Senior Advisers, not only to meet the expressed appetite of 'middle-management' staff in schools, but also to provide from the LEA's viewpoint an opportunity to clarify and enumerate the range and quality of its expectations of senior staff in schools.

These courses ran over four terms, with a mixture of two-day blocks, and weekly local working sessions, and were largely tutored by practising Heads, supported by Advisers and Officers. Their style and content was eclectic – but largely task-orientated.[21] What we did not fully grasp at first was the importance of the local groups with their individual tutors whose leadership characteristics and behaviour proved highly influential. This did emerge, however, on the Primary course when, at the concluding stages, major intergroup simulation exercises were mounted, throwing up a good deal of evidence about the levels of cohesiveness and effectiveness of the individual local groups and their leaders and turning our minds to dynamic aspects of group process which had been implicit throughout but not directly confronted.

The Secondary course, at an early stage, involved paradigms external to Education, and a group of managers and behavioural scientists from ICI (via the North-Hardwick group) were introduced in order to mount residential modules with a wide range of techniques and exercises familiar in Industrial management training, but new and exciting to many teachers.

The development of materials and planning of courses by the tutor teams of Heads and Advisers established training groups whose skills and motivation were now keenly aroused. These teams began to look in new directions, as I will discuss in the next section.

The sense of success and excitement generated by these courses emboldened us to recognize that many of the skills and techniques we were exploring were as relevant to serving as to aspiring Heads and, in 1976, we began a series of annual residential in-service events for Heads, organized and staffed by the Cleveland Advisory Service. Through the vehicle of some thirty courses since that time a climate has been established in which Heads have accepted what seemed at first high-risk techniques: while some may have experienced role-play, simulation, group problem-solving and structured experiences as individuals on outside courses, they were now confronted with such approaches on their own territory, not only in the presence of their peers but often tutored by fellow Heads in partnership with Advisers and Officers of the Authority. These 'Goathland Events', with their Staff College atmosphere, have done much to develop a cohesiveness of approach and a sense of mutual understanding across the Authority as well as sharing and legitimizing new analyses of management problems.

If we look at the first three years of these programmes (from 1975–1978) we find that some 1150[22] senior staff participated in such extended courses with an approximate total commitment of 60,000 student-hours. The next section will examine some of the work arising from this initial phase of management development.

Growth and Development

The Goathland courses soon established a tradition in which Heads were able to welcome intellectual and personal challenge presented by colleagues and by the Authority's staff. Furthermore, by exploring issues such as accountability, self-appraisal, resource contraction and staff development (under rather opaque headings such as 'What makes a good school?', 'The School and the Community', 'Education in the 1980s'), they were themselves influencing the climate in which major policy matters were to be confronted ('Sensing the Issues', as some problem-solving models see this phase). Thus, when I review the themes established by Advisers for these courses, it is possible to find a strong 'proactive' flavour through which key issues which were likely to arise but whose resolution seemed uncertain, could be rehearsed and clarified in an interactive way with Heads. This is not to deny that many such events were indeed 'reactive', and devoted primarily to responses to external circumstance or legislation. It should perhaps be emphasized that while these courses were offered as merely one part of a very wide in-service programme, some 70 per cent of all Heads attended one or more of the three day events in the first two years. This, in itself, sharpened the sense of participation and 'ownership' which had been established principally by the use of local Heads and Advisers as the major tutor force.

The cadre of Heads and Advisers who had gained considerable experience at tutors, course planners and material writers, seemed now to demand additional skills and background to enable them not only to expand their work into new areas but to cope with the stresses of tutoring other professionals in areas which often took them to the frontiers of their own confidence and experience. This seemed especially marked in the management of interpersonal relationships, where some groups had exhibited dysfunctional behaviour which could be traced to the quality and style of tutor leadership experienced. This phenomenon led to some self-exclusion from the tutoring role but, by 1977–78, a group of some twenty primary and twelve secondary Heads, together with some six Advisers, could be identified as a committed and relatively skilled group of course leaders and facilitators (over the ensuing three years, this group has undergone natural flow in membership, but has increased in size by 50 per cent).

The inevitable response to this phase was to launch 'Training the Trainers' events which have been provided since that time for this 'core-group'. The functions of such events have been complex, but include: refreshment and rededication; evaluation of past events; exploration of new target areas; training in new techniques; self-exploration and team-building. It may prove helpful to describe, briefly, the earliest such event, which will be balanced by a later discussion of a more recent training session.

The 'Beamish Hall' training session (a two day residential course) was designed for some twenty-four Primary Head-Tutors and Advisers. They had themselves specified the goals as lying largely in the group-management and interpersonal areas of leadership, to which was added a related consideration of new course plans and design. As with later events, the intention of the leaders (the Senior Primary Adviser and myself) was to offer training and insight in group process and to apply this to real issues as perceived by the membership. In this case, for example, structured exercises on group consensus and leadership preceded the 'real' task of evolving plans for new programmes and approaches, which were to be designed under conditions of group consensus, distributed leadership and limited time-span (such an experiential-transfer model has always seemed attractive to me, but I have sometimes doubted whether the intellectually seductive transitions from simulation to reality are always effectively communicated to the membership – often because we leave ourselves too little time to reinforce or consolidate learning in the early stages).

This first training event was, however, widely appreciated and was found not only personally stimulating but also productive of effective new course designs.

The success of the early work with Heads prompted a desire to attempt more 'experimental' approaches in which new models or techniques could be investigated. As a consequence of links with training personnel within ICI, I organised, in 1977, a two day seminar for some twenty people – senior staff of the Education Department; Headteachers, and Senior Managers and Personnel Officers from ICI, Billingham. The overt theme was to explore ways in which a large industrial employer had coped, over the past decade, with severe contraction in employment while maintaining apparently positive support and involvement from the workforce. The spectre here, of course, was the dramatic decline in school pupil numbers which was then just making its first impact on the education service (and in the 1980s would effect a 30 per cent reduction in school rolls). The descriptions of ways in which bold staff and in-service development had facilitated major retrenchment and reorganization, while retaining both acceptable profitablity and a humane policy of staff participation, set an exciting challenge. This was reinforced by the apparent high-risk climate in which managers had exposed themselves in events at a deeply personal level alongside staff of all levels of responsibility. This contrasted (to my mind somewhat shamefully) with the rigid caste-distinctions within which the education service habitually seemed to protect its own hierarchy, and the tacit conspiracy that effectiveness as an educational manager could be entirely segregated from one's own personal growth, sensitivity and self-awareness.

From this arose a contract to work on one of the following year's Goathland Heads' courses with a team from ICI who had used such a training package as an effective tool of organization development, employing the 'Open Systems' model as the conceptual framework. I will not describe the content in any detail at this stage, except to point out that it relies on an initial break-through into trust and individual self-disclosure (using 'life-line' and 'Imagery' techniques) and moves outwards to a confrontation of group or institutional blockages in the hope of releasing creative solutions.

Each of the four ICI tutors (three of whom were *not* training officers but engineers by background) were 'paired' with an Adviser as co-tutor, and I had structured the membership to include Primary and Secondary Heads, Advisers and senior staff of other educational services (Higher Education, Careers Education, Educational Psychologists, Teachers' Centre Wardens, etc.). This was, I suppose, the first formally sanctioned management course in which senior staff were expected, as part of the unfolding structure, to share with their peers sensitive personal material. While these kinds of training challenges have been commonplace in many professions, the notion of using them on a local 'in-house' event prompted considerable initial anxiety among my colleagues.

My own description and evaluation of this course (which provided great personal insight for me) is less material than the more formal evaluation I conducted eighteen months afterwards (with a 75 per cent response rate). This is summarized in Appendix A and comments have been reproduced as received.

This consideration of the use of techniques which may have seemed exotic or alien to tradition has periodically caused difficulty. There is, of course, a widespread folk-lore around the alleged 'damage' to psychological health and stability caused by such approaches, and at various times official, as well as unofficial, frowns have been directed at programmes with which I have been associated.

Our overall in-service programmes have indeed encouraged a wide range of approaches outside the traditional range of structured courses, and have included a major commitment to group-focused sensitivity training with the National Marriage Guidance Council; Gestalt approaches to creativity and communication skills; and later developments of the Open Systems concept. Nevertheless, throughout the training programmes I have been conscious of a 'task-centred – person-centred' polarity to which I have had to remain alert, and deal with openly whenever it becomes a live issue for trainers and participants.[23]

I mentioned earlier the 'Norton-Hardwick' group, as a multi-professional support group, whose personnel gave valuable impetus to the development of programmes. By 1978, their own unity and confidence was such that they were invited to organized a regional event (based on Durham University) in order to disseminate to other areas the notion of such collaborative management development. The success of their efforts was certainly marked by the establishment of two other such 'cells' in Cleveland involving Education (largely at Headteacher level) and Industrial and Training Officers in a continuing active exploration of management skills. (Though it would seem less well transplanted to other parts of the Northern Region.) The original group has also developed a self-appraisal document for Headteachers which will itself form part of a Management Development progamme for Heads.

A further extension of one of the earlier elements (the 'induction' programmes for new Heads) has been the establishment of on-going support groups for recently appointed Heads. Three such groups (one secondary and two primary groups, of about twelve Heads each) have been established to meet approximately monthly and to explore, in a self-directed way, common issues and concerns with myself and other Senior Advisers as coordinators. While the style of group varies considerably, there has been much attention to staff management, conflict-handling and inter-personal relations. For the group with which I am associated this has involved peer-counselling, role-play demonstrations of staff-appraisal, and attention to cognitive models of human behaviour – as in presentations I have given of the application of the theory of Transactional Analysis to staff development.

It may also be useful to take a further example of extension by looking at the most recent 'Training the Trainers' residential course (April, 1980). This differed from the earlier Beamish event in the following ways:

> It was double in size (45 members).
> It combined Primary and Secondary Heads.
> It was tutored by 'outsiders' (an ICI Training Officer, the coordinator of the Teesside Industrial Mission, and myself).
> It was concerned with the design of four different long courses. The content was planned not only to give cohesiveness to the four teams and help them in their work, but also to offer them individual 'take-away' skills for their own institutions.

Whether the course enabled such diverse targets to be attained, may not be entirely certain, but later productivity and a high level of client satisfaction suggest that the structure was helpful. What may, in truth, be more crucial, is the growing level of autonomy and maturity of the Head-tutors. One consequence of this increasing independence and resourcefulness is a sense of redundancy among the initiators in the Advisory service. This has certainly been recognized and is now being worked through, but there is an inevitable sense of loss and regret when the original client-groups take responsibility for their own development. Although relatively unplanned, this may be seen as one of the more hopeful outcomes of the work in Cleveland.

Analysis and Discussion

At the head of my notes for this section stands a stark slogan *'Con or Reality?'* Nor is this question merely the putative challenge of a sceptical observer; it must, I believe, mirror my own self-questioning on the effectiveness of the work I have described.

The initial tentativeness and vulnerability to other day-to-day pressures has already become clear; what may seem at first sight less pardonable is the lack of clarity and overall purpose in the design and structure of the programmes, and the absence of formal evaluative mechanisms. A possible remedy which seems to me worth investigating would be the appointment of an external evaluator who could be sensitive to the process issues involved, and astute enough to disentangle genuine from spurious effects. Whether an analysis of Heads' management skills programmes could be undertaken in separation from a review of 1) the Authority's wider in-service programmes and 2) the empirical and material circumstances which may have accelerated or inhibited the growth of management skills, must be open to doubt.

The ethical and practical difficulties of establishing research and control samples; the contamination of causal with developmental factors; the shifting and spontaneous natures of the programmes themselves; the elimination of artefacts – all are obstacles with which 'action-research' in the educational fields has long been familiar. In addition, the very special dynamic of the relationship between Heads and educational Advisers is a factor which may be particularly characteristic of the United Kingdom over the past decade (see note 10).

Despite this lack of 'hard-edged' evaluative data, I will go on to indicate some personal responses, offered from a position of caring if subjective commitment.

From the ICI experience earlier described, I have been taken with the concept of the management 'umbrella', which functions as a protective shelter giving permission to those within the system to innovate and experiment with safety. While that shelter can be erected purely by managerial 'fiat', it seems to me that its credibility and durability is increased if there is seen to be a personal commitment at senior staff level to the new styles being promoted. That is why I and my senior colleagues have been careful to be seen not simply to 'dish out' the new kinds of experience. At an anecdotal level, this was demonstrated in some of the earliest role-play scenarios where we played, for example, the candidates for relatively junior posts who were interviewed by Heads, and in our general participation in activities requiring self-disclosure. This 'modelling' effect seems to reinforce, often in subtle ways, the power of the learning, giving rise to what has been called the 'Cascade Process'. If Advisers and Senior Officers can relate in an open and spontaneous way with Heads and other teaching staff, without resorting to implicit rank or power distinctions, it becomes more likely that such a process will become safe and acceptable within schools. Culture change, in effect, can be transmitted downwards as a conscious policy model, provided that there is underlying trust and genuineness in the transactions across the various levels of the system.

An accusation which is often implicitly voiced is that the 'core-group' of Heads has by now constituted a 'charmed circle' whose identification with the training team of Advisers has practical and political advantages. I can only say that in our day-to-day relationships where priorities or resources are at issue, I detect no evidence of such links being exploited or of the Heads concerned becoming reticent in using mechanisms to achieve their goals – including those of opposition or direct confrontation to Adviser colleagues in the training team.

It is hardly surprising, moreover, that, under conditions of threat, crisis or human overload, Heads who have taken most enthusiastically to such innovative programmes and concepts regress to earlier modes of behaviour – autocratic, dependent, manipulative or depressed. Increasingly, however, they are able to turn to Advisers or fellow Heads on a consultancy basis, to work through such episodes which only a naive training group would aspire to eliminate entirely.

I have suggested that the creation of an overall climate for change, which is based on genuine mutual respect and participation appears to offer, in an Authority like Cleveland, the best basis for the growth and renewal of schools as institutions. There are, however, other models currently purveyed which argue for greater and more direct intervention from the centre. This has been marked in the long and continuing series of papers originating from the DES which suggest, in part, that schools are failing to deliver outcomes consonant with national success. Such approaches have also been manifested in the 'self-appraisal' instruments promoted by LEAs (such as Oxfordshire, ILEA, Solihull), and in the Institutional Development Programme applied by IMTEC in Scandinavia and explored by several LEAs, including Cleveland, in 1979.[24] A similar, but more modest and perhaps more promising, instrument is that produced by Elliott-Kemp and Williams, under the title 'The DION Handbook'.[25]

Such approaches may appear mechanistic but, in their own way, they offer a point of entry to management and relationship issues within the school which have for too long remained undisturbed. Whether they can be imposed or successfully implemented on a wide scale, without first creating the appropriate climate of trust and consent conducive to a change of culture, I cannot speculate. Nothing, however, is likely to prevent the superstitious adoption of instant solutions in the wake of the latest ill-digested or misunderstood research. (The fate of Rutter's investigation of London Secondary schools,[26] whose conclusions on school 'ethos' have been selectively cannibalized by some Heads to prove, for example, that the imposition of standard school uniform or the setting of homework will *per se* guarantee success, is a contemporary example of the venerable fallacy '*post hoc non propter hoc*'.)

Public disenchantment with state schooling in the late 1970s, accompanied by (and perhaps causally related to) a relative decline in expenditure and resources has sharpened the need for institutional change. Rapidly contracting pupil numbers have dramatically modified career aspirations and profiles; the switch from a search for external rewards to the promotion of intrinsic satisfactions can be seen as favourable to school renewal, with its promise of stability and continuity. Excessive local and national political direction, bearing both on resource allocation and on the shape and content of the curriculum can perhaps be best averted by the development of purposeful, creative and self-critical schools. The capacity for rational and effective innovation in times of great difficulty requires a flexibility which may only be lasting if it is based on widespread trust and commitment among staff.

To find a point of leverage in the complex and theoretically decentralized management structure of a large LEA (with its several hundred 'Cottage Industries' each with its own 'Chief Executive') seems to me a critical but elusive goal. At times I may seem to have argued that there is a bald choice available between external intervention with prescriptive models and authoritarian solutions, or a school-focused, individualized process of autonomous discovery and self-actualization. The Cleveland experience, however, may suggest that other ways are possible, even if they appear to lack some of the crispness or directness of the given alternatives.

Reflections and Conclusions

The sketch I have offered in this paper, of what might be described as 'OD initiatives in Cleveland' may appear to encompass a somewhat discursive and unplanned range of activities. It was to confront this challenge and to respond to those who, using industrial training analogies, were pressing for 'an Organisation Development Unit' in the County that we established, in 1979, a co-ordinating group composed (in broadly equal numbers) of Advisers, Primary and Secondary Headteachers and external support agencies (including Industrial trainers).[27] My personal response to a year's work within that group evokes a sense of disillusion which may well, in turn, elicit the charge that I and my colleagues have not cared enough about its success to make it work; that we are fearful of losing control over programmes; and that we treat participative planning as a worthy goal for others but irrelevant to ourselves.

It must, however, be reported that the group's work has felt laboured and purposeless at times; activities (including the collection of resources and the running of training events) have often seemed gratuitous – not least in the sense that they could have been achieved adequately under other auspices. It has also displayed classic symptoms of a dysfunctional group: differences have been avoided or suppressed; commitment has been low; sub-groups have remained unchallenged; the role of others has often been discounted; goals have been unclear or divergent. The classic remedy was accordingly invoked in the person of an external consultant who spent a day with the group (as well as pre- and de-briefing sessions with me) exploring these issues. One major observation which emerged was that I had failed to offer sufficiently positive leadership, given the authority which my job imparts in these fields. While I accept this diagnosis, I also observe that all the goals which the group set for itself are in train of active achievement through other more natural working formations and that the establishment of the group as a visible token of commitment to the work may have been less important than the fostering of such spontaneous developments.

I have spent time exploring this passage in our history in order to illuminate a central and critical question, relevant not only to OD but more generally to the '*modus operandi*' of British Local Authorities: can detailed central planning – even in strategic terms – promote the best practice and outcomes in a human, small-scale Industry like Education?; even if a statement of end-goals was adopted, would it inevitably hover between a bland guarantee of minimum action and a rigidity of detail that would provoke resistance or sabotage?

In discussing such matters, reference is usually adduced from other, allegedly centralized, educational systems, notably in Europe and North America, and it is striking that Cleveland's self-generated efforts often appear trivial by comparison with the commitment to OD interventions by external consultants cited in the literature.[28] In such contexts the apparent openness and permeability to change of other systems seems enviable by contrast with our own more enclosed and tradition-bound structures. And yet, while other LEAs (who are now deciding – under whatever banner – to embrace programmes of school change and development) may well profit from economies of scale and design and from the experimental errors of other pioneers, we should not forget that such development is as much about process and growth as about effective system-building. Cleveland schools that we have seen struggle over some years to reach a modest developmental level (as measured by formal criteria of goal-clarification, survey-feedback, or structural sophistication – see note[24]) have harvested other fruits of personal self-awareness, creativity and autonomy that are the more impressive for being internally engendered and nourished.

If helping to run a local education system lays down a challenge to mobilize creative and humane means to effect instrumental goals,[29] then I and my colleagues can perhaps provide a better service through the kind of slow evolutionary discoveries which I have portrayed, than by commissioning ready-made, self-improvement packages which have been manufactured elsewhere. Our personal involvement and visible commitment to our own continuing growth and learning is not to be discounted for it has, I believe, foreshadowed and facilitated the professional and personal growth we have seen in Heads who have participated actively in these programmes and who have, in their turn, proved able to release the energies and creativity of their own staffs and pupils.

The immense difficulties of morale and resources which now threaten the English education system[30] can be viewed, in this perspective, as the most urgent challenge to personal and institutional growth in schools. The immediate future threatens turbulence and rapid change: the search for individual significance may show itself in socially uncomfortable or disruptive manifestations. Education is nothing if not the shape and spirit of that quest for meaning.

Appendix A

Open Systems Course – Goathland, October 1978

Review Document

Summary of Responses

(Please tick boxes, as appropriate).

1. How would you now assess the course as a broad *Educational* experience?

Of no value	Of little value	Of some value	Of considerable value	Of the highest value
☐	1	6	12	3

2. How would you now assess the course as a broad *personal* experience?

☐	☐	2	15	5

3. With how much success was the Open Systems Model communicated to you on the course?

Not at all	A little	Some	A good deal	Very much
☐	☐	9	10	3

4. Would you have liked fuller explanation or further experience of the Open Systems Model at the time?

2	2	3	7	5

Management Development for Headteachers

5. How relevant have you found the Open Systems Model to your work situation?

   ☐　　5　　8　　6　　3

6. How much use have you made of the Open Systems Model in your work since the course?
   (a) As a means towards understanding your organization and its functioning:

   2　　5　　10　　3　　1

   (b) As a management tool in planning or in resolving problems:

   3　　4　　8　　3　　3

   (c) As a training or development technique with colleagues:

   7　　7　　4　　3　　1

   (d) As a means to greater personal understanding, (not necessarily within the work setting).

   ☐　　2　　7　　8　　4

7. Please describe your estimate of the *value* of the various techniques employed on the course:
   (a) Life Line:

   1　　2　　5　　7　　7

   (b) Imagery:

   1　　7　　4　　5　　5

   (c) Domain Mapping:

   ☐　　☐　　5　　10　　7

   (d) Boundary Negotiation:

   ☐　　2　　6　　8　　6

   (e) Core Process:

   ☐　　3　　9　　6　　3

8. How far is the Open Systems Model a tool you would wish to see offered

to colleagues in similar positions to your own?

| 1 | 1 | 6 | 7 | 7 |

9. How far would you be prepared to use the model in training or developing others within your own field?

| 1 | 2 | 5 | 11 | 2 |

10. Do you feel any need or wish for further work with the Open Systems Model?

| 2 | | 9 | 5 | 5 |

Further Comments

A valuable exercise: obviously personal opportunity for implementation limited except as a general tool for in-service approach and influence on personal approach and insight.

I would rather have been involved in this work during a holiday period. Firstly to allow relaxation during the 'event' and secondly to aid recovery afterwards.

As a 'prescriptive tool' for others I have found the Open Systems Model of great value – but as a means of examining any other organization the possibility doesn't seem to be there; I think this may well be how I see my own status in the two circumstances.

Although convinced of the value of the Open Systems Course, it does not lend itself to my particular work situation very readily. As a personal experience and an ongoing reminder of my own development, I find it very useful.

I think Q.4 a time lag is needed from the original presentation and further explanation would have been superfluous. We have been influenced most by the problem solving contribution and have adopted this as our approach.

One feeling that has remained was that the course was very much a demonstration of, rather than confrontation with, open systems and thereby not the total learning experience it could have been.

One of the groups spent some time discussing 'role negotiation' (as *per* Roger Harrison). It has been in mind since that this would be a very profitable area to pursue. A further point is whether a PRIMARY group for those interested might be useful at this time. I would see it being initiated to meet on a regular basis to discuss, explore further, refresh, undergo further training, etc. It would help in confidence building and perhaps be worth exploring.

The techniques introduced were clear at the time. At this distance and without an opportunity to reinforce they have become generalized and a bit confused one with another. Perhaps I should have taken some initiatives to develop them but one becomes involved in day to day expedients – the old problem of the course not being integrated with ongoing responsibilities.

I found the course most re-assuring in that it presented the concept of management in a way that is particularly attractive to me. As a Head, one spends a great deal of time listening to and re-assuring colleagues. In this respect the course provided a similar therapeutic service for Heads.

The effective use of the Open System Model for me would be enhanced if my staff were with me during the learning stage.

Difficult to assess after such a long period – to be honest the Open Systems Model itself left me cold. Some of the transactions arising from the group work were valuable but would have been even more valuable if tied to a more appropriate vehicle.

It would have been of some value to have had an opportunity to relate one or more of these techniques to a school based problem solving situation – either real or simulated.

The course was too short, i.e. too intense. A series of evening lectures with some associated reading might well have suited me better.

From my answers I seem not to have used the techniques at all. In fact I found the course an intense personal experience and my responses to problems have been influenced generally, i.e. overall. Ironically the technique that I found pointless at the time, Imagery, is the one that comes unbidden at times of stress.

I have found some of these questions extremely difficult to answer because of the overlap of some of the concepts involved, e.g. 1 and 2: 6a and 6b.

This was a most enjoyable course. There were moments of personal apprehension possibly a fear of revealing too much of one's hidden self but this was always overcome. The 'mixture' of course members helped a lot. Much of the work was new to me and needed some digesting. Parts of it may still need further reflection and study on my part – given time. This course, coupled with the Rugby PR experience, has been of great value.

Staff involvement and participation have certainly benefited considerably. Senior management discussions have increased in number, content and general evaluation of the school and staff. Perhaps these two points would have been covered without the course as a natural development – may be not!

I feel a course should be run for the senior management of special schools.

Notes and References

1 Department of Education and Science Circular 10/65 'The organization of secondary education' may serve as one famous illustration of the attempt to blend a central and controversial political decision with an educational justification for major structural change.
2 The analysis of innovation at the Countesthorpe School by Professor Bernbaum, Leicester University, well illustrates the 'unintended consequences' of radical change: See HOLMES B. (1973) *Leicestershire UK* Case Studies of Educational Innovation, Paris, OECD.
3 Compare the 'Impact and Take-Up Survey' conducted by the Schools Council

into the effectiveness of its own programmes. This is described and discussed by the secretary, John Mann, in the Schools Council Report (1979–80), pp. 4–5.
4 The Schools Council's newly adopted 'Programme of Work', March, 1980, marks a radical shift away from its traditional focus on classroom and subject-based materials. See in particular *Programme 1* 'Purpose and Planning in Schools' and *Programme 2* 'Helping Individual Teachers Become more Effective' described in Schools Council News Release 80/9. The programme descriptions are periodically updated as releases by the Schools Council. The original outline was described in a pamphlet 'Principles and Programmes', Summer, 1979.
5 Such 'illuminative' evaluation has been described by PARLETT, M. and HAMILTON, D. (1972) 'Illuminative evaluation: A new approach to the study of innovatory programmes', Occasional Paper No. 9. University of Edinburgh Centre for Research in Educational Sciences, and by MCDONALD, B. 'Curriculum evaluation today', in TAWNEY, D., Macmillan.
6 HELLER, H. (1979) 'Organization development within a local education authority', *Educational Change and Development*, 2(1), Autumn, pp. 1–16.
7 Such initiatives were widely prescribed both at Central and Local Government level, and were formally adopted into many planning systems. The Coventry Education Department was one which adopted a 'Management by Objectives' approach. See also DAVIES, J.L. (1973) 'MBO in local education authorities', *Educational Administration Bulletin*, 2(1): 38–54.
8 These figures are taken from Cleveland County's Statistics, 1980. Research and Intelligence Department.
9 *National Association of Inspectors and Educational Advisers Journal*, 1(3): 5–7 and 11–14 and Internal Survey Report 1976.
10 BOLAM, R., SMITH, G. and CANTOR, H. (1978) *LEA Advisers and the Mechanisms of Innovation*, NFER.
11 Papers on this have been issued separately (and jointly) by NAIEA, and the Society of Education Officers, 1974, *et seq*.
12 See the Report of the Public Enquiry into the William Tyndale Schools, conducted by Robin Auld Q.C., ILEA, 1976.
13 Speech by the Prime Minister, James Callaghan, Ruskin College, Oxford, 18 October, 1976; followed by DES Green Paper, 'Education in schools – A consultative document', July, 1977.
14 *The Guardian*, editorial, 11 February, 1976.
15 HMI (1977) 'Ten Good Schools', *Matters for Discussion*, No. 1.
16 Heads, as well as Industrialists, have readily responded to concepts, such as Adair's 'Action-Centred Leadership', originally designed to train Army Officers. See Adair, J. (1973) *Action-Centred Leadership*, Gower Press.
17 The Centenary of the Forster Education Act was widely celebrated in 1970 as illuminating current values and goals in the education Service.
18 So-called 'Democratic Evaluation' and accountability in the schools system have been advocated, in particular by MACDONALD, B. (1978) 'Accountability, standards and the process of schooling', in BECHER, A. and MACLURE, S., *Accountability in Education*, Slough, NFER.
19 Cleveland County Education Department – Curriculum Review documents. (A series of 22 papers, written by Phase, Curriculum and Special Interest groups.)
20 The Taylor Committee Report – 'A New Partnership for our Schools'. DES/HMSO, 1977.

21 The outline syllabus of these courses was as follows:
Primary Course Themes
A. *Data*
   1. Roles and Duties. 2. Boundaries. 3. Procedures and Policies.
B. *Management Skills*
   1. Problem Solving. 2. Managing Groups. 3. Priorities and Resources.
   4. Job Description. 5. Decisions and Communication.
   6. Managing Change.
C. *Organization*
   1. Strategies of Staff Deployment. 2. Strategies of Pupil Deployment.
   3. Justification and Rationale, Effects.
D. *Curriculum*
   1. Why, How, When... (and What). 2. Assessment Procedures.
Secondary Course Themes
A. *Resources*
   1. Change and Flexibility. 2. Human Resources and Motivation.
   3. Staff Development. 4. Staffing Structures.
B. *Curriculum Management*
   1. Aims and Implementation. 2. Curriculum Change. 3. Assessment.
C. *Pastoral Issues*
   1. Systems. 2. Curriculum Links. 3. Home and Agencies.
   4. The Community.
D. *Decision-Making*
   1. Democracy. 2. Communication. 3. Participation.
   4. Feedback Systems.
22 There were approximately 6,200 teachers employed in schools within Cleveland through this period – although some double-counting must be assumed in the student figures.
23 Despite the reservations of SCHUTZ, W.C. (1974) Pfeiffer and Jones Annual Handbook, University Associates, pp. 279 ff, a useful treatment of this issue is found in LIEBERMAN, M.A., YALOM, I.D. and MILES, M.B. (1973), *Encounter Groups – First Facts*, Basic Books.
24 IMTEC Foundation, Oslo; Institutional Development Programme.
25 ELLIOTT-KEMP, J. and WILLIAMS, G.L. (1980) 'Diagnosis of individual and organizational needs for staff development and in-service training in schools', in *The DION Handbook*, Sheffield City Polytechnic.
26 RUTTER, M., MAUGHAN, B., MORTIMORE, P. and OUSTON, J. (1979) *Fifteen Thousand Hours*, London, Open Books.
27 The goals of this group (approved by the Education Committee of the Cleveland LEA) are to:
   (i) establish a 'clearing house' or 'Consultancy Service for Schools', so that relevant expertise could be directed towards helping schools resolve specific problems in their management or development;
   (ii) design further management courses both for individual schools and for groups of teaching staff within the Authority;
   (iii) investigate how far such courses might be appropriate or available to those engaged in educational management outside schools – such as for example Further Education, the Careers Service, the Youth and Community Service, and the Education Department.

28 Compare, for example, North American descriptions such as: SCHUTZ, W. (1977) *Leaders of Schools*, University Associates, and SCHMUCK, R.A. and MILES, M.B. (1971) *OD in Schools*, National Press Books.
29 Hence, perhaps, the still prevalent British tradition of recruiting educational administrators from the classroom.
30 In the three years from 1976 to 1979, Local Government Spending, in the UK, as a proportion of Gross Domestic Product, fell from 15 per cent to 12.6 per cent, and within that total there is evidence that the share of expenditure devoted to the Education Service declined relative to other local services, Chartered Institute of Public Finance and Accountancy – Statistics, 1980.

Research into Educational Innovation

Michael Fullan
Ontario Institute for Studies in Education

Over the past twenty years research on educational innovation has moved from a preoccupation with general theories and uncritical advocacy of the latest fads to a concern with what is actually happening *in practice*. This article focuses on current knowledge and directions in research on implementation of educational innovations. The vast majority of the research on which it is based comes from Canada and the United States, although many of the basic findings are similar to those in other western countries. It is divided into four main sections: I. What is Implementation; II. What Factors Affect Success or Failure; III. Principles and People in Implementation; and IV. Reflections on Implementation Research.

I. What is Implementation?

Effective implementation or changing practice at the classroom and school level in regard to a new program or policy was rare enough in the 1970s to be called a 'non-event' (Charters and Jones, 1973) – it was so rare in the 1960s that it wasn't called anything. Understanding the meaning of implementation

---

Editor's note: The essential activity that is managed in educational organizations is the curriculum. Sometimes curriculum is perceived as little more than syllabuses, more often it is perceived as the whole teaching-learning activity that makes a school a school and a college a college.

Because educational institutions tend to consolidate and conserve whatever practices have grown up around curriculum, changes tend to occur as lurches and sudden bursts of energy between long periods of quiescence. Yet in the last twenty years, there have been many attempts to change curriculum, a number of great movements of educational innovation. The nature of such changes must be understood by educational managers and consultants though it is only in recent years that a questioning of previous optimism has come about.

In his chapter, Michael Fullan describes the matter of the implementation of educational change and indicates how much further we have to go if we are to help people in educational institutions to deal with effective innovation, so that there is a true institutional dynamism rather than a cosmetic change in appearances.

and associated problems is not as straightforward as it seems at first glance. In fact, one of the basic reasons why so many innovations have failed is that implementation tasks have been underestimated and misunderstood. Implementation is *changing practice* (with the emphasis on actual rather than assumed use). More fully, implementation is the process of altering existing practice in order to achieve more effectively certain desired learning outcomes for students. The terms innovation, change, and revision are all frequently used in the context of describing implementation. Change is the generic term with innovation usually referring to a more radical or thorough change than does revision. In either case, implementation is involved when a person or group of people attempt to use a new or revised program for the first time.

What does 'changing practice' mean? In examining any proposed curriculum or policy document the initial implementation question is, 'What aspects of current practice would change if this document were to be used effectively?'. The complexity of implementation begins to surface in that there appear to be at least three aspects or dimensions of change involved. Implementation is multi-dimensional. To take a curriculum guideline or document as an illustration, we can immediately discern that at least the following three kinds of changes are at stake – possible use of new or revised *materials*; possible use of new *teaching approaches* (e.g., teaching strategies), and the possible incorporation of new or revised *beliefs* (e.g., philosophical assumptions and beliefs underlying the particular approach). All three aspects of change are hypothetically directed at achieving more effectively some new or existing educational goal (see also Leithwood, in press).

Virtually every curriculum change states or implies the three aspects of change whether we refer to language arts, geography, history, science, special education, etc. Thus, for each of these programs there may be a set of materials (guidelines, textbooks, local curriculum documents, audio-visuals) which, if used in the classroom, represent one indicator that implementation is taking place. But these same curricula also contain implications for what teachers and others might do differently; those skills and actions which would engage a teacher if he or she were putting the curriculum into practice. Teaching students listening skills, problem-solving skills or an understanding of Canada and its peoples, for example, involve the use of certain pedagogical approaches, methods of diagnosing student learning, planning, and evaluation which, if not carried out by the teacher, result in failure to achieve desired objectives for students. I am not suggesting that curriculum documents do a good job of identifying and presenting ideas for teaching strategies, only that teaching behaviour is a fundamental component of change which must go along with replacement or revision of materials.

Finally, curricula are based on certain assumptions, philosophies, or beliefs about education. These beliefs are often critical to effective implementation (because they shape the teacher's thinking and subsequent actions). They are also extremely difficult to change. To take a simple example, the teacher who believes (whether or not explicitly recognizing it) that acquisition of facts and individual student memory work is basic, will think and behave much differently from the teacher who believes that students should be exploring knowledge, formulating and testing ideas, and interacting with fellow students. Implementation of a new curriculum, therefore, may necessitate changes or adjustments in the belief system of teachers as they work through it (see Werner, 1980). In summary, an innovation or a revised program consists of potential alterations in materials, approaches and beliefs. Implementation refers to whether or not these alterations occur in practice.

Given at least the three dimensions within which curricular change may occur (materials, teaching approach, and beliefs), it is clear that any individual may implement none, one or two, or all three dimensions. A teacher could use new curriculum materials in the classroom without using related teaching strategies (e.g., teaching inquiry oriented materials in a lecture oriented format). Or a teacher could use at least some of the teaching strategies and materials without coming to grips with the underlying beliefs. We should also make it clear that we are making no assumptions at this stage about who decides on or formulates the beliefs or other aspects of what should change. Teachers for example, can participate fully in defining beliefs and teaching approaches. This depends on the process (Section II) but, whatever the process, one of the main aspects of implementation consists of beliefs.

The three dimensions have also been presented in increasing order of complexity for implementation. Materials, most visible and tangible of the three, are the easiest to produce and to use literally. Alterations in teaching approach or style present greater difficulty when significant new skills must be acquired or additional time to plan must be found. Changes in beliefs are yet more difficult to bring about: they challenge the core values held by a person regarding the fundamental purposes of education and they are often not explicit or recognized, but rather buried at the level of unconscious assumptions. The relationship between behavioural change (e.g., teaching approach) and changes in beliefs is complicated. Logically one might think of beliefs changing first which, in turn, lead to new behaviour associated with the belief. Practically, however, there is considerable socio-psychological evidence to support the view that beliefs are learned through experience (see Elliott, 1978, McLaughlin and Marsh, 1978). Perhaps it is sufficient for our purposes to recognize that the relationship between beliefs and behaviour is reciprocal – trying new practices sometimes leads to questioning one's underlying beliefs; examining one's beliefs can lead to attempting new behaviour.

Why worry about all three aspects of change? Why not be satisfied to produce better curriculum materials and encourage their use in classrooms. The answer is simply that such a limited change would be unlikely to result in the kind or amount of student learning usually aspired to by a curriculum program or policy change. Curriculum materials alone focus the student on particular types of content. The teacher's behaviour shapes the learning experiences of students as they confront that content. And the teacher's belief system provides a set of criteria or a screen for sifting valuable from not so valuable learning opportunities that inevitably arise spontaneously during instruction.

What implementation is, can now be restated. *Implementation consists of alterations from existing practice to some new or revised practice (potentially involving materials, teaching, and beliefs) in order to achieve certain desired student learning outcomes.* The logic of implementation is depicted in Figure 1.

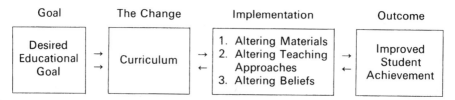

Figure 1. *The Logic of Implementation*

There are three main observations to be made about Figure 1. First, implementation is the hypothesized means of accomplishing improved student achievement. If implementation does not occur or only partially occurs (as when materials change but teaching approach does not), it is, of course, unlikely that the desired outcome will be achieved.

Second, the implementation process represented in the figure is not necessarily linear. The two-way arrows denote that curriculum change frequently gets defined or redefined in practice. This point is extremely important because it relates to the complicated question of what the role of the classroom teacher is in implementation. There is widespread agreement that the teacher has a role in defining and adapting curriculum. In fact, some researchers such as Connelly caution that the very use of the concept 'implementation' tends to cast teachers in the role of adapters rather than full partners (see Connelly and Elbaz, 1980, and Connelly and Ben-Peretz, 1980 and Roberts, 1980). For my part, I use the term 'altered practice' to mean that it could occur *either* through minor adaptations by teachers *or* through significant individual teacher development in working with new curricular ideas or programs. I stress this issue because there is a tendency to read Figure 1 from left to right, while not giving equal weight to the possibility that the reverse process occurs and may be equally important in bringing about improved practice. It is useful to keep in mind the two-way nature of implementation as I describe in the next section the factors that affect whether or not altered practice comes about. [As I take up in Section II, there are at least two different research perspectives on implementation. One is called the 'fidelity' or 'programmed' approach in which researchers attempt to assess the degree of implementation in terms of the extent to which actual use corresponds to the developer's intentions; the other is called the 'adaptive' or 'mutual adaptation' approach in which the researcher attempts to identify the interaction of the innovation and the setting in order to determine how they influence or alter each other (see Fullan and Pomfret, 1977; and Berman, 1980).]

The third point I would make about Figure 1 is that it is not always possible to measure or prove that a certain student learning outcome has been achieved, especially if it involves some of the more complex cognitive (e.g., decision-making skills) or affective (e.g., valuing Canada's multi-culturalism) educational objectives. Whether or not, and how, to measure student achievement raises some difficult philosophical and practical questions which I cannot adequately explore in this article. Some educators would be content to establish specific new activities and experiences, that is, to alter practice and to presuppose that learning outcomes will be accomplished without actually measuring them. On the other hand, assessing achievement levels can raise important questions about what program improvements and altered practices may be needed.

In concluding this section, I should like to mention that the ideas of implementation also apply to broader program or policy changes as well as to curriculum revision. For example, special education legislation is one of the more complex educational reforms on the current educational scene, and as such it highlights the dimensions of implementation – the need for new or revised specialized curriculum materials, alterations in teaching practices of special education teachers and of regular classroom teachers, changes in the relationship between regular classroom teachers and special education teachers, an examination of beliefs about the education of children with special characteristics, and a whole host of assessment and decision-making procedures involving parents, teachers, and administrators (for one description of the implementation of special education reform, see Weatherley, 1979).

As we turn to identify and discuss those factors which affect whether or not implementation happens, I might anticipate the overall problem by saying that most efforts at curriculum and policy change have concentrated on curriculum development and on 'paper' changes. Put more forcefully, the implementation process has frequently overlooked people (behaviour, beliefs, skills) in favour of things (e.g., regulations, materials) and this is essentially why it fails more times than not. While people are much more difficult to deal with than things, they are also much more necessary for success.

II. What Factors Affect Success or Failure

Now that we have some idea of what is involved in changing practice, we can ask, 'Why are some proposals for change implemented and others not? Why do some curricula receive effective implementation in some classrooms, schools, and districts, and fail to be implemented in others?'. While more research is needed to unravel the complexity of the implementation process, existing evidence consistently emphasizes twelve factors as especially critical to changing practice (see Table 1). In addition to these twelve factors we could discuss other possible causes pertaining to personality (e.g., dogmatic resistance to change) or demographic characteristics (e.g., age), but I do not see this as fruitful. These factors cannot easily be altered. Moreover, much of what appears to be resistance may be a result of lack of planning, inadequate incentives and resource support for implementation, and thus not intrinsic to individual personalities, although the latter certainly can make a difference.

Table 1. *Factors Affecting Implementation*

A. *Characteristics of the Innovation or Revision*
   1. Need for the change
   2. Clarity, complexity of the change
   3. The quality and availability of materials
B. *Characteristics at the Local Education Authority (LEA) Level*
   4. History of innovative attempts
   5. Expectations and Training for Principals
   6. Teacher input and Technical Assistance for Teachers (in-service, etc.)
   7. Board and Community Support
   8. Time line and Monitoring
   9. Overload
C. *Characteristics at the School Level*
   10. The Principals' actions
   11. Teacher/Teacher relations and actions
D. *Factors External to the School System*
   12. Role of the Government Departments of Education, and other Educational Agencies

A close examination of the factors listed in Table 1 leads to the conclusion that they operate in a dynamic fashion as a *process* over time, and that they form a *system of variables which interact*. If any one, two, or three factors are working against implementation, the process will be less effective. Put positively, the more factors supporting implementation, the more effective it will be. In the next several pages I discuss how these twelve factors operate to influence implementation. The purpose of this description is to explain what causes practice to change.

A. *Characteristics of the Innovation or Revision*

The first three factors influencing implementation are related to the nature of the change itself. Teachers, for example, frequently do not see the need for a change that is being advocated, are not clear about what they ought to do differently in their classroom, and find the materials inadequately developed, impractical, or unavailable. These three factors – need, clarity/complexity, and quality and availability of materials – affect the likelihood that implementation will occur (see Gross *et al*, 1971, Charters and Pellegrin, 1973, and Ponder and Doyle, 1977–78).

In regard to need, any given change may not be needed or valued in some situations. Even when there is a potential need, as when teachers want to improve some area of the curriculum, the change may be presented in such a way that it is not an obvious solution. Or the change may not be sufficiently well-developed to be 'implementable'. Whatever the case, we do know that lack of clarity about what teachers would actually do when implementing a curriculum or policy change frequently discourages them from using new curricula. The more complex and unclear the change appears, the more likely it will be avoided (see Robinson, 1980).

Materials that are vague or not practical to use, contribute to this complexity and lack of clarity. But it is possible to have 'false clarity' in which the change is interpreted in an oversimplified way (in other words, the proposed change has more to it than people perceive or realize). For example, an approved textbook may easily become *the* curriculum in the classroom, yet fail to incorporate significant features of the curriculum guideline on which it is based. Such reliance on the textbook may detract attention from behaviours and underlying beliefs critical to the achievement of desired student outcomes. The dismissal of proposed curriculum change on the grounds that 'we are already doing that', provides a somewhat different illustration of the same problem. Frequently, this assertion refers only to content aspects of a curriculum, ignoring suggestions for change in teaching approaches and beliefs. [On the problems of false clarity and superficial change, see Goodlad and Klein, 1970, Bussis *et al*, 1976, and Berman and McLaughlin, 1979).]

In summary, the need for change, the lack of a clear, practical picture of the discrepancy between current practice and what is proposed, and the development or acquisition of quality materials constitute one major set of barriers to implementation. The solution is frequently not to present ready-made, highly specific curricula, but to set up a process through which the need for change and its implications for concrete action can be developed with a group of people over time. As with other aspects of change, clarification should be seen as a process with people, not something that can be achieved on paper at the development stage.

B. *Characteristics of the LEA*

Implementation of the same curriculum is often relatively successful in one school system, and relatively fruitless and discouraging in another. What factors are operating differently across these systems that account for this? A substantial amount of evidence (both large scale studies and case studies of successful and unsuccessful school systems) points toward six such factors or variables as indicated in category B, Table 1 (see Berman and McLaughlin, 1977, Emrick and Peterson, 1978, Fullan and Pomfret, 1977 and Yin *et al*, 1977). The first variable concerns previous experience – the history of innovative attempts in the system (Sarason, 1971, ch. 13). The more that previous attempts at change have been painful and unrewarding, the more skeptical people will be about the next change that comes along. This variable operates relatively independently of the innovation, because it stems from a general belief people have acquired through experience; the belief that subsequent changes will follow the same ineffective pattern as previous ones. We might wish that this belief did not exist, but it does for many people because of their experiences over the last fifteen years. This factor helps explain why so many people initially view proposals for change in a highly skeptical light.

The effects of the next five factors depend substantially on the quality of the school district or Local Educational Authority plan guiding the implementation process. Many LEAs do not have a well worked out plan at all; others have plans which omit or underestimate key elements. Implementation has worked more effectively when LEAs have explicitly planned for factors 5 through 9 in Table 1. [The reader should be reminded that the specific formulations are based on research evidence in North American settings.] Specifically, the chances of changing practice are enhanced when LEAs: 1. have had clear expectations and provided training and follow-up that permits and encourages *principals* to take responsibility for facilitating implementation in their schools (Fullan, 1980); 2. have set up a system for obtaining *teacher input* about the need for a given change and have provided technical assistance on a continuous basis during implementation (technical assistance includes provision of good materials and resources, in-service training, and some opportunity for one to one assistance) – teacher input means that teachers are giving and receiving help and helping to define the change in practice (Berman and McLaughlin, 1977); 3. have obtained *parent and board support* for the direction of change, including the willingness of boards to allocate budget for implementation activities (some boards allocate substantial money to in-service education and other resources for principals and teachers, while others allow only minimal amounts); 4. recognize implementation as a process which takes some *time*, and which requires a *monitoring or information system* during the implementation period – an implementation plan should permit work associated with a new guideline to take place over a period of time (two, three or more years) and should incorporate an information gathering system which can be used by teachers and administrators to address implementation problems; and 5. take some steps to address the *overload* problem which occurs when teachers are attempting to implement several curricula simultaneously – effective LEA plans include the determination of priorities and their sequencing over time (this does not eliminate the overload problem, but it makes it more manageable).

It takes considerable planning skill to influence the record of innovative experiences and the other five school system factors just mentioned. Obviously, the role of the chief LEA administrator is crucial. Effective implementation is much more likely when he or she works with system and school staff to put together a comprehensive, broadly endorsed and understood plan for implementation than when implementation is left to the chance of curriculum products, written directions, one-shot workshops, and infrequent meetings.

C. *Characteristics of the School*

What happens at the school level finally determines whether implementation occurs effectively. The actions of the principal and teacher interaction are the two key factors. There is very strong evidence in North America that principals who play a direct *active* role in leading the process of change influence the extent of implementation much more so than principals who carry out more of an administrative role leaving implementation to the individual teacher or department (see Fullan, 1980 for a review of the evidence). We need more detailed descriptions of what constitutes effective principal behaviour. The evidence we do have suggests that principals who provide leadership for change at the school level are not necessarily experts in the content of the curriculum. Rather, their leadership is in curriculum planning and implementation – becoming familiar with the general nature of what a guideline implies for a program, and working with staff to set up and carry out a plan for change at the school level. Of course, if the LEA administration expects and helps principals in this role, it is much more likely to happen. If the system does not do this, the influence of the principal will depend on the individual interests and skills of principals – some will become involved and others will not. Involved or not, the principal has a major impact on change.

Teachers also vary in their interest in working on a new curriculum. In those school situations where, for whatever reasons, teachers interact with each other on some ongoing basis, implementation is much more likely (Berman and McLaughlin, 1979, Rosenblum and Louis, 1979, and Miles *et al*, 1978). When teachers in a school have, or create, the opportunity to assist each other in addressing and attempting to resolve the many issues raised in the implementation of a significant change in the classroom, change in practice will more likely occur. Implementation, as I have said, involves the development of new teaching approaches and examination of underlying beliefs. Teachers as a group in a school are likely to have the collective ability to help one another acquire many of the skills and understandings associated with a change. Teachers' colleagues are a preferred source of knowledge and skill. One of the greatest obstacles to effective implementation is that teachers do not have the time to interact with each other about their work, and changes therein. Again, the LEA and the school through the principal can help create the conditions for teachers to interact with other teachers in the division, with the department head, the principal, and with system consultants and other resources external to the school. While pre-implementation orientation sessions are necessary and useful for certain purposes, it is *during* attempts at implementation that most specific issues arise and must be addressed. In brief, effective implementation requires some ongoing, systematic face-to-face *small scale interaction* among teachers and between teachers and others.

D. Factors External to School System[+]

While a number of societal forces affect educational change, government departments of education at the regional and national levels represent the main vehicle through which specific policies and programs are proposed. What changes are presented, and how the government does this, have a major impact on the likelihood of success. Implementation has received varied and inconsistent attention by government agencies over the past fifteen years during which time our knowledge of implementation was only gradually emerging. As a result, many new programs were produced for implementation in too short a time, with little support provided. Many of these changes were not implemented adequately. There will always be problems arising from the fact that government proposals for change reflect a political reality; an expectation from 'society' that policy changes get implemented fully and in short order. Variations in how many changes are proposed at one time, how rapidly they are expected to be implemented, how clearly the need for change and the nature of the change are developed and specified in comparison to current practice, how carefully the orientation is carried out, and how supportive the government is in providing guidelines and resources for implementation all affect the chances of success.

III. Principles and People in Implementation

Principles

The previous two subsections have said, in effect, that implementation or change in practice is not a thing, a set of materials, an announcement, or a delivery date; rather, *it is a process of learning and resocialization over a period of time involving people and relations among people in order to alter practice*. Socialization requires interaction and support, especially among peers and between peers and others close to their situation. Change in practice may also be thought of as a process of learning in which adults are the main learners; all the main principles derived from knowledge about socialization or learning theories apply.

In reflecting on principles of change one should recognize that the three aspects of implementation (materials, teaching approach, and beliefs), and the twelve factors affecting implementation interact in any given LEA as a *system* of variables. Although I will not attempt to present additional research evidence for the following ten principles, I present them in order to make more explicit what seems to be the underlying thinking or assumptions behind current implementation research:

[+] This section represents only a general treatment of the role of government agencies, because I have been more interested, in this article, in examining change in practice at the local level. For those interested in the increasingly sophisticated treatment of the role of government agencies in implementation, please see Elmore, 1980, Bardach, 1979 and Berman and McLaughlin, 1978a and b).

1. *Implementation is a process not an event.* It is self-defeating to think of implementation as completing one task or event, forgetting about it and proceeding to the next one. Implementation occurs gradually or incrementally over time – usually two or more years for most significant innovations, during which time all twelve factors must be *continuously* addressed.

2. *The innovation will get adapted*, further developed and modified during use – this may be either a good or bad thing depending on the adaptation and the solution, but it will happen. Adaptation can be a good thing if it improves the fit of the innovation to the situation, or if it results in further development, specification or other improvements in the innovation.

3. *Implementation is a process of professional development and growth.* It is at once a highly personal and a social experience. It is personal because it is the individual who finally makes change (in practice and thinking). It is social because effective personal change occurs in the context of a socialization process.

4. *Implementation is a process of clarification* whereby individuals and groups come to understand and use a change involving new materials, behaviour, and thinking.

5. Because implementation is a socialization and clarification process it follows that *interaction and technical assistance are essential.* Regular opportunities for professional interaction, mutual help and external assistance are required.

6. There are many practical obstacles to implementation which occur naturally. *Planning at the school and at the system level is a necessity if obstacles are to be addressed.* Systematically identified strategies have a noticeable effect in overcoming obstacles.

7. *The LEA and school plans to guide action must incorporate several features*: (a) they must be based on and be true to the principles listed here; (b) they must systematically address the three implementation outcomes (materials, teaching approaches, and thinking) and the twelve factors which affect implementation by employing coordinated strategies; and (c) they must monitor and otherwise gather information during the process which is used to assess progress and to address problems which are encountered. There is no one best plan, but all plans should include the above features.

8. *Developing and using a plan is itself an implementation problem.* As with any innovation it cannot be laid on. People must learn to use it, modify it, etc. over a period of time.

9. *One hundred percent implementation is probably not desirable, and in any case is impossible.* An effective plan is one in which the implementation process and outcomes are better for more people than they would be if it were done another way or left to chance. Another version of this is that the new plan brings about more improvements than the previous plan. Thus, effectiveness of a plan can be measured in terms of the progress that has been made compared to previous approaches, not in terms of whether it solves all the problems – the latter will never occur.

10. *The ultimate goal of implementation is not to implement X or Y particular innovation, but to develop the 'capacity' for LEAs, schools, and individuals to process all innovations and revisions.* The goal is to have this implementation capacity built into the LEA as a normal, regular procedure. Implementation of any specific innovation will probably get easier as this basic capacity gets established.

People

The one common factor underlying effective principles and plans is the recognition that the success of change is dependent solely on what people do and are prepared to do. It is necessary to consider the role of some of the main participants at the school and LEA level, although in the short space available it is not possible to provide more than a good glimpse of the main issues. *Teachers* are legitimately preoccupied with coping with the everyday demands of classroom and school life. Discipline, extra-curricular duties, meetings, marking tests, planning the next day or next week's lesson, covering the curriculum can easily take all the teacher's energy. There is little normal time and opportunity for reflection and serious interaction with fellow teachers on instructional matters. Moreover, norms promoting individualism and non-interference with fellow teachers have reinforced the likelihood that teachers will grapple with their professional instructional concerns pretty much alone (or at best with one close colleague). There are some exceptions to this (particularly if the principal and staff have set out to do it differently) but, by and large, teachers do not carry out regular, ongoing discussion with fellow teachers about curricular matters (see House, 1974, Sarason, 1971).

Adding new demands (i.e., implementing a new curriculum) creates further problems. We need more practical research about what teachers consider or ask themselves when they examine a proposed change. There is some evidence that they ask at least two questions: 'Will it benefit the students (including whether it is procedurally clear and practical)?' and 'What are the costs in terms of my time, energy, and anxiety in learning to use it?'. Teachers usually choose not to change when the answers to these two questions are not positive – a very rational choice (what Ponder and Doyle (1977–78) call 'the practicality ethic of teachers'). A teacher who is preoccupied with the demands involved in maintaining the existing program, cannot be expected to change readily when the change does not seem needed, is unclear or unrealistic in timeline or resource support, is not understood by the principal, may seem politically motivated, and is likely to be reversed or altered in the near future based on new political pressures.

Implementation will occur to the extent that *each and every teacher* has the opportunity to work out the meaning of implementation in practice. Involving teachers on curriculum development committees is helpful, but not sufficient. Once the curriculum is produced, it is just as new or foreign to those teachers who have not been involved (the majority of teachers) as when it comes from any external source. Because every teacher cannot participate in development, it is essential that the implementation process permit and encourage involvement of every teacher. The teacher is a professional who should be learning from fellow teachers and external resource people as well as contributing to learning by his or her peers. The process should allow adaptation, further development and specification of any new or revised curriculum by teachers as individuals and groups.

In sum, the very substantial demands faced by teachers, their perspective on those demands, and an opportunity to discuss and address the needs and meaning of practices new or revised, must be recognized in any effective plan.

Principals are also faced with pressure to keep up with the daily demands of their work, demands which have become greater in range over the past twenty years (see Fullan, 1980). One of the many new responsibilities added to their role is the expectation (written in role descriptions) that the principal should be a leader or facilitator of implementing curriculum guidelines. There seem to be three basic problems in doing this. First, there is not enough time. It is quite easy to spend all of one's time handling conflicts, administrative matters, and going to meetings. Second, some school systems do not *really* expect or help their principals to be agents of change, but rather to be administrative managers who keep things running smoothly. Third, it is not at all clear what principals should do to be effective leaders of change. Generalities that the principal is the gatekeeper of change or the instructional leader do not provide any practical clarity about what to do. Moreover, principals normally do not receive pre- or in-service training for their roles as curricular change leaders (although some in-service programs have now been developed).

The principal's problems are compounded by the multiplicity of curriculum changes being introduced. It was noted above that some of these proposed changes will not meet a high priority need from the teachers' point of view, will not be clear, and will be introduced in a way which does not provide resources to support implementation. In short, many principals find themselves in an overloaded and ambiguous situation. If the LEA administration keeps its own house in order and provides training opportunities to help principals in their roles as curriculum facilitators, problems for the principals can be greatly reduced. The principal is facing not only many new program

changes, but also changes in his or her role, namely, to provide more effective assistance in guideline implementation. This involves planning at the school level to address and manage the factors associated with change. The principal is the critical person for better or worse, when it comes to school planning.
Trustees, Parents, Students. Very little research is available on the views of trustees, parents and student groups about curricular change. Evidence that does exist indicates that board and individual parent support is essential for effective implementation. School boards which are relatively successful in bringing about curricular implementation also have established good relationships between the community and the Board. These latter groups are not necessarily actively involved in implementation, but the successful board maintains a good information flow about new programs. It is possible for some implementation to occur without the community (e.g., when the community is content to leave everything to the professional educators). However, implementation benefits from the more active knowledge and support of parents. The community and board can force adoption of a new policy or program, but not change in actual practice if they are not willing to listen to teachers, and to provide support for a process of implementation that will allow for further modification or development of new ideas.

The little that is known of relevance about these three groups can be summarized as follows: the board needs to receive enough program information in order to know what new activities are going on and to make judgements on the goals of change. It is particularly important that the board become more sensitive to the requirements of implementation so that they will support (financially and otherwise) the training and resource needs during that period. Individual parents often experience great difficulty in understanding the purpose, meaning, and quality of new programs. One can surmise (and there are a few studies which confirm it) that the more knowledgeable and involved parents become, the more effective implementation is likely to be (see Armour, 1976). As for students, they are almost always thought of as passive recipients of change in terms of achievement, job market, etc. It is worth reflecting on the possibility of treating students as *participants* when it comes to implementing new programs. What would happen if a teacher spoke to students in his or her classroom about the purpose and meaning of new activities, especially if that involved a new role (e.g., problem solving, independent study) for students? We do not have a firm basis for answering this question, but it is worth exploring.
The LEA administration is the last group to be considered. They are referred to as a group consisting of the director, superintendent, area or zone superintendents, coordinators, and consultants. This group receives many conflicting demands from a variety of sources including the government, the trustees, parents, principals, teachers and teachers groups. What administrators can do about these demands is not the subject of this paper (see Fullan and Leithwood, 1980). Suffice it to say here that there are large variations among LEA administrations in the effectiveness with which they consider,

select, and implement program change. The way in which they do this can make a great difference in the realities of change of all other district staff.

IV. Reflections on Implementation Research

There are two broad implications which I would like to consider: one concerns the notion of implementation outcomes or success, the other relates to problems on how to do implementation research given the fidelity vs variation possibilities.

What is implementation success in terms of outcomes? Hypothetically, implementation is the *means* to attaining a desirable educational goal. One of the most serious problems in research on innovations is that the extent of implementation is frequently not examined (see Charters and Jones, 1973). However, one of the larger questions is whether more thorough implementation is always a good thing. Clearly it is not. Figure 2 depicts four logical possible implementation outcomes.

		Implementation Yes	No
Need for and/or Quality of the Innovation	HIGH	A	B
	LOW	C	D

Figure 2. Implementation Outcomes

Implementation 'success' can be seen as outcomes A and D, while situations B and C can be thought of as 'failures'. Thus, non-implementation (rejection) of a bad or unwanted idea (case D) gives school systems protection against questionnable program decisions. On the other hand, non-implementation of a needed policy (case B) represents a major problem. Of course, it is not very easy to gain consensus on whether an innovation is needed and possesses quality, but the heuristic idea of conceptualizing outcomes as in Figure 2 seems to be a necessary perspective.

The second major problematic area concerns the uniformity versus variation dilemma. If innovations get adapted (vary), and should be adapted as they are used in a variety of situations, how can one assess implementation? This is a complicated research question, but the general response is that it is possible to approach implementation in a programmatic way or in a more open-ended manner. The methodological issues are too detailed to discuss in this paper, but need to be considered carefully in designing any implementation research (see Berman, 1980, Fullan, forthcoming, Murphy, 1980, Shipman, 1974, and Elmore, 1980).

Problems in implementing many policies and programs may be less those of dogmatic resistance to change (although there is no doubt some of that) and more those of the difficulties related to planning and coordinating a multilevel social process involving hundreds of people. It is up to research on implementation to identify, unravel and in general to enlighten what is happening, and with what results, as new or revised policies and programs are developed and tried.

References

ARMOUR, D. (1976) *Analysis of School Preferred Reading Programs in Selected Minority Schools*, Santa Monica, California, Rand Corporation.
BARDACH, E. (1979) *The Implementation Game: What Happens After a Bill Becomes a Law*, Cambridge, Mass, MIT Press.
BERMAN, P. (1980) 'Thinking about implementation design: Matching strategies to situations', in MANN, D. and INGRAM, H. (Eds.), *Why Policies Succeed and Fail*, Berkeley, California, Sage Publications.
BERMAN, P. and MCLAUGHLIN, M. (1977) *Federal Programs Supporting Educational Change, Vol. VII: Factors Affecting Implementation and Continuation*, U.S. Office of Education, Dept. of Health, Education and Welfare.
BERMAN, P. and MCLAUGHLIN, M. (1978a) *Federal Programs Supporting Educational Change, Vol. VIII: Implementing and Sustaining Innovations*, U.S. Office of Education, Dept. of Health, Education and Welfare.
BERMAN, P. and MCLAUGHLIN, M. (1978b) 'Federal support for improved educational practice', in TIMPANE, M. (Ed.), *The Federal Interest in Financing Schooling*, Cambridge, Mass., Ballinger Publishing Company.
BERMAN, P. and MCLAUGHLIN, M. (1979) *An Exploratory Study of School District Adaptation*, National Institute of Education.
BUSSIS, A.M., CHITTENDEN, E.A. and AMAREL, M. (1976) *Beyond Surface Curriculum*, Boulder, Colorado, Westview Press.
CHARTERS, W.W. and JONES, J. (1973) 'On the risk of appraising non-events in program evaluation', *Educational Researcher*, 2(11).
CHARTERS, W.W. and PELLEGRIN, R. (1973) 'Barriers to the innovation process: Four case studies of differentiated staffing', *Educational Administrative Quarterly*, 9, pp. 3–14.
CONNELLY, F.M. and BEN-PERETZ, M. (1980) 'Teachers' roles in the using and doing of research and curriculum development', *Journal of Curriculum Studies*, 12(2): 95–103.
CONNELLY, M.F. and ELBAZ, F. (1980) 'Conceptual bases for curriculum thought: A teacher's perspective', in FOSHAY, A. (Ed.), *1980 Yearbook, Association for Supervision and Curriculum Development*, Alexandria, Virginia, Association for Supervision and Curriculum Development, pp. 95–119.
ELLIOTT, J. (1978) 'How do teachers learn?', Cambridge Institute of Education, prepared for OECD.
ELMORE, R. (1980) *Complexity and Control: What Legislators and Administrators Can Do About Implementing Public Policy*, National Institute of Education, Washington, D.C.
EMRICK, J.A. and PETERSON, S. (1978) *A Synthesis of Findings Across Five Recent Studies in Educational Dissemination and Change*, San Francisco, California, Far West Laboratory.
FULLAN, M. (1980) 'The role of human agents internal to the school districts in

knowledge utilization', in LEHMING, R. (Ed.), *Improving Schools: What Do We Know*, Berkeley, California, Sage Publications.

FULLAN, M. (in press) 'The relationship between evaluation and implementation in curriculum', forthcoming chapter in LEWY, A. (Ed.), *Evaluation Roles*, United Kingdom, Gordon Breach Publications.

FULLAN, M. and LEITHWOOD, K. (1980) *Guidelines for Planning and Evaluating Program Implementation*, prepared for Ministry of Education, British Columbia.

FULLAN, M. and POMFRET, A. (1977) 'Research on curriculum and instruction implementation', *Review of Educational Research*, 47(1): 335–397.

GOODLAD, J.I., KLEIN, M.F. and Associates (1970) *Behind the Classroom Door*, Worthington, Ohio, Charles A. Jones Publishing Company.

GROSS, N., GIACQUINTA, J. and BERNSTEIN, M. (1971) *Implementing Organizational Innovations*, New York, Basic Books.

HOUSE, E. (1974) *The Politics of Educational Innovation*, Berkeley, California, McCutchan.

LEITHWOOD, K. (in press) 'Dimensions of curriculum innovation', *Journal of Curriculum Studies*.

MCLAUGHLIN, M.W. and MARSH, D. (1978) 'Staff development and school change', *Teachers College Record*, 70(1).

MILES, M.B., SIEBER, S., WILDER, D. and GOLD, B. (1978) *Final Report, Part IV: Conclusions – Reflections on the Case Studies and Implications*, New York: Project on Social Architecture in Education, Center for Policy Research.

MURPHY, J. (1980) *Getting the Facts*, Santa Monica, California, Goodyear Publishing.

PONDER, G. and DOYLE, W. (1977–78) 'The practicality ethic in teacher decision-making', *Interchange*, 8, pp. 1–13.

ROBERTS, D. (1980) 'Theory, curriculum development and the unique events of practice', in MUNBY, H., ORPWOOD, G. and RUSSELL, T. (Eds.), *Seeing Curriculum in a New Light: Essays from Science Education*, Toronto, OISE Press.

ROBINSON, F. (1980) 'Superordinate curriculum guidelines as guides to local curriculum decision-making: An Ontario case study', in LEITHWOOD, K. (Ed.), *Studies in Curriculum Decision-making*, Toronto, OISE Press.

ROSENBLUM, S. and LOUIS, K.S. (1979) *Stability and Change: Innovation in an Educational Context*, Cambridge, Mass., Abt Associates.

SARASON, SEYMOUR (1971) *The Culture of the School and the Problem of Change*, Boston, Allyn and Bacon, Inc.

SHIPMAN, M.D. (1974) *Inside a Curriculum Project*, London, Methuen.

WEATHERLEY, R. (1979) *Reforming Special Education: Policy Implementation from State Level to Street Level*, Massachusetts, MIT Press.

WERNER, W. (1980) 'Implementation as belief', Faculty of Education, University of British Columbia.

WILLIAMS, W. (1980) *The Implementation Perspective: A Guide for Managing Social Service Delivery Programs*, University of Berkeley, California, University of California Press.

YIN, R., HEALD, K. and VOGEL, M. (1977) *Tinkering With the System*, Lexington, Mass., Lexington Books.

Problems of Institutional Management in a Period of Contraction

Tom Bone
Jordanhill College of Education

The management of educational institutions in a time of contraction, along with the tensions which accompany this, is a subject which has attracted a good deal of attention in recent years (e.g. Morris, 1980) and may expect to be of continuing interest throughout much of the 1980s because of the falling rolls which will be affecting first schools and then colleges and universities throughout that period. This chapter is written from the perspective of the head of an institution of higher education in the United Kingdom, and is based partly on personal experience within that institution, and partly on more general experience derived from membership of the Education Committee of the Council for National Academic Awards, which has given the author the opportunity to become acquainted with institutional problems in many other parts of Britain. An attempt has been made to relate that experience to some of the writing on the subject.

In a number of instances throughout the United Kingdom, although not

---

Editor's note: Tom Bone is a practising manager but one who is familiar with management ideas. He is interested in personal and interpersonal relationships and his human perspective is quite clear in his chapter on institutional decline. One of the most important ideas he works on is that management skills are not different in contraction and expansion but are essentially the same. The central problem of much management in education is that institutions were not managed well in benign times and that is why they are managed badly in bad times. Furthermore, management does not come naturally by virtue of the position but requires help and training.

The current period of educational organizational change shows up the quality of theory and practice. An enormous amount needs to be learned that many managers have never even dreamed of. Even in this book many ideas and approaches are still being developed though the directions of development are daily more clear. Many institutions fare much more badly than the one described in Bone's chapter and that is because under expansion leadership was often over-confident and arrogant. Starting with this chapter as a bench mark for progress, readers can return to examine the theories put forward in the book and their relevance – hopefully, they will prove more useful than some of the current myths about management and leadership.

in the author's own, the basic problem for management in the past year or two has been that of the survival of the institution as falling student numbers have brought its viability into question. Such a situation creates exceptional pressures both on an institution and within it and there are some effects which may be beneficial, like the sense of corporate unity which is engendered, but the position is so unusual and normally so brief in its duration that it has little to offer others not similarly placed. Likewise there have been particular management problems raised when two or more institutions have been forced to merge (Barker, 1976, Dearden, 1974, Rickett, 1974), but these are only of interest to persons affected by the same conditions. No attempt is therefore made to deal with them here.

A much more common position however, indeed one that is becoming almost the norm, is that in which an institution is able to survive but finds that its resources are contracting because of a decline in student numbers and income. Sometimes there is direct pressure for the reduction of staff. What happens then is that there has to be consideration given to the reduction in the number of academic and non-academic staff employed, and it is the group of problems associated with that reduction which is the first to be given some detailed treatment in this chapter.

Before any reduction in staffing actually takes place there is usually a period in which attempts are made to avoid this and, while there may typically be some people in the organization who simply hope that the problem will go away, there are possibilities for constructive planning at this stage which may be beneficial to the institution and to the community it serves as well as to the individuals whose jobs may be saved. In the author's experience there are three steps that may well be taken, two of which will probably be ineffective and one which may in fact be useful. The first step, which is perfectly natural but which will probably fail, is that both the management of the institution and the leaders of the staff unions will argue for some change in the basis for the calculation for staff entitlement so that the funding body will allow more staff to be employed for any given number of students. Often good arguments will be put forward for this, but the case should have been pressed at a time of more generous treatment, and it is likely that in times of financial stringency governments will not accept it. They are seeking to make cuts in public expenditure, and a reduction in student numbers seems to offer them a legitimate means of doing so (Bone, 1980).

The other technique, which will be even more certain of failure, is to avoid reducing staff by cutting expenditure in other ways – e.g. by making savings on equipment, the maintenance of buildings, departmental expenses, etc. This fails simply because it does not save enough, and because any savings that are made are likely to be totally offset by consequent necessary expenditure in future.

The one constructive step that may be taken at this stage, before staff is actually lost, is that attempts can be made to diversify the service provided, or to make use of staff in ways that have always been justified but which have not been happening in more comfortable times. In England and Wales the colleges of education were encouraged by the James Report (1972) and by the DES (1972 and 1973) to develop Dip.H.E. courses of a general kind, and did so in the mid 1970s with varying success (Lynch, 1979). The Scottish colleges of education were able between 1977 and 1980 to preserve the posts of 214 academic staff across the system by a major movement into school-focused in-service training of teachers, and in the author's own college further posts were saved by a significant expansion of externally funded research, as well as by the attraction of students from overseas countries whose governments were prepared to pay for special courses. All of these things required members of the staff to move into new forms of work, and made demands upon them which might not have been so readily accepted in another climate, but in the situation which existed at that time there was an energetic and enthusiastic response. A significant number of staff, for example, were willing to go away from their own homes for periods of as long as a year to acquire new qualifications and expertise.

Yet there are limits to the possibilities of diversification, and it is unlikely to do more than ease the problem. Any institution worthy to have been there in the first place will not have totally neglected all its opportunities for interesting work and, when it begins to widen its field of activity, it is likely quite quickly to encounter the sphere of influence of some other institution. In the United Kingdom the colleges of education, which have thus far suffered more than any others in respect of declining rolls, have often found that their attempts to diversify have brought them into conflict with the colleges of further education and the polytechnics, which in the 1960s and '70s had expanded their work to cover most of the areas in question. Indeed for the principals of many of the English colleges, caught between the conflicting demands of the Department of Education and Science and neighbouring universities or the CNAA, and with the psychological stresses arising from the attempt to keep as many options open as possible, the process of diversification proved a particularly exhausting one (Shaw, 1978).

Quite quickly there will come an acceptance of the need to reduce the numbers of staff, and there are three normal ways of doing this. The first is to make use of natural wastage by not filling the posts which become vacant as people die, retire and move away to other fields. This will be accepted by the staff in general, as doing least harm to any individual within the institution, but by itself it is inadequate and unsatisfactory as a method for dealing with the problem. It is inadequate because it is slow and because there are not enough people who leave at such a time (partly because promotion opportunities are becoming less available elsewhere), and it will only work in places where the decline in numbers is occurring very gradually, like some secondary schools. It is unsatisfactory because it is so unpredictable, and because it produces imbalances within the general pattern of staffing. Deaths and retirements tend to occur in a random way which may spread themselves evenly across an institution over a lengthy period, but which certainly do not do so in the short term, and promotions to posts elsewhere are more likely to be available to some kinds of staff than to others. For example those involved in such fields as physics and mathematics, if they are good, will continue to be mobile, but those who teach in such areas as art, music, drama, physical education, etc. are likely to be less so, while in recent years those who have taught history, geography, economics, etc. have had very few prospects at all. The result is that reliance upon natural wastage is likely to lead to too many staff in certain areas, and too few in others, and it is in the areas with most staff that there will probably be the greatest decline in student numbers. That certainly has been the case in teacher training. If this is allowed to continue without any check, it will be very damaging to morale within the staff in general.

There is, therefore, almost always a move to supplement natural wastage by a process of early retirement or voluntary redundancy, with both assisted by financial treatment more generous than the usual. Contrary to what might have been our expectation some years ago, this is not always inadequate, but experience suggests that it is still unsatisfactory. It is not always inadequate because a surprising number of members of staff are likely to opt for redundancy if the financial settlement is sufficiently generous, especially if the process is not rushed and there is time for those who are more cautious to wait to see how things turn out for their colleagues. It is not simply those who are approaching retirement who will choose to go, for experience shows that there are many, especially married women in their late forties and early fifties, who have been working partly for satisfaction but also partly for money and who will find the financial settlement more attractive than the prospect of continuing to work until they are sufficiently old to secure the normal pension. In the Scottish colleges of education nearly 400 staff, out of a total of around 1400, chose voluntary redundancy between 1978 and 1980 (under the Grant Aided Colleges (Compensation) (Scotland) Regulations of 1977).

Yet even if the voluntary process proves numerically adequate, it will be attended by serious disadvantages, especially for the management of the institution. Like natural wastage it will not affect all departments similarly and, if all volunteers were accepted, there would be both general imbalance and a loss of staff in fields where they could not readily be spared. The management will have to refuse some volunteers, and great care will have to be taken if this is not to antagonize the unions and staff in a damaging way. That point will be taken up in a later paragraph. Even if that problem is avoided, there is another aspect which will be just as serious. Inevitably the voluntary redundancy terms will attract some of the senior staff, including heads of department and key personnel, and it will be difficult for the management to replace these persons from within the institution without loss. Normally it will be possible, where good relationships exist, for the staff unions to be persuaded that a lecturer in mathematics can not be released because his department is not over-staffed but, if it is clear that the department of history is over-staffed and the head of that department seeks redundancy, it is too much to hope that the staff unions will accept that no one else within that department is fit to assume his position. Yet that could be the case. The result is that voluntary redundancy will produce too many internal promotions and the institution will suffer from this, as is indicated more fully in a later paragraph.

In this position there is another alternative, that of forced redundancy, and this is likely to be considered both by the funding body or government and by the management of the institution. It is frequently employed in industry and commerce, and there is no obvious reason why education should be exempt from it. If it is used it may have the merit of being quick, and it can be effective in tackling specific problems – e.g. cuts can be made where they are felt to be most necessary instead of being left to the random working of natural wastage or voluntary redundancy, and it may be possible for the institution to shed those persons who are regarded by management as being least effective, so that the staff is reduced to the desired level with the minimum damage to the college's work. The power of unions is so strong today, however, that it may be over-optimistic to count on this happening, and even when compulsory redundancy is employed it is possible that some formula may have to be agreed which will result in the candidates for redundancy being selected on criteria other than the effectiveness of their contribution. 'Last in, first out' may not always be insisted on, but it is a phrase which represents a typical union attitude, and it is simply not to be expected that unions will readily agree to any system which distinguishes among workers on the basis of such factors as energy, intelligence, or application to duties. Thus even compulsory redundancy may not result in the best solution from the point of view of management.

The main objection to compulsory redundancy, however, is concerned with its side-effects, which can not all be predicted and which usually are harmful to the institution. Redundancy of a forced kind is always accompanied by fear, suspicion and tension, and is very damaging to the morale of the staff. Perhaps if one quick cut was all that was necessary the fear and suspicion would not be long-lasting, and the tension would gradually evaporate, but even in industry staff reductions are rarely effected on a necessary scale at one blow and, in education, where student numbers tend to fall annually for a period, it is almost impossible that this could happen. Any prolonged period of fear and suspicion will be thoroughly damaging, and will result in the working behaviour of staff regressing to a kind which is entirely motivated by a need for security rather than by professional thinking. To take only one example, it will become very difficult to secure agreement to any changes in courses, regardless of how desirable these may be, since any member of staff who agrees to a lower teaching commitment will automatically have increased the likelihood of being selected for redundancy.

There is, therefore, no way of reducing staff which will not produce problems for management and in education what will happen in most cases is that there will be a dependence on a combination of natural wastage and voluntary redundancy, with an attempt being made to minimize the worse effects of the latter. If forced redundancy is employed, it will probably only be in specific and very limited areas. In the author's experience, however, based upon what he has seen in a number of colleges of education in the United Kingdom, the same basic methods of tackling the problem can produce very different results, depending upon the ways in which they are implemented. In his view there are certain management tools which are essential if the damage to the institution is not to be so great that it ceases to carry out its basic functions effectively.

The first of these tools is the employment of a regular and effective system of communication with the staff in general (Fielden and Lockwood, Chapter 7, 1973). What individual members of that staff find hardest to bear is uncertainty, and it is vital that they should be kept informed as accurately and as fully as possible of what is happening. It is the task of management to do this, and it is unwise to delegate something so important to any other group such as a union, which may view the matter from a different point of view. As is well known, over-communicators are ineffective communicators in that people cease to listen to what they are saying, but there are few who are uninterested in matters affecting themselves, and in a redundancy situation, it is a more serious mistake to communicate too little than too much. Naturally it is best if a variety of methods can be employed, and if the people doing it are personally good at it. Those in senior positions in education ought to be. What certainly must be avoided is the encouragement of any small clique of people who know what is going to happen before others do and who take pleasure in dropping hints of their knowledge.

If the management communicates regularly with the whole staff, it must also, however, have an effective system of consultation with the unions, and in a time of redundancy this will probably have to be quite formal. In the United Kingdom the law (Employment Protection Consolidation Act of 1978) actually requires consultation with the unions on this matter, but in countries where that is not the case it is nevertheless desirable. The author found it helpful that, in his own college some years before student rolls ever began to fall, he had taken the initiative in establishing a joint management/union committee, based upon a procedural agreement whereby all decisions affecting the conditions of service of staff collectively had to be the subject of consultation before they could be implemented. Over a period of several years this system had come to work fairly well, and a relationship of some trust had been built up, which was to be of great value in the period of most severe contraction.

As any study of communication will show, it is not enough for people to get together to talk about a problem; they must be able to talk about it in a common language. In discussion of redundancy it is essential also that there is an agreed system of calculating both the general entitlement of the institution to staff, and the particular entitlement of units within it. Often the first will exist before the need for contraction arises, having been instituted at some time by the funding body and, while it is inevitable that it will come to be criticized as inadequate once contraction begins to bite, it will nevertheless provide parameters for the internal negotiations. It is helpful if the formula is sufficiently simple to be readily understood by most people.

What is most difficult is to secure agreement to a means of calculating the entitlement of individual units within the institution. If management is fortunate this will have been agreed in days of expansion, but it is all too possible that it will never have been felt necessary to face the question, since additional staff could always be obtained where it was seen that they were required. Once contraction has been entered upon, members of departments will quickly see that any method of calculating entitlement, whatever it happens to be, will be dangerous to them as long as it works within the parameters laid down by the overall institutional complement. Inevitably it will show that some departments are over-staffed, and as long as there is fear of compulsory redundancy this will be tantamount to admitting that some of their close colleagues must go. Institutions of higher education are complex in their working, and it will not normally be possible for management to calculate a department's entitlement exactly without the co-operation of its head, who can explain how the staffing resources are deployed over a wide variety of courses. If management happens to know in some instances it is unlikely to know in all, and so the co-operation of the heads of department will be needed.

In one instance the author was familiar with, the management of an institution attempted to carry out a survey of the use of staffing resources, only to find that some heads of department, under union pressure, refused to give the necessary information. Probably wisely the managers refrained from any attempts at discipline or pressure on the heads concerned, withdrew the survey, and let some time pass before trying a different tack.

Time does help in such situations, and if compulsory redundancy can be avoided staff will themselves gradually see the effects of the imbalances created by its alternatives. If they can be persuaded that no one will be forced to leave, but that all that will happen will be attempts to persuade some to retrain for other forms of work within the institution, then they may agree to some means of calculating entitlement.

As Burns and Stalker (1961) have shown, normal bureaucratic structures in which each person plays his own specialist role are suitable only in relatively stable conditions and, in a period of rapid change, when new and unfamiliar problems are having to be tackled, more 'organismic' structures have to be set up, drawing on appropriate resources regardless of formal position. As far as this process of staff reduction is concerned, probably the most important instrument of all is that the task of overseeing it should be in the hands of some group which includes both members of the management team and highly respected members of the teaching staff itself. In the author's own college the government body set up an 'establishment committee' which brought together external governors, members of administration, and some heads of department elected by the staff. There was one such establishment committee for the academic staff and another for the non-academic staff. These committees were then given the responsibility of making recommendations to the governors on all changes in establishment i.e. if a member of staff left it was for the committee to recommend whether the post should be filled again or not; if a department was seeking additional staff on the grounds of increased work, it was for the committee to recommend whether this should be agreed or not; and if an individual member of staff offered himself for voluntary redundancy, it was this committee which recommended whether the offer should be accepted or not. These recommendations then had to be the subject of consultation with the staff unions in a formal 'consultative committee', before finally going to the governors for decision. Often the consultative committee agreed, because the unions respected the care with which their own colleagues had looked into the problems, but even when they did not agree the governors, as was their right, still accepted the recommendations from the establishment committee. In three vital years there was no occasion when such a recommendation was rejected, although there were two cases when the committee was asked to consider new evidence which had been supplied.

The advantage of this establishment committee was that it brought some of the most important heads of department, people who had considerable influence among their colleagues, to regard the problem of retraction as their problem, and not merely one which the management had to face. They appointed a sub-committee which, with the agreement of staff, measured the entitlement of each department and, in the first instance, withheld knowledge of that entitlement from the governors, giving it only to the individual departments themselves, so that they could know where they stood and could judge for themselves whether or not it was appropriate to ask the committee for replacements, or whether one of their number should possibly apply for one of the opportunities of re-training currently being offered. The establishment committee received applications for voluntary redundancy from individuals and interviewed heads of department if these applications were opposed. Sometimes they regretfully denied it. When departments genuinely had a need for additional staff, or for the replacement of those leaving, the establishment committee sometimes persuaded the department heads to carry on with one short of complement for the general good; sometimes they suggested that the opportunity of transfer to these departments should be made to others within the college, with re-training if necessary; and sometimes they agreed that a request had to be made to the funding body (in this case the Scottish Education Department) for an external replacement. They gave a good deal of time to all this, but it was time well spent, and the general reaction of the staff appeared to be that they were 'fair', a point which research on the subject of teacher satisfaction shows to be of importance, and which undoubtedly related to the participation of staff members in the decision-making (Belasco and Alutto, 1975).

From what has been said in the previous three or four paragraphs, it may seem that the author is claiming success for his own institution and for his own methods in handling a very difficult situation. That is not the case: the best that the author can claim is that the position could have been very much worse, for the consequences of all this were still harmful.

A process of steady retraction in any institution is inevitably accompanied by a decrease in the recruitment of new blood, and over a period of some years this becomes increasingly serious. In higher education it is essential that there is a steady flow into universities and colleges of people who have recently been working at the frontiers of their subjects (Blau, Chapter 4, 1974). In a university department of mathematics or physics, for example, it is common to find that people do their best work when they are relatively young, while in a teacher training institution it is vital that there is a regular supply of people who have themselves recently been facing the problems of teachers in ordinary classrooms and in ordinary schools. When the supply of such people begins to dry up it may be hardly noticed at first, especially if the institution is then preoccupied by what appear more serious difficulties, but the effects will show fairly soon and they may last for a long time (Hirsh and Morgan, 1978). At the very worst (and the author has not yet seen this happen, since contraction is still a relatively fresh phenomenon in the UK) an institution could lose its natural authority, in that it might cease to have a sufficient number of people with personal experience of what they are teaching others about.

The problem is seen most clearly when too many internal promotions take place. As already explained, the combination of natural wastage and voluntary redundancy will almost certainly take a greater toll among the senior staff than among the junior, and there will be a higher than usual incidence of heads of department posts becoming vacant. Although everyone will recognize that these should be advertized nationally, this will probably not happen – partly because the institution is over-staffed and the funding body can not agree to the rejection of any opportunity to reduce that problem, and partly because staff in the institution (and the union) will oppose any external recruitment which might increase the danger of existing staff being made redundant in a compulsory way. So with regrets the management will advertize such posts within the institution alone, and will have to take the best person that can be found there. Often this will be a good person, one who in many ways is suitable for the post, or who would be suitable for appointment to a similar post in another institution. But if he has worked in the department for a number of years, the changes which he will wish to make will tend to be relatively small and, although of course there are exceptions to this, it is unlikely that he will adopt any radical policies which will be unsettling to all his colleagues. If several such appointments have to be made at one time, the disadvantages will hardly be noticed, indeed it will appear that everything is going very smoothly, but a price is being paid in terms of the institution's development which may well be serious, and the current managers could be taking steps which their successors will regret in the future.

Staff development is important in any institution at any time, but in a period of contraction it becomes even more so. The lack of fresh blood and the probable spate of internal promotions make it essential that there be a deliberate and systematic plan designed to strengthen the experience and qualifications of those who are going to remain in the institution for some time to come. This is widely recognized and any external body looking at the quality of an institution, not only in its current work but in its plans for the years ahead, will certainly wish to examine its staff development programme. In the United Kingdom the Council for National Academic Awards has placed considerable emphasis on this (CNAA, 1974 Section 9) in its institutional reviews and has looked for a strong programme of this kind in the polytechnics and colleges which teach for its degrees. It has not merely been a matter of seeing that some individual lecturers have gained the qualifications and experience necessary to undertake new tasks, but rather the emphasis has been placed on the existence of an environment in which the continuing education of staff is seen as important. Institutions which in recent years have proclaimed and supported the call for recurrent, life-long education for others, should certainly be able to show that they believe in this to the extent of putting it into practice themselves.

There is an extensive literature devoted to staff development (e.g. Piper and Glatter, 1977, Greenway and Harding, 1978, Teather, 1979), and attention is being paid here only to the ways in which it may be encouraged in a time of contraction. It is assumed that the idea of staff development is in no way new to the institution, and that it has always been common for some staff to be engaged in study designed to raise their qualifications through masters' or doctors' degrees etc., that there have always been some staff who are engaged in research, that many have contributed to and attended conferences, that some have gone back for periods of development work in the field with which their teaching is concerned, and that some have served on national committees, working parties etc. The first danger in a time of contraction is that arguments may be presented for the curtailment of these activities on two grounds, one being that if reductions in expenditure have to be made, they can most simply be made by reducing attendance at conferences etc., and the other being that the institution must devote all its resources to activities which earn staff. And thus, for example, it could be argued that in a teacher training college the provision of in-service courses for others, which counts towards the staff entitlement, should be supported by staff even to the exclusion of the raising of their own qualifications or membership of national committees. Both these arguments are fallacious. There can justifiably be a reduction in the support for some of the peripheral conferences which grow up in times of expansion, and whose benefits are almost entirely social (although there is some value to institutions in that too), but even if the total budget has been cut and financial restraints are necessary, in a time of contraction it is still important to encourage staff to raise their personal qualifications and widen their experience. Fees for attendance at courses elsewhere should still be paid, and other forms

Problems of Institutional Management in a Period of Contraction

of financial support should also be considered. The suggestion that the institution should concentrate all its activities on teaching others so that it earns the maximum number of staff must be firmly repudiated, since it has no right to set out to teach others unless it continues to be a learning environment itself.

Most people would accept that statement, but since contraction is accompanied by fears, suspicions and tensions, it is too much to hope that there will not be some lecturers who will not resent having to carry the burden of teaching work while they see their colleagues going off to courses and conferences, especially if it is suspected that this will enhance the likelihood of their colleagues being promoted at a later stage. For this reason it is important that the matter be discussed openly within the institution, and that decisions as to which individuals should receive the financial support for courses etc., should be taken by a group which includes representatives of staff interests. In times of expansion it will probably have been left to a member of the management team, without anyone caring very much about it because any reputable cause has always been supported, and management could well wish to hold on to this power when contraction comes, in that it helps to control an element of expenditure at a difficult time, but this is a mistake. The element of patronage which has always existed in such matters will now be perceived and resented, and although the management will be suffering from a loss of power in a number of ways, as will be discussed more fully in a later paragraph, it should be prepared to give up some of this, retaining only that share which is the legitimate interest of the financial guardians.

In the author's own college this work has come to be shared by two groups. The establishment committee, already referred to, identifies the cases where it is necessary to encourage people to transfer from one department to another, and authorizes the advertisement of such opportunities, including the prospect of retraining, with the institution paying all costs. Another committee, equally representative, deals with applications for sabbatical leave, financial support for external degrees, and attendance at those conferences which will require major periods of absence. Smaller conferences are left largely for departments to make decisions on, operating within a budget which has been allocated at the beginning of each session.

Sabbatical leave, mentioned above, many pose particular problems. The institution will probably have had a policy of granting such leave in the past, with conditions relating to length of service and worthiness of intention, and probably in the past it will have been open to any member of staff who could meet these conditions. When contraction occurs a stage will arise in which some departments will have lost so many staff that they are genuinely unable to allow anyone to be away for a lengthy period, while other departments will have a surplus which would make this comparatively easy. The other problem is that the fear of compulsory redundancy will probably remain in the background for some time, and individuals may be afraid to ask for leave in case this shows that they can readily be done without, and therefore may be making

273

themselves prime targets for that redundancy. What the author has found himself, and has indeed observed elsewhere, is that applications for sabbatical leave tended to dry up, and this has been in some ways convenient for the institution's management, but if it were to continue too long it would represent a serious diminution in staff development, taking away the longest periods available for uninterrupted refreshment of experience.

At a time of contraction however the emphasis has to be on specific rather than general enrichment, and institutions will commonly find themselves seeking to have members of their staff re-equipped for fresh tasks. For example in the United Kingdom in the late 1970s there has been a great deal of interest in the education of the handicapped (Warnock Report, 1978) and that of those with learning difficulties (Scottish Education Department, 1978), and there has been a desire that teacher training institutions should both expand and reorganize their provision in these areas. In a time when education authorities have found it difficult to release staff from schools, it can still be possible to do this for these purposes, and the colleges of education and polytechnics providing training courses have been presented with an important opportunity for development. The problem has been in some that they have not really been equipped to take advantage of this opportunity, since they have not had enough staff with specialist qualifications and/or experience. This area has therefore presented a good example of the possibilities of retraining, since lecturers in such fields as art or social studies, surplus to other requirements, have sometimes been sent away for attendance at remedial courses, and to work for periods in schools teaching the handicapped, so that after a time (usually between one year and two years) they would be able and ready to play a worthwhile part in this fresh service to the schools.

That example is a useful one for discussion in that it shows both the opportunity and the problems associated with it. Staff who have to undertake a new task of such a demanding kind require to have credibility if they are to be received by the teachers with whom they will have to work, and their credentials will not be automatically accepted, especially if the teachers are themselves sensitive to the fact that major changes are being suggested in their area. In particular, if new qualifications are being introduced, as in Scotland (where a Diploma in Learning Difficulties is replacing the previous qualifications for remedial teachers from 1981) those who have worked in the field with the old qualifications are bound to be suspicious of the change. In such a situation they are not going to accept help from redundant lecturers of art or social studies unless they are convinced that this help will be well founded. Probably re-training will not be enough, and there will have to be some recruitment of highly experienced and respected persons at the same time, but re-training can make a major contribution provided it is well done. There are two imperative conditions; first that the people concerned are of high quality, and are not those least wanted for other work; and secondly, that the training need is foreseen sufficiently far in advance and adequate time allowed for it. If the institution makes the mistake of using weak people, its courses will fail to attract and its reputation will suffer; if it is too slow in re-equipping staff for the task, the opportunity will be missed and the prospective students will go elsewhere.

The most important need for staff development however may not be at the grade of ordinary lecturers, but rather at that of head of department, for two reasons. The first is that conditions both inside and outside the college will be changing very rapidly; the second is that, as has already been explained, there is likely to be an unduly high incidence of internal promotion to head of department posts. If the departments have a fairly high degree of autonomy in the institution, as is very common in higher education, then a head of department who is not responsive to changing conditions, or who wishes simply to keep matters ticking over in a routine way, can impose a very serious brake on progress. It is essential that all heads of department should continue to have opportunities to develop themselves and to be placed in situations which will encourage creative and constructive thinking.

Such opportunities can sometimes be provided by experience away from the person's own institution, and an attempt should be made to ensure that as many as possible gain from this. All too often there are a few heads of department in an institution who have a national reputation and who are invited to participate in all sorts of external bodies and committees, while the remainder receive little experience of this kind. The management of the institution does not have the power to issue these invitations, but should do what it can to see that the opportunities go round as far as possible. It is especially important that those newly appointed to the head of department posts should be found the chance to widen their vision and understanding.

Probably the best single experience of this kind available throughout the United Kingdom in recent years has been that of serving the Council for National Academic Awards through membership of one of its committees, panels, or boards. These take their members to visit other institutions for consideration of the validation of new course proposals or for the review of the working of whole institutions, and both of these situations, while very demanding on the membership of the visiting parties if they are doing their job well, provide almost unrivalled opportunities for gaining fresh experience, understanding and insights. The members are taken away from the restraints of their own institutions and placed in a situation which is not simulated but real, in which they can learn a great deal from both the senior members of the visiting party and from the institution being visited. They have to test their skills and their ideas against those of their peers, and few members would deny that their early experiences in serving such visiting parties have been of considerable benefit to them personally. The institutions being visited do not suffer, since the Council's officers and the senior members of the party will ensure that undue weight is not given to the views of those who are still in the process of being bloodied, and this form of association with the CNAA is something that is highly valued. Institutions receive opportunities to nominate members of the committees, panels and boards every four years, and of course the number who go from any one college is fairly limited, but across the country the CNAA involves more than one thousand people in its work, and this has been of great benefit to the higher education system (CNAA, 1979).

CNAA experience is probably best because it is all directly relevant to the person's own work, and because it fairly quickly brings about contact with a wide range of comparable institutions, but another form of external experience which is of tremendous value is that of working for a time in another country. Many universities and colleges have links with counterparts in various parts of the world, and these often provide an opportunity for staff to be exchanged for periods of a session, semester, a term, or perhaps only a month. The longer the period is the more is probably gained, but for family reasons not everyone can manage to go away for as long as a year, and the shorter periods can also be very helpful. They allow a person to see problems from another perspective, to realize that the difficulties faced at home are not unique and that the solutions found there are not inevitable, and a person frequently returns from such an experience ready to try out some new approach to part of his work. There is a danger in a time of contraction that institutions will agree to fewer of these exchanges, putting the existing schemes into abeyance for a period, but the potential value is so great that this should be resisted. Furthermore there is benefit to the institution in having a visitor from overseas work within a department for a time, since he or she may be a refreshing influence there.

In addition to such inter-institutional links, there are often opportunities provided by the Council of Europe or the British Council for members of staff to go abroad for a time, and these can be particularly valuable.

Perhaps best of all in this kind of experience is the opportunity to teach in a summer school in a North American university. This provides very little difficulty for the home institution, in that its member of staff is away at a time when he or she would be less required in his or her own post, and it is very attractive to the persons concerned in that they are paid for the work and usually take their families abroad with them for a pleasant summer vacation. What matters most however is that the style of teaching tends to be different from that of the European institution in a number of ways, and the lecturer gains from working with students who are more mature (often themselves in posts of some responsibility), very highly motivated, and bringing to the class a wide variety of experience of different situations. The learning tends to be of a more participative kind, and any conscientious lecturer will find quite heavy demands made upon him if he has to meet the needs of the class. If the author could arrange it he would wish all of his heads of department to have an experience of this kind every three or four years, but of course the universities in North America which provide such summer schools are inevitably restricted in their issuing of invitations, and only a few members of staff in a European institution are likely to receive these. Moreover, the invitations cannot be controlled in any way by the college administration. Nevertheless people who do go are likely to be among the most influential, and if they come back with new ideas after a summer in North America at least some of these are likely to spread to those around them.

Outside the institution there are many other useful, if less prestigious, forms of staff development available. Whatever the financial difficulties of the time, it is worthwhile to see that heads of departments, especially new heads of department, attend important conferences, are placed on local working parties and committees, and find themselves where it is likely that they will have to discuss their ideas with others engaged in similar and related work. It is particularly important that they are kept conscious of the views of the professions for which they are training future members.

The best forms of staff development take place within the institution itself, and they tend to be associated with the practice of participative management. They are therefore side-effects of something which is introduced for its own and even more important purposes – purposes with which this chapter now goes on to deal – but side-effects are very helpful too.

Education as a whole has been slower to adopt the participative style of management than has industry, probably because failure to achieve objectives in education generally has less calamitous results for the managers, and a relatively old-fashioned style of authoritarian leadership remains not unknown in many schools. In higher education however there has been a quite distinct and widespread movement towards the location of control in the hands of academic boards and committees, partly because of external pressure (as through the Weaver Report, DES, 1966, and the work of the CNAA in England and Wales) and partly through internal pressure from academic unions and from the institution's own social scientists. There also has been considerable influence exerted, especially in the United States and in Canada, through the courses in educational administration which are commonly taken by those who aspire to promoted posts, and gradually this is having its effect on the schools sector too.

The basic concept of participative management is that an organization will be more effective, in the sense of achieving its goals, when the work groups most affected by the consequences of any decisions which are required are actively involved in making those decisions. The approach is a direct application of the motivation theories and social systems theory of the 1950s, '60s, and '70s, especially as these were expressed in the writings of Kurt Lewin (1947), Abraham Maslow (1954), Douglas MacGregor (1960) and Frederick Herzberg (1966). Although later writers have found weaknesses in Herzberg's two-factor theory of motivation, and there has been a movement towards the more sophisticated expectancy theory as formulated by Vroom (1964) and others, so that it is now recognized as necessary to individualize the incentive system to satisfy the varying needs of employees, it is still generally accepted that the organization will be more effective if workers can be given the opportunity to participate in making the decisions on what they themselves will have to do. And while MacGregor's theory X/theory Y is an over-simplification which has been shown even by some of its supporters (e.g. Maslow, 1965) to have limitations in application, it has nevertheless been the most powerful single contribution to the movement away from paternalistic control and towards the sharing of power.

The most obvious feature of participative management is that decisions are generally taken in boards and committees, and there is nothing particularly new in this even in education, where universities have had their senates for a very long time. Nevertheless the role of the president or principal has perceptibly changed in the last twenty years or so and, in smaller institutions of higher education where the influence of one individual tended in the past to be greater, the position and stature of academic committees has certainly grown. Although the legal position varies, and there are places where academic boards are still in theory advisory, in practice all major academic decisions, along with the responsibility for academic standards in the institution, lie with the academic board, which normally has a system of sub-committees which give an opportunity for a large number of academic staff to play a part in the process. Strong support for this position is provided by the Council for National Academic Awards, which validates degree courses in most polytechnics and colleges in the United Kingdom, since this is one of the 'minimum requirements' for the award of degrees:

> The Council believes that advanced work can only flourish in an institution which has made considerable progress towards becoming an academic community within the sphere of advanced further and higher education. Normally this can only be achieved if there are opportunities for the staff and student body to participate in the formation of academic policy, in the determination of priorities as between the various activities in the institution, and in the other major issues, which are likely to arise.
>
> (CNAA, 1974)

The arguments for such devolution of power within an institution are strong, and provided that it has not been carried to excessive lengths (as is rumoured to have happened in some institutions in North America) those who have experience of a change in this direction would not readily return to the previous position. This is true of the managers as well as of the teaching staff, for there are positive advantages for them too. When problems are being tackled, more minds are brought to bear on them and it is helpful to have the views of those who are nearer to the situation and have more immediate experience of it. There is more likelihood of fresh ideas, and communication throughout the whole of the staff is enhanced as more have first hand knowledge of what is happening. Since authority lies in a body on which everyone has either membership or representation, it is less remote and less likely to be misunderstood. If members of the teaching staff are involved in looking at the whole of a problem rather than only at their own little piece of it, they are more likely to share in contributing to the common good, and interdepartmental co-operation becomes more probable. Most important of all, when a much larger proportion of the academic community is involved in making a decision, there come to be far more people committed to making that decision work.

Although a large number of people may come to participate in management, there will nevertheless be a small group of people who are regarded as the managers, and while the participative style has benefits for them, as indicated in the preceding paragraph, it also makes considerable demands on this managerial group. In an authoritarian situation they would have decided what required to be done and would have told others to do it. Now they are setting out to harness the knowledge and experience of the teaching force in order to decide what requires to be done, and are trying to bring everyone to see problems as collective rather than pertaining to small groups or to the administration. That can require skills of a high order, and the chairman of an academic board, or the chairman of one of the major committees of such a board, is no detached and neutral figure, like the Speaker of the House of Commons, but one who is vitally involved in the proceedings and very conscious of the objectives of the meeting. They have an authority which is attached to their positions, but their effectiveness depends much more on their ability to deploy a wide range of skills appropriate to such meetings. The good chairman, for example, will not wish too often to have to resort to taking votes in meetings, since this polarizes views and actually puts some people into a position where they have publicly indicated their opposition to the idea which is going to have to be implemented, but it takes far more time, patience and skill to achieve a consensus than merely to decide to do something by oneself.

Participative management has created problems of other kinds for the appointed managers, since there are now normally members of the teaching staff on the governing bodies of the institutions as well as on the academic boards. This is entirely appropriate, since so many of the decisions taken there will affect the working conditions of staff, but it makes the managers accountable in a new way to their colleagues. *De jure* the principal has always been accountable to the governing body, but *de facto* that body has tended to leave the day-to-day management of the institution entirely to the principal, who has only had to give full explanations to governors when something has very clearly gone wrong. Now, because of the presence of staff and student members, the governing body is likely to be much more conscious of the major issues within the institution.

It is at a time of contraction (Bone, 1979) that the principal is likely to be most conscious of these pressures. If student numbers are declining and there have to be reductions in staff, as discussed in the early part of this chapter, then attitudes of resentment and fear may come to exist among at least some of the staff, and defensive behaviour may be exhibited by individuals who are, quite naturally, giving a higher priority to their own security than to the needs of the institution. Whereas previously it may have been common for many members of staff to content themselves with doing their own jobs, leaving matters of policy to the principal, in a contracting situation, everyone quickly becomes conscious of the importance of general policy for themselves, and staff are much more likely to be watchful of what the principal is doing in negotiations with central and local government, or of what he says in external committees and at conferences, or of anything that he does which might affect their position. Trade unions will assume greater importance than in times of relative quiet, and both in academic boards and in governing bodies there may be times when staff members tend to follow a union policy.

All this affects the position of the institution's managers and if, as the contingency model asserts (Fiedler, 1967), different types of situations require different types of leadership, the management style will have to adjust to the new situation of contraction. According to Fiedler, the extent to which the leader can exert influence is affected by three major factors – the position power, task structure and leader/member relations – and all of these can change at a time of contraction. While the position power (i.e. the way in which the individual's power comes from his formal position) may appear to be the same, in fact it is modified in at least two ways: partly as he becomes accountable in more matters than would normally be the case, and partly as his opportunities for patronage diminish, since there are fewer promotions etc. available. As far as the second factor is concerned, when tasks are highly structured, with clear goals and well tried procedures for achieving these, the leader, like the captain of a ship coming into port, can expect that his decisions will be accepted without question, and the success or failure of the enterprise will depend mainly on him. But for the manager of an educational institution in a time of contraction the task is much less structured, since the goals are ambiguous, the solutions are not clear-cut, and a multiplicity of approaches may be under consideration. Certainly in terms of Fiedler's analysis, the leader/member relationships will also be affected in a time of contraction, to some extent because people behave differently when their basic security appears in danger of being threatened, and also because the opportunities for stress are much more frequent.

If Fielder's analysis is accepted, a situation of contraction is much less favourable to the leader than is one of expansion, and although the educational manager cannot abdicate from his or her responsibilities, and will obviously have tried to operate with as much skill and good sense as possible at all times, the management style will almost inevitably change. As has been suggested earlier in this chapter, in the discussion of the machinery adopted in the writer's college for dealing with questions of redundancy, filling of vacancies etc., there can be considerable advantage in the bringing together of various groups – administration, lay members of the governing body, and respected members of the teaching staff – to find solutions to the most difficult questions. Even if the task is, in Fiedler's terms, ambiguous, and if a variety of different approaches are being employed, some experimentally, the leadership is more likely to be accepted and trusted if it is thus shared among the various interests concerned.

This does not mean that the appointed managers are operating on a level of pure equality with those they are supposed to lead. Just as in an academic board the chairman does not merely chair the meetings, but accepts it as one of his main responsibilities to ensure that the board faces up to the most important questions of the day, so in tackling the questions of contraction the manager may employ a power sharing structure, but will still regard it as his business to see that the problems are tackled by that structure. He will have renounced the concept of ultimate responsibility because he will have gone consciously into a negotiating position with nothing sealed off (Gray, 1975), and will have to go along with whatever decisions are reached in the new representative body, but, as the person who has most influence on the agendas etc. of that body, he will be seeking to ensure that the institution's problems are tackled. The essence of the structure will be open negotiation, and he will be openly pressing what he sees as the needs of the institution. That will not be resented; what would be resented would be for him to be perceived as acting to protect his own position and authority.

In all this the appointed managers do not make their work any easier; what they do is to make it less impossibly difficult than it would be if they attempted, in a time of contraction, to deal with all the problems themselves.

There is another matter which the educational manager should never forget, regardless of the extent of the other problems afflicting him, and that is to see that the institution is constantly developing and revising its courses to meet the changing demands which society and the professions will make of its graduates. But that is material for another chapter.

References

ASSOCIATION OF LECTURERS IN COLLEGES OF EDUCATION IN SCOTLAND (1980) *Policy Statement on the Possibility of the Closure of Some Colleges*.

BARKER, K. (1976) 'Some questions raised by the amalgamation of colleges', *Coombe Lodge Report*, 9(1).

BELASCO, J.A. and ALUTTO, J.A. (1975) 'Decisional participation and teacher sales/action', in HOUGHTON, V., McHUGH, R. and MORGAN, C. (Eds.), *Management in Education*, London, Ward Lock.

BLAU, P.M. (1974) *The Organization of Academic Work*, New York, Wiley.

BONE, T.R. (1979) 'Accountability in teacher education', *Educational Analysis*, 1(1), Falmer Press.

BONE, T.R. (1980) 'Current trends in initial training', in HOYLE, E. and MEGARRY, J. *op. cit.*

BURNS, T. and STALKER, G.M. (1961) *The Management of Innovation*, London, Tavistock Publications.

COUNCIL FOR NATIONAL ACADEMIC AWARDS (1974) *Regulations and Conditions for the Award of the Council's First Degrees*, London, CNAA.

COUNCIL FOR NATIONAL ACADEMIC AWARDS (1979) *The Council: Its Place in British Higher Education*, London, CNAA.
DEARDEN, N.G. (1974) 'Experiences of amalgamating two colleges of education', *Coombe Lodge Report*, 7(8).
DEPARTMENT OF EDUCATION AND SCIENCE (1966) *The Government of Colleges of Education* (the Weaver Report), London, HMSO.
DEPARTMENT OF EDUCATION AND SCIENCE (1972) *White Paper, A Framework for Growth*, London, HMSO.
DEPARTMENT OF EDUCATION and SCIENCE (1972) *Teacher Education and Training* (the James Report), London, HMSO.
DEPARTMENT OF EDUCATION AND SCIENCE (1973) *Development of Higher Education on the Non-University Sector*, Circular 7/73, London, HMSO.
Employment Protection Consolidation Act, (1978)
FIEDLER, F. (1967) *A Theory of Leadership Effectiveness*, New York, McGraw Hill.
FIELDEN, J. and LOCKWOOD, G. (1973) *Planning and Management in Universities*, London, Chatto and Windus.
FIELDER, F. (1972) 'The effects of leadership training and experience: A contingency model interpretation, *Administrative Science Quarterly*, 17.
GRAY, H.L. (1975) 'Exchange and conflict in the school', in HOUGHTON, V., MCHUGH, R. and MORGAN, C. (1975) op. cit.
GREENWAY, H. and HARDING, A.G. (1978) *The Growth of Policies for Staff Development*, Research into Higher Education, Monograph No. 34, University of Surrey.
HERZBERG, F. (1966) *Work and The Nature of Man*, Cleveland, World Publishing Company.
HIRSCH, W. and MORGAN, R. (1978) 'Career prospects in British universities', *Higher Education*, 7.
HOUGHTON, V., MCHUGH, R. and MORGAN, C. (Eds., (1975) *Management in Education: The Management of Organizations and Individuals*, London, Ward Lock Educational.
HOYLE, E. and MEGARRY, J. (1980) *The Professional Development of Teachers*, the World Yearbook of Education, London, Kogen Page.
LEWIN, K. (1947) 'Frontiers in group dynamics', *Human Relations*, 1(5).
LYNCH, J. (1979) *The Reform of Teacher Education in the United Kingdom*, Surrey, Society for Research into Higher Education.
MASLOW, A.H. (1954) *Motivation and Personality*, New York, Harper and Row.
MASLOW, A.H. (1965) *Eupsychian Management*, Homewood, Illinois, Irwin.
MCGREGOR, D. (1960) *The Human Side of Enterprise*, New York, McGraw Hill.
MORRIS, J. (1980) *Management, Stress and Contraction*, Sheffield, Association of Colleges for Further and Higher Education.
PIPER, D.W. and GLATTER, R. (1977) *The Changing University*, Slough, National Foundation for Educational Research.
RICKETT, R.M.W. (1974) 'Polytechnics and colleges of education', *Coombe Lodge Report*, 7(8).
SCOTTISH EDUCATION DEPARTMENT (1978) *Pupils with Learning Difficulties*, Edinburgh, HMSO.
SHAW, K.E. (1978) 'Contraction and mergers of United Kingdom colleges of education: Some logistic comments', *The Journal of Educational Administration*, 16(2), Armidale, N.S.W., Australia.
TEATHER, D.C.B. (1979) *Staff Development in Higher Education, an International Review*,

New York, Kogan Page.
VROOM, V. (1964) *Work and Motivation*, New York, Wiley.
Warnock Report (1978) *Special Educational Needs*, London, HMSO.

Contributors

Tom Bone is Principal of Jordanhill College of Education, Glasgow. He is a member of the Council of the British Educational Management and Administration Society and has written widely on educational topics. In 1975 he was visiting professor at the Ontario Institute for Studies in Education, Toronto.

Thomas J. DeLong is an assistant professor of secondary education at Brigham Young University. Trained in colleges of business and management (BYU, Purdue, and MIT), Delong finds the world of schools to be an exciting arena in which to practise his knowledge and skills. He continues to consult with, research and write about business and industry.

C. Brooklyn Derr is an associate professor of management in the Graduate School of Business, University of Utah. He has taught educational administration at Harvard and UCLA. Being trained in business schools and currently teaching in the college of business, he continues to consult for and write about his work in school districts.

Michael Fullan is Chairman of the Department of Sociology at the Ontario Institute for Studies in Education, Toronto. His main interest is the planning, implementation and assessment of educational change.

Harry Gray is Principal Lecturer in Education Management at Huddersfield Polytechnic. He is secretary of the Network for Organization Development in Education and editor of the journal *Educational Change and Development*.

Harold Heller is Chief Adviser to the Cleveland Education Authority. He is interested in counselling, group methods and the management of schools.

Donald Layton is Associate Professor in Educational Administration at the State University of New York at Albany. His main interest is educational planning and policy making. In 1976–77 he was Visiting Fellow at the Anglian Regional Management Centre, N.E. London Polytechnic.

Geoffrey Lyons is Principal Lecturer in Education Management at the Anglian Regional Management Centre, N.E. London Polytechnic. He has researched widely into the administrative tasks and needs of heads and acted as consultant overseas.

Iain Mangham is Professor of Management Development and director of the Centre for Organizational Change and Development at the university of Bath. He is interested in Organization Development and the human side of management.

Mike Milstein is professor of educational administration at the State University of New York at Buffalo. He is interested in educational change and has taught at N.E. London Polytechnic and the University of Tel Aviv.

Bill Mulford teaches educational administration at the Canberra College of Advanced Education. He has worked at OECD and developed OD in Australia.

Dick Schmuck has developed the practice of OD in the US, researched and written widely in the field. With his colleague, Phil Runkel, he produced the classic American texts on OD in Education, *The Handbook of Organization Development in Education*, and the *Second Handbook in Organization Development in Education*. He is a professor at the University of Oregon, Eugene, Oregon.

Roger Simon is Associate Professor in the Department of Educational Administration at the Ontario Institute for Studies in Education, Toronto, Canada. He is interested in psycho-sociological and political models of educational organization, particularly the study of educational change.

Len Watson is head of the Department of Education Management at Sheffield Polytechnic. A New Zealander by birth he has travelled widely as a consultant in education management and is a member of the Council of the British Educational Management and Administration Society.

Peter Webb is an HMI in Wales concerned in the development of programmes in Education Management alongside his other inspectorial interests.

Author Index

Ackoff, R.E. 26
Adair, J. 242
Agernsap, T. 26
Alderfer, C. *(see Cooper and Alderfer)*
Allison, G.T. 124, 126
Althusser, L. 72, 83
Alutto, J.A. *(see Belasco and Alutto)*
Amarel, M. *(see Bussis et al)*
Amis, K. 53
Anastasio, E.J. *(see Landis et al)*
Apker, W. *(see Sandow and Apker)*
Apple, M., 69–71, 78, 83
Arends, J. et al., 160, 161 *(see also Runkel et al & Schmuck et al)*
Arends, R. *(see Arends et al & Schmuck et al)*
Arlene, S. and Skolnick, J.H. 136
Armour, D. 258, 260
Aronowitz, S. 83
Association of Lecturers in Colleges of Education in Scotland, 281
Atkinson, J.W. 131, 135

Bailey, F.G. 56–7, 62
Bailyn, L. *(see Van Manaan et al)*
Baldridge, J.V. and Deal, T.E. 136
Barker, K. 264, 281
Bardach, E. 260
Baron, G. 1, 14
Bassin, M. et al., 148, 161
Becher, A. and Maclure, S. 242
Beckhard, R. 135
Belasco, J.A. and Alutto, J.A. 270, 281
 (see also Milstein and Belasco)
Bell, C.H. *(see French and Bell)*
Benne, K.D. *(see Bennis et al)*
Bennett, R. 26
Bennis, W.C. 165, 177
Bennis, W.G. et al., 180, 215
Ben-Peretz, M. *(see Connelly and Ben-Peretz)*
Bentzen, M.M. 209–10, 215
Berger, P. and Luckman, T. 29, 42
Berman, P. and McLaughlin, M.W. 135, 163, 165, 177, 249, 251, 252, 253, 259, 260
Bernstein, M. *(see Gross et al)*
Biddle, B.J. 52, 62
Bidwell, C.E. 129, 135, 163, 177
Bishoprick, D.W. *(see Rice and Bishoprick)*

Blake, R.R. and Mouton, J.S. 135, 182, 215
Blau, P.M. 26, 271, 281
Blanchard, K.H. *(see Hersey et al)*
Blegen, H.M. 26
Blum, A. *(see Tamir et al)*
Blumer, H. 62
Bolam, R. 151, 161
Bolam, R. and Porter, J. 210, 211, 215
Bolam, R. et al., 223, 224, 242
Bone, T.R. 263–83 *(see also Harrison et al)*
Borowitz, E.B. 63–9, 83
Boyd, W.L. 113, 126
Bradbury, M. 53, 55, 56, 62
Braybrook, D. and Lindblom, C. 185, 215
Bredo, E. 189, 215
British Educational Administration Society, 3, 14
Buergenthal, D.A. and Milstein, M.M. 167, 177
Burgoyne, J. *(see Morris and Burgoyne)*
Burns, E. 61
Burns, T. 86, 98, 108
Burns, T. and Stalker, G.M. 269, 281
Burr, A. *(see Runkel and Burr)*
Bussis, A.M. et al., 251, 260
Byrne, D.R. et al., 108

Callan, M.F. and Kentta, W.P. 170, 177
Cameron, W.G. 182–3, 215
Campbell, R.F. and Mazzoni, T.L. 122, 126
Campbell, W. 187, 192, 215
Cantor, H. *(see Bolam et al)*
Carlson, S. 86, 97, 98, 108
Carr, V. *(see Keast and Carr)*
Charters, W.W. and Jones, J. 245, 259, 260
Charters, W.W. and Pellegrin, R. 250, 260
Chickering, A.W. 215
Chin, R. *(see Bennis et al)*
Chittenden, E.A. *(see Bussis et al)*
Chung, H.H. 135
Cistone, P.J. *(see Iannaccone and Cistone)*
Clark, P.A. 30, 42
Coad, R. 212, 215
Cogan, M.L. 66, 83
Cohen, A.M. and Smith, R.D. 182, 215
Cohen, M. and March, J. 59, 62
Coldren, S.I. *(see Frances and Coldren)*
Cole, D. 61

Author Index

Conabere, A.B. *(see Mulford et al)*
Connell, R.W. 83
Connelly, F.M. 79-80, 83
Connelly, F.M. and Ben-Peretz, M. 248, 260
Connelly, M.F. and Elbaz, F. 260
Conway, J.A. *(see Milstein and Conway)*
Cooley, 47
Cooper, C. 218
Cooperative Project for Educational Development (COPED), 146, 161
Corrigan, D. 214
Corsini, R. 33, 42
Council for National Academic Awards (CNAA), 272, 276, 278, 281, 282
Crittendon, A. 133, 135

Dahl, R.A. 27
Dale, R. 30, 42
Dalin, P. 151, 159, 161, 162, 186, 215
Dalton, G.W. *et al.*, 166, 177
Davies, D. 114-15, 126
Davies, J.L. 242
Deal, T.E. *(see Baldridge and Deal)*
Dearden, N.G. 264, 282
DeLong, T.J. 127-37
Department of Education and Science (DES), 241, 242, 265, 277, 281
Derr, C.B. 127-37
Deutschberger, P. *(see Weinstein and Deutschberger)*
Dewey, J. 143, 161
Doyle, W. *(see Ponder and Doyle)*
Dunn, W. and Swierczek, F. 186, 215

Easton, D. 27, 111, 125
Edwards, R. 69-71, 84
Elbaz, F. *(see Connelly and Elbaz)*
Elkland, H. 211-12, 215
Elliott, J. 247, 260
Elliott-Kemp, J. and Williams, G.L. 235, 243
Elmore, R. 259, 260
Emrick, J.A. and Peterson, S. 251, 260
Englert, R.M. *(see Scribner and Englert)*
Eraut, M. 180, 211, 215

Fairlie, H. 133, 136
Fiedler, F. 280-1, 282
Fielden, J. and Lockwood, G. 268, 282
Ford, J.E. *(see Hampstead et al)*
Frances, C. and Coldren, S.I. 27
Francisco, R. *(see Runkel et al)*
Franklin, J.L. 208, 213, 215
French, J. and Raven, B. 153, 161
French, W.L. and Bell, C.H. 136, 165, 177
Frye, N. 82, 84
Fullan, M. 208, 245-61 *(see also Miles et al)*
Fullan, M. and Leithwood, K. 258, 260
Fullan M. and Pomfret, A. 249, 251, 261
Fullan, M. *et al.*, 148-59, 165, 177, 200, 215
Fuller, F.F. 131-2, 136

Further Education Staff College, Coombe Lodge, Bristol, 2, 14

Galbraith, J. 136
Giaquintin, J.B. *(see Gross et al)*
Gibson, O. and Stetar, M. 166, 177
Giddens, A. 83
Giroux, H. 72-3, 77, 83, 84
Glaser, E. 187, 216
Glass, G. 187, 196, 198, 216
Glatter, R. *(see Piper and Glatter)*
Goffman, E. 47-8, 52, 61
Gold, B. *(see Miles et al)*
Goodlad, J.I. *et al.*, 251, 261
Gorton, R.A. and McIntyre, R.E. 108
Gouldner, 61
Gramsci, A. 83
Grant, W.R. 116-17, 126
Gray, H.L. 1-14, 27, 29-43, 139n, 151, 161, 281, 282
Greenfield, T.B. 1, 14, 30, 42
Greenway, H. and Harding, A.J. 272, 282
Gregersen, J. 188, 211, 216
Greiner, L.E. *(see Dalton et al)*
Gross, N. *et al.*, 52, 136, 250, 261
Gross, T. *(see Bassin et al)*
Grumet, M. 68-9, 80-1, 84
Gurel, L. 187, 216

Habermas, J. 83, 84
Hagen, R.E. *(see Hall and Hagen)*
Hall, A.D. and Hagen, R.E. 27
Hall, G. 203, 214
Hall G. and Loucks, S. 193, 216
Hamachek, D.E. 32, 42
Hamilton, D. *(see Parlett and Hamilton)*
Hampstead, T.F. *et al.*, 216
Harding, A.G. *(see Greenway and Harding)*
Harman, G. 112, 125-6
Harrison, M. *et al.*, 27
Havelock, R.G. 180, 184, 216
Heald, K. *(see Yin et al)*
Hearn, P. and Ogilvie, D. 187, 216
Heller, H. 139n, 219-44
Hersey, P. *et al.*, 182, 216
Herzberg, F. 277, 282
Hickson, D.J. and McCullough, A.E. 27 *(see also Pugh et al)*
Hines, S. *(see Byrne et al)*
Hinings, C.R. *(see Pugh et al)*
Hird, W.N. *(see Hampstead et al)*
Hirsch, W. and Morgan, R. 271, 282
Hodgkinson, C. 3, 14, 41, 42
Hofstein, A. *(see Tamir et al)*
Holmes, B. 241
Holmes, R. 53-4, 56, 62
Holt, J. 14
Homans, G.C. 32, 42
Horne, J.H. and Lupton, T. 86, 108
Hornstein, H.A. 210, 216

288

Author Index

Houghton, V. *et al.*, 42, 281, 282
House, E. 256, 261
Howey, K. 214
Hoyle, E. and Megarry, J. 282
 (see also Harrison et al)
Huberman, A.M. 203, 216
Huck, J.R. 213, 216
Hughes, M.G. 42

Iannaccone, L. and Cistone, P.J. 112, 125
Illich, I.D. 14
IMTEC, 235, 243
Ingram, H. *(see Mann and Ingram)*

Jacoby, R. 83, 84
James Report, 265
Jehenson, R. 33, 42-3
Jones, J. *(see Charters and Jones)*
Jones, J.E. 182, 216
Jordon, P. *(see Bassin et al)*
Jung, C.C. 181, 216

Keast, D. and Carr, V. 159, 161
Keith, P.M. *(see Smith and Keith)*
Keller, J.A. *(see Mulford et al)*
Kellner, D. 78, 84
Kelly, J.P. *(see Salancik et al)*
Kentta, W.P. *(see Callan and Kentta)*
Keys, C. 148, 150, 161
Kirst, M.W. *(see Wirt and Kirst)*
Klein, M.F. *(see Goodlad et al)*
Knowles, M. 203, 216

Lafornara, P.A. *(see Milstein and Lafornara)*
Landis, D. *et al.*, 27
Langmeyer, D. *(see Schmuck et al)*
Lash, C. 133, 136
Lasswell, H. 111, 125
Lawler, E.E. 131, 136
Lawrence, P.R. and Lorsch, J.W. 165, 177, 180, 216 *(see also Dalton et al)*
Layton, D.H. 109-26
Leavitt, H.J. 27
Leithwood, K. 246, 261 *(see also Fullan and Leithwood)*
Lewin, K. 8, 14, 140, 143, 145, 161, 277, 282
Lewy, A. 260
Lieberman, M.A. *et al.*, 243
Lindblom, C. 185, 216 *(see also Braybrook and Lindblom)*
Lippitt, G. and Lippitt, R. 181, 216-17
Lippitt, R. *(see Lippitt and Lippitt)*
Lockwood, G. *(see Fielden and Lockwood)*
Lodge, D. 53
Loevinger, J. 204, 217
Lorsch, J.W. *(see Lawrence and Lorsch)*
Loucks, S. *(see Hall and Loucks)*
Louis, K.S. *(see Rosenblum and Louis)*
Luckman, T. *(see Berger and Luckman)*
Lukacs, G. 83, 84

Lupton, T. *(see Horne and Lupton)*
Lynch, B.P. 27
Lynch, J. 265, 282
Lynton, R.P. 27
Lyons, G. 45, 85-108

McCall, G.J. and Simmons, J.L. 48, 61
McCarthy, T. 83, 84
McCleary, L.E. 105, 108 *(see also Byrne et al)*
McClelland, D.C. 131, 136
McCullough, A.E. *(see Hickson and McCullough)*
MacDonald, B. 242
McElvaney, C. and Miles, M. 145, 161
McGregor, D. 131, 136, 277-8, 282
McHugh, R. *(see Houghton et al)*
McIntyre, R.E. *(see Gorton and McIntyre)*
Mackenzie, W.J.M. 27
McLaughlin, M.W. *(see Berman and McLaughlin)*
McLaughlin, M.W. and Marsh, D. 247, 261
Maclure, S. *(see Becher and Maclure)*
Mangham, I.L. 31, 43, 45-62
Mangham, I.L. and Overington, M.A. 62
Mann, D. 185-6, 217
Mann, D. and Ingram, H. 260
March, J. *(see Cohen and Marsh)*
Margulies, N. and Raia, A. 181, 216
Marland, M. 83, 84
Marsh, D. *(see McLaughlin and Marsh)*
Maslow, A.H. 131, 136, 192, 217, 277-8, 282
Maughan, B. *(see Rutter et al)*
Mazzoni, T.L. *(see Campbell and Mazzoni)*
Mead, G.H. 47, 61
Megarry, J. *(see Hoyle and Megarry)*
Meltzner, B.N. *et al.*, 61
Menzel, R.H. 180, 217
Merton, R.K. 52, 62
Meyer, J. and Rowan, B. 197, 217
Miles, M.B. 145, 184, 188, 213, 217
 *(see also Fullan et al.; Lieberman et al.;
 McElvaney and Miles; Schmuck et al)*
Miles, M.B. *et al.*, 217, 253, 261
Miller, D.L. 61
Milstein, M.M. 148, 161, 163-78
 (see also Buergenthal and Milstein)
Milstein, M.M. and Belasco, J.A. 27
Milstein, M.M. and Conway, J.A. 177
Milstein, M.M. and Lafornara, P.A. 177
Mintzberg, H. 86, 87, 97, 98, 99-102, 105, 107, 108
Moos, R.H. 27
Morgan C. 208, 217 *(see also Houghton et al)*
Morgan, G. 61
Morgan, R. *(see Hirsch and Morgan)*
Morris, C.W. 61
Morris, D. 34-5, 43
Morris, J. 263, 282
Morris, J.F. and Burgoyne, J. 32, 43
Mortimore, P. *(see Rutter et al)*
Mosher, R. and Purpel, D. 66, 84
Mouton, J.S. *(see Blake and Mouton)*

Author Index

Mulford, W.R. 139n, 151, 159, 161, 179–218
Mulford, W.R. *et al.*, 217
Munby, R. *et al.*, 261
Murphy, J. 259, 261

Natemeyer, W.E. *(see Hersey et al)*
National Committee for Citizens in Education, 122, 126
Nisberg, J.N. *(see Tichy and Nisberg)*
NWRL, 168

Oakes, P. 61
Ogilvie, D. 187, 188, 217 *(see also Hearn and Ogilvie)*
Organization for Economic Cooperation and Development (OECD), 214
Orpwood, G. *(see Munby et al)*
Ouston, J. *(see Rutter et al)*
Overington, M.A. 61, 62

Packard, J. 136
Parlett, M. and Hamilton, D. 242
Parsons, 52
Pellegrin, R. *(see Charters and Pellegrin)*
Perinbanayagam, R.S. 48, 61
Perkins, J. 62
Peterson, P.E. 112, 124, 125, 126
Peterson, S. *(see Emrick and Peterson)*
Petras, J.W. *(see Meltzner et al)*
Pfeiffer, J.W. 216
Pfeffer, J. *(see Salancik et al)*
Pierce, L. 126
Piper, D.W. and Glatter, R. 272, 282
Pomfret, A. *(see Fullan and Pomfret)*
Ponder, G. and Doyle, W. 250, 256, 261
Poole, R. 31, 43
Porter, J. *(see Bolam and Porter)*
Porter, L.W. *(see Steers and Porter)*
Postman, N. and Weingartner, C. 14
Psathas, G. 43, 46, 61
Pugh, D.S. *et al.*, 27
Purpel, D. *(see Mosher and Purpel)*
Pusey, M. 188, 217

Raia, A. *(see Margulies and Raia)*
Rand Corporation, 163, 177–8
Rapoport, R. and Rapoport, R.N. 133, 136
Rapoport, R.N. *(see Rapoport and Rapoport)*
Raven, B. *(see French and Raven)*
Reason, P. 29, 43
Reddin, W.J. 179, 201–2, 218
Reimer, E. 14
Reynolds, L.T. *(see Meltzner et al)*
Reynolds, M. 218
Rice, G.H. and Bishoprick, D.W. 59, 62
Rickett, R.M.W. 264, 282
Ritchie, T. 83
Roberts, D. 248, 261
Robinson, F. 251, 261
Roeber, R.J.C. 136

Rogers, C. 32, 43
Rosenblum, S. and Louis, K.S. 253, 261
Rowan, B. *(see Meyer and Rowan)*
Runkel, P.J. and Burr, A. 157, 161
Runkel, P.J. *et al.*, 142, 161, 164, 165
Russell, T. *(see Munby et al)*
Russell, T.J. *(see Harrison et al)*
Rutter, M. *et al.*, 108, 236, 243

Sabar, N. *(see Tamir et al)*
Safilios-Rothschild, 133, 136
Salancik, G.R. *et al.*, 27
Sandow, S. and Apker, W. 126
Sarason, S.B. 27, 188, 218, 251, 256, 261
Schein, E.H. 133, 136, 183, 218 *(see also Van Maanen et al)*
Scheinfeld, D. 148, 162
Schmuck, R.A. 27, 37, 139–62, 211, 218 *(see also Arends et al)*
Schmuck, R.A. and Miles, M.B. 129, 136, 161 162, 181–2, 244
Schmuck, R.A. *et al.*, 164, 165, 170, 177
Scholem, G. 65, 84
Schools Council, 242
Schutz, W. 243, 244
Scottish Education Department, 274, 282
Scribner, J.D. and Englert, R.M. 110, 111, 125 126
Seiler, J.A. 27
Sergiovanni, T. and Starratt, R. 67, 82, 84
Sharp, R. 83
Shaw, G.B. 50
Shaw, K.E. 265, 282
Shipman, M.D. 259, 261
Sieber, S. *(see Miles et al)*
Simon, R.I. 63–84
Simon, R.I. and Willinsky, J. 84
Simkins, T.J. 27
Simmel, 47
Simmons, J.L. *(see McCall and Simmons)*
Singer, E.A. and Wooton, M. 213, 218
Skolnick, J.H. *(see Arlene and Skolnick)*
Slivak, R.M. *(see Landis et al)*
Smith, G. *(see Bolam et al)*
Smith, L.M. and Keith, P.M. 136
Smith, R.D. *(see Cohen and Smith)*
Snow, C.P. 53
Spady, W.G. 136
Stalker, G.M. *(see Burns and Stalker)*
Starratt, R. *(see Sergiovanni and Starratt)*
Steele, F. 201–2, 218
Steers, R.M. and Porter, L.W. 131, 136
Stern, G.G. 27
Stetar, M. *(see Gibson and Stetar)*
Stewart, R. 86, 97, 98, 105, 108
Strauss, A. 61
Swierczek, F. *(see Dunn and Swierczek)*

Tamir, P. *et al.*, 83
Taylor, G. *(see Fullan et al & Miles et al)*

Author Index

Teacher, D.C.B. 272, 282-3
Terkel, S. 133, 136
Thomas, 47
Thompson, E.P. 83
Thompson, J. and Tuden, A. 218
Thompson, J.D. 27
Tichy, N. and Nisberg, J.N. 183-4, 218
Tucker, H.J. and Zeigler, L.H. 126
Tuden, A. *(see Thompson and Tuden)*
Tyack, D. 136
Tye, K.A. 164

Van Maanen, et al., 133, 137
Vickers, B.C. 27
Vogel, M. *(see Yin et al)*
Vroom, V.H. 131, 137, 277, 282

Walberg, H.J. 27
Walker, J.W. 133, 137
Warnock Report, 274, 282
Watson, L.E. 15-28
Weatherley, R. 249, 261
Webb, P.C. 45, 85-108
Weber, M. 47, 61
Weick, K.E. 163
Weingartner, C. *(see Postman and Weingartner)*
Weinstein, E.A. and Deutschberger, P. 61

Weiss, C. 122-3, 126
Werner, W. 247, 261
Wexler, P. 83
Whetten, D.A. 28
White, J. *(see Harrison et al)*
White, P. *(see Harrison et al)*
Wilder, D. *(see Miles et al)*
Williams, G.L. *(see Elliott-Kemp and Williams)*
Williams, W. 261
Willinsky, J. *(see Simon and Willinsky)*
Willis, P., 83, 84
Wirt, F.M. and Kirst, M.W. 122, 123, 124, 125 126
Wise, A.E. 118-19, 126, 185, 218
Wolff, K. 61
Wooton, M. *(see Singer and Wooton)*
Wrapp, H.E. 99, 108
Wrong, D.H. 28
Wyant, S.H. 209, 218

Yalom, I.D. *(see Lieberman et al)*
Yin, R. et al., 251, 261
Young, O.R. 28

Zeigler, L.H. *(see Tucker and Zeigler)*
Zinkel, C. *(see Mulford et al)*

Subject Index

action research, 30, 145
administration, *passim*
  concept of, 3
administrative duties
  of teachers, 87–107
administrative skills
  of teachers, 100–1
administrative theory
  and management theory, 7–9
advisers, 223–44
Africa, 2, 7
andragogy, 203–7
Asia, 2
assessment, 187
Australia, 1, 6, 8, 9, 139n, 151, 154, 155, 159, 179–218
authority, 10–13, 40–1
autonomy
  in social organizations, 78–82

bargaining, 113, 116–17
behavioural research, 85–108
British Council, 276
Buffalo, USA, 165–77
business
  and education, 128–9
business management, 127–37

Canada, 1, 6, 8, 9, 10, 148–51, 200–1, 245–61, 276–7
centralization
  of decision making, 117–119
clearinghouse
  and Organization Development, 156–8
Cleveland, UK, 219–44
communication, 19, 143, 268
community involvement
  in education, 113–16
conflict
  and Organization Development, 144
consultancy
  and education systems, 179–218
  and Organization Development, 154
control
  in organizations, 69–71, 73–8, 82
cooperation
  among teachers, 179–218

Cooperative Project for Educational Development (COPED), 146
Council of Europe, 276
Council for National Academic Awards (CNAA), 263, 265, 275–6, 277, 278
counselling, 33, 101, 139n
creation
  and leadership, 64–9
critical Marxism, 71–3
  see also Marxism
cultural perspectives, 6–7
cultural system
  and educational situations, 18, 20, 25–6
curricular materials, 70–1
curriculum, 245–61

decision making, 117–19
  and Organization Development, 144–5
Denmark, 4, 188, 211
Department of Education, USA, 116, 119
Department of Education and Science, UK, 87, 265
desegregation
  in schools, 169–74
diary technique
  in research, 86–107

economic pressures, 12–13, 263–83
economic system
  and education, 18, 21–3, 24–5
economics
  and educational organization, 7
education
  and business, 128–9
  community involvement in, 113–16
  and consultancy, 179–218
  and economic system, 18, 21–3, 24–5
  managerial activities in, 85–108
  parent involvement in, 113–16
  and policy making, 113, 117–19
  politics of, 109–26
educational administration, *passim*
educational innovation
  and research, 245–61
educational management, *passim*
enrolments, 128, 130
  see also falling rolls

292

Subject Index

evaluations
 in schools, 179-218

falling rolls, 263-5
France, 3, 9

geographic system
 and educational situations, 18-19
goals
 and Organization Development, 144
Goathland courses, 230-4, 238-41
governance system
 and educational situations, 18, 20-1, 25
group meetings
 and Organization Development, 144

handicapped
 education of the, 274
headteachers, 87-107
 management training for, 219-44
human resource management, 132-5

ICI, 221, 222, 228, 231-2, 234
ideology, 71-8
imagery
 and Organization Development, 153
implementation
 of change, 79-80, 163-78, 179-218, 245-61
individuals
 and organizations, 45-62
innovation
 and educational institutions, 163-78, 245-61
 see also implementation of change
in-service education, 139n, 210-11, 223-44
In-Service Education and Training (INSET), 139n, 210-11
institutional management, *passim*
 see also business management
International Movement Toward Educational Change (IMTEC), 148m, 158, 159

language policy
 in schools, 74-5
leadership, 6, 40-1, 63-84, 100-1, 166-9, 175, 182, 280
learning by doing, 143
legal situation
 and educational situations, 20-1, 25
'levels of use' concept, 193, 207, 214
Local Education Authority (LEA), 219-44, 250, 251-3, 255-6, 257, 258
Luria, Isaac, 63-9

management, *passim*
management theory
 and administrative theory, 7-9
management training, 219-44
managerial activities
 and education, 85-108
managerial skills
 of teachers, 100-1
managers, 86-95
Marxism, 4
 and management of educational institutions, 63-84
motivation
 in schools, 130-2
mysticism
 and management, 63-84

National Institute of Education, 200
National Training Laboratories, 145
Nigeria, 5, 6
norms
 and organization in schools, 141-2
North America, 1, 200-1, 253, 276-7
 see also Canada, United States of America
Norway, 4, 148, 151

open systems courses, 232, 233, 238-41
open systems theory, 4-6, 7
Oregon, University of, 146-8, 156-8
Organization Development (OD), 5-6, 31, 37, 85, 127-8, 134, 139-62, 163-78, 179-218, 226-7
organization theory, 29-43
organizational adaptation
 in schools, 132-5
organizations
 and authority, 40-1
 and causation, 40
 and change, 38-9
 and determinants of behaviour, 35-6
 and functioning, 39-40
 and individual interests, 36-7
 and leadership, 40-1
 and management, 41-2
 models of, 45-62
 and objectives, 35
 and objectivity, 37
 and order and disorder, 33-4
 and reality, 37-8
 and structure, 34-5
 and subjectivity, 37
 see also Organization Development

parent involvement
 in education, 113-16
participation, 114-16, 277-9
personality theory, 32
phenomenology, 4-6, 29n, 30
policy making, 113, 117-19
political system
 and educational situation, 18, 22, 23-4
politics
 of education, 109-26
 and Organization Development, 154
politics of education research, 119-25
power
 and Organization Development, 153

293

Subject Index

problem solving, 140-4
problematics, 71-8

Radford scheme, 187
rationality, 72-3
redundancy, 266-74
research
    diary technique in, 86-107
    and educational innovation, 245-61
    and Organization Development, 155-6
    and politics of education, 123-5
role theory, 52
roles, 141-2
    and consultants, 180-6
    of teachers, 99-106
retirement, 266
retraining, 274-5

sabbatical leave, 273
school evaluations, 179-218
School Improvement Resource Team (SIRT), 169-74
schools
    and business management, 127-37
    and change, 163-78
    desegregation in, 169-74
    and educational innovation, 245-61
    evaluation in, 179-218
    management in, 219-44
    and Organization Development, 139-62
social actors, 45-62
social setting
    of education management, 15-28
spatial system
    and educational situations, 18-19
staff development, 272-7
staffing, 265-70
'stages of concern' concept, 193-4, 199, 207, 214
subjective theory, 29n, 30-42
SUNY/Buffalo, 165-9, 174-7
supervision, 63-84
Sweden, 4, 86, 151, 211-12
systems theory, 15, 18

task system
    and educational situations, 18, 19
teachers
    administrative duties of, 87-107
    cooperation among, 179-218
    isolation of, 187-9
    management training for, 219-44
    managerial skills of, 100-1
    power of, 113, 116-17
teaching styles, 10-11
technology, 19
    and Organization Development, 140-5
theatre
    higher education as, 45-62
trade unions, 267-8, 280
training
    of educational administrators, 120-2
    for headteachers, 219-44
training groups (T-groups), 58, 145
Tyndale affair, 224, 227
'tzimtzum', 63-9, 71, 73

United Kingdom, 1, 2-12, 23, 25, 30, 86, 105, 109-10, 139n, 151, 154, 155, 159, 210, 219-44, 263-83
United States of America, 1-12, 86, 105, 109-26, 127-37, 139-62, 163-78, 188, 200-1, 211, 245-61, 276-7

value systems, 11-12
voluntary redundancy, 266, 268, 271

294